Preparedness and Response for Catastrophic Disasters

Preparedness and Response for Catastrophic Disasters

RICK BISSELL

CRC Press
Taylor & Francis Group
Boca Raton London New York

CRC Press is an imprint of the
Taylor & Francis Group, an **informa** business

CRC Press
Taylor & Francis Group
6000 Broken Sound Parkway NW, Suite 300
Boca Raton, FL 33487-2742

© 2013 by Taylor & Francis Group, LLC
CRC Press is an imprint of Taylor & Francis Group, an Informa business

No claim to original U.S. Government works

Printed in the United States of America on acid-free paper
Version Date: 20120823

International Standard Book Number: 978-1-4665-1189-7 (Hardback)

This book contains information obtained from authentic and highly regarded sources. Reasonable efforts have been made to publish reliable data and information, but the author and publisher cannot assume responsibility for the validity of all materials or the consequences of their use. The authors and publishers have attempted to trace the copyright holders of all material reproduced in this publication and apologize to copyright holders if permission to publish in this form has not been obtained. If any copyright material has not been acknowledged please write and let us know so we may rectify in any future reprint.

Except as permitted under U.S. Copyright Law, no part of this book may be reprinted, reproduced, transmitted, or utilized in any form by any electronic, mechanical, or other means, now known or hereafter invented, including photocopying, microfilming, and recording, or in any information storage or retrieval system, without written permission from the publishers.

For permission to photocopy or use material electronically from this work, please access www.copyright.com (http://www.copyright.com/) or contact the Copyright Clearance Center, Inc. (CCC), 222 Rosewood Drive, Danvers, MA 01923, 978-750-8400. CCC is a not-for-profit organization that provides licenses and registration for a variety of users. For organizations that have been granted a photocopy license by the CCC, a separate system of payment has been arranged.

Trademark Notice: Product or corporate names may be trademarks or registered trademarks, and are used only for identification and explanation without intent to infringe.

Library of Congress Cataloging-in-Publication Data

Bissell, Rick.
    Preparedness and response for catastrophic disasters / Rick Bissell.p. cm.
    Includes bibliographical references and index.
    ISBN 978-1-4665-1189-7 (hardcover : alk. paper)
    1. Emergency management. 2. Preparedness--Government policy.
3. Disaster relief--Finance. 4. Emergency management--United States. 5. Preparedness--Government policy--United States. 6. Disaster relief--United States--Finance. I. Title.

HV551.2.B57 2013
363.34'7--dc23   2012031645

Visit the Taylor & Francis Web site at
http://www.taylorandfrancis.com

and the CRC Press Web site at
http://www.crcpress.com

Contents

Foreword: Why Catastrophes?..vii
Editor ix
Contributors xi
Introduction..xiii

Chapter 1
What Is a Catastrophe, and Why Is This Important?...............................1
Rick Bissell

Chapter 2
Understanding Catastrophes: A Discussion of Causation, Impacts,
Policy Approaches, and Organizational Structures................................27
David A. McEntire

Chapter 3
Ethics in Catastrophe Readiness and Response.....................................45
Anna K. Schwab and Timothy Beatley

Chapter 4
Political and Legal Issues 77
John C. Pine

Chapter 5
Economics of Catastrophes and Disasters..109
Kevin M. Simmons

Chapter 6
Logistics and the Management of Critical Supplies Following Catastrophes.......131
José Holguín-Veras, Tricia Wachtendorf, Miguel Jaller, and Theresa Jefferson

Chapter 7
Overview of Critical Infrastructure in Catastrophes 151
Matthew J. Levy and Rick Bissell

Chapter 8
Public Health Role in Catastrophes 171
Rick Bissell and Thomas Kirsch

Chapter 9
Catastrophes, Mass Displacement, and Population Resettlement 185
Anthony Oliver-Smith

Chapter 10
Emergent Organizations and Networks in Catastrophic Environments 225
Tricia Wachtendorf

Chapter 11
Methods of Planning and Response Coordination 257
Jasmin R. Ruback, A. Scott Wells, and Brian J. Maguire

Chapter 12
Catastrophic Disaster Recovery: An Institutional Network Perspective 281
Gavin Smith

Chapter 13
Pandemic Scenario 301
Rick Bissell and Thomas Kirsch

Chapter 14
Training and Exercises for Catastrophes 319
Myra M. Socher

Chapter 15
Catastrophes in Haiti and Japan 341
Thomas Kirsch, Nobuaki Kiriu, and Rick Bissell

Chapter 16
Summary and Call to Action 377
Rick Bissell and Jasmin R. Ruback

Epilogue 387
Acronyms and Abbreviations 389
Index 391

Foreword: Why Catastrophes?

This is the book that I wish had existed when I directed the Federal Emergency Management Agency (FEMA) (1993–2001). The insights, reasoning, and policy challenges presented here would have made it easier to move government and non-governmental emergency management and response organizations in new and more effective directions. However, this was not to be. This is because the diverse scientific base so aptly cited by the authors of *Preparedness and Response for Catastrophic Disasters* was not yet far enough along. When I came into office at FEMA, the organization was only a little more than a decade old. There was little consensus regarding what a national-level emergency preparedness and response coordination agency's roles would be, or should be. Should the national government be a response agency, or only coordinate and stimulate planning efforts? How should federal assets be deployed ... upon evidence of their need, or only after formally requested by state governments? What roles should a national agency play in mitigation and recovery, and what tools should be available and used?

The power and scale of Hurricane Hugo in September of 1989 helped provide us some insights regarding the challenges of responding to such a large-scale event. It made us painfully aware of the inadequacy of the then-existing roles, methods and plans for confronting extraordinarily large multi-country (including Caribbean islands) and multi-state disasters. Shortly before I took office at FEMA, Hurricane Andrew provided yet more incentive to pay attention to the task of re-thinking how national, state, and local entities can most effectively work together to protect the population from emergencies and disasters of all sizes.

During the 1990s and early into the new century, a group of emergency managers and researchers in North America, and around the world, began the process of critically re-thinking some of the previously held assumptions about how to prepare for—and effectively respond to a broad variety of events—events with radically different challenges. The sciences of sociology, public health, and logistics had developed to the point where their viewpoints could provide critical insight into disaster research. Some of the authors of this book were among those who began to recognize that very large multi-jurisdictional disasters have dynamics and properties that are fundamentally distinct from the more common disasters whose direct effects often do not extend beyond the boundaries of a single state or province.

After much analysis, consensus and recognition began to emerge that the methods of preparing for and responding to such mega-events needed significant revision. The hard reality is that mega-events, which we now call catastrophes, are too multidimensional, too confusing, and have such broad impacts that no single plan, organizational methodology, or agency type can effectively manage the myriad important tasks—nor, perhaps, even consider all that needs to be done—to minimize both immediate and downstream consequences. In quick succession, the world experienced the attacks of September 11th, 2001, the December 2004 Indian Ocean tsunami, and the onslaught of Hurricanes Katrina and Rita, all of which provided additional evidence that new thinking and new methods needed to be developed to successfully confront catastrophes.

The authors of this important book have combined their broad expertise in sociology, anthropology, public health, economics, engineering, ethics, political science and policy, planning methods, logistics, and on-the-ground field operations to provide a volume that describes the many ways in which catastrophes differ from disasters. The book discusses challenges in a rapidly changing world, critiques, and assesses new approaches to addressing catastrophes. The chapter on the responses to the 2010 Haitian earthquake and the 2011 earthquake/tsunami/nuclear power plant meltdown in Japan demonstrates how far the world has yet to go. But the research and suggestions found in these pages leave me hopeful that the world will develop and implement effective new strategies and tools for confronting catastrophes.

This book is a must-read for anyone responsible for the well-being of people worldwide who will be affected by catastrophic events in the years to come.

James Lee Witt
Director of FEMA 1993–2001

Editor

Rick Bissell, PhD, is a professor and graduate program director at the University of Maryland Baltimore County (UMBC) Department of Emergency Health Services. He started his career in emergency response working as a paramedic in Northern California in the early 1970s. He combined studies in international relations, preventive medicine, health services administration, and emergency management in order to pursue a career in emergency and disaster public health. He has lived and worked in the United States, Austria, Germany, the Dominican Republic, Mexico, Chile and Bolivia, and has worked in a dozen more countries on four continents. Dr. Bissell has responded to disasters in Mexico, the Dominican Republic, Bolivia, Chile, Costa Rica, and the United States. His research focuses on disaster epidemiology, health sector response to disasters, public health–emergency management collaboration, emerging global emergency management challenges, earthquake impact on health services, and various topics related to EMS (emergency medical services).

An early collaborator with the U.S. National Disaster Medical System, Dr. Bissell headed the team that developed and provided online training to more than 16,000 Public Health Service personnel regarding response operations in challenging circumstances, and built and directed the team that developed the Catastrophe Readiness and Response Course for FEMA's Emergency Management Institute. He has consulted for the USAID Office of Foreign Disaster Assistance, the German National Committee for Global Change Research, the Centers for Disease Control and Prevention, the Federal Emergency Management Agency, the American Red Cross, the Saudi Red Crescent Society, the American Ambulance Association, and various state health departments.

Dr. Bissell serves as chair for the Preparedness Subcouncil of the American Red Cross Scientific Advisory Council, and also serves as the unpaid emergency preparedness coordinator for the Garrett County Health Department in rural western Maryland. Dr. Bissell has more than 35 publications in peer-reviewed journals and six book chapters.

Contributors

Timothy Beatley
Department of Urban and Environmental Planning
School of Architecture
University of Virginia
Charlottesville, Virginia

Rick Bissell
Department of Emergency Health Services
University of Maryland Baltimore County
Baltimore, Maryland

José Holguín-Veras
Department of Civil and Environmental Engineering
Rensselaer Polytechnic Institute
Troy, New York

Miguel Jaller
Department of Civil and Environmental Engineering
Rensselaer Polytechnic Institute
Troy, New York

Theresa Jefferson
Center for Technology, Security, and Policy
Virginia Polytechnic Institute and State University
Arlington, Virginia

Nobuaki Kiriu
Critical Care Medicine and Trauma
National Disaster Medical Center
Tachikawa, Japan

Thomas Kirsch
Office of Critical Event Preparedness and Response (CEPAR)
Center for Refugee and Disaster Response (CRDR)
Department of Emergency Medicine
Johns Hopkins University School of Medicine
Baltimore, Maryland

Matthew J. Levy
Department of Emergency Medicine
Johns Hopkins University School of Medicine
Baltimore, Maryland

Brian J. Maguire
Central Queensland University
School of Medical and Applied Sciences
Queensland, Australia

David A. McEntire
Department of Public Administration
University of North Texas
Denton, Texas

Anthony Oliver-Smith
Department of Anthropology
University of Florida
Gainesville, Florida

John C. Pine
Research Institute for Environment, Energy and Economics
Appalachian State University
Boone, North Carolina

Jasmin R. Ruback
Ruback Associates, LLC
State College, Pennsylvania

Anna K. Schwab
Center for the Study of Natural Hazards
  and Disasters
University of North Carolina at
  Chapel Hill
Chapel Hill, North Carolina

Kevin M. Simmons
Department of Economics and Business
  Administration
Austin College
Sherman, Texas

Gavin Smith
Center for the Study of Natural Hazards
  and Disasters
University of North Carolina at
  Chapel Hill
Chapel Hill, North Carolina

Myra M. Socher
TriMed, Inc.
Rockville, Maryland

Tricia Wachtendorf
Disaster Research Center
University of Delaware
Newark, Delaware

A. Scott Wells
InSight Inc.
Washington, Virginia

Introduction

Hurricane Katrina, the 2010 earthquake in Haiti, the 2004 South Asia tsunami, and the 2011 earthquake, tsunami, and nuclear plant meltdown in Japan are all recent examples of disasters that had, and still have, national and international ramifications. When an event is so large and impactful that an entire country ... or multiple countries ... are affected, we change the vocabulary from "disaster" to "catastrophe." This is far from being a simple word change; as we will see in this book, it recognizes that the entire dynamics of preparing for and dealing with the event and its impacts are in many ways vastly different from what is expected in a disaster that is limited to a particular region of a country. This book provides an overview of these changes and why catastrophes can be expected to increase in coming years. It also brings the reader useful understanding of why many current assumptions about disaster preparedness and response may not be useful in catastrophes, and presents alternative considerations, techniques, and methodologies to help societies to prepare themselves to be more resilient in the face of future catastrophes.

We began the work that serves as the basis for the book in 2007 when the U.S. Federal Emergency Management Agency's (FEMA's) Emergency Management Institute (EMI) initiated the process of preparing a course to be used in university and graduate-level programs in emergency management, designed to parallel FEMA's new work focused on helping the United States to better prepare for and respond to the next Hurricane Katrina (or larger) sized event. FEMA's work was largely predicated on evaluations done post-Katrina[1-4] that, when analyzed as a whole, indicated that super-large disasters have fundamental characteristics and dynamics that are different from events that are restricted to a single jurisdiction or region, and that these fundamental differences require alternative approaches to mitigating, preparing for, and responding to them. Simultaneously, several European and North American scholars, emergency managers, and policy analysts came to similar conclusions about what they termed the "hypercomplexity" of super-large multi-jurisdictional events, and, under the leadership of Erwan Lagadec at Johns Hopkins University, launched a North Atlantic consortium effort to study the phenomenon and develop new understandings. As described in Chapter 1, both the FEMA and consortium groups came to the conclusion that catastrophes are not just big disasters, but rather constitute phenomena that are in many ways fundamentally different from disasters.

The goal of this book, crafted by some of the brightest disaster scholars and practitioners in the United States, is offered to provide the reader with a substantial understanding of why catastrophes are different from disasters and why they need to be approached differently if we are to be ultimately successful in protecting our populations in times of new and changing hazards, the increased vulnerability of ever-expanding populations, and rapidly accelerating resource depletion. While the authors are mostly U.S. based, many have spent substantial time working and living in other parts of the world; it is our intention that this book be available to readers from virtually everywhere, taking into account that many of the examples are from the United States but are not intended to apply only to U.S. circumstances. This book does not pretend to offer all the solutions, but rather to challenge much current thinking and to offer potential new directions based on new understandings of rapidly evolving realities.

The authors collectively extend their thanks to the FEMA Emergency Management Institute for funding the early work from which this book takes its roots, with particularly warm thanks to Dr. Wayne Blanchard, now retired from FEMA.

REFERENCES

1. The White House. The Federal Response to Hurricane Katrina: Lessons Learned. 2006. Available at: http://georgewbush-whitehouse.archives.gov/reports/katrina-lessons-learned/. Accessed 29 Jan 2012.
2. U.S. House of Representatives. 2006. A Failure of Initiative: The Final Report of the Select Bipartisan Committee to Investigate the Preparation for and Response to Hurricane Katrina. Available at www.katrina.house.gov. Accessed 29 Jan 2012.
3. United States Government Accountability Office. 2006. Hurricane Katrina: GAO's Preliminary Observations Regarding Preparedness, Response and Recovery. Available at http://www.gao.gov/new.items/d06442t.pdf. Accessed 14 April 2012.
4. Quarantelli, E.L. Catastrophes are different from disasters: Implications for crisis planning and managing drawn from Katrina. 11 June 2006, Social Sciences Research Council, available at http://understandingkatrina.ssrc.org/Quarantelli.

CHAPTER 1

What Is a Catastrophe, and Why Is This Important?

Rick Bissell

CONTENTS

Definitions 4
Continuum of Magnitude 6
Historic Examples of Catastrophes 7
    Middle Ages Black Plague 7
    Little Ice Age in Europe 9
    Irish Potato Famine 10
    The 1918–1919 Influenza Pandemic 12
    Hurricanes Katrina and Rita 13
Potential Future Catastrophes 16
    Sea Level Rise 17
    Drought and Desertification 18
    Global Pandemic 20
    New Madrid Mega-Earthquake 21
    Summary: Factors Common in Catastrophes 22
    Overview of the Book 23
References 24

When Hurricane Katrina slammed ashore near New Orleans in August 2005, it was bad news for millions of residents of the Gulf coast. Some 1,200 to 3,500 people lost their lives in the storm and related flooding, and many thousands more sustained injuries.[1] Hundreds of thousands had to evacuate their homes, often to places hundreds of miles away, and then many of those could not return to destroyed homes, neighborhoods, and businesses. Houston, Texas and many other communities around the country absorbed "Katrina refugees," often at great cost and discomfort. Motorists in most of the United States found themselves paying higher prices for gasoline due to compromised pumping and refining facilities in the

Katrina-damaged area. Homeowners in the Mid-Atlantic and New England states wondered whether sufficient fuel oil would be available as summer turned to fall. And, in faraway places such as Namibia, Bangladesh, and Angola, the provision of affordable or charity-donated food grains to the starving and very hungry was diminished and threatened by the shut-down of barge traffic and docking facilities at the far-away mouth of the Mississippi River, through which a huge percentage of the exported grains from the American Midwest and Canadian breadbaskets are shipped. Once the severity of the impacts of Hurricane Katrina was beamed out to the world through virtually instantaneous media, disaster responders from various countries offered their assistance, and some actually showed up without request. The storm left direct damages in six states: Alabama, Florida, Georgia, Kentucky, Louisiana, and Mississippi, all of which subscribed to the national all-hazards hierarchical incident management system, and all of which had their own different hurricane response plans. A single hurricane, hitting at the right place, had both national and international implications, many of which were not amenable to the assumptions of a national incident management system that assumed that a larger event simply demanded a larger response. In fact, the US Federal Emergency Management Agency (FEMA) and its host, the Department of Homeland Security, had been hard at work since the attacks of September 11th, 2001, revising and developing the way that the United States responds to large disasters, but found the events surrounding Hurricane Katrina much more complicated than even the newly enhanced planning efforts had assumed.

A year and a half earlier, on December 26, 2004, a massive earthquake was unleashed below the ocean off of Indonesia (see Figure 1.1), triggering equally

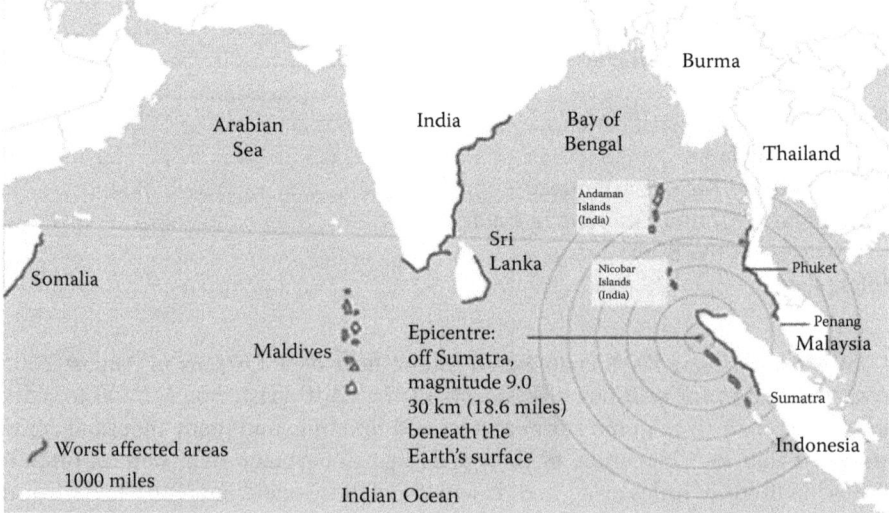

Figure 1.1 Epicenter of, and countries affected by, the 2004 Indian Ocean Tsunami. (http://image.guardian.co.uk/sys-images/Guardian/Pix/maps_and_graphs/ 2004/12/29/asia_quakemap5.gif.)

massive tsunami waves that ended up killing an estimated 225,000 people, and leaving homeless between 1.2 million and 10 million people in 11 countries.[2] Because this was a coastal disaster, response requirements were spread out in countries that had long exposed coastal zones, not to mention the fact that it also covered 11 very different nations. To make matters more difficult, in two tsunami-affected areas, Banda Aceh, Indonesia, and in Sri Lanka, active insurgencies were underway. The response to this event required resources from around the world; many of the affected countries did not have the resources to meet their own needs, and no single response organization anywhere had all the resources required to effectively respond to the needs presented by the earthquake and tsunami. More than 50 countries contributed aid of various kinds, as well as a large (unknown) number of multinational, bilateral, and non-governmental assistance organizations representing a broad range of sizes, capabilities, and foci.

On January 12, 2010 a strong earthquake[3] (7.0 Mw) struck the south-central part of Haiti, with its epicenter close to the capital Port-au-Prince. Even without the earthquake, Haiti was incapable of providing for the basic needs of its population in a self-sufficient sustainable manner. So, one could argue that it was in "chronic disaster mode" prior to the earthquake. However, the earthquake killed more than 230,000 people and injured more than 300,000 while simultaneously destroying housing for millions, basic road, water supply, and communications infrastructure for a broad swath of the most populated part of the country, and crushing many of the government ministry buildings housing a significant percentage of the very people who, in normal times, would be expected to guide the country through tough times. Not only could Haiti not respond to its own event, even all of its combined Caribbean neighbors did not have enough resources to respond effectively. In fact, response teams and supplies came in from throughout North and South America, Europe, the Middle East, parts of Asia, and the South Pacific. Even with monetary and direct assistance from dozens of countries, at the time of this writing in the summer of 2011, one and a half years after the earthquake, very little of the rubble has been removed, most who lost their homes have not been able to rebuild permanent replacements, healthcare is still scattered and inadequate for the vast majority of the population, and permanent solutions to destroyed infrastructure are few. More detailed information on Haiti will be given in Chapter 15.

All three of these events have some common characteristics: (1) They were too large to have their effects contained by a single country; (2) they involved responses by several countries and multiple response systems; and (3) they created highly complex after-effects that impacted core societal functions across many polities and societies, such as food distribution, production and distribution of fuels, electricity and other power sources, transportation of goods and services, banking system interruptions, displacement of healthcare systems and their workers, and perhaps even resulted in changes in a society or country's overall security or viability (i.e., Sri Lanka). This complexity requires a new kind of planning, preparedness and response, and, perhaps, some new vocabulary.

DEFINITIONS

We humans use words to help us conceptualize and understand the world in which we live. When we define and use our words carefully, we can convey our concepts and understandings quite concisely, which can greatly facilitate our ability as humans to build on the thoughts and experiences of individuals in a way that benefits humans in general through science, technology, policy, and other activities that involve many people over numerous generations. It is difficult, however, to develop new vocabulary such that everyone will understand what is meant, or, even to use old familiar words in a new context, to convey new meanings. Who would have thought 25 years ago that the mathematical term "google" (a one with one hundred zeros behind it) would not too many years later become both a trademark and a verb (to Google [search] for information on the "web")?

Recognizing this, several scholars who study disasters, FEMA, and emergency managers in several countries worked to develop new vocabulary to describe the very complex and large events that clearly have some characteristics that require rethinking regarding how we approach preparedness and response. FEMA and several U.S. scholars decided to use the word "catastrophe" to refer to this new concept.

FEMA defines a catastrophe as:

> ... any natural or manmade incident, including terrorism, that results in extraordinary levels of mass casualties, damage, or disruption severely affecting the population, infrastructure, environment, economy, national morale, and/or government functions (p. 42).[4]

Note that a government definition is carefully worded, recognizing the fact that such official wording ends up being used to implement policy and funding.

Famed disaster sociologist E.L. Quarantelli has developed a list of six criteria that help distinguish catastrophes from disasters.[5] His definition includes indicators that can be recognized at the community level as well as addressing national actors. Quarantelli's definition has become well-used in the limited but growing sociological literature on catastrophes.

Quarantelli's six criteria:

1. In catastrophes most or all of a community's built structure is impacted, including facilities of emergency response organizations.
2. Local response personnel are unable to assume normal roles due to losses of personnel and/or facilities and equipment.
3. Help from nearby or even regional communities is not available because all are affected by the same event.
4. Most, if not all, of the everyday community functions are sharply and concurrently interrupted.
5. News coverage is more likely to be provided by national organizations over a longer period of time.
6. National government and very top officials become directly involved.

Let us look at Quarantelli's criteria for a moment. Note that the criteria do not form a definition, but criteria that help the reader see that catastrophes really are different in some observable ways. Not every criterion needs to be met, and most are qualified by relative terms such as "most." The first criterion indicates that infrastructure cannot be counted on for local or regional response. However, nearly all writers in this field, both in and out of government, agree that a high-mortality pandemic could or would qualify as a very serious catastrophe, even though it would not touch our physical infrastructure. It would affect our human infrastructure ... those who meet the needs of the population on all levels, thus withdrawing needed services at the very moment they are most needed. In our opinion, this is the real meaning of Quarantelli's first criterion: The resources we most need are directly affected by the catastrophe and rendered unavailable.

The second criterion says the same thing, but focuses on personnel and equipment. The third points out that mutual aid is not to be counted on, because the event is of such size that "neighbors" are all similarly affected and unable to come to the aid of others. This is a clear departure from much of the thinking in disaster preparedness, and calls for different planning parameters.

The fourth criterion, noting that community functions are sharply curtailed, like the third criterion, indicates that outsiders will be responsible for providing what the affected population needs. This could mean that higher levels of government will begin to take primary responsibility at local levels, or even that non-governmental organizations from outside of the affected area will become primary service providers. In either case, decisions regarding the use of resources at the local level may be coordinated and decided by outsiders. If we read this right, the combination of criteria two, three, and four breaks with the longstanding concept that outsiders will come in to help in a response that is still directed by capable and knowledgeable locals.

Criteria five and six add more evidence to the shift from local to national or higher levels of participation. The movement of foci away from the local, while still focusing on meeting the needs of local populations throughout the entire affected region, provides a hint at the complexity of catastrophes. This is one of the key concepts of catastrophes, as identified by several European planners and writers (Lagadec and others).

Readers should note that none of the definitions we have offered thus far has a single clear tipping point at which an event converts from being a disaster to taking on the characteristics of a catastrophe. This "loose definition" phenomenon is one of the enduring (if not endearing) qualities of extreme event preparedness and response.

In my own writing, I have posited a shorter, perhaps more concise definition of catastrophe:

> A catastrophe is an event that directly or indirectly affects an entire country, requires national or international response, and threatens the welfare of a substantial number of people for an extended period of time. Synonym used in several European countries: hypercomplex emergency.

This definition brings into discussion the concept that an entire nation is affected for an extended period of time, and that international response assistance may be needed. In doing so, it incorporates one of the base concepts of disaster

... that outside assistance is needed ... only this time the "jurisdiction" is much larger. The "hypercomplexity" term is increasingly used in some European countries to describe catastrophes, using a functional perspective of how catastrophes are different from a response viewpoint. This is covered well in one of Erwan Lagadec's books: *Unconventional Crises, Unconventional Responses: Reforming Leadership in the Age of Catastrophic Crises and Hypercomplexity*. (Lagadec E: *Center for Transatlantic Relations*, 2007. ISBN 10: 0-9788821-8-0.) Note that both the book you are now reading and the work by Lagadec make numerous references to international aspects of catastrophes due to their habit of not respecting national boundaries.

Embedded in this definition is the concept that size of the event is only one of the variables that distinguishes catastrophes from disasters. Catastrophes differ *in kind* as well as size. By this we mean that their complexity and their various impacts are so significant that the ordinary planning, preparedness, and response tools are no longer sufficient ... or may even be counterproductive. One of the core concepts entailed in this definition is the complexity described by Lagadec, based on the realization that modern social and economic systems are so thoroughly intertwined with multiple diverse actors that no single command-and-control system will be effective in bringing all needed resources to bear on a response. Once this is realized, alternative approaches to resource acquisition and utilization can be envisioned.

CONTINUUM OF MAGNITUDE

Catastrophes exist on a conceptual continuum, ranging from emergencies to events that can or would bring about the extinction of the human species. For reference, here are some summary definitions of the four levels of events used in this book:

Emergency: An event, usually sudden, that puts at risk the life or well-being of at least one person. Local emergency response resources are adequate to meet the immediate needs of those who are affected by the incident. The response is directed/coordinated by personnel from within the same jurisdiction as the responding agencies.

Disaster: An emergency involving multiple people, of such magnitude that local response resources are *not* adequate to meet the immediate needs of those who are affected by the event, requiring that additional resources be brought in from outside jurisdictions. The response is directed/coordinated by personnel from within the jurisdiction where the event occurred, but many of the responders may be from other jurisdictions, increasing the challenge of response coordination.

Catastrophe: Use one or a combination of the definitions offered above. The response is from so many different jurisdictions, levels of government, and different kinds of organizations, and the needs of the affected population are so diverse and spread out, that no single entity can coordinate it all. Many needs will go unmet, at least in the short term.

Extinction level event: An event so severe that humans may not survive. No useful organized interventions can be anticipated.

HISTORIC EXAMPLES OF CATASTROPHES

To help understand what a catastrophe is, let us look at several historical examples. Obviously, many of the conditions and capabilities of societies in the past may be different from those of our own times, and one might argue that a given historical catastrophe in the past would not be one today. Right. That realization helps us understand that the socioeconomic and technical contexts of an event strongly influence what is a disaster and what is a catastrophe, and why the same event might be a catastrophe in a place like Haiti but not a disaster in Germany or Australia.

Before introducing the first historic example of a catastrophe, we think it is important to import a concept from public health, as it helps us understand how catastrophes can challenge human societies, and how we might identify useful intervention points. In public health and medical sciences we talk about an *etiology* of a disease or condition. It means the causes of, and typical pathways of a disease or other pathological state. As such, this is a very useful term for emergency managers looking into the future, who can envision calamities as pathologies with distinct causes, pathways, and consequences. In medicine, knowledge of the etiology of a pathology helps bring understanding regarding where successful interventions can be made. For example, understanding that malaria is caused by a microbe that has to complete part of its transmission cycle in the *Anopheles* mosquito, has allowed humans to greatly decrease (but not exterminate) the disease by way of controlling mosquito breeding opportunities and using window screens or netting to keep them from biting. To date, we have not been able to eliminate the microbe that causes malaria, just as we cannot eliminate earthquakes, but knowing that we can minimize the transmission of malaria by way of controlling *Anopheles* mosquitoes helps us limit malaria's impact on human well-being. We will see in the first historic example of a catastrophe that the lack of knowledge of the etiology of a microbe led to a horrible catastrophe.

Middle Ages Black Plague

Situation: A massive change in world trade patterns coupled with an overpopulated Europe suffering from 50 years of famine. Famine was partially due to rapid climate change toward colder, less predictable weather. A new microbe, *Yersinia pestis* entered Europe in the late 1340s via ships from Asia, by way of fleas on ship-board rats.

Brief background: The Plague is a disease that is still around today, caused by the bacterium *Y. pestis*, which can infect a variety of mammals. The typical etiology of *Y. pestis* is that it is transmitted from wild rodent hosts (rats, squirrels, etc.) to humans via the bite of fleas that had infested the rodents and picked up the bacterium in their blood meals. *Y. pestis* can also be transmitted, although with considerably less frequency, by way of contact with the flesh, blood, sputum or pus of infected humans or animals.[6] The disease can kill people in several ways, including massive body-wide sepsis and pneumonia. It is common that victims turn a dark color as the disease progresses, hence the term "black plague." The case fatality rate can run from 50% to nearly 100%. *Y. pestis* is mysteriously highly infectious sometimes and not so much on other occasions, and has been targeted as a potential biological weapon.[7]

Figure 1.2 Painting depicting the Black Death in Europe. (http://www.historyguide.org/ancient/death.html.)

At the time of the onset of the Black Plague, Europe had been undergoing numerous significant changes, several of which teamed with the introduction of *Y. pestis* to wipe out huge portions of many local populations (see Figure 1.2). Successful European agriculture had led to a significant population increase, which, in turn, led to more crowded living conditions. European-Asian commerce had begun to grow. A sudden change to a colder climate decreased crop yields and food availability to the large population, leading to famine at the time that *Y. pestis* entered Europe via shipboard rodents coming in from the East. The European population had no experience with plague and scientists expect that many had compromised immune response systems due to hunger. The result was a massive disease outbreak that lasted decades and eventually resulted in structural changes to society.

The consequences of this catastrophe are virtually unimaginable in today's social consciousness ... loss of up to 70% of the population! There was no germ theory-based medicine at the time and no treatments that offered relief. One of the scenes in Monty Python's *Holy Grail* movie, depicting carts being pulled through cities to collect the bodies of those who died over night, is probably pretty accurate (minus the jokes). Late during this period, a few governments started to take some responsible action, mostly imposition of quarantines and what we now call "social distancing" even though the etiology of the pathogen was not at that

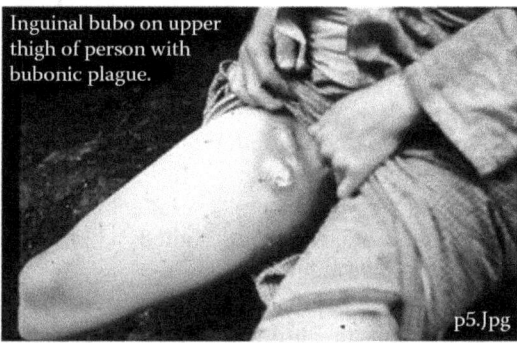

Figure 1.3 Modern bubonic plague victim. (http://www.cdc.gov/ncidod/dvbid/plague/p5.htm.)

time understood. At the end of all the suffering, the Black Plague led to several improvements:

- Governments began to take some responsibility for the well-being of their people.
- Some mitigative actions, such as quarantine and social distancing, became known as ways of decreasing disease propagation.
- The huge loss of population, especially among the landless peasant class, led to revised labor relations, giving rise to a "middle" class of merchants and artisans who worked for themselves, not for aristocracy. Given the relative scarcity of labor, workers could demand more recompense and better living conditions.

Note that modern medicine is capable of *decreasing* the lethality of plague, but not stop it (see Figure 1.3). More worrisome is the specter of the use of genetically altered *Y. pestis* as a bioweapon, against which none of the current control strategies would be efficient.

Little Ice Age in Europe

Situation: From roughly 1300 to 1850 the climate in the Northern Hemisphere became significantly colder, with three minima: 1650, 1770, and 1850. Crop-dependent populations hungered and starved. Famine decimated the Scandinavian population in Greenland.

This was a slow-onset event of 3.5 centuries duration. The effects for any particular locality differed over the years and they differed also from region to region, but they were serious. For more information, see Fagan.[8]

Climatologists tell us that climate change can bring about local and regional catastrophes. The Little Ice Age was relatively mild in terms of the actual temperature change, less than 1°C, according to the Intergovernmental Panel on Climate Change.[9] The calamity it provoked, however, was nothing near mild. Humans had been able to greatly expand their population, based largely on increasingly successful agricultural techniques. The downside, then as now, is that we were also very dependent upon continuing success in growing food, which is ultimately largely dependent on temperature, the availability of water, and viable soils. Many of the crops people used from the 1300s through the 1800s are little different from what we depend on today, with a relatively narrow range of temperature and moisture for optimal growth. When crops failed during this period, they did not just fail locally, but across wide territory, making it difficult or impossible to bring in food from the outside to stem starvation.

Some Europeans sealed their own fates by refusing to change their eating habits. For example, Scandinavians who had begun several colonies on Greenland, starved to death when their crops and grass-fed cattle failed, while the local native people survived eating marine mammals and fish.

The losses of some European populations met or exceeded 50%, such as was the case in Iceland. It was not only in Europe that people succumbed to starvation or related disease; the records of deaths in North America are poor, but there is evidence of some groups, including American Indians, banding together to avoid starvation.[10] This event obviously meets the definition of catastrophe: huge numbers of people suffered and died across many countries, and little could be effectively done about it.

It may be worth noting that, while modern society has better heating and food distribution systems, we are just as dependent on favorable weather to grow crops as we were in the 1600s. One of the paradoxical *potential* sequelae of climate change, as reviewed in the JEM article by Bissell et al.,[11] is a rapid-onset ice age, which would likely make it quite difficult to support agriculture and other life-support activities affecting 300 million modern Europeans. For more about this, see Schwartz and Randall.[12]

It is also worth noting that both of our first two examples of historical catastrophes were not rapid-onset events. It is important to keep in mind that the worst catastrophes we may face in the future might well be caused by the types of slow-onset dynamics that have killed so many in the past. Once again our climate is changing, and with it, potentially many threats that we will explore a little later in this book.

Irish Potato Famine

Situation: A combination of English land grabs of Irish farmland, the virtually complete dependence of a huge percentage of the Irish population on potatoes as their base food stock, and the accidental importation of a rapidly spreading fungus (or blight) left vast hunger, starvation, disease, and death in Ireland. The blight and crop failure became evident in 1845. The British response was confused: First they provided some imported Indian corn, but then stopped and assumed a laissez-faire approach, believing things would sort themselves out.

This catastrophic event was a combination of natural insult (the potato fungus) and poor decisions made by both the English rulers and the Irish peasants. Prior to the onset of the blight, Ireland had been occupied by England, and virtually all land was forcibly transferred from Irish farmers to new English landlords, essentially making Irish farmers peasants without land rights. The new landlords demanded the planting of wheat and oat crops for export to England, diminishing the land available for Irish agricultural self-sufficiency, thus placing the Irish population in a position of significantly enhanced vulnerability.

Even after the potato blight became a clear reality with obvious consequences for the landless Irish peasants, most of the new British landowners did not allow the Irish to expand the amount of land used for subsistence farming, nor did they allow the Irish to consume the cash crops of grains that were grown on Irish soil for English sale and consumption.

The British government formed an office to provide a response to the Irish potato blight, but then provided this program with very little in terms of staffing or supplies. For a short while the British provided Indian corn imported from the Americas to the Irish, but then discontinued this practice. While it is fair to say that there were concerned groups of people in England who tried to apply political pressure to force their government to act in a more decisive way, the majority of the British political class reached the conclusion that things in Ireland would sort themselves out on their own. The British army actually escorted shipments of Irish-grown wheat and oats out of Ireland so that British investors would not lose their profits, while Irish peasants died by the thousands. To add to the suffering, the winter of 1846–1847 was one of the coldest in recorded history, in a country where winter temperatures are usually mild. Seeing no alternatives, many Irish started to out-migrate by whatever means they could find available, often to North America or Australia as indentured servants, with a significant percentage of them dying while underway. Those who remained behind made the fatal mistake of once again planting potatoes as their primary subsistence crop. We might read into this history some conclusions about the willingness or ability of desperate populations to make rational decisions and take helpful actions to enhance their own survival in situations of catastrophic losses. The effects of malnourishment on brain function are well known and may be considered when making decisions regarding response and recovery operations for populations facing starvation.

The death toll estimates run from 775,000 to 1,500,000 (1845–1851) and it is estimated that another 1.5 million emigrated to North America and Australia during that time period. I think it is important to note that the Irish Potato Famine was the result of a natural event being converted into a catastrophe by human behavior and human decision making. The potato fungus would not have been capable of such a high toll in deaths, had the British not disregarded the well-being of the Irish, and had the Irish not stuck to a single-item diet (which had previously served them reasonably well). This is in no way a phenomenon that could be considered an historical relic. If we look at some of the catastrophes that are underway in Sub-Saharan Africa as this book is being written, we see that starvation, war, and genocide in places like Darfur, Somalia, Sudan, and the Ethiopia-Eritrea region are a combination of long-term drought, loss of arable land, competition for scarce survival resources, and the use of military and other means of force to assure the predominance of one group over another.

The examples of historical catastrophes we have looked at thus far also bring out a phenomenon that is much more typical of catastrophes than disasters, but which does not figure in any of the mentioned definitions of catastrophe: the fact that catastrophes often force or motivate survivors to migrate elsewhere, which can raise disastrous or catastrophic consequences as new populations attempt to move in with people who have been there for generations. That is to say that the catastrophe stimulates massive out-migration, and the out-migration itself can become the root of a secondary catastrophe. We will address this in much more depth in Chapter 9.

The 1918–1919 Influenza Pandemic

Situation: A strain of the influenza A virus with which humans had no previous experience hit in three waves in 1918 and 1919 with rapid worldwide spread and cumulative mortality that is estimated by various sources to be in the range of 40–100 million.[13–15] Symptoms started like typical influenza but often rapidly progressed to severe pneumonia.

The difference between an epidemic and a pandemic is that the epidemic has limited geographical reach, while a pandemic has worldwide spread (even if not all regions are affected equally). Influenza is a viral disease that typically has annual outbreak cycles, with each year's outbreaks generally affecting people who had no previous experience with that particular version of the virus (or one similar to it). The virus that caused the 1918–1919 pandemic was genetically different enough that virtually no one had immunity to it. The disparity in fatality numbers is due to the poor recording of death statistics in many countries at that time, exacerbated by the destruction and disorganization that resulted from World War I.

Chapter 13 of this book is focused on the modern concern over the potential of another influenza pandemic, which could have equally catastrophic or even worse consequences than the 1918–1919 pandemic. Both this present discussion of the 1918–1919 pandemic and the later chapter that is dedicated to a potential new influenza pandemic are included in this book to make it clear that a catastrophic pandemic is just as possible today as was the Black Plague of the 1300s. Pandemics also present an interesting set of challenges for emergency managers who are contemplating catastrophe preparedness, in that the lead responders to the pandemic would be medical and public health people who know comparatively little about emergency management. However, public health, as is described in Chapters 8 and 13 of this book, does not have the resources to mount and coordinate a societal response to a pandemic, and will have to rely on emergency managers who know comparatively little about the tools and strategies of epidemiology, public health, and medicine. Coordination in this kind of catastrophe (that attacks humans rather than physical infrastructure) will be so complicated that the only approach to assuring any kind of effectiveness is to engage in serious multi-disciplinary, multi-agency pre-planning, and exercising.

It is thought that the 1918–1919 pandemic began at a military base in Kansas, having been passed from pigs to humans in the area.* The military base provided a densely populated locale for incubation and propagation of the virus, and also a portal for outmigration to other areas of the world as the troops were assigned elsewhere. This particular version of the influenza virus was unusual in its behavior, in that it attacked healthy young adults with more frequency and more strength than people in older age groups. Because of military movements at that time, toward the

---

* For more information on this catastrophe, see *Flu: The Story of the Great Influenza Pandemic of 1918 and the Search for the Virus that Caused It* by Gina Kolata.

end of World War I, the virus moved quickly to Europe and then on to other parts of the world. After a large outbreak in Spain, Americans took to calling it the Spanish flu, mostly unaware that the disease likely started in the United States. The end of the war stimulated the migration of millions of people, either out of war zones and back to their homes, or out of their home territory toward countries deemed safer, thus providing yet another pathway for the virus to be transported. It is likely that the presence of post-war hunger and poor sanitation also contributed to the seriousness of the disease once it took hold in a new "virgin" population.

In the United States, clinical care facilities were rapidly overwhelmed, as were also mortuaries and morgues. Alternate care sites were set up in several East Coast cities, but throughout the country many people chose to suffer at home rather than go to a huge ward for the very sick. Many jurisdictions in the country established social-distancing rules and forbad gatherings of people. Some jurisdictions also attempted, some successfully, to isolate themselves entirely from outsiders. In a 2007 article in the *Journal of the American Medical Association*, Markel et al. demonstrated that American cities that adopted the practice of using selected isolation and quarantine during the 1918–1919 pandemic significantly decreased transmission of the disease.[16] More about this kind of strategy is discussed in Chapters 8 and 13 of this book.

Note that some characteristics of life in the United States during that time enabled people to do what might be very difficult or even impossible today, namely, essentially isolate oneself from outsiders during the peaks of the disease. During that time period food came from nearby, and many, if not most people had stores of food they had "canned" from their own gardens. The economy was more organized around local production and consumption, making it more robust in face of vast worker absences or deaths. Today's economy is much more centralized and interdependent, with widespread use of "just in time" delivery models of crucial resources. This makes the entire economy much more vulnerable to disruptions in critical functions, which is exacerbated by a very large percentage of the population not having a self-sufficient storage of basic foodstuffs. It is not inconceivable that a pandemic could result in widespread hunger and a significant temporary disruption of the monetary economy, in addition to the already horrendous suffering and loss of human life.

Just as has been the case in previous pandemics, the actual death toll of the 1918–1919 influenza pandemic is not precisely known. Historians and epidemiologists are comfortable with the assertion that over 500,000 people died of the disease in the United States, but an exact number will never be known. It is more difficult to come to exact numbers of those lost in other countries. For many years, historians guessed at a figure somewhere around 20 million. However, in more recent studies with more effective information gathering and better epidemiologic models, that figure has been re-estimated to fall between 40 and 100 million worldwide.[17] Keep in mind that there were fewer than one-third as many people on the planet then as compared to now.

Hurricanes Katrina and Rita

Situation: Two Category 5 (at one point) hurricanes hit the U.S. Gulf Coast in 2005. The eye of Hurricane Katrina hit some 30 miles east of New Orleans,

LA (NOLA) on August 29, bringing with it a storm surge above 20 feet in many places. The morning after Katrina's landfall, several of the levees protecting below-sea level New Orleans failed, flooding the majority of the city and significant portions of the surrounding suburbs (see Figure 1.4). More than 1,500 people were killed as a result of the storm. Hurricane Rita followed on September 24, making landfall on the Texas–Louisiana border, forcing the evacuation of much of the area around Houston and diverting resources from response to the needs of Katrina victims.

While it is, perhaps, debatable as to whether Hurricane Katrina and its aftermath qualify as a catastrophe, we add it here as a large event with many catastrophe-like characteristics, one that resides in the collective memory. We recommend that you read the Cooper book on *Hurricane Katrina* in order to obtain a much more thorough understanding of the event than we can cover in this book.[18] Cooper's book provides a good discussion of the various causes of the response going so badly, including the overwhelming character of some aspects of the events, poor understanding by federal authorities of their own planning documents, poor relationships between levels of government, poor local preparedness, power plays, and interference with incident command at many levels, and misunderstandings among the public as to what government would or could do. At the time of writing this current book, numerous new research publications on Hurricane Katrina and its aftermath are available through the Disaster Research Center at the University of Delaware and the Natural Hazards Center at the University of Colorado. We recommend that you peruse the titles of

Figure 1.4 New Orleans under water after Hurricane Katrina. (http://www.fema.gov/photolibrary/photo_details.do?id=19230.)

available papers and review those that speak to the issues most important to your own understanding. It is this event that forced the United States to start thinking about catastrophes as different and real.

There are several ways in which these storms had catastrophe-like characteristics. One of the characteristics of catastrophes is their multi-jurisdictional coverage. Hurricane Katrina damaged transportation and communications routes in four states, which greatly complicated the tasks of damage assessments, needs assessments, logistics planning and coordination, and communication from those who were directly affected to those who could provide assistance.

Healthcare became an issue almost immediately, both for the lack of availability and the need to safely evacuate patients out of hospitals and nursing homes to new locations. The damage was so widespread that solutions were not to be found in the next county (parish) over, or even the next state. In the end, many patients were transported as far away as the Midwest, East Coast, and Southwest regions of the country, often without medical records or a responsible companion or family member.

As was pointed out in the Quarantelli description of catastrophes, the locus of decision-making often changes away from local, up to state or national, or even international. In the city of New Orleans (NOLA), local pre-storm decisions made a huge difference in how difficult the situation would ultimately become. The city did not issue an evacuation order until it was too late to get everybody out, and poorly coordinated the manpower and mobile resources needed to evacuate those who did not have vehicles. These decisions had significant repercussions on death rates and on the well-being of those who stayed behind. Once the storm and flooding had hit, the city was no longer capable of mounting a response, due to the vast infrastructure damage and the evacuation of a large number of its workers. NOLA became dependent upon state and federal level resources, as did many other coastal and near-coastal communities in Louisiana, Mississippi, Florida, and Alabama. For several weeks the major decisions regarding New Orleans were largely made by state and federal authorities after the city's government was rendered ineffective due to its losses of human and physical infrastructure.

Hurricane Katrina hit four states and the federal response to all four was confused, at least initially. However, in Mississippi, Texas, and Alabama, the response coordination became increasingly better, whereas it did not in Louisiana for quite some time. This demonstrates the importance of that middle level of response ... the state ... in bringing about a well-coordinated response.

All four of the states that received primary impact from Hurricane Katrina operated under a standard all-hazards emergency operations plan, at both state and local levels. One of the concepts of the all-hazards standardized National Incident Management System (NIMS) approach is that it minimizes confusion as new resources come in from the outside to provide assistance. They all have the same authority structure and use the same vocabulary. However, the involved states did not have the same response plans for the event type at hand, and this created significant problems in the response to Hurricane Katrina. The disarticulation between plans was not only between state and federal plans, but also between the various local jurisdictions within a given state. This was particularly problematic in Louisiana, and contributed to the response confusion that reigned in that state for some time. Another area of disarticulation was between federal agencies, and, at times, between federal-level political operatives and emergency managers. The breakdown of the incident management system that resulted from political-level interventions led to such confusion that it sometimes took days, or even weeks to reconstitute organized command.*

Obviously, lessons have been learned, and are still being learned. Texas learned from the late evacuation of NOLA and, when faced with Hurricane Rita a month later, initiated and operated a much more effective evacuation of vulnerable populations. FEMA learned that some kinds of massive events, the focus of this book, require multi-jurisdictional, multi-agency, and multi-government joint planning and testing if a region is going to be able to have a coordinated response to predictable events. One of the lessons picked up upon by researchers such as Lagadec[19] and some of the coauthors of this book is that the vastness of the needs caused by the event, and the confusion caused by attempts at response, led to a level of complexity that was too much for the current response system design to handle effectively.

New Orleans' population 1 year after Katrina was about 40% of the pre-storm level; in early 2008 it was estimated at about 50%. It is clear that the long-term outmigration of more than 200,000 former inhabitants of the city is one of the effects of the storm. One of the characteristics of catastrophes is that they have long-term effects, one of which is that many catastrophes will provoke significant out-migration.

POTENTIAL FUTURE CATASTROPHES

The historical examples of catastrophes provided here demonstrate that catastrophes are part of the human experience, and often leave lasting consequences far beyond the place and time in which they occur. Even with the very small sample of historical catastrophes we have just described, we recognize that they are not extremely rare occurrences, and that they will continue to happen. This book is based on the premise that humans can be better prepared to confront catastrophes in such a manner that minimizes the huge potential damage and suffering these events bring. Before moving to more detailed descriptions of the challenges and potential remedies, let us take a few moments to consider a small sample of potential future catastrophes, so that we have at least a sketchy understanding of some of the dynamics we may be facing. We present here only a very few of the numerous potential events.

---

* Readers may want to go to some of the official evaluations released in 2006 by the White House and congress. (http://www.whitehouse.gov/reports/katrina-lessons-learned/). Note that the Government Accountability Office (GAO) has issued numerous reports on various aspects of the response to Hurricane Katrina. You can peruse and acquire them at http://www.gao.gov/docsearch/locate?searched=1&o=0&order_by=rel&search_type=publications&keyword=Hurricane+Katrina&Submit=Search.

Sea Level Rise

Situation: With global warming taking place, there is significant melt-off of Arctic, Antarctic, and terrestrial glaciers, with resulting waters going to the oceans. Estimates range between 1 and 3 m (3 to almost 10 ft) sea-level rise in the next century, but current melt-offs are progressing much more quickly than any model had predicted.[20]

Sea level rise is both a direct threat and an indirect one. Let us concentrate first on the two direct threats ... the ocean will flood areas that are currently populated, and it will contaminate the ground water of many areas that are close to the new coast line but not yet flooded. In the first case, populations will have to migrate or drown; in the second, they will lose significant agricultural productivity in a world that is already moving toward food inadequacy. Island countries are particularly hard hit, as many of them are low-lying and have nowhere else to go. If authorities can manage peaceful out-migration to another country, the loss of the island might be a significant inconvenience, but if peaceful migration is not allowed, the situation could become catastrophic. For example, consider the cases of two island countries (Tuvalu and the Maldives) that, at the time of this writing, are considering the need to evacuate their entire populations to another country, due to rising sea levels. Worldwide, more than 300 million people are estimated to live within the 1-m flood zone. Note that many European and international planning agencies are now setting their planning targets based on the assumption of a 5-m (15+ ft) sea level rise by the end of this century (see Figure 1.5).[21,22]

An indirect result of sea level rise is that storm surges will have deeper reach into populated areas. This comes at a time when climatologists are predicting increasingly powerful storms. This raises the fear that Katrina-like events could become commonplace. Either way, mass population relocation will be an inevitable result of the sea level rising, and it would not just be people moving around within their own countries. As we have already mentioned, mass migration is much more likely to result from catastrophes than disasters, and such migrations, in and of themselves have the possibility to become a secondary catastrophe. There are very few examples of mass migrations in the past 500 years of human history that have been accomplished peacefully. Where do you move the 300 million people living in coastal lowlands? And, how can you do this peacefully? Who will pay for mass resettlement and massive civil engineering projects?

Much valuable agricultural land around the world lies in deltas, often less than a meter above mean high tide level. This is particularly true in places such as Bangladesh, India, Thailand, Cambodia, Myanmar, China, the Netherlands, and even the Chesapeake Bay area of the United States. In many of these areas the produce of the delta agriculture is important to the survival of populations that are already at risk of starvation. Sea level rise will ruin agriculture by way of inundation for those on or near the coastline, and can also affect agriculture further inland by way of contaminating aquifers with salt water. Such is the predicted case with low-lying Florida, whose produce is sent around the world (see Figure 1.6).[23] How will we make up for the lost agricultural productivity, especially when at the same time many inland areas are succumbing to desertification?

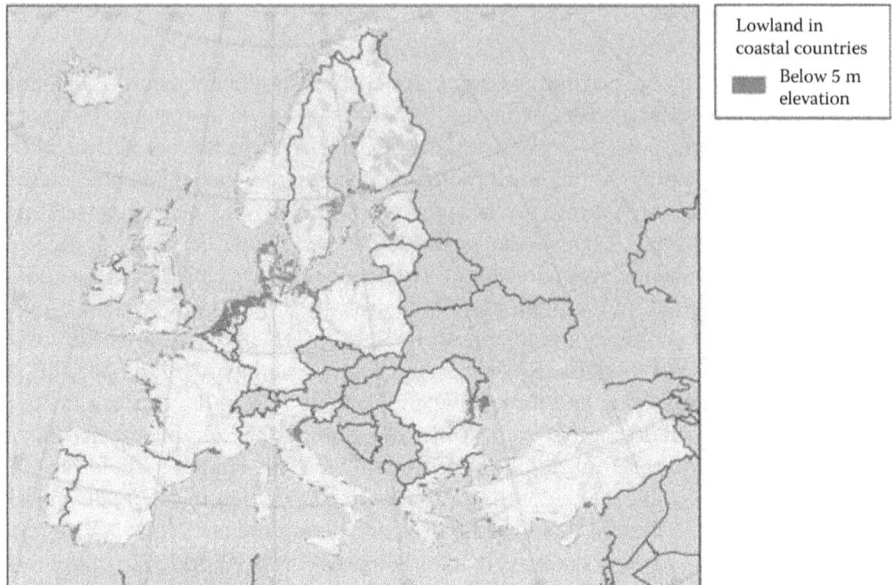

Figure 1.5 Likely European land loss to a 5 m or less sea level rise. (Darkened coastal areas are likely to be lost.) (http://www.eea.europa.eu/data-and-maps/figures/european-coastal-lowlands-most-vulnerable-to-sea-level-rise/insert-to-box-9.eps/insert%20to%20box%209.eps.75dpi.png/at_download/image.)

Drought and Desertification

Situation: A combination of global warming and poor land use practices is resulting in loss of overall fresh water available in some significant parts of the world, resulting in the loss of land capable of supporting either crops or natural vegetation. Without vegetation, land converts to desert.

This is another natural event that we can see coming ... the process is already underway and is well documented. Photos from sites of new desertification can really help you see this as a reality. For starters, go to http://www.abc.net.au/science/photos/desertification/ or http://managingwholes.com/photos/index.htm. There has already been major loss of agricultural lands in already over-populated countries such as China, India, and Nigeria. For example, in China the current rate of losing arable land to desert is 3,600 km^2 per year, and in Nigeria it is 3,510 km^2.[24] This is a problem in many parts of the world, and, if Darfur and Somalia are any example of the human response to drought and desertification, conflicts over increasingly scarce arable land may prove as dangerous as starvation. The rapid loss of underground aquifers adds to the consequences of drought, in many places removing future options to irrigate land that is dry on the surface. The drought in the American Southwest could also lead to radical relocation in the United States if the predicted loss of Lake Meade becomes a reality.

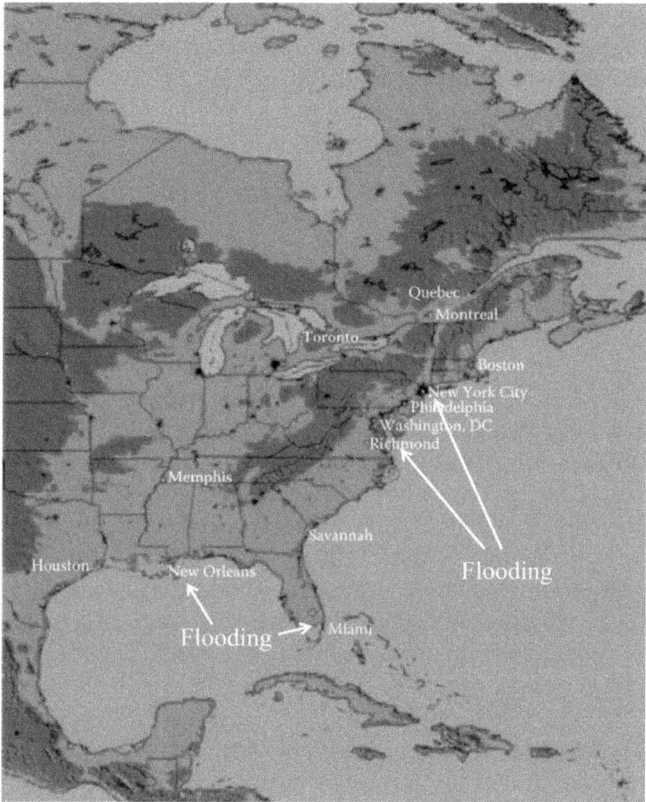

Figure 1.6 Predicted coastal flooding in the United States with a 3 m sea level rise. (http://vrstudio.buffalo.edu/~depape/warming/EastCoast003-480.jpg.)

From a global perspective, climate change-generated drought in the American *Midwest* could prove far more catastrophic than the loss of Lake Mead, because millions of people around the world directly or indirectly depend on grains from the North American breadbasket, even in normal times. As global warming decreases crop yield in many parts of the world, each source of grains will become that much more important.

By this point it should be becoming apparent that the hazards and threats we are talking about here may originate years before reaching catastrophic proportions, and may have an etiology that originates on other continents. A drought in the North American bread basket can result in many thousands, if not millions of deaths in Asia and Africa. Year-after-year loss of snowpack in Colorado can result in millions of people in Arizona, Nevada, and Southern California migrating to places with a more secure water supply. Economists have traditionally assured us that if there is a demand, somebody will figure out how to supply the goods demanded. That is clearly not the case where the basic resources we call on are in short supply. These are not just ecological issues; they are the progenitors of potential catastrophes. What skills will emergency managers need in order to contribute to efforts to minimize the effects of slow-moving but massive hazards like drought and desertification? What skills will they need when mitigation fails? What kinds of coalitions and agreements need to be initiated now so that we have access to vital tools and strategies when conditions migrate from bad to catastrophic?

Global Pandemic

Situation: A pathogenic virus or other microbe mutates (either naturally or by purposeful weaponization) and spreads out into a human population that has no natural immunity to it. There is a significant lag time between the spread of the disease and the ability of medical and pharmaceutical researchers to develop and produce enough vaccines or medicines to effectively counteract the microbe.

The scenario of a pandemic presents a real challenge to both experienced and up-coming emergency managers. This is partly because emergency managers tend to have limited understanding of the science behind disease control. The scenario also runs counter to the more frequent disaster events, in which some outside force damages physical structures and hurts humans in the process. In the pandemic situation, the physical infrastructure is not destroyed, but humans are the locus of damage. The chapter on pandemics later in this book presents much more detail and helps you learn more about the basics of disease control, and suggests meaningful ways in which emergency managers can contribute to improving the outcome from a pandemic.

One of the challenges in a high-mortality pandemic is that the functioning of the human-built *organizational* (not physical) infrastructure will be severely affected, including perhaps some basics like the transport and distribution of food and other basic commodities. The medical system we depend on to take care of sick people will be rapidly overwhelmed, making it necessary to make really tough choices. It is not inconceivable that even basic public safety and security will become challenged as public safety personnel fail to come to work due to disease, death, family needs, or fear.

Pandemics, by definition, affect many or most of the countries on Earth. A pandemic that has a high death rate would present a situation in which political jurisdictions, whether counties or countries, could not expect to receive outside assistance because virtually all countries would be faced with the same situation in which their resources are insufficient to be able to meet the needs of their own people. It may also be virtually impossible to migrate out of contagion zones, as authorities would attempt to halt migration as a means of minimizing contamination. As you can see, even with this superficial description, a high-mortality pandemic would not just be an issue for public health and medical authorities to address; coordinated emergency management would be required to attempt to overcome deficits in security, food distribution, energy supplies, movement of vaccines, and other medical supplies, as well as both commercial and physical infrastructure, and these challenges would be faced at a time that emergency managers themselves may be sick or limited because of illnesses in their families. Is there a way to prepare for this kind of scenario, so that even if billions around the world are affected, planned and coordinated responses could at least minimize the suffering and dying?

New Madrid Mega-Earthquake

Situation: The New Madrid fault line along the Mississippi River repeats its 1811–1812 production of one or more Richter-level 8 earthquakes. The region from Memphis TN to Illinois and from Arkansas to parts of the Eastern Seaboard would be affected. This area has very little anti-seismic construction, including transportation infrastructure, water, gas, and electricity transmission, critical public buildings such as hospitals and fire stations, as well as private housing.

What converts this event into a catastrophe is the combination of the size of the event (magnitude), the lack of appropriate building codes or building designs, and the important roles the area plays in the national transportation network, power supplies, and economy. As is the case with virtually all disasters, this event becomes a catastrophe because of the vulnerability humans built into the constructed environment, private and public, as well as the design of service systems in a way that assumes there will be no meaningful earthquakes.

The New Madrid fault line was not recognized by seismologists until the last few decades, and by emergency managers and building standards regulators even more recently. The area covered follows the Mississippi River and includes the states of Illinois, Indiana, Missouri, Arkansas, Kentucky, Tennessee, and Mississippi. It is a major fault line that produced two very large earthquakes in 1811 and 1812 (magnitude 8 or higher), at a time when there were few human structures in the region, and those that did exist were light and presented little danger. However, the earthquakes were forgotten for about 150 years, and, in the meantime, the area was heavily settled and covered with buildings, roads, bridges, and pipelines that were not designed to resist seismic activity.

If a new earthquake of similar magnitude (or even in the 7 range) were to hit today, a 5–8 state region would be affected, making mutual aid compacts useless (see Figure 1.7). Depending on magnitude and timing, deaths could be in the tens of thousands and injuries in the hundreds of thousands. Many bridges over the Mississippi River would likely collapse, including those that carry major interstate freeways and railroads, greatly impeding much national commerce. Of course, local bridges and roads would also be damaged, and in the cities, roads would be covered with debris. The in-transport of response personnel and supplies, and out transport of the injured would be very difficult. Pipelines carrying natural gas and oil to much of the East Coast would be affected, perhaps for many months. Many places in the world that depend on grains transported down the Mississippi River from the American and Canadian "breadbaskets" would suffer. The sheer quantity of damage would render rapid reconstruction impossible, perhaps resulting in a significant out-migration of populations and businesses.

In summary, the extreme volume and spread of the damage would affect the entire United States in many ways, as well as affecting people around the world who depend on products that come from or are shipped through the New Madrid fault line

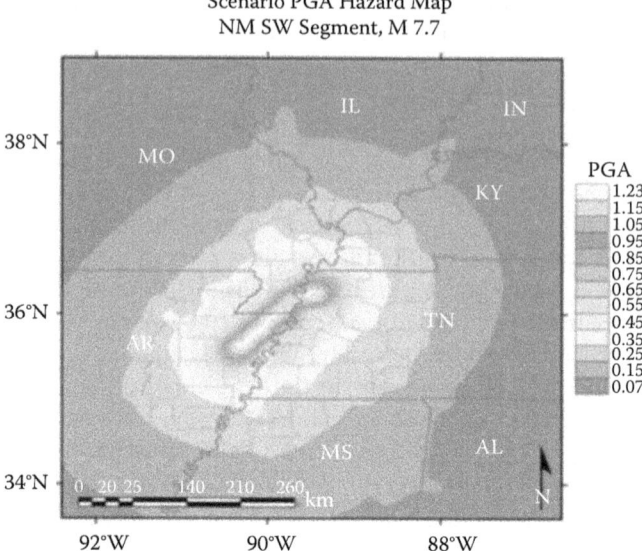

Figure 1.7 Projected peak ground acceleration intensity in a major New Madrid Seismic Zone earthquake. (http://earthquake.usgs.gov/regional/ceus/products/regional.php.)

area. Local mutual aid compacts would be useless at the same moment that many communities would find themselves effectively cut off from the rest of the world. The United States does not have sufficient search and rescue teams, disaster medical assistance teams, emergency engineering personnel, emergency food supplies nor transportable emergency shelters (should, God forbid, this earthquake happen in the winter) to meet the needs of such a large number of people spread out over such a huge area. And ... the tasks of coordinating national and international aid to such a large area would outstrip our traditional national response management capabilities. In a word, this would be a catastrophe.

Summary: Factors Common in Catastrophes

Now that we have looked at several past and likely future catastrophes; we can summarize the factors that are common to catastrophes, recognizing that not all catastrophes will exhibit all of these characteristics. The characteristics or factors common to catastrophes are

- The events involve many jurisdictions simultaneously.
- Jurisdictions are unable to respond effectively alone, but the breadth of the event makes outside help difficult or impossible.
- Response demands outstrip the capabilities of traditional government leadership and resources.

- In many affected localities, major decision-making will move upstream to larger jurisdictions.
- With the reality being that many communities suffering a rapid-onset event will not see outside resources for days or weeks, immediate survival will require both local skills and non-traditional approaches to bringing assistance to those who are in need.
- Many catastrophes do not have an extremely rapid onset.
- Many catastrophes' direct effects have long endurance, decades or even centuries.
- Mass migration is a common potential outcome of catastrophes.
- Many causes of both past and future catastrophes are outside of the current emergency management planning mentalities.
- The complicated etiologies of most causes of catastrophes require strong and sustained interaction between science and emergency management in order to provide any chance of successful mitigation or response planning.
- Poor government response can significantly enhance the peril (e.g., Irish Potato Famine).

This book is designed to help us all understand better the etiologies of catastrophes, and to begin to develop new and different approaches to preparing for and responding to these hypercomplex events.

Overview of the Book

Most of the chapters in this book address issues, problems, or relationships we already know about in the disaster context, moving the discussion to how they play out, or change in importance in catastrophes. It is not our intention to re-educate the reader about the basics of disaster preparedness and response, but rather help the reader move beyond his or her current knowledge and perceptions to a new set of understandings that will help the reader provide some real leadership in preparing for and responding to catastrophes. In fact, we hope that the new understandings conveyed in this book will also help you decide how you might want to alter your own family preparedness plans. In the last third of the book we concentrate a bit more on providing alternative approaches to planning for and responding to catastrophes, realizing that we do not have all the answers but rather suggestions based on accumulated learning and current activities in several countries to address the catastrophe potential. The Great Eastern Japan Earthquake and Tsunami of 2011 occurred during the writing of this book, and so we have added to the original plan a chapter that compares the responses to that event and the 2010 Haitian earthquake, each of which has strong but different catastrophe characteristics.

The layout of the book is designed to provide three kinds of information. This first chapter has set a general context for catastrophes, how they differ from disasters, with a quick overview of some past and potential future catastrophes to help the concept become more real and practical. Chapters 2 through 5 provide topic-oriented background information so that you will have a broad understanding of some of the dynamics, challenges, and limitations related to catastrophes, upon which you can build more specific plans and strategies. Chapters 6 through 14 provide the best current discussion on such important catastrophe preparedness and response topics such as logistics, critical infrastructure, public health, mass displacement, emergency organizations, response, recovery/reconstruction, pandemic response strategies and preparedness, and tools for exercising and refining plans. Chapter 15 provides a review of the 2010 earthquake in Haiti and the 2011 earthquake/tsunami/nuclear plant failure in Japan, to help us gain insight into the dynamics of catastrophe response in one of the world's poorest countries and one of the wealthiest. The final chapter provides a review of the most salient points in this book and challenges you to move forward the world's level of preparedness for catastrophes. We also provide a list of resources at the end of the book that should serve to help you dig deeper into the catastrophe content, and keep up with developments as they happen.

A word about the global context of this book: Although most of the team of authors who have worked on this book reside in the United States, many of us have spent considerable time living and working in other parts of the world. Catastrophes are not limited to any one country or region, although some are more vulnerable than others, and so, although many of the organizational contexts mentioned in this book are US-centric, the broader thoughts and many of the examples are meant to be global in context. We trust that we have achieved a balance between "domestic" and international content that will prove helpful and comfortable to everyone.

REFERENCES

1. Olsen, L. Who died in Hurricane Katrina? *Houston Chronicle*, 31 Aug 2010: http://www.chron.com/disp/story.mpl/nation/7177268.html, accessed 15 July 2011.
2. WHO. http://www.who.int/hac/crises/international/asia_tsunami/en/, accessed 15 July 2011.
3. 7.0 Mw earthquake (USGS). http://earthquake.usgs.gov/earthquakes/eqinthenews/2010/us2010rja6/, accessed 22 July 2011.
4. US Department of Homeland Security National Response Framework. Chapter 2: *Response Actions*, 42. Available at http://www.fema.gov/pdf/emergency/nrf/nrf-core.pdf.
5. Quarantelli EL. Catastrophes are different from disasters: Some implications for crisis planning and managing drawn from Katrina. 11 June 2006, Social Sciences Research Council. Available at http://understandingkatrina.ssrc.org/Quarantelli/.
6. Heyman DL, ed. *Control of Communicable Diseases Manual.* 2008, APHA Press, Washington, DC. ISBN: 978-08755-31892.
7. Orent W. *Plague: The Mysterious Past and Terrifying Future of the World's Most Dangerous Disease.* 2004, Free Press, New York. ISBN: 0-7432-3685-8.
8. Fagan B. *The Little Ice Age: How Climate Made History.* 2000, Basic Books, New York. ISBN: 0465022723.
9. Intergovernmental Panel on Climate Change (Third Assessment). *Was There a "Little Ice Age" and a "Medieval Warm Period"? Working Group 1: The Scientific Basis. Chapter 2: Observed Climate Variability and Change.* Available at: http://www.grida.no/publications/other/ipcc_tar/?src=/climate/ipcc_tar/wg1/070.htm.
10. *NASA: The Sun's Chilly Impact on Earth. Scientific Visualization Studio.* Available at http://svs.gsfc.nasa.gov/stories/iceage_20011207/.

11. Bissell RA, Bumbak A, Levy M, Echebi P. Long-term global threat assessment: Challenging new roles for emergency managers. *Journal of Emergency Management*, 2009, 7(1), 19–37.
12. Schwartz P, Randall D. *An Abrupt Climate Change Scenario and Its Implications for United States National Security*. Report produced on contract to the US Department of Defense, 2003. Available at: http://oai.dtic.mil/oai/oai?verb=getRecord&metadataPrefix=html&identifier=ADA469325.
13. Patterson KD, Pyle GF. The geography and mortality of the 1918 influenza pandemic. *Bulletin of the History of Medicine*, 1991, 65(1), 4–21. PMID 2021692.
14. Taubenberger JK, Morens DM. 1918 Influenza: The mother of all pandemics. *Emerging Infectious Diseases*. 2006, 1–8. Available at http://wwwnc.cdc.gov/eid/article/12/1/pdfs/05-0979.pdf.
15. Johnson NP, Mueller J. Updating the accounts: Global mortality of the 1918–1920 "Spanish" influenza pandemic. *Bulletin of the History of Medicine,* 2002, 76(1), 105–15.
16. Markel H, Lipman HB, Navarro JA, Sloan A, Michelsen JR, Stern AM, Cetron MS. Nonpharmaceutical interventions implemented by US cities during the 1918–1919 influenza pandemic. *JAMA*, 2007, 298(19), 2260.
17. Johnson N, Mueller J. Updating the accounts: Global mortality of the 1918–1920 "Spanish" influenza pandemic. *Bulletin of the History of Medicine,* 2002, 76(1), 105–115.
18. Cooper C, Block R. *Disaster: Hurricane Katrina and the Failure of Homeland Security,* 2006. Times Books, New York. ISBN-13: 978-0-8050-8130-5.
19. Lagadec E. *Unconventional Crises, Unconventional Responses: Reforming Leadership in the Age of Catastrophic Crises and Hypercomplexity,* 2007. Johns Hopkins University Press, Washington, DC. ISBN 10: 0-988821-8-0.
20. World Glacier Monitoring Service: *Glacier Mass Balance Bulletin. Bulletin No. 11, 2008–2009.* 2011. Available at http://www.wgms.ch/mbb/mbb11/wgms_2011_gmbb11.pdf, accessed 14 April 2012.
21. Dasgupta S, Laplante B, Maisner C, Wheeler D, Yan DF. *The Impact of Sea Level Rise on Developing Countries: A Comparative Analysis*, 2007. World Bank Policy Research Working Paper No. 4136. Available online at http://econ.worldbank.org/resource.php?type=5.
22. Olsthoorn X, van der Werff P, Bouwer L, Huitema D. *Neo Atlantis*: *Dutch Response to Five Meter Sea Level Rise*. Working Paper FNU75. Institute for Environmental Studies, Vrije Universiteit Amsterdam. Available at http://www.uni-hamburg.de/Wiss/FB/15/Sustainability/waishollandwp.pdf.
23. Reese RS. *Hydrogeology and the Distribution of Salinity in the Floridan Aquifer System, Southwestern Florida*. 2000, U.S. Department of the Interior, U.S. Geological Survey.
24. Brown L. *Plan B 3.0 Mobilizing to Save Civilization,* 2008. Norton Books, New York. ISBN: 978-0-393-33087-8.

CHAPTER 2

Understanding Catastrophes
A Discussion of Causation, Impacts, Policy Approaches, and Organizational Structures

David A. McEntire

CONTENTS

Introduction	27
Hazards, Vulnerability, and Catastrophes	27
The Complex Interaction of Variables	35
The Impact of Catastrophes on Society	37
Required Intervention Points for Potential Catastrophes	39
Organizational Structures and Catastrophes	40
Conclusion	42
References	42

INTRODUCTION

The following chapter explores how hazards and vulnerability interact to produce catastrophes. It underscores the complexity of catastrophes as well as the significant impact that these events have on individuals, organizations, communities, and societies. Possible intervention points to mitigate, prepare for, respond to, and recover from catastrophes are mentioned. The chapter includes a discussion about two competing response structures, but concludes that all pertinent agencies should remain flexible in order to more effectively deal with the significant challenges posed by catastrophic events.

HAZARDS, VULNERABILITY, AND CATASTROPHES

Similar to a disaster, a catastrophe will occur when a hazard interacts with (or multiple hazards interact with) human-created vulnerability. Unlike a disaster, however, a catastrophe will involve a hazard (or hazards) of substantial magnitude along with extreme forms of vulnerability. These significant differences distinguish an unusual catastrophe from more common disaster situations.

A hazard is defined by Edward Keller and Robert Blodgett as "a process that poses a threat to human life or property" (2006, 6). Such hazards have been categorized as being natural, technological, or anthropogenic in origin. Examples of natural hazards include earthquakes, hurricanes, droughts, and epidemics. These result from natural processes within the physical or biological environments (e.g., the movement of tectonic plates, the hydrological cycle, or transformation of disease). Examples of technological hazards include industrial explosions, chemical releases, and nuclear accidents. Such hazards result from the failure of modern technology or the mistakes made by those handling computers, industrial machinery, aircraft, hazardous materials, and so on. Examples of anthropogenic (or civil) hazards include riots, terrorism, and war. These anthropogenic hazards result from social and political conflicts within or across societies.

Although there are distinct types of hazards, they all trigger or initiate the unfolding events called disasters or catastrophes. In some cases, the magnitude of hazards can be excessively severe. For instance:

- 50,000 years ago, a 54-yard meteorite struck the earth in North Western Arizona at a speed of at least 28,000 mph. It produced crater 4,000 feet in diameter and nearly 600 feet deep. The meteorite is estimated to have displaced 175 million tons of rock over a 100 square mile area. Even though this was a relatively small meteor, all life would have been destroyed within a 3–7 mile radius of the impact zone.
- The 1918–1919 Spanish Flu Pandemic killed between 20 and 40 million people. The influenza A virus affected 50% of the population and was a virulent killer. This event brought up numerous questions about quarantines and adequate medical care.
- On December 3, 1984, workers at a Union Carbide plant accidentally released 40 tons of methyl isocyanate gas, causing pulmonary edema and instant death of over 5,000 people living near the industrial facility. Over 100,000 people were injured, making it one of the largest industrial disasters in history.
- The 9/11 terrorist attacks caused the collapse of the World Trade Center Towers 1 and 2, resulting in 1.2 million tons of debris. The attacks had far-reaching economic and political impacts in the United States and even around the world.
- The Great Sumatra earthquake, which occurred on December 26, 2004, is another example. It registered at least 9.1 on the Richter scale and produced a tsunami (at least 30 feet high) that traveled between 300 and 600 mph. In some cases, the tsunami reached over 1 mile inland and killed an estimated 250,000 people.
- Hurricane Katrina generated sustained winds of 160 mph and included, in some places, a storm surge of 28 feet. The storm broke several levees, which flooded 80% of New Orleans. One million people were displaced and forced to evacuate to cities around the United States.
- According to scientists, the May 12, 2008, earthquake that struck China registered between 7.8 and 8.0 on the Richter scale. Thousands of buildings as well as countless

roads and bridges were damaged or destroyed in the event. Many communities were isolated from others for hours, days, and even weeks.
- The April 2010 eruption of the Eyjafjallajökull volcano in Iceland had significant consequences on aviation travel across the Atlantic Ocean. It has been estimated that over a period of at least 8 days, more than 100,000 flights were cancelled which stranded 10 million passengers.

The occurrence of such severe hazards has not only been experienced in the past; the potential of devastating events will certainly be witnessed in the future. As an example, it is anticipated that the Midwest and West Coast (running from California to Canada) will experience major earthquakes in the next 30–100 years. A major slip of the Tokai fault South West Tokyo is also overdue, possibly resulting in an estimated 8.4 earthquake. Loss of transportation, electrical, and water infrastructure will accompany these massive events. It is also believed that major hurricanes will threaten Miami, Florida, and even New York City. These major urban areas are predicted to experience substantial negative consequences from intense storms like the one that affected the Gulf Coast in 2005. A massive tsunami is anticipated to occur in the future when a rock slide occurs in La Palma (Canary Islands). The resulting wave could reach between 150 and 2,000 feet, and affect over 100 million people in Southern Europe and countries across the Atlantic Ocean. A future nuclear attack against the United States would kill hundreds of thousands of Americans. An estimated $1 trillion in economic damages would result if the detonation took place in a major city.

Although the intensity of hazards can at times be almost unimaginable, focusing on hazards as the sole cause of catastrophe is problematic (McEntire 2005). In most cases, people have very little control over asteroids, earthquakes, volcanic eruptions, and hurricanes. Also, giving excessive attention to hazards tends to downplay the human element in disasters and catastrophes. For this reason, "scholars have long proposed that we reconsider the 'naturalness' of disasters, arguing that we must acknowledge the social construction of such events" (McEntire 2005, 10). Ken Hewitt, quoting Claude Gilbert, states that there is "danger with ... the hazards paradigm: a viewpoint that classifies, explains and responds to disasters as if they were wholly or essentially a function of the agent that impinges upon a vulnerable society" (Hewitt 1998, 78). "Under the hazards view, society—at least, communities, the public or populations—are made to appear passive victims of natural and technological agents" (Hewitt 1998, 78).

E. L. Quarantelli, the editor of the book, *What Is a Disaster? New Answers to Old Questions* (2005), holds similar views. He suggests that "the imagery of hazards as leading to disasters is a very misleading one. To be sure, a hazard may at times be involved. However, the hazard ... is one factor at best, and not necessarily the most important one" (Quarantelli 2005, 342). Quarantelli further contends that "it is a misnomer to talk about 'natural' disasters as if they could exist outside of the actions and decisions of human beings and their societies.... For instance, floods, earthquakes, and other so-called 'natural' disaster agents have social consequences only because of the activities of human beings and their societies" (2005, 343). Finally,

Quarantelli states that "a focus on disaster calls attention to the social nature of such happenings; a focus on hazards tends to emphasize physical and natural phenomena. With rare exceptions little can be done about the latter; much can be done about the former" (2005, 342).

With this logic in mind, it is imperative that those involved in emergency management rethink past and current theoretical perspectives. Britton argues that "academics need to 'unlearn' in order to learn what the issues are ... and how they could contribute to issue solution" (Britton 2005, 116). Quarantelli declares that "what is needed is ... the creation of a new paradigm for disaster research" (Quarantelli 1998, 235). Cutter likewise notes that "a number of researchers have commented on the need for a redirection of risk, hazards, and disasters research into understanding vulnerability and reorienting disaster policy" (Cutter 2005, 44). Perry agrees that "hazards researchers studying disasters have moved slightly from what might be considered an 'agent centered' approach to a greater focus on vulnerability" (Perry 2006, 9). Quarantelli also concurs that "the recent shift in much of the literature from a primary focus on hazards to one on vulnerability is a step in the right direction" (2005, 343–344). These comments bring up the human role in catastrophes.

While it is true that hazard agents can be formidable, it is also evident that people play a significant role in disasters and catastrophes. Rick Bissell's paper, "Long-Term Global Threat Assessment: Challenging New Roles for Emergency Managers," outlines several human activities that will lead to future catastrophes (see also Brown 2008). For instance, while global warming has become more controversial due to the falsification of data by some scholars, the use of carbon-based fuels may nonetheless add to greenhouse gasses in the atmosphere. This change could potentially alter weather patterns significantly and lead to five problematic consequences:

1. Tropical diseases may spread due to warmer temperatures and the lack of immunity in areas that have historically had a cooler climate.
2. Desertification, or the loss of arable lands, may expand as deserts encroach upon fertile and forested areas.
3. Sea levels may rise and flood low-lying coastal areas as polar ice caps melt.
4. An abrupt ice age may occur, as the melting of the ice caps may dilute the salinity of the water that contributes to the distribution of life-supporting tropical waters to the Northern Hemisphere.
5. Storms may increase in frequency and intensity, and occur in places that are not accustomed to such climatological phenomena.

Other examples of human impact on disasters and catastrophes can be given. First, because of rising fertility rates and declining death rates, the population is expanding at significant rates. Population growth may encourage or force people to move to hazard-prone areas (e.g., flood plains) or live in densely populated urban areas that will result in more deaths or impacts when hazards occur. Second, humans are consuming more and more resources as time goes by. As a consequence, watersheds and forests may be lost due to increasing environmental pollution; forests and wetlands are in jeopardy due to the encroachment of a growing population, and biodiversity is lost in conjunction with these trends. Water is also becoming scarce due to the pumping of aquifers while food security is in question due to expanding demand. Petroleum-based economies may likewise collapse as demand is anticipated to exceed future supplies. Third, medical practices and human social interactions are resulting in the introduction of new, more virulent, and contagious diseases. Antibiotics may be accompanied by microbial mutations, and global transportation services are allowing disease strains to span the earth within days and even hours. Fourth, conflict among humans shows the potential of becoming more deadly as compared to the past. Terrorists continue to make threats and launch attacks, and civilians could be targeted in addition to uniformed soldiers with weapons such as nuclear weapons, dirty bombs, germ, and chemical warfare. As can be seen, humans are not blameless—particularly in reference to anthropogenic catastrophes. This brings up the important concept of vulnerability.

Vulnerability is the critical variable (or set of variables) in a disaster or catastrophe. In other words, a hazard agent can be witnessed independent of human activity (a tornado in a remote and isolated area cannot produce a disaster or catastrophe). In contrast, it is only when a hazard interacts with vulnerability that a disaster or catastrophe may occur. Accordingly, "vulnerability ... refers to the proneness of people to disasters based on factors such as their geographic location, exposed property and level of income. The ability of individuals, organizations, and communities to deal with disaster also has a close relation to vulnerability" (McEntire 2007, 2). There are two schools of thought pertaining to vulnerability: the social vulnerability school and the holistic school. Both are related, but the second is perhaps more comprehensive than the first.

The social vulnerability school discusses the social, political, and economic structures that perpetuate vulnerability and this viewpoint identifies those persons who are most vulnerable in society. This school is represented best by the work of Hewitt (1983), Wisner et al. (2004), Peacock et al. (1997), and Fothergill et al. (1999), among others. According to this view, social relationships, which are maintained by government policies as well as economic institutions and political structures, are to blame for vulnerability. In other words, emergency management law, employment relationships, and class divisions benefit some more than others. For instance, dangerous industries are almost always located far from wealthy neighborhoods. The rich have better jobs, which allow them to purchase insurance that can be used to replace property and other financial losses from a disaster or catastrophe. Because of available economic resources, some people are more educated than others. This allows them to make better response decisions when a hurricane approaches or an earthquake occurs. The rich also have close and reliable social networks (family, friends, or professionals) to help them through the difficult recovery period. In contrast, and because of economic constraints, the poor are more likely to live in hazard-prone areas and in dilapidated housing. They are often unprepared for disasters and catastrophes because they less able to purchase emergency supplies, and are less likely to have an education level that enables them to accurately judge risks and take preparatory and mitigative actions. The poor are least able to respond effectively to a disaster because they lack transportation and have limited funds for hotels during evacuation. Those with fewer economic means will also recover more slowly than others because they do not have savings or other social resources to help them get through challenging times.

Haiti and Poverty

The January 12, 2010 earthquake in Haiti is an excellent example that supports the social vulnerability paradigm. Haiti is the poorest nation in the western hemisphere and, indeed, is one of the least wealthy in the entire world. About 80% live below the poverty line in Haiti and about half earn less than $1.00 per day. Under these dire economic conditions, people often have little choice but to live in substandard housing. They often build houses themselves and with the materials they are able to acquire. In addition, people do not follow any building codes and their homes often lack the proper mixture of rebar, cement, rock, and sand. Consequently, when the 7.0 earthquake struck about 25 km distance west/south west of the capital city of Port-au-Prince, catastrophe resulted. The heavy and unstable roofs, walls, and floors gave way and collapsed like pancakes on the inhabitants within. Over 214,000 people are estimated to have died in the event.

Making matters worse, the country lacked any meaningful plans to respond to the event as well as trained personnel and sufficient equipment to help with search and rescue, medical care, and sheltering. Mass fatality management and debris removal also suffered as a result of poor preparedness efforts. Because of the lack of insurance and monetary resources, Haiti will be almost entirely dependent on international disaster assistance. These conditions will likely delay recovery and lead to a condition of increased vulnerability to future hazards.

Besides those who are disadvantaged due to structural relationships in society, the social vulnerability school identifies others who are vulnerable to disasters and catastrophes. This includes minorities, women, children, the elderly, the disabled, prisoners, and many others. In the United States, African Americans, Hispanics, and other ethnic groups are often poor and may struggle with warnings distributed in the English language. Many other countries have similar social or cultural groups who have relatively fewer self-protection capabilities. Women, particularly single mothers in places such as Africa or Latin America, may have limited economic resources, which increase their vulnerability. Women and their children may not be as able as men to protect themselves physically when hazards strike. Older individuals live on fixed incomes, and they are often frail in terms of health and physical abilities. The blind, deaf, physically ill/disabled, and mentally handicapped/ill face obvious challenges that put them at a distinct disadvantage in a disaster or catastrophe. Those incarcerated may be trapped when a disaster occurs (e.g., they are unable to evacuate to higher ground during a flood due to the metal bars and other barriers that prevent them from escaping). Others—homeless individuals, patients, college students, tourists, people with pets, and countless individuals—face unique circumstances that may make them especially vulnerable to disasters and catastrophes.

The second, or holistic theoretical school, accepts the premises of the social vulnerability perspective, but adds additional variables that must be taken into consideration. This school has been introduced by McEntire (2004, 2005). The holistic vulnerability school argues that the social vulnerability school is indeed correct. Social structure obviously augments vulnerability in numerous ways and there are countless individuals and groups that suffer as a result. That being said, the holistic school asserts that vulnerability is socially constructed through many variables—and not just economic structure alone. There are almost countless examples that can be given to support this claim:

- Some people choose to live in hazard-prone areas because of scenic views and temperate climates.
- Improper engineering designs and faulty construction practices may result in vulnerable infrastructure.
- Certain occupations, such as fire fighting and law enforcement, may make men more vulnerable than some women.
- Environmental degradation can augment vulnerability to flooding and famine.
- The perception that emergency management deals with disaster responses alone discourages the implementation of much needed mitigation measures.
- Failure to establish redundant warning systems and interoperable communications technology may limit the sharing of information needed to protect property and lives.
- Operational mistakes or errors may result in major accidents and disasters at industrial facilities.
- People may choose not to evacuate an approaching hurricane due to projected traffic jams and re-entry delays.
- Writing plans to fulfill mandates instead of build capability does nothing to reduce vulnerability.
- The move away from an agricultural economy and a reliance on a just-in-time shipping strategy could make people vulnerable to food shortages after a major catastrophe (at least initially).
- The presence of an established emergency operations center could be one of many factors that determine successful response operations.
- Apathy about disasters and catastrophes (due to their infrequent occurrences) discourages adequate preparedness measures.
- Urbanization may augment the vulnerability of cities to disasters due to a larger number of people in a smaller geographic area.
- People's diet and physical health determine, to some extent, their susceptibility to disease or inability to quickly escape.
- Our reliance on technology may limit what we can do when the conveniences of life are taken away when disaster strikes.
- Certain religious doctrines may be accompanied with fatalistic attitudes (although this is not always the case).
- Demographic patterns may result in a higher number of nursing home residents, who are highly dependent upon the care of medical and other personnel.
- Ignoring the need for public education and CERT teams will ensure a population is more vulnerable to catastrophe than it would be otherwise.
- Insufficient education and training may result in incorrect decisions by emergency managers, first responders, or the public.

- Poor coordination among all levels of government is likely to aggravate the impact of disasters and catastrophes.
- The convenience of fast food discourages the development of skills pertaining to planting, harvesting and cooking, which may be needed in times of a disaster or catastrophe.
- Lax border control could permit the infiltration of terrorists who wish to attack the United States.
- Disaster relief programs may at times subsidize risk and encourage people to avoid taking personal responsibility for their own vulnerability.
- Viewing emergency management as a public sector function only ensures that the private sector and individuals do little to reduce their vulnerability to disasters.
- Decisions made during recovery will certainly have an impact on future vulnerability (e.g., rebuilding vs. relocation).

In short, there are countless variables that make individuals, groups, organizations, communities, and nations vulnerable to disasters and catastrophes.

Hurricane Katrina and the Multi-Causality of Catastrophes

Hurricane Katrina was undoubtedly a monster storm that ravished the Gulf Coast, including Mississippi and Louisiana. Katrina reached category-3 storm status when it struck New Orleans and it contained strong winds, a large storm surge, and impressive amounts of precipitation. However, the damage and impact on this city cannot be blamed on Mother Nature alone. For instance:

- The city did not maintain and repair levees, and these gave way to the intense flooding.
- Public officials did not always warn people or make decisions about evacuation with sufficient time, and did not follow through with its plan to shuttle people to safety by school bus.
- The Superdome was not stocked with adequate supplies (e.g., cots, water, food) even though these were clearly identified as needs in the Hurricane Pam exercise one year earlier.
- The state government was unable to provide details about damages and request specific resources for response and recovery.
- The federal government had jeopardized emergency management severely in prior years with the focus on terrorism, the creation of a new National Response Plan, and the political battles over the direction and autonomy of the Federal Emergency Management Agency.
- Citizens failed to adequately prepare for a known hurricane threat while first responders, hospitals, and nursing homes could not meet the demands placed upon them.

While poverty certainly played a role in the outcome of Hurricane Katrina, so did poor decision making, insufficient preparedness, limited understanding of federal aid requirements, the creation of the Department of Homeland Security, intergovernmental politics, and a culture of apathy.

THE COMPLEX INTERACTION OF VARIABLES

As noted above, disasters and catastrophes are produced from the interaction of hazards and vulnerability. Nonetheless, the equation *"hazard agent + vulnerability = disaster or catastrophe"* is much too simple. Many disasters and catastrophes are not always sudden occurrences, but are instead gradual processes that develop over time. For instance, both drought and problematic agricultural policies may be present for several years before a famine is witnessed. A hurricane will not generate a catastrophe unless development over several decades puts thousands or millions of people in harm's way. An earthquake becomes catastrophic when construction practices over a significant period of time have not kept up with the reality of the threat of major building collapses.

What is more, a single hazard may also trigger other hazards and expose vulnerabilities in dynamic ways. An earthquake may produce devastating tsunamis as we observed in the Indian Ocean, but it may also adversely impact nuclear power plants and emit radioactive contamination as was witnessed in Japan recently. Earthquakes may also produce landslides that inhibit disaster assistance (as was illustrated by the broken roads and bridges in China after the Sichuan earthquake). Fires from broken gas lines may rage since water lines are also damaged as well (thereby making fire suppression difficult or impossible as in the case of the Kobe earthquake). An industrial accident involving hazardous materials may reveal the deficiencies of detection systems, the lack of education and training among some first responders, and insufficient medical equipment, supplies, and personnel (e.g., the Union Carbide plant in Bhopal, India). The terrorist attack on 9/11 is also illustrative of the cascading effect of certain disasters. The intentional crashing of the planes into the World Trade Center buildings damaged the structures and created intense fires. The structures were weakened further by the fires, which ultimately resulted in them falling to the earth. The collapse of the buildings severed the subway and road systems in addition to damaging electrical and water lines below. The loss of power and water subsequently made the response to the attack even more difficult.

Of course, it should be pointed that that future events are likely to be equally—if not more—complicated. The use of a nuclear weapon in a terrorist attack on a major city would kill millions of people instantly. Fires would quickly spread in the surrounding area, destroying hundreds of the buildings still standing. The accompanying electromagnetic pulse from the nuclear device would render most vehicles useless so evacuation from the affected area would lag as a result. The radiation fallout would create both short- and long-term health consequences. The loss of electricity or overloading of hospitals in nearby areas would hinder medical care and outstretch physician abilities. The expanding and interacting consequences are almost unimaginable.

As can be seen, the systems and variables that lead to disasters and catastrophes interact in chaotic and, at times, unpredictable ways. David McEntire (2004, 2005) has developed a model of vulnerability that explores how a myriad of variables work together to reduce or augment disasters and catastrophes. In the model, some hazards are external in nature (e.g., resulting from earthquakes, tornadoes, volcanic eruptions, etc.) while others have internal origins and are produced from human actions that augment vulnerability (e.g., mistakes that lead to hazardous material spill or computer malfunctions, cultural disagreements that lead to terrorist attacks, etc.). Both external and internal hazards may also interact at times in complicated ways (e.g., human activity that causes deforestation could exacerbate flooding and mudslides from excessive precipitation). When the hazard or hazards interact with vulnerability, a disaster or catastrophe may result.

The Interactions of the Natural, Social, and Built Environments

Disasters and catastrophes unfold in extremely complicated ways. Dennis Mileti, in his important work, Disasters by Design, suggests that "losses from hazards and disasters in the United States in the next millennium will be determined, as in the past, by a large number of factors. These variables can be grouped into three broad categories: the natural environment, the social world, and the human-made constructed environment" (1999, 105). The physical environment is "the earth's physical systems (the atmosphere, biosphere, cryosphere, hydrosphere, and lithosphere)" (Mileti 1999, 107). The social environment includes "human systems (e.g., population, culture, technology, social class, economics, and politics)" (Mileti 1999, 107). The built environment is comprised of "the constructed system (e.g., buildings, roads, bridges, public infrastructure, and housing)" (Mileti 1999, 107).

The East Bay Hills fire in California on October 22, 1991 provides a good glimpse of these systems and their interaction (McEntire 2007, 361). The East Bay Hills area is prone to fire hazards. A combination of abundant vegetation, drought conditions, strong winds, low humidity, and steep terrain created tinderbox conditions. The construction of homes and infrastructure in the area increased vulnerability. Residences included a great deal of flammable wood in their construction. Narrow roads hindered evacuation and the arrival of first responders. Water systems relied on electricity, but power lines were severed by the high winds and were responsible for the ignition of the fire. Many social factors aggravated the disaster. People moved to the hazardous location because of scenic views overlooking the valley below. Regulations on construction and fire suppression were dismissed due to popular outcry and the expense of enforcing them. The use of different sized hoses created problems for first responders who arrived to provide mutual aid. The net result of these challenges was the scorching of over 1,500 acres, the destruction of 3,000 houses, the death of 25 people, injuries to at least 150 others, 10,000 people left homeless, the evacuation of 20,000 to 30,000 others, and $1.5 billion in losses.

Another aspect of this model deals with human activities that have a bearing on vulnerability. People live and interact in and with the physical environment. The physical environment includes their choice of settlement, how they construct buildings and infrastructure, and their use of technology. Humans live and interact in the social environment as well. This includes many variables ranging from politics and economics to culture and psychology. The social environment may also influence how humans are organized and what planning efforts they implement in emergency management.

Human activities therefore have a bearing on the attributes of the physical and social environments. These attributes are known as liabilities and capabilities. Liabilities are factors that augment vulnerability by increasing exposure/risk and susceptibility. Capabilities are factors that reduce vulnerability by increasing resistance and resilience. The levels of risk/exposure, susceptibility, resistance, and resilience interact, according to the model, in complicated ways. For instance, the variables related to:

> risk, susceptibility, resistance, and resilience are not mutually exclusive or exempt from interaction. Each category ... may influence, or is influenced by, every other category. Risk may be increased if resistance is lowered (e.g., higher exposure to a hazard in a poorly constructed building), while resilience may be decreased if susceptibility is heightened (e.g., poverty may preclude purchasing insurance to aid recovery). At the same time, risk and susceptibility, as well as resistance and resilience, often interact in mutually reinforcing ways (e.g., social, cultural, political, technological, and economic environments may encourage people to live in dangerous areas, while weak infrastructure makes response and recovery more difficult). Furthermore, risk could jeopardize resilience (e.g., living on or near certain soils will make response and recovery after an earthquake more difficult), while resistance and susceptibility may have an inverse relationship (e.g., safe construction will lower susceptibility, and constraining cultural attitudes may discourage the careful use of technology for resistance). Complex, interdependent relationships exist among risk, susceptibility, resistance, and resilience (McEntire 2004, 25).

While disasters and catastrophes may be complex in any given situation, they may also be compounded over time. Disasters and catastrophes may augment future vulnerability since people will lose precious resources in the disasters they have experienced. Increased vulnerability will result so significant preventive, mitigative, and preparatory activities must be undertaken to reduce it in the future. For example, individuals or families may need to be relocated to avoid repetitive losses in the future, but this may not be possible without insurance or other forms of disaster assistance. The model therefore suggests that response and recovery efforts must also take into consideration future vulnerabilities. As can be seen, the reduction of liabilities and building of capacity are extremely challenging problems that cannot be solved through simplistic policies or in isolation of other variables.

THE IMPACT OF CATASTROPHES ON SOCIETY

Disasters, and by extension catastrophes, have been described by sociologists as non-routine social problems. "The phrase 'non-routine events' distinguishes disasters as unusual and dramatic social happenings from the reservoir of everyday routines and concerns which human beings encounter" (Kreps and Drabek 1996, 133). Disasters and catastrophes are not frequently experienced, although it is evident that the rate of occurrence appears to be increasing. Disasters and catastrophes are thus unique occurrences that are usually outside the normal frame of human reference. That is to say, many people have never been directly impacted by disasters and catastrophes.

Consequently, disasters, and especially catastrophes, create new and sometimes unforeseen challenges in society. According to Bates and Peacock, "a disaster occurs when an environmental event overwhelms ... the use of established, institutionalized, routine or 'normalized' patterns of activity or behavior" (1989, 352). A simple example of household routines helps to elucidate such challenges. Frederick Bates and Walt Peacock illustrate that households perform several important and life-sustaining functions on a daily basis. These include shelter, food preservation/cooking/serving, clothes washing, dishwashing, bathing, waste disposal, sleeping, heating/air conditioning, and communication (1992). However, in a disaster or catastrophe, such functions may become impossible for households. People cannot protect themselves from the elements (e.g., heat, cold, wind, rain, snow, etc.) if their home has been damaged or destroyed by a hurricane or a tornado. Since there is no electricity, gas, or water systems after major disasters or catastrophes (i.e., these lifelines are severed by earthquakes and mudslides), it will be difficult to prepare and serve food and water. The lack of water or scarcity of clean water also prohibits the washing of clothes and dishes, bathing, and waste disposal. Because personal property is often rendered useless in a disaster, other functions (e.g., sleeping, heating/air conditioning, and communication) become impossible. Beds become soggy mattresses in floods, gas or power for heating and air conditioning is unavailable, and phone lines are disabled.

Such challenges are amplified at the community, state, and even national levels when catastrophes occur. For instance, transportation becomes problematic due to the loss of roads and bridges. This complicates not only routine commerce for business purposes but also emergency medical care, damage assessment, debris removal, and all other forms of disaster assistance. Additional problems may include the psychological impact of thousands or hundreds of thousands of deaths and injuries in major disasters, the environmental consequences of unique hazardous materials releases, the overwhelming of the medical system during pandemics, or the probable social disruption resulting from weapons of mass destruction.

In light of these significant non-routine social problems, citizens as well as city, state, and even national governments may not have the ability to deal effectively with disasters and catastrophes. In disasters and catastrophes "a sociocultural system's capacity to adapt" is severely hampered (Bates and Peacock 1989, 352). "A disaster in the sociological sense, is then, a failure in the social structure or organization of the social system. The failure is brought on by an environmental event which is out of the range of the system's internal adaptive capacity" (Bates and Peacock 1989, 352). For instance, emergency medical care becomes problematic if doctors, nurses, and paramedics have been killed. Sheltering is difficult if thousands are left homeless and the housing stock has been decimated. Public information is nearly impossible when radio and TV stations have been knocked out of service. Clean up and debris removal cannot take place when heavy equipment has been damaged and when fuel is no longer available. Rebuilding time is lengthened as resources have been destroyed or demand for goods and services outstrips supply. The need for outside involvement is therefore a key characteristic of major disasters and catastrophes.

In cases of catastrophes, impacted societies cannot address basic needs of daily life—let alone the urgent demands of the response and recovery phases of disaster. For instance, when evacuees returned to Galveston after Hurricane Ike, there was nothing to return to. Buildings were destroyed, roads were damaged, electrical and water systems were not functioning. In this situation, survivors of catastrophes may not be able to take care of the necessities of life. Outsiders will have to help with the provision of food and shelter, the distribution of relief, and the restoration of services.

REQUIRED INTERVENTION POINTS FOR POTENTIAL CATASTROPHES

Since the consequences of catastrophes are so substantial, a variety of proactive steps must be taken to minimize their impact. This may require mitigation, preparedness, response, and recovery efforts that go beyond normal or traditional emergency management principles and practices.

For instance, in terms of mitigation for all types of hazards, communities and nations might need to undertake more serious and thorough risk assessments, develop more stringent land-use policies, and begin a calculated withdrawal from the most hazard-prone areas. Environmental protection through expanded educational programs, further environmental monitoring, and the administration of fines for ongoing degradation will be required. Improved construction standards and practices, paying special attention to the development of policies that promote resistance, must be implemented. Increased regulations, caution with hazardous materials, and the back-up of systems relying heavily on computer programs will be necessities if industrial and technological disasters are to be minimized. Enhancing the health status of citizens and building capabilities in the medical community (e.g., inoculation programs, epidemiological surveillance, and surge capacity) will be imperative. Preventing terrorism via more deliberate foreign policy directions, valued information sharing among intelligence agencies, better-equipped counter-terrorism forces, and more fully trained law enforcement personnel should be pursued as well.

Regarding preparedness, there is a need to focus on true and verifiable capacity building rather than planning (i.e., the writing of documents) alone. This includes the determination and enhancement of all pre-disaster functions ranging from community education and first responder training to grant management and exercises. It would also cover ways to increase the probability of success for all post-disaster functions (particularly those pertaining to warning, communications, and decision making as well as the often-neglected components of long-term recovery).

For response, the intervention points are relevant to any post-disaster activity. However, special attention must be given to the needs of vulnerable populations, major evacuation and sheltering operations, rapid damage and impact assessments, flexible deployment of search and rescue and emergency medical resources, effective use of inter-state and international mutual aid compacts, and an orchestrated coordination of donations and volunteers from around the affected country or world at large. The point here is to consider scale and not just routine operations.

Finally, when speaking of recovery, it will be imperative that emergency managers and all organizations in society implement well-crafted plans that identify the best ways of overcoming the impacts of disasters in both the short- and long-term. Particular emphasis should be given to removing massive quantities of debris, helping thousands or millions of people through disaster assistance programs, and finding ways to speed up re-establishment of lives, businesses, and communities through effective partnerships.

ORGANIZATIONAL STRUCTURES AND CATASTROPHES

As has been illustrated above, a variety of measures must be taken to effectively deal with disasters and catastrophes before, during, and after they occur. If the organizational approaches that could be utilized to address disasters or catastrophes are examined, they typically fall into one of two ideal type categories: the bureaucratic and problem-solving models (Dynes 1994; see also Neal and Phillips 1995).

The first approach to organize emergency management efforts is referred to as the Bureaucratic Model. The model has four significant features. First, the bureaucratic model takes a very centralized approach to disasters and catastrophes. Decisions and activities, under this model, are made and completed by politicians, government leaders, military officials, and incident commanders. The reasoning is that these individuals are the experts who have the requisite knowledge and resources to tackle the problems related to catastrophic events. Second, this model is top-down in orientation. That is to say, policies and decisions are distributed from key leaders to intermediate managers and those who implement decisions among the lower levels of government or within individual organizations. It is believed that this approach is best suited to ensure communication and coordination among the participants as they deal with catastrophes. Third, this approach is very rigid. Under this perspective, it is advocated that standard operating procedures be followed before and after calamitous disasters. Finally, the bureaucratic model may assume the worst about human behavior in catastrophes. Specifically, this perspective is often associated with the belief that humans will panic, become dependent on others, and engage in anti-social behavior (e.g., looting).

The second organizational approach is very different than the command and control viewpoint. It has been referred to as the Problem Solving model. This approach also has four significant features that lie in stark contrast to the bureaucratic viewpoint. First, the Problem Solving model is decentralized. It recognizes that there are countless players and stakeholders from the public, private, and non-profit sectors involved in disasters and catastrophes. Therefore, government officials, military officers, and incident commanders will not be alone in dealing with catastrophes. In fact, the problem-solving model suggests that responses will be improved when everyone is engaged in emergency management activities. Second, the Problem Solving model is bottom-up in orientation. In other words, those actually in the field or on the front lines are more likely to understand what is happening and are in the best position to make decisions and implement policies. This approach consequently stresses efficiency and rapid reactions to problems. Third, the Problem Solving model is flexible. It recognizes that departing from plans and standard operating procedures is inevitable in most disasters. The model instead values creativity and improvisation when dealing with the challenges presented by catastrophes. Finally, the Problem Solving model asserts that people will not become self-serving individuals in catastrophic situations. Instead, it is assumed that individuals and groups will work together to solve mutual problems and show concern for well-being of others.

As can be seen, each model has dramatically different implications. For instance, the bureaucratic model relies more on government, concrete organization, and standardized policies. It also assumes that people will need assistance and oversight in a catastrophe. In contrast, the problem-solving model recognizes that numerous partners beyond government will be involved in catastrophes including the private sector, non-profit organizations, and even citizens. This model asserts that government will not be able to solve all of the problems evident in catastrophes, and understands that most people will do all they can to take care of their own needs and those of others.

As a result of these substantial differences, it may be a mistake to rely on any single model before, during, or after a catastrophe. For instance, the Bureaucratic model helps with governmental planning, the identification of standardized processes, and occasions when social order becomes fragile. However, the command and control model is less able to integrate new participants into the organizational structure and adapt to the situation as it unfolds. In contrast, the Problem Solving model is open to the involvement of any entity which has resources that can be applied to the challenges of catastrophes, it recognizes that flexibility is required when dealing with uncertainty, and it assumes that everyday citizens can be part of the solution in emergency management. However, the Problem Solving model may downplay the role of experts in catastrophic situations or their ability to marshal vast resources to react to disasters. For these reasons, both models must be applied at different times and in different contexts due to the unique nature of catastrophes. In fact, it may be argued that the application of both models is inevitable in catastrophes. However, more certainly needs to be known about when to act under one perspective versus the other or integrate both models into a more complete approach.

Lagadec's work on catastrophic crises and hypercomplexity follows this latter recommendation. He argues that our "basic concepts and tools defined from the 1980s onward in the field of crisis management fall short of what is needed today" (Lagadec 2007, 1). In particular, Lagadec acknowledges that the nature of catastrophes automatically requires the involvement of a cornucopia of participants in both number and variety. This includes "spontaneous, unanticipated coalitions among unlikely partners" ... as well as more "traditional leaders" in crisis situations (Lagadec 2007, 2). Because of this unique mix of stakeholders in catastrophic crises, leaders should ensure that information is transmitted both to and from the local actors (Lagadec 2007, 25). In unconventional crises, hierarchical and stovepiped organizations must give way, at least in part, to ambiguities of leadership and expanded networks that rely on inter-sector coordination (Lagadec 2007, 30–35). Planning and response efforts should not always focus on the prescribed course of action, but also focus on innovative and alternative solutions to hypercomplex problems (Lagadec 2007, 43). Put differently, Lagadec asserts:

> When catastrophic or hypercomplex crises hit, a culture that is geared towards preserving the coherence of chains of command and behaviors through inflexible prescriptions is not a strength, but a lethal weakness—as it impedes the creativity, indeed the audacity necessary to respond to chaotic and unpredictable events.... Response efforts must take place among a hypercomplex map of actors whose identity and motivations are unclear (2007, 49).

Leaders must therefore accept the unconventional nature of catastrophes. They should deploy "rapid reflection forces" that make sense of unfolding events and are open to finding solutions in new partners even if the decision runs in opposition to prior held notions of how the response would be organized and implemented (Lagadec 2007, 52–53). Failing to make this adjustment in leadership will result in continued disappointment when catastrophic events occur in the future.

CONCLUSION

This chapter has attempted to illustrate that catastrophes—much like disasters—result from the interaction of hazards and vulnerability. However, it was illustrated that catastrophes are likely to include a larger number of variables that interact in very complicated ways, and this difference has a dramatic and disruptive impact on the routine functions in society. Because catastrophic events are so unique and overwhelming, it is imperative that additional efforts be given toward mitigation, preparedness, response, and recovery activities. The size and scale of catastrophes are the major considerations that have to be taken into account when designing and implementing emergency management policies. In addition, the chapter indicates that emergency managers and others involved in catastrophes must think critically about the organizational approach they utilize since each model has dramatically different assumptions and implications. While much more undoubtedly needs to be known about catastrophes, it is hoped that this chapter has increased understanding of these events along with the need for new policies and emergency management activities. More importantly, it will be imperative that emergency managers engage all relevant partners in the preparedness process. Catastrophes require not only substantial and effective responses, but also proactive planning and capacity building initiatives among all sectors of society.

REFERENCES

Bates, F.L. and W.G. Peacock. 1989. Long term recovery. *International Journal of Mass Emergencies and Disasters* 7(30): 349–365.
Bates, F.L. and W.G. Peacock. 1992. Measuring disaster impact on household living conditions: The domestic assets approach. *International Journal of Mass Emergencies and Disasters* 10(1): 133–160.

Bissell, R.A., A. Bumbak, M. Levy, and P. Echebi. 2009. Long-term global threat assessment: Challenging new roles for emergency managers. *Journal of Emergency Management* 7(1): 19–37.
Britton, N.R. 2005. *What's A Word? Opening Up the Debate*. pp. 60–78 in R.W. Perry and E.L. Quarantelli (eds) *What is a Disaster? New Answers to Old Questions*. International Research Committee on Disasters: Bloomington, IN.
Brown, L.R. 2008. Plan B 3.0: *Mobilizing to Save Civilization*. W.W. Norton: New York.
Cutter, S.L. 2005. *Are We Asking the Right Question?* pp. 39–48 in R.W. Perry and E.L. Quarantelli (eds) *What is a Disaster? New Answers to Old Questions*. International Research Committee on Disasters: Bloomington, IN.
Dynes, R.R. 1994. Community emergency planning: False assumptions and inappropriate analogies. *International Journal of Mass Emergencies and Disasters* 12(2): 141–158.
Fothergill, A., G.M. Enrique, and D.D. JoAnne. 1999. Race, ethnicity and disasters in the United States: A review of the literature. *Disasters* 33(2): 156–173.
Hewitt, K. 1983. *Interpretations of Calamity*. Allen & Unwin: Boston, MA.
Hewitt, K. 1998. Excluded perspectives in the social construction of disaster. pp. 75–92 in Quarantelli, E.L. (ed). *What Is a Disaster? Perspectives on the Question*. Routledge: New York.
Keller, E.A. and R.H. Blodgett. 2006. *Natural Hazards: Earth Processes as Hazards, Disasters and Catastrophes*. Pearson: Upper Saddle River, NJ.
Kreps, G.A. and T.E. Drabek. 1996. Disasters are non-routine social problems. *International Journal of Mass Emergencies and Disasters* 14(2): 129–153.
Lagadec, E. 2007. *Unconventional Crises, Unconventional Responses: Reforming Leadership in the Age of Catastrophic Crises and Hypercomplexity*. Center for Transatlantic Relations, Johns Hopkins University: Washington, DC.
McEntire, D.A. 2004. Tenets of vulnerability: Assessing a fundamental disaster concept. *Journal of Emergency Management* 2(2): 23–29.
McEntire, D.A. 2005. Revising the definition of "Hazard" and the importance of reducing vulnerability. *Journal of Emergency Management* 3(4): 9–10.
McEntire, D.A. 2005. Why vulnerability matters: Illustrating the need for a modified disaster reduction concept. *Disaster Prevention and Management* 14(2): 206–222.
McEntire, D.A. 2007. *Disaster Response and Recovery: Strategies and Tactics for Resilience*. Wiley: Hoboken, NJ.
Mileti, D. 1999. *Disasters by Design: A Reassessment of Natural Hazards in the United States*. Joseph Henry Press: Washington, DC.
Neal, D.M. and B.D. Phillips. 1995. Effective emergency management: Reconsidering the bureaucratic approach. *Disasters* 19(4): 327–337.
Peacock, W.G., E. Enarson, and B.H. Morrow. 1997. *Hurricane Andrew: Ethnicity, Gender and the Sociology of Disasters*. Routlege: New York.
Perry, R.W. 2006. What is a disaster? pp. 1–15 in Rodriquez, H., E.L. Quarantelli, and R.S. Dynes (eds). *Handbook of Disaster Research*. Springer: New York.
Quarantelli, E.L. 1998. *What Is a Disaster? Perspectives on the Question*. Routledge: London.
Quarantelli, E.L. 2005. A social science research agenda for the disasters of the 21st century: Theoretical, methodological and empirical issues and their professional implementation. pp. 325–396 in R.W. Perry and E.L. Quarantelli (eds). *What Is a Disaster? New Answers to Old Questions*. International Research Committee on Disasters.
Wisner, B.W., P. Blaikie, T. Cannon, and I. Davis. 2004. *At Risk: Natural Hazards, People's Vulnerability and Disasters*. Routledge: London.

CHAPTER 3

Ethics in Catastrophe Readiness and Response

Anna K. Schwab and Timothy Beatley

CONTENTS

Overview	46
Setting the Stage: Could *Survival of the Fittest* Be the New Ethical Paradigm?	47
Sources of Ethical Thinking	48
Terms and Definitions	49
Ethics Typologies	50
Applied Ethics	50
Triage: A System of Real-Time Decision Making	51
Medical Triage	52
Professional Ethics and Codes of Conduct	52
International Association of Emergency Managers Code of Ethics and Professional Conduct	53
Professional Duty and Self-Preservation	54
Professional Codes of Ethics for the Media	55
New Media and Social Networking	56
Relationship between Ethics and Law	58
Constitutional Rights	58
Civil Rights and Anti-Discrimination Laws	61
Americans with Disabilities Act/Rehabilitation Act	62
International Law: Recognizing Basic Human Rights	64
Legal Basis of Human Rights Law	64
The Human Rights of Disaster Victims	64
Defining the Dimensions of the Moral Community	65
U.S. Aid to Foreign Nations	67
Volunteer Organizations and Private Donations	69
The Problem of "Donor Fatigue"	70

The Moral Community: Focusing on Vulnerable Populations 71
From Disaster to Catastrophe: Increasing Security by Addressing
Social Inequities 72
Summary 73
References 74

OVERVIEW

This chapter is designed to introduce readers to some of the ethical and value issues that emergency management professionals might confront while in the line of duty during a natural or manmade catastrophe. It is important to note up front that while there is much study into the ethics of particular aspects of disaster (e.g., crisis communication and role of the mass media; allocation of resources in times of scarcity; equitable treatment of disparate population groups), there is not a substantial body of literature that deals with ethics in disaster per se, let alone the ethics of catastrophe as it pertains specifically to the emergency manager. As a result, this chapter discusses a wide range of issues that fall under the broad umbrella of "ethics" in the catastrophe setting. Much has been borrowed from the public health sector, where significant work has been conducted in laying out an ethical framework for decision-making in the health field, for example, in terms of pandemic influenza planning. Other parallels to the emergency management profession are found in medicine, law, nursing, journalism, and other disciplines that cross paths with the emergency manager.

The chapter opens with a description of the term ethics, followed by an exploration of the various branches of ethical philosophy. The chapter then identifies and discusses some of the major ethical quandaries and dilemmas faced in preparing for and responding to a major natural disaster or catastrophic event. We next identify the range and variety of ethical and moral concepts that could help guide response planning and decision-making.

In addition to a discussion of ethical duties and moral obligations that exist before, during, and after a catastrophe, this chapter also describes some of the many sets of principles and codes that help establish the parameters of ethical decision making in the professions, hopefully helping readers understand the reasoning behind such rules of practice. This, in turn, should help practitioners apply basic tools and techniques of ethical analysis to catastrophic events, and to glean insights about morally appropriate and ethical response actions and decisions. The chapter also includes a discussion about the relationship between ethics and law, with emphasis on particular segments of the population that are, or should be, protected by disaster law. We conclude the discussion of ethics by defining the dimensions of our "moral community," including a brief examination of the types of social conditions that lead to extreme vulnerability of certain segments of the population, bringing up questions about the basic construct of our social, political, and economic systems that might cause a disaster to morph into a catastrophe.

SETTING THE STAGE: COULD *"SURVIVAL OF THE FITTEST"* BE THE NEW ETHICAL PARADIGM?

Imagine an event of catastrophic proportion involving mass casualties, disrupted or non-existent services (power, transportation, communications), scarce food and water, limited emergency personnel and medical supplies, overwhelmed hospitals, perhaps contamination from biohazard materials or nuclear fallout, and so on. The world as we knew it has turned upside down. The systems and resources that we rely upon are gone, or working at diminished capacity. Perhaps hundreds or thousands of homes, businesses, and government buildings are damaged, untold numbers of residents are killed or injured. Law enforcement and emergency response personnel may be working in greatly reduced numbers. Elected leaders and government officials may be among those killed or missing (see Figure 3.1).

Without a pre-conceived decision framework that deals with the worst-case scenario, might survivors turn to a "survival of the fittest" set of rules? If so, would precious limited resources be directed to or commandeered by the strongest and most powerful for exclusive use of the able-bodied—those who could contribute to continued maintenance and eventual recovery of the population? Would the decision framework take into account those who might require a disproportionate share of resources to live? Would those who might not survive or are otherwise compromised be given lower priority for distribution of assistance, including food supplies and medical treatment?

Figure 3.1 The 2010 Haitian earthquake damaged critical social and government buildings in the capital Port-au-Prince, killing officials and religious leaders along with thousands of ordinary citizens. The country was left short of political and social decision-makers in the midst of crisis, a leading factor in the ensuing chaos. (Courtesy of The American Red Cross.)

If, in this new paradigm, decision-makers were to set criteria for determining the "fittest" for survival, upon what criteria would those decisions be based?

- The richest and most powerful?
- Young men and women with the highest sperm and ova counts?
- Strategic thinkers who might carry forward lessons likely to help humans survive in a changed environment?

How would these criteria be measured and applied?

- How would we "value" people who work in areas essential for human survival such as food production and medical care, as opposed to educators and artists?
- Would leaders be chosen or imposed? Would we look to existing political figures (assuming their survival)? Religious leaders? Military commanders?
- How would we deal with the sick, aged, institutionalized, and immobilized? The poor? Illegal immigrants? Orphans?

Is such an approach "*ethical*"? Is it "*moral*"? Is this approach even *legal*?

Without any formal discussion of what ethics are and how ethical decisions might be made in the midst of crisis, we can already see that the ethical problems are endless, but are basically summed up by asking ourselves, "Is every human life of the same value as others?" There are many among us who are uncomfortable even thinking about such a dilemma; yet, it is not unfathomable that emergency response personnel on the scene of a catastrophic event might face just such a question as they decide whom to help and who they must leave behind.

Keep these questions in mind as we explore the field of ethics, and search for ways to help emergency managers and policy-makers alike to think and plan for the tough choices that might lie ahead in the wake of a catastrophe.

SOURCES OF ETHICAL THINKING

In this section, we define the term "ethics" and discuss the various typologies within ethical philosophy. We begin by describing some of the sources of ethical thinking, including the capacity of humans to think and reason.

"WHAT DO ETHICS MEAN TO YOU?"

Sociologist Raymond Baumhart once posed this question to a group of business people, and received the following replies:

- Ethics has to do with what my feelings tell me is right or wrong
- Ethics has to do with my religious beliefs
- Being ethical is doing what the law requires
- Ethics consists of the standards of behavior our society accepts
- I don't know what the word means

Although these questions were posed in the business context, they easily translate to the views an emergency manager might have when considering one's "ethical" duty in carrying out professional responsibilities. There is clearly no single correct answer to the question "what are ethics?" But there is a long history of scholarship and applied practice that attempt to describe some of the basic tenets of the concept.

Many believe that at the heart of what makes human beings special or unique is the ability to engage in ethical and moral reasoning, and to act and live according to ethical principles. The goal of a good and meaningful life, then, is living a *principled* life.

Where and how we derive our moral sensibilities as a species remains debatable. For many there are important *religious* sources to morality and ethics (e.g., the Bible, the Koran, the Torah, and other religious texts). On the other hand, scholars in the field of biology—E.O. Wilson, for instance—have argued that moral standards and codes are born of *evolutionary needs*; ethics codes and standards provide important guidance for cooperation, and thereby survival.

Many moral philosophers commonly appeal to *rationality* in one form or another to defend moral principles that govern behavior. We need and adopt moral principles because it is rational to do so, as explained by Gert:[1]

> Examination of the content of common morality makes it clear that it is a system that would be rational for all persons to want everyone to be taught and trained to follow because of the protection that it provides.... It is rational for all persons to want everyone to obey rules such as "Do not kill;" "Do not deceive;" and "Keep your promises."

In other words, there are many different points of reference in making ethical judgments. One's individual perspective, upbringing, and beliefs will color one's concept of what is "ethical."

TERMS AND DEFINITIONS

As an *academic discipline*, ethics is a branch of philosophy that is concerned with moral issues:

> "The branch of philosophy that deals with the general nature of good and bad and the specific moral obligations of and choices to be made by the individual in his relationship with others."[2]

As a *practice*, ethics refers to standards of human behavior:

> "Ethics refers to standards of conduct, standards that indicate how one should behave based on moral duties and virtues, which themselves are derived from principles of right and wrong."[3]

More specifically, ethics often refers to a set of standards for a particular *profession*:

> "The rules or standards governing conduct, esp. of the members of a profession."[4]

We will discuss professional and applied ethics in more detail later in this chapter.

ETHICS TYPOLOGIES

There are various branches or theories of ethics, each of which might pertain in the context of catastrophe management. One classic distinction in moral philosophy is between *teleological* theories of ethics and *deontological* ethics.

Teleological ethics, also known as the utilitarian perspective or consequentialism, demands that the rightness or wrongness of an action or policy is assessed by its consequences, specifically by looking at the comparative balance of positive versus negative results. *Utilitarianism* is the dominant version of teleological ethics. For example, cost–benefit analysis is a type of teleological decision-making, where the ratio of the "cost" of an action is weighed against the outcome or benefit.

In contrast, deontological ethics implies that there is an inherent rightness or wrongness to an action or choice, regardless of the outcome or consequence. Certain obligations are considered an ethical duty, and should not be subject to utilitarian reasoning. In deontological ethics, an action is considered morally good because of some characteristic of the action itself, not because the product of the action is good. Deontological ethics holds that at least some acts are morally obligatory regardless of their consequences for human welfare. Expressions such as "Duty for duty's sake," "Virtue is its own reward," and "Let justice be done though the heavens fall" are descriptive of the deontological approach.

APPLIED ETHICS

Applied ethics is a discipline of philosophy that attempts to apply ethical theory to real-life situations. The discipline has many specialized fields, such as bioethics and business ethics, all of which attempt to determine how a moral outcome can be achieved in specific situations.

As noted by Roberts and DeRenzo:[5]

> Human beings have been thinking and writing about ethics in general, disaster management in particular, and the application of ethical ideas to public policy for as long as we have been thinking and writing. Literally 5000 years ago, the Egyptians struggled with their idea of *maat*—by which they meant the appropriate good order of society— and the role of the Pharaoh in preserving or restoring that when the annual Nile floods got out of hand.

Applied ethics is not an abstract or academic endeavor; on the other hand, there are no simple, formulaic schemes for making ethical choices. What does exist is the opportunity to develop a systematic approach—an ethics algorithm—that can be used to apply basic ethical principles and theories to a particular situation. For example, various ethical approaches—from utilitarian to virtue-based—have been used to allocate disaster relief funds in a manner that is fair and just as opposed to merely efficient.

Note: To see different ethical approaches applied to the management and distribution of disaster relief funds following 9/11, see Santa Clara University Markkula

ETHICS IN CATASTROPHE READINESS AND RESPONSE 51

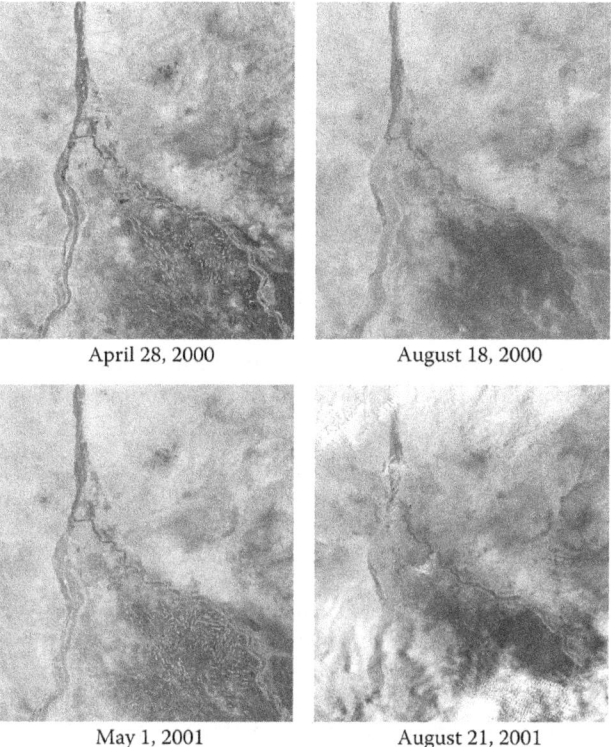

Figure 3.2 Throughout history, the rising and falling waters of the mighty Nile River have directly impacted the lives of the people who live along its banks. (Courtesy of NASA.)

Center for Applied Ethics, "The Ethics of Disaster Relief" at http://www.scu.edu/ethics/publications/briefings/philanthropy.html.

The need for a pre-established set of principles is even more critical at the response stage of a major disaster when rapidly changing conditions and an environment of pressure and stress can make deliberative decision making difficult. These conditions require more than quick wits and nerves of steel. The emergency manager must have a solid framework to enable the "right" choice to be made for the circumstances.

TRIAGE: A SYSTEM OF REAL-TIME DECISION MAKING

Triage is a system for making real-time decisions by prioritizing needed actions based on available resources, manpower, and so on during crisis conditions. Most commonly used in the context of a medical emergency or on the battlefield, triage helps sort the injured or sick into groups for treatment based on the seriousness of the condition or injury. We can also speak of "legal triage" or "response triage" for making non-medical decisions in the immediate crisis situation.

Medical Triage

Many of the catastrophe situations posed in earlier chapters involve serious risk of bodily harm or death to hundreds if not thousands of individuals within a short span of time. These sorts of mass casualty incidents (MCI) will demand rapid and efficient triage of victims. Triage may appear to be an ethically neutral system of allocation of medical care. For example, the START protocol—Simple Triage and Rapid Treatment—is a systematic process for the prioritization of medical treatment. START is a method for identifying salvageable victims from those with imminent mortality based on the objective criteria of vital sign measurements including respiratory rate, pulse rate, and best motor response.

While triage may seem to be a purely objective system for decision making, triage has an inherently "ethical" component since it attempts to identify the parameters for choosing who might live and die. In effect, the triage system was developed because incorrect decisions may have far-reaching consequences. Triage is an area in which decision-makers must know what they are doing, why they are doing it, and which actions to take to achieve a satisfactory outcome.

As noted in the commentary by James Childress:[6]

> Rules of triage, the allocating of scarce medical resources in an emergency such as a bioterrorist attack, can engender moral distress for healthcare professionals who have to implement them. Yet we need rules such as a "capacity triage plan," established in advance of emergencies, so that everyone will know how to respond. Otherwise, confusion and even chaos will reign. Although rules of triage must be formulated with the best medical information available, they are not merely medical in nature. They also reflect important moral values.
>
> Triage is one way to ration healthcare when caregivers cannot meet everyone's needs at the same time and to the same degree. Systems of triage, whether informal or formal, all have an implicit or explicit utilitarian rationale—they are designed to produce the greatest good for the greatest number by meeting human needs most effectively and efficiently under conditions of scarcity. They are structured to satisfy the formal criterion of justice (to treat similar cases similarly and equal cases equally), and their minimal material criteria for distribution of treatment are some combination of patients' needs and the probability of successful treatment.
>
> Traditional codes of medical ethics did not adequately address situations of triage because of their focus on physicians' responsibilities for individual patients. In most situations, it is appropriate for physicians to attend first to the worst-off in the confidence that others can wait their turn without undue burden or risk. It is difficult to shift from assigning priority to patients who are the sickest to assigning priority to patients who are most likely to survive.

PROFESSIONAL ETHICS AND CODES OF CONDUCT

Professional ethics can be considered a subset of applied ethics, since it involves establishment and adherence to a moral code that helps guide members of that profession in the proper conduct of their duties and obligations in real-life situations. Most if not all professions that involve trained, certified specialists observe a code of professional conduct. There are codes established by professional and trade organizations ranging from the American Football Coaches Association to the Yacht Architects Association. Doctors, for instance, are famously guided by the "Hippocratic Oath" taken upon their entrance into the field of medicine, where the primary guiding principle is "First, do no harm." Individual business organizations and government agencies also promulgate professional codes of responsibility, which range in complexity from a simple statement of ideals to detailed rules of conduct covering multiple situations and conditions.

Most professional codes are developed as a guide for carrying out responsibilities in a manner consistent with quality service and ethical obligations of the profession. The code serves as a framework for decision making and ethical analysis, establishing a standard of conduct that is meant to be non-negotiable and immune to ad hoc revision or amendment. Above all, professional codes are established with the intent that they be usefully applied to actual case situations.

International Association of Emergency Managers Code of Ethics and Professional Conduct

The International Association of Emergency Managers (IAEM) is an international organization dedicated to promoting the goals of saving lives and protecting property by mitigating, preparing for, responding to, and recovering from disasters/emergencies. Because maintenance of public trust and confidence is central to the effectiveness of the emergency management profession, the IAEM has a Code

PRINCIPLES OF THE INTERNATIONAL ASSOCIATION OF EMERGENCY MANAGERS CODE OF PROFESSIONAL CONDUCT

- *Respect*: Respect for supervising officials, colleagues, associates, and most importantly, for the people we serve is the standard for IAEM members. We comply with all laws and regulations applicable to our purpose and position, and responsibly and impartially apply them to all concerned. We respect fiscal resources by evaluating organizational decisions to provide the best service or product at a minimal cost without sacrificing quality.
- *Commitment*: IAEM members commit themselves to promoting decisions that engender trust in those we serve. We commit to continuous improvement by fairly administering the affairs of our positions, by fostering honest and trustworthy relationships, and by striving for impeccable accuracy and clarity in what we say or write. We commit to enhancing stewardship of resources and the caliber of service we deliver while striving to improve the quality of life in the community we serve.
- *Professionalism*: IAEM is an organization that actively promotes professionalism to ensure public confidence in emergency management. Our reputations are built on the faithful discharge of our duties. Our professionalism is founded on education, safety, and protection of life and property.

of Professional Conduct that seeks to address a range of issues that impact emergency management professionals in their day-to-day work. The Code of Ethics of the IAEM, with its emphasis on the principles of respect, commitment, and professionalism, is generally accepted as the standard for emergency managers.

Following the preamble, the IAEM Code of Ethics lists several specific rules of conduct designed to guide professional emergency managers. These rules cover issues of quality, independence, objectivity, competence, conflict of interest, and other areas of professionalism and responsibility. Upon certification, emergency managers agree to abide by the principles and standards of the Code. (For more information about the IAEM Code of Ethics and Professional Conduct, visit the IAEM website at www.iaem.com.)

PROFESSIONAL DUTY AND SELF-PRESERVATION

Legal obligations and professional codes compel professionals in many fields to act on duty, and even to confront danger. Sometimes, this duty can lead to conflict with personal responsibility to oneself. In the health professions, for example, ethics codes generally make strong moral claims in the context of a mass casualty event. The American Medical Association stops short of postulating a duty but nevertheless calls for physicians to "apply their knowledge and skills when needed though doing so may put [them] at risk."[7] At the same time, the National Association of Emergency Medical Services Physicians notes that pre-hospital care providers have no duty to place themselves at risk for the benefit of another. Similarly, according to the American Nurses Association, nurses are obligated to provide care in certain circumstances, yet they also have duties to themselves, namely to preserve their integrity and safety.

While many codes thus reveal tensions between obligations to others and to self, emergency professionals are often left to determine which holds the most moral weight. *Proportionality* is an important principle that can help resolve the conflict between meeting professional duty and self-endangerment. The actions of

THE FUKUSHIMA 50: AVERTING NUCLEAR MELTDOWN IN JAPAN

On March 11, 2011, a magnitude 9 earthquake occurred about 70 kilometers off the coast of northern Japan, generating a massive tsunami striking the Japanese coastline with immense ferocity. The damage and destruction were immense: more than 15,000 people lost their lives, and entire coastal towns and communities were swept away. Some 300,000 buildings were destroyed, and much of the infrastructure of roads, bridges, rail lines, now gone. In the aftermath, there were (and still are) many ethical questions and quandaries, but perhaps none so heart wrenching as the plight of workers inside the Fukushima Daiichi nuclear power plant, where the first stages of a nuclear meltdown began to occur just days after the initial impact of the giant wave. During the unfolding disaster, there were difficult questions about how to manage the crisis, and the extent to which emergency crews should be expected to risk their own lives.

The Fukushima 50 is the name given by the media to the team of nuclear power plant workers, estimated to be 50–70 in total, who faced extreme personal risk while they worked to avert greater catastrophe at the stricken Fukushima facility. Their coworkers and nearby residents were evacuated, as radiation leaks at the site increased after a series of aftershocks, explosions, and fires occurred at the plant. Workers inside the plant had limited communication as they scrambled to open vents, pump in seawater to cool the reactor, and perform incredible feats of bravery to maintain the last of the plant's integrity. At one point in the disaster, power was lost and critical monitoring equipment malfunctioned. The workers went out to the parking lot and brought in their car batteries in order to restore the plant's measuring instruments.

Most if not all of the "50" were older, experienced workers without young families. Their naturally shorter expected lifespans made them less susceptible to the long-term ramifications of radiation exposure than the younger men and women who worked at the plant. Nuclear reactor operators say that their profession is typified by the same kind of esprit de corps found among firefighters and elite military units. Lunchroom conversations at reactors frequently turn to what operators would do in a severe emergency. The consensus is always that they would warn their families to flee before staying at their posts to the end.

professionals in crisis situations are ethically justifiable when the risks of harm to self are minimized and reasonable in proportion to the anticipated benefits of the response effort.[8]

PROFESSIONAL CODES OF ETHICS FOR THE MEDIA

Often called the fourth branch of government, the media plays an instrumental role in successful democracy. Journalists and other media have a duty to report the news truthfully and disseminate it to the public in a responsible manner. Principles of ethics and good practice for the media are found in a variety of codes or canons drafted by professional journalism associations. Individual print, broadcast, and online news organizations also issue codes of ethics. Like many broader ethical systems, journalism ethics includes the principle of "limitation of harm."

The ethical principles that govern journalists' actions can be tested during times of crisis, when situations are quickly unfolding, lines of communication may be distorted or broken, and the urge to engage in sensationalist reporting in order to boost ratings can be strong. The rising use of social media adds an additional layer of complexity to ethical implications of instantaneous "news" and other messaging. In some respects, the ethics of traditional journalism have not kept pace with the rapidly changing ways in which information is transmitted and shared during a disaster.

Crisis Communication: Communication during a crisis is essential, and the media can often assist getting much needed messages out to the public in emergency situations. In his review of the behavior of mass communications systems in disasters, Quarantelli[9] concluded that passing on warnings is "Without doubt, the clearest and most consistent role [of mass media] in a disaster ...."

In an emergency, effective risk communication is vital because it helps the public respond to the crisis, reduces the likelihood of rumors and misinformation, and demonstrates good leadership. In many occasions, the media has served as the glue that binds communities together, facilitating collaboration and resource sharing during emergency response and fostering volunteerism and donations (including blood donations) following the event. The media is also instrumental in reporting on recovery and reconstruction and can help keep issues in the public eye and on the political agenda, as well as play a role in healing and sense-making in the post-event setting. The media can also play an important role in highlighting deficiencies in government services, prompting corrective action on the part of officials and decision makers.[10]

Perpetuating Disaster Myths: But there are also issues concerning responsible journalism in times of crisis; the media have been blamed for many of the misconceptions that exist about disaster, misconceptions that may lead to errors of judgment when disaster strikes.

For instance, it is a common belief that people become paralyzed with fear, or act irrationally when told of impending danger. Delay or failure to issue official warnings has been attributed to the myth that people panic, a myth often perpetuated by the media. Yet disaster research has shown that victims are typically *not* dazed and confused but instead participate directly in initial search and rescue efforts. Research has shown that panic is so rare it is difficult to study and that the real problem is not panic but an unwillingness to believe warnings.[11] Another myth that is compounded by journalists' treatment of the disaster scene is that rampant crime, violence and looting always occur. Research has shown that looting in the wake of disasters does happen, but it is relatively rare. Usually, crime rates actually fall in the immediate aftermath of disaster.[12] Consider, for example, reports of the situation in New Orleans following Hurricane Katrina. Media coverage of the Superdome—where thousands of evacuees were sheltered as floodwaters rose in the city—included stories of marauding gangs, shootings, murders, and rape. The vast majority of these stories were later discredited, chalked up to exaggeration and unchecked rumor. Reports of looting and vandalism in the city were also later found to be much exaggerated, although certainly crimes did take place as law enforcement was stretched beyond capacity and conditions deteriorated.

NEW MEDIA AND SOCIAL NETWORKING

Whereas we were once dependent upon the ability of journalists to access a disaster scene to receive reports of an evolving crisis, today's new media allow "citizen journalists" to broadcast information far beyond the boundaries of traditional reporting. The use of Facebook, Twitter, Youtube, and other forms of social media have translated to a type of peer-to-peer communication that enables participants to forgo traditional media outlets as a source for the latest news. And while traditional media is bound by a code of ethics, including a duty to report truthfully and impartially, there are far fewer restrictions on ordinary individuals and informal organizations who can gather and relay information with near impunity.

Increasingly, technology and telecommunications are playing a leading role in many disaster response activities through non-government and "unofficial" channels. Innumerable emergent groups have formed specifically to advance the use of open source data in crisis management, and to provide aid and disaster relief worldwide. For example, SparkRelief, which shares information during a crisis and lets volunteers find ways to help, began in Boulder, Colorado to help victims of wildfires quickly find food and housing, and to coordinate people who wanted to supply aid. In response to the Japanese earthquake and tsunami catastrophe, the nonprofit launched a site to help survivors find housing. The site lets people enter their housing needs, and aims to connect them with those who can help.

Similarly, CrisisCommons has developed as an open forum for practitioners, first responders, humanitarian aid workers, technology specialists, and others to come together to enhance the capabilities of crisis response organizations and impacted communities. The group focuses on using technology to build tools and search and translate data to solve problems arising from crisis situations. For example, projects supporting the Haitian earthquake disaster included creating a hack to expand long-distance Wi-Fi connectivity, developing a Creole mobile translation application, and creating a variety of open source street maps that depict on-the-ground conditions, including areas of damage, aid stations and shelters, and places where displaced residents had gathered.

Aside from individuals and emergent groups who are using technology and telecommunications for crisis response on a volunteer basis, professional emergency managers are also making strides in their use of online and mobile applications of social media, particularly in support of real-time reporting of events. Yet the lack of systematic control and coordination of information sharing from social media sources makes some officials leery of their use for purposes of increasing situational awareness at early stages of a crisis. However, research into social media in disaster shows that these concerns, while valid, may be overstated. For instance, during the Virginia Tech Massacre of 2007, when a gunman opened fire on campus killing 33 people including himself, communications between members of Facebook groups was found to be extremely well-coordinated. Individuals took turns monitoring and verifying one another's postings.[13]

It is clear that we have just begun to tap the potential of social networking to facilitate catastrophe readiness and response. However, while emergent groups are often meeting needs that would otherwise be unmet, there remain serious issues with the use of volunteers who—although well-meaning and with good intentions—may be untrained and unfamiliar with the basic tenets of emergency management and crisis intervention, and who are not bound to any standard ethical code. Other areas of concern in the use of social media for disaster management include the need to verify sources and content of shared information, the unintentional or deliberate creation or use of misinformation, and the potential danger of invasion of privacy. These questions should be considered when emergency managers apply these new forms of communication in the catastrophe setting.

RELATIONSHIP BETWEEN ETHICS AND LAW

Thus far in this chapter, we have explored some of the sources of ethics that apply to the professional emergency manager. We have seen that formal and informal frameworks for decision making can help guide EM workers in the context of catastrophe (e.g., the use of a triage system to provide response services during a mass casualty event), and that codes and standards of conduct serve to promote ethical behavior in both everyday and crisis situations (e.g., the principles of respect, commitment, and professionalism promoted by the International Association of Emergency Managers). In addition to these types of guiding principles, a variety of laws directly govern activities carried out by professional emergency managers in the course of their duties. Many of these laws are covered in depth in Chapter 4 and so are not discussed in detail here; instead, this section of this chapter focuses on the relationship between ethics and law, and how certain elements of the legal system can help emergency managers make ethically informed decisions when planning for and responding to catastrophic events. Among the laws addressed here are constitutional laws, civil rights laws, laws governing vulnerable populations, and international human rights laws.

Before we begin our discussion of law and ethics, we note that although emergency workers must look to the law for official guidance to develop advance directives and to implement policy, legal guidance alone does not provide the answer to every difficulty that may arise. Laws do not always address the entire breadth of ethical imperatives in emergency response, and the laws that do exist can vary widely from state to state. In fact, the law itself does not always reflect ethical behavior. For example, case law has stated that a person who knows how to swim has no legal obligation to rescue a drowning child, but is this an *ethical* position?

As a result, it is important that emergency managers supplement legal guidance with ethical analysis for a more robust framework for determining moral duty, obligation, and conduct. Having said that, however, it is also important to note that ethical analysis does not substitute for appropriate legal guidance. When anticipating dilemmas, when initiating policy and protocols, or when updating existing procedures, informed legal advice is mandatory. An attorney familiar with disaster challenges and well-versed in relevant statutory and case law can help emergency management practitioners to define legally acceptable actions.

CONSTITUTIONAL RIGHTS

Many of the issues we must deal with in a disaster of any proportion, and certainly of a catastrophic nature, will have legal as well as ethical implications. Among these issues are constitutionally guaranteed rights, which are based on moral and ethical principles dating to the founding of our nation. These rights are guaranteed not only during ordinary times, but also during emergencies. Whether they may ever be violated or suspended during a crisis of catastrophic proportion is a serious area of concern from both a legal and ethical perspective. Consider the following brief descriptions of Constitutional guarantees and how they may be impinged during a catastrophe.

First Amendment Rights: The First Amendment to the U.S. Constitution protects our right of free speech and freedom of the press. In a crisis situation, government officials may desire to tightly control the messaging that goes out to the public in order to maintain order and ensure the efficient and effective deployment of resources and delivery of services. However, the need for operational procedures to run according to protocol must be balanced with the well-established right of the press to publish freely, even if the information disseminated is critical of government response efforts.

The Right to Due Process: Due Process is best defined in one word: *fairness*. Due process embodies the idea that both the law itself as well as all legal proceedings must be fair and equitably applied. The right to due process is found in the Fourteenth Amendment to the U.S. Constitution, and guarantees that the government cannot take away a person's basic rights to life, liberty, or property without due process of law.

Following Hurricane Katrina, judicial procedure in New Orleans broke down because court documents and records, material evidence, judicial calendars, and the court buildings themselves were decommissioned or destroyed because of the storm. Defendants awaiting trial, plaintiffs bringing civil suits, and even incarcerated prisoners were in some instances denied their rights to due process, because the legal system itself was literally under water.

The Right to Equal Protection: The Equal Protection clause of the Fourteenth Amendment to the Constitution states: *"No State shall ... deny to any person within its jurisdiction the equal protection of the laws."* This right ensures that all persons have the same access to the law and courts, and have the right to be treated equally by the law and courts, both in procedures and in the substance of the law. It is akin to the right of due process, but in particular applies to equal treatment as an element of fundamental fairness.

The Equal Protection Clause most clearly prohibits race-based discrimination by the government. Precedent demonstrates that plaintiffs can assert successful equal protection claims in cases of serious, intentional governmental discrimination. Thus, if authorities deliberately underserve or mistreat a minority community, such as African Americans or other minority group during an emergency because of race, that group could have a valid equal protection claim. Furthermore, regardless of potential litigation outcomes, the Equal Protection Clause articulates a clear antidiscrimination principle that guides governmental authorities at all times, including during times of emergency preparedness and response.[14]

Habeas Corpus: Simply stated, *Habeas Corpus* (from the Latin, "you have the body") protects people from being detained by the government indefinitely without appearing before a judge or magistrate to hear the charges against them. In times of dire emergency, habeas corpus has been suspended, for example, by President Lincoln during the Civil War; by President Grant during Reconstruction; and in 2001 during the War on Terrorism.

Consider the following description of the demise of the legal system in New Orleans, and the de facto violations of habeas corpus, due process and equal protection that resulted from institutional neglect and lack of preparedness for a disaster the size of Hurricane Katrina—a "perfect storm" that illuminated how unprepared local criminal systems are for a severe natural disaster or terrorist attack.[15]

Hurricane Katrina washed away the New Orleans criminal justice system. As residents evacuated, the jails flooded to inmates' chests and police scrambled to enforce order without any communication. The water receded weeks later revealing thousands of detainees awaiting hearings and trials ... thrust into a legal limbo without courts, trials, or lawyers, resulting in what one judge called "a constitutional crisis." This dire situation lasted not just during the initial period of severe disruption, but for upwards of a year. While courts eventually reopened, they failed to act as 8,000 people languished for months "doing Katrina time" in prisons. Most were arrested for petty offenses such as public drunkenness, reading tarot cards without a permit, or failure to pay traffic tickets, and then detained based solely on a police affidavit. Most then served long past their likely sentences without ever receiving a judicial hearing. Nor did these thousands of detainees, mostly indigent, meet with lawyers. Only six public defenders remained in New Orleans, which the Chief Judge of the criminal court called "a full-blown disaster." In effect, Louisiana courts suspended habeas corpus for six months.

The Eighth Amendment: The impact of Hurricane Katrina on the judicial system in New Orleans has included alleged violations of constitutional rights of due process, equal protection, and habeas corpus; as serious as these abuses have been, even more gruesome are accounts of experiences in the city's jails during the storm itself and immediately thereafter. Some of the events during Katrina may have risen to the level of violating the Eighth Amendment, which governs the treatment of incarcerated individuals and prohibits the infliction of "cruel and unusual punishment." While the general population has no right to healthcare or to have other services provided by the government, prisoners are entitled to food, clothing, shelter, and medical treatment because they are not free to obtain these necessities for themselves. These entitlements are *not* suspended during disasters.[16]

Consider this description of the treatment of prisoners in New Orleans during and immediately following Hurricane Katrina:[17]

> The Orleans Parish sheriff did not evacuate inmates before the storm, stating that he could never have convinced other sheriffs to house his thousands of prisoners. Instead the prison conducted some very last minute preparation and planned on "vertical evacuation" to higher floors if the city flooded.
>
> The large concrete buildings survived the storm itself well, but not the levee break that followed after the storm had passed. Waters rose quickly overnight and ruined the emergency generators. The prison lost lights and air circulation (in 90-degree weather); soon the sewage backed up as well. The rising water filled the ground floor cells with chest-deep water, and transformed the jail into an "island of fear and frustration."
>
> Electronic cells could not be opened and food could not be safely distributed. Guards brought inmates to higher floors, where they were crowded in with other prisoners. "[T]he man who failed to pay his traffic ticket was shoulder to shoulder with the man serving 20 years for manslaughter. They were afraid of each other; they were afraid of dying; they were afraid no one would ever come back for them."
>
> Many deputies simply deserted; some deputies that remained attempted to use force to keep prisoners in their flooded cells, though some helped break windows in order to let in some air. Prisoners signaled for help by setting fire to blankets and shirts and hanging signs outside the windows reading "We Need Help," "Help Us," and "One

Man Down." There are reports of a few prisoners escaping in the chaos, swimming through the floodwaters.

The next day, the Louisiana Department of Corrections arrived with boats to carry prisoners to an elevated overpass on the nearby interstate (where New Orleans residents rescued from their homes also awaited transportation). Deputies parked buses as close as floodwaters allowed, and ferried prisoners day and night to other jails around the state.

Most prisoners were brought to a staging area for processing, an outdoor football field at the Elayn Hunt Correctional Facility in St. Gabriel, Louisiana. The numbers at Hunt grew so large that guards did not feel safe patrolling inside the gated field and retreated beyond the fences. An inmate described, "[y]ou had to sleep on the wet grass. They didn't have anywhere we could urinate or defecate. We didn't have hot food. We didn't have cold water. In fact, they come once a day and throw peanut butter sandwiches over the gate. They wouldn't even come in the gate."

In ordinary times, negligence by prison authorities is not usually a constitutional violation, and most prison regulations are upheld as sufficiently linked to valid goals of the penal system. But if prison authorities do not have or do not follow established emergency plans and abandon prisons en masse—leaving inmates to fend for themselves as happened after Hurricane Katrina—an Eighth Amendment violation may exist.[18]

CIVIL RIGHTS AND ANTI-DISCRIMINATION LAWS

Large-scale events in the United States such as the 9/11 attacks and Hurricane Katrina have focused nationwide attention on emergency preparedness and on the specific needs of people with disabilities, older adults, people with low incomes, people with limited English proficiency, and other special populations. In planning for very large impact emergencies, these groups may require specialized attention to ensure their rights are upheld—both as a matter of law and ethical imperative (see Figure 3.3).

Specifically, legislation such as Title VI of the Civil Rights Act of 1964; the Americans with Disabilities Act; Section 504 of the Rehabilitation Act of 1973; and the Age Discrimination Act of 1975 provide that no person in the United States may be denied benefits or be excluded from participating in any federally funded program or activity on the basis of race, color, national origin, disability, or age. Because a presidentially declared disaster often generates a great deal of federal disaster aid for impacted communities, officials must ensure that these funds are allocated in a nondiscriminatory manner. For example, under the Public Assistance provisions of the Disaster Mitigation Act of 2000, a disaster declaration triggers grant funds to help local and state governments repair damaged public infrastructure such as water and sewer treatment plants, roads and bridges, schools, government buildings, and other critical facilities. Although discriminatory intent can be hard to prove, Title VI mandates that the federal disaster aid cannot be withheld from specific neighborhoods based on the fact that residents are predominantly low-income, minority, or members of other protected groups.

Figure 3.3 Federal and state laws prohibit discrimination and require accommodations for special-needs populations in the provision of government services. This figure depicts a designated section for deaf evacuees at the emergency shelter in the Houston Astrodome during Hurricane Katrina. (Courtesy of FEMA.)

Americans with Disabilities Act/Rehabilitation Act

The Americans with Disabilities Act and the Rehabilitation Act establish a dual mandate of nondiscrimination and accommodation to meet the needs of individuals with disabilities. This dual commitment is particularly important in the context of emergencies, when individuals with physical and mental impairments have many special needs. Emergency managers may find themselves in violation of the statutes if they fail to take affirmative steps to protect the safety of individuals with disabilities when planning for large-scale disasters. For example, disaster plans should include strategies to ensure that officials can adequately communicate with, evacuate, and shelter disabled individuals in a disaster of any scale (see Figure 3.4).

THE FEDERAL TRANSIT ADMINISTRATION IMPLEMENTS ANTI-DISCRIMINATION LAWS

Implementation of the various laws against discrimination in disaster response can take many different forms. For example, the Federal Transit Administration's Office of Civil Rights developed a report, titled *Transportation Equity in Emergencies*, which provides guidance and technical assistance to officials in metropolitan regions to better incorporate attention to populations with specific mobility needs into their ongoing emergency preparedness planning activities. In conjunction with the report, the FTA has developed Geographic Information System (GIS) maps of 20 metropolitan regions. These maps highlight areas with high concentrations of minority and low-income populations, persons with limited English proficiency, and households without personal vehicles. These maps are targeted for use by state departments of transportation, metropolitan planning organizations, and transit agencies in identifying and assisting populations that may need assistance in an emergency evacuation. The full report and maps can be found at http://www.fta.dot.gov/civilrights/12324.html.

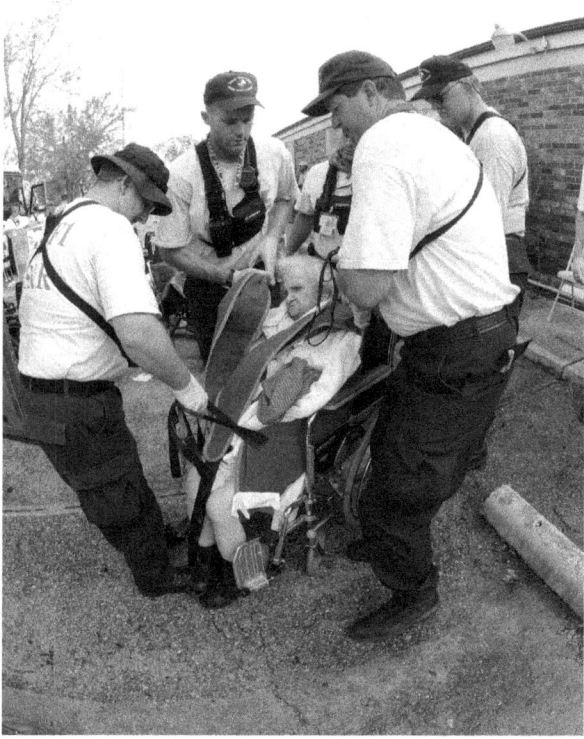

Figure 3.4 Emergency evacuation plans must include provisions to evacuate people with limited mobility or other special needs, including hospital in-patients, residents of nursing and convalescence homes, and residents without cars, as well as individuals and families living in homeless and battered women's shelters. In this photograph, a resident of a New Orleans nursing home is assisted to a bus going to an emergency shelter during Hurricane Katrina. (Jocelyn Augustino/FEMA.)

INTERNATIONAL LAW: RECOGNIZING BASIC HUMAN RIGHTS

There is a large body of international law that embodies a sense of "ethics" in recognizing and articulating basic human rights. These rules are often pushed to the limit in the chaos of a major international disaster, but the rights of all disaster victims remain intact regardless of circumstances, including the most basic right of all—to live life with dignity.

Legal Basis of Human Rights Law

International human rights law is actually a complex system of laws—including domestic, regional, and international—designed to promote human rights through various international agreements, which are binding on signatory countries. Human rights law is related to, but not the same as international humanitarian law and refugee law.

A few of the relevant international human rights laws, standards, and policies pertaining to humanitarian action as well as to human rights in disaster situations include

- The International Universal Declaration of Human Rights
- The International Covenant on Civil and Political Rights
- The International Covenant on Economic, Social, and Cultural Rights
- The Convention on the Elimination of All Forms of Discrimination against Women
- The Convention on the Rights of the Child

Other relevant policies and standards include

- The Sphere Humanitarian Charter and Minimum Standards in Disaster Response
- The United Nations Inter-Agency Standing Committee Internally Displaced Persons Policy
- Code of Conduct for The International Red Cross and Red Crescent Movement and NGOs in Disaster Relief

The Human Rights of Disaster Victims

Traditionally, natural disasters have been seen as situations that create challenges and problems mainly of a humanitarian nature. However, increasingly it has come to be recognized that human rights protection also needs to be provided in these contexts. The tsunamis, hurricanes, and earthquakes which hit parts of Asia and the Americas in the last decade highlighted the need to be attentive to the multiple human rights challenges victims of such catastrophes may face. All too often the human rights of disaster victims are not sufficiently taken into account.

Unequal access to assistance, discrimination in aid provision, enforced relocation, sexual- and gender-based violence, loss of documentation, recruitment of children into fighting forces, unsafe or involuntary return or resettlement, and issues of property restitution are just some of the problems that are often encountered by those affected by the consequences of natural disasters. In addition, a high number of persons also become internally displaced when volcanic eruptions, tsunamis, floods, drought, landslides, or earthquakes destroy whole communities, forcing entire populations to leave their homes in mass exodus. Experience has shown that the longer the displacement lasts, the greater the risk of human rights violations. In particular, discrimination and violations of economic, social, and cultural rights tend to become more systemic over time.

As proclaimed by the United Nations Interagency Standing Committee, human rights must be the legal underpinning of all humanitarian work pertaining to natural disasters. At a minimum, steps should be taken to alleviate suffering and provide assistance in areas critical to human survival, including providing the following to all non-combatant victims of disaster:

- Potable water
- Water sanitation
- Nutrition
- Access to food
- Adequate shelter
- Healthcare services

Under international human rights law, these basic necessities must be provided without discrimination in accordance with the humanitarian principles of humanity, impartiality, and neutrality.

HUMAN RIGHTS VIOLATIONS IN THE UNITED STATES?

Before Hurricane Katrina hit the Gulf Coast in 2005, the human rights issues raised in the context of international disasters would seem to many Americans to have little relevance to the United States; most of us would take such basic necessities for granted, and assume that water, sanitation, food, shelter, and medical care would be provided in ample supply and timely fashion after a disaster of any size that occurred within our borders. Yet descriptions of the aftermath of Hurricane Katrina graphically demonstrate that even in America these basic human needs for survival may go unmet for certain vulnerable segments of society. Referring to essays from the Understanding Katrina collection published at the website of the Social Science Research Council (http://understandingkatrina.ssrc.org), discuss whether internationally recognized human rights laws were violated during Hurricane Katrina, and whether planning for catastrophe readiness and response should explicitly incorporate recognition of these rights.

DEFINING THE DIMENSIONS OF THE MORAL COMMUNITY

Contemplating and evaluating to whom we owe ethical obligations in a catastrophe are significant and important questions. The philosophical concept of the "moral community" refers to the people and things to which we might have ethical duties, if only because they share a common existence with us. Consider these questions about the potential dimensions of the moral community, and decide which might be relevant for the emergency manager when planning for catastrophic events.

Biological Dimension: Are only humans part of our moral community? Or, do we have ethical duties to take into account the welfare and interests of other forms of life? If so, which ones? Does this include only sentient species (those that can feel pain), or all life forms? Are only certain animals, say ones that we have actively cared for like household pets, owed respect and consideration?

PET RESCUE: MORAL DUTY OR WASTEFUL SERVICE?

Consider that rescuing and caring for pets during and after disasters is a major task and can be controversial when it takes away from time and resources that could be devoted to human rescue and care. However, emergency managers have become much more aware in recent years of the need to provide for pet rescue, including establishing pet-friendly evacuation shelters, because of the number of people who have risked their own lives, and that of first responders, in attempting to save pets from flooding and other disasters (see Figure 3.5).

Temporal Dimension: Are only residents living today a part of our moral community, or do we also have ethical duties and responsibilities to future generations, and future residents? If we have a duty to consider the impact of our actions on the future, how far into this future does our moral community extend?

Geographical Dimension: What is the geographical range or extent of our moral community? Do we have duties to people and cultures far away, to respond to catastrophic events and impacts that take place in other nations, in other parts of the world? To what extent are those who are poor and vulnerable, but living in another country also to be considered part of our moral community and thus due respect and consideration?

Arguments can be made that we should consider the plight of those who live in other countries from a purely ethical standpoint, and that a moral view would require the offering of assistance. Others have pointed out the impact that foreign disasters can have on our own economy, and that disaster assistance is an investment in domestic security. Consider the following example:

Hurricane Mitch, which struck Central America in October, 1998, left almost 10,000 people dead and another million homeless, revealing the extreme degree of social and ecological vulnerability of Central America as a region. Particularly hard hit were Honduras and Nicaragua, which suffered massive flooding, mudslides, and devastating loss of crops and livestock. As a result, a northward migration of thousands of Mitch refugees occurred over the ensuing decade as indigenous populations sought the means of making a livelihood outside of their native land. While international aid agencies, volunteer organizations and charities worldwide donated significant funds for emergency assistance, would adequate aid provided for reconstruction and mitigation against future disaster have made staying in the region a more viable option? What are the long-term ramifications of waves of disaster refugees to our country?

Figure 3.5 Because of the number of disaster victims who have refused to evacuate without their pets, the Federal Emergency Management Agency now provides guidance to communities to develop plans for managing animals in an emergency. An increasing number of evacuation shelters provide accommodations for household pets in addition to service animals. (Courtesy of FEMA.)

U.S. AID TO FOREIGN NATIONS

The United States has a long history of extending non-military aid to foreign countries, primarily through the United States Agency for International Development (USAID), whose roots date back to the Marshall Plan for reconstruction of Europe following World War II. The Office of U.S. Foreign Disaster Assistance (OFDA) within USAID is responsible for facilitating and coordinating U.S. government emergency assistance overseas. The OFDA responds to all types of natural disasters, including earthquakes, volcanic eruptions, cyclones, floods, droughts, fires, pest infestations, and disease outbreaks. OFDA also provides assistance when lives or livelihoods are threatened by catastrophes such as civil conflict, acts of terrorism, or industrial accidents. In addition to emergency assistance, OFDA funds mitigation activities to reduce the impact of recurrent natural hazards and provides training to build local capacity for disaster management and response.[19] Many other countries have official government agencies that operate like OFDA, serving the needs of people affected by disasters outside of their own borders, sometimes in conjunction with United Nations agencies, sometimes not.

U.S. AID TO HAITI: MEETING DIRE NEEDS, FINDING RESILIENT SPIRITS

While the United States has a long history of providing aid to foreign countries, the amount of that aid has often been the subject of both political and popular debate. The earthquake disaster in Haiti opened anew ethical questions about the extent of the obligations of developed countries of the world, and the United States in particular. Although the United States is a generous nation, the level of development aid provided by it as measured by percentage of Gross Domestic Product is very low, indeed the lowest among international donor governments. Wracked by political turmoil, government corruption, resource depletion, and overwhelming poverty *before* the earthquake, the Haitians suffered disproportionately when the natural disaster hit. It can be argued as a matter of global ethics and fairness that Haiti needs stronger commitments of aid for the long-term—above and beyond present levels—to help speed up the agonizingly slow process of recovery and rebuilding.

In his book *One World* (2002), Philosopher Peter Singer argues that the ethical principle of impartiality requires us to come to the aid of people and countries in need. While the slowness of the earthquake recovery process and the ongoing instability of the political and institutional conditions in Haiti may make some doubt that the country has the requisite capacity to put any amount of aid to efficient use, a closer look at the people of Haiti themselves could help change those perceptions. Haitians, especially the women who serve as the backbone of the community, are incredibly resilient. Despite the televised images of rubble in the streets, tent cities full of refugees, thousands of men without jobs, and children suffering from malnourishment, cholera, and other disease outbreaks, there is another side to Haiti. For decades, the Haitians have had a unique capacity to survive and even thrive amid dire living conditions and harsh political regimes. Their strength comes from family and faith, and an incredible creative spirit. This spirit is evident in the work of Haitian artists and artisans, who often use recycled and found materials to create colorful paintings, sculptures, hangings, and decorative objects that inspire and uplift all who see them.

Perhaps the evocative works of Pierre-Louis Prosper can serve as ambassador of Haiti's undying spirit. His life illustrated the difficult living conditions of his native country (he died barely reaching his 50s), but also the unique mix of creativity, ingenuity, and spirituality that infuses this troubled land, and which at the end of the day will likely be as important as anything to long-term recovery and renewal (see Figure 3.6).

Figure 3.6 The works of Pierre-Louis Prosper are symbolic of the resilient spirit of the Haitian people. (Courtesy of Timothy Beatley.)

VOLUNTEER ORGANIZATIONS AND PRIVATE DONATIONS

In addition to governmental aid for disaster relief, private citizens have donated generously to help those at home and abroad recover from catastrophe. Relief organizations such as the American Red Cross, the Federation of Red Cross and Red Crescent Societies, OXFAM, Save the Children, Salvation Army, AmeriCares, Catholic Charities, CARITAS, Mennonite Disaster Service, Médicens sans Frontieres, Second Harvest and others that are part of the National Voluntary Organizations Active in Disaster (NVOAD) and its international affiliates, as well as thousands of smaller non-profit and faith-based organizations, accept, process, and deliver emergency and longer-term recovery assistance around the globe. Many of the individuals who work within these organizations clearly consider those who are impacted by disaster to be within their "moral community," deserving of charity and compassion, no matter where they live.

Modern technology has stepped in to allow more individuals to give directly—and instantaneously—to causes they wish to support. In this age of multi-tasking, expressions of personal commitment and financial help are only a text message away.

The Haiti earthquake is a dramatic illustration of how mobile phones and modern communications might be effectively harnessed to bring the world together in response to various crises around the globe. The American Red Cross received more than $3 million in $10 increments in just the first several days of the Haiti response, proving text messaging to be a very effective form of philanthropy.

The Problem of "Donor Fatigue"

Despite the new methods and continued generosity of aid organizations and individual donors, the rapid succession of disasters of near-catastrophic proportion that has struck at home and abroad in the span of a few short years has caused what some call "donor fatigue" or "disaster fatigue"—the sense that these events are never-ending, uncontrollable, and overwhelming. Consider this partial list of recent catastrophes, and the huge need for international assistance they represent:

- 2004: Indian Ocean Tsunami leaves hundreds of thousands dead and homeless in Asia
- 2005: Hurricanes Katrina, Wilma, and Rita devastate the Gulf Coast of the United States
- 2006: Killer mudslides in Central America
- 2006: Magnitude-7.6 earthquake kills tens of thousands in Pakistan
- 2008: Cyclone Nargis leaves widespread destruction in Myanmar
- 2008: Massive earthquake hits China, killing thousands and destroying entire communities
- 2010: Earthquake in Haiti kills over 100,000; rebuilding is slow and thousands remain in temporary shelters subject to flooding, cholera, and abject poverty
- 2011: Earthquake and tsunami in Japan leave 20,000 dead or missing; thousands evacuate as radiation leaks from destroyed nuclear plant

For many charities and aid groups, the slew of disasters are taxing already limited resources in what now seems to be a constant flow of requests for donations, manpower, and supplies, as described below:[20]

> As bodies pile up in disaster after global disaster, even the most sympathetic souls can turn away. This problem came up after the 2004 Asian tsunami, an event that brought an avalanche of $1.92 billion in charity from the United States. Hurricane Katrina eight months later generated even more, $5.3 billion. But then fatigue seemed to set in. The earthquake in Pakistan that killed nearly 80,000 people generated just $150 million from Americans. And the Guatemala mudslide shortly thereafter that killed at least 800 was virtually forgotten.
>
> Ironically, the more bad news there is, the less likely people may be to give. According to some reports, "Hearing about too many disasters makes some people not give at all, when they would have if it had been just one disaster." For example, compared with disasters such as the Asian tsunami and Hurricane Katrina, those in China and Myanmar generated just a trickle of aid.
>
> A number of factors may be at play in a slowing American response, including a lack of sympathy for the repressive governments of China and Myanmar, doubts about whether aid will get through, and an inclination to save pennies because of shaky economic times at home.

But Americans may have also been influenced by the quick succession of monumental catastrophes in distant lands. "For the vast number of Americans, if they just gave to some disaster far away and then another disaster happens, in their mind that's clumped as 'faraway disaster.'"

THE MORAL COMMUNITY: FOCUSING ON VULNERABLE POPULATIONS

Whether the populations in need of assistance due to catastrophe are at home or abroad, many believe that we owe an even greater obligation to the most vulnerable among us. Earlier in the chapter we discussed some of the constitutional protections and state and federal laws that require a degree of equity in planning for emergency response, but these protections are not sufficient to address the needs of socially vulnerable populations in a holistic fashion. There has been a significant amount of research into the topic of "social vulnerability," including attempts to identify and define the characteristics of populations that are most susceptible to the negative impacts of disaster. It is fairly clear from this work that we can dispel a popular myth about natural disasters:[21]

> *Myth:* Disasters kill people without respect for social class or economic status.
> *Reality:* The poor and marginalized are much more at risk of death than are rich people or the middle classes.

This myth-buster was made abundantly clear during the aftermath of Hurricane Katrina; the hurricane itself was merely a phenomenon of nature, without ethics or purpose. And yet, those who were killed, displaced, or made homeless were disproportionately low-income African Americans with no means to evacuate the region.

The demographics and management issues of the socially vulnerable have been addressed elsewhere, and this is a rapidly growing field among disaster researchers. Rather than attempt to summarize the latest work in this area, we instead merely list some, but certainly not all, of the factors that can increase social vulnerability:

- Race, culture, and ethnicity
- Age
- Gender
- Disability
- Literacy
- Language barriers
- Social class
- Income disparity
- Foreign birth
- Illegal residency
- Domestic violence/violence against women
- Substance abuse/mental illness
- Homelessness
- Non-traditional families

The population groups that fall into the categories above are not an insignificant proportion of our society. At the global level, we would add to this list those living with HIV/AIDS as well as populations displaced or otherwise impacted by genocide, war, civil unrest, famine, and drought, all of which serve to make these populations disproportionately vulnerable to the impacts of natural hazards.

In the United States alone, vulnerable populations include tens of millions of people. Consider the following statistics from an article addressing the needs of the vulnerable in preparing for disaster:[22]

> According to the United States Census Bureau, in 2006, 41.3 million non-institutionalized Americans over the age of 5 had disabilities. Many more may have physical or mental impairments that may impact their welfare during an emergency but are not deemed to be serious enough to constitute reportable disabilities. In 2006, approximately 35.5 million individuals were 65 years of age or older and 38.8 million Americans were living in poverty. Children constitute approximately 25% of the United States population. Meanwhile, at the end of 2007, approximately 2.3 million individuals were incarcerated in U.S. prisons and jails.
>
> Some subset of each of these groups will almost certainly have special needs during disasters. Inadequate preparation for the needs of vulnerable populations can lead to catastrophic consequences. The disadvantaged could suffer large death tolls, as illustrated by Hurricane Katrina, in which over 1,800 individuals died because they were unable to evacuate the city, many of whom were elderly, poor, disabled, or infirm.

FROM DISASTER TO CATASTROPHE: INCREASING SECURITY BY ADDRESSING SOCIAL INEQUITIES

Thus far in this chapter, we have listed some of the characteristics of vulnerable populations—they tend to be poor, elderly, disabled, not fluent in the national language, or otherwise compromised. In general, they have little or no ability to prepare in advance for disaster; imagine, for example, the difficulty of stockpiling three days' worth of food and water when day-to-day living is a struggle. As a result, these populations require additional attention when planning for catastrophes because their vulnerability necessitates a higher level of response than populations that have greater capacity for self-sufficiency.

It is important to remember that preparedness for disadvantaged groups is not done in isolation. This is part of a larger picture, one that involves the root of disparities that exist in our communities. In other words, social vulnerability is a result of "pre-event" conditions in our society, as described by noted sociologist Susan Cutter:[23]

> Social vulnerability is partially a product of social inequalities—those social factors and forces that create the susceptibility of various groups to harm, and in turn affect their ability to respond and bounce back (resilience) after the disaster. But it is much more than that. Social vulnerability involves the basic provision of healthcare, the livability of places, overall indicators of quality of life, and accessibility of lifelines (goods, services, emergency response personnel), capital and political representation.

To be fully prepared for large-scale disasters, we must take a holistic approach, and confront the need for security of all members of the community. In this sense, "population security" is distinct from but closely related to the concept of "national security," because in the context of disaster, the one hinges upon the other. In practical terms, population security includes the following social and economic factors:

- Housing security
- Food security
- Health security
- Job security
- Access to education
- Access to credit
- Mobility, both within communities and across state lines
- Participation in community decision-making
- Exercising the right to vote

The underlying social construct in which preparedness and response play out are the very factors that necessitate the disproportionate level of resources and effort in times of disaster that are (or should be) directed toward vulnerable populations. In fact, it is these very factors that can allow a disaster to escalate into crisis; the more vulnerable the population is going into the disaster, the more likely the situation will morph into a catastrophe. It follows, then, that population security in its broadest context will make us all less vulnerable to catastrophe. This, it can be argued, may be at the heart of ethics in the context of catastrophe readiness and response.

SUMMARY

This chapter has considered a few of the ethical issues that may confront emergency managers in the context of catastrophe readiness and response. We discussed the point that, although subjective at times, there are branches of ethical philosophy that can provide guidance for making difficult decisions when the stakes are high in crisis situations; in particular, the various methods of applied ethics, as well as the availability of ethical codes and professional standards can help establish parameters of value judgments in advance of disaster events. Lessons learned from other professions, such as the use of *triage* by the medical and public health communities, can also help emergency managers make critical choices when time is short, resources are limited, and needs are great. We learned that ethics and law are not necessarily coterminous, and that the law stops far short of providing answers to all of the ethical dilemmas that can arise during planning and responding to disaster. Many laws do exist, however, that protect our fundamental rights, including the constitutional guarantees of freedom of the press, the rights to due process and equal protection, the prohibition against cruel and unusual punishment, as well as the protection from unlimited detainment, or habeas corpus. We discussed the ideal that these rights are not suspended during times of catastrophe, and yet instances of violations of constitutional protections have occurred, such as the breakdown in the justice system that transpired in the wake of Hurricane Katrina. We also briefly touched on some of the federal and state civil rights laws that prohibit discrimination in disaster aid, and the requirement that government agencies adequately provide for special populations in emergency response, necessitating advance planning that accounts for individuals with disabilities and other compromised groups such as low-income, minority, and non-English-speaking people. We then explored the various dimensions of our moral community, including biological, temporal, and geographic, which lead to a discussion of international human rights laws, as well as humanitarian aid and charitable giving, where we made the discovery that while one or two disasters can be galvanizing, several in a row can be paralyzing to the point of donor "disaster fatigue."

We started out the chapter by setting a scene of utter devastation and chaos in the wake of a hypothetical catastrophe, and asked readers to imagine the types of ethical dilemmas they might face in such a situation. We posed a scenario where first responders and other emergency professionals were directed to follow a "survival of the fittest" standard, where all decisions were directed to ensure continuation of selected segments of the population. We ended the chapter by exploring some of the social inequities that cause disparate impacts of disaster on less resilient populations, noting that the measure of our entire society's capacity to recover from major calamity might be jeopardized by those of us with limited means to survive on a daily basis. In stark contrast to a theory of "survival of the fittest," a paradigm that advocates "protection of the vulnerable" would require that our moral community includes the *least* able to survive a catastrophe. Whether one extreme or the other prevails, it is essential for emergency management professionals to understand that readiness and response requires thinking about the ethical implications of decision making long before the catastrophe occurs.

REFERENCES

1. Gert, B. 2005. *Morality: Its Nature and Justification*. New York, NY: Oxford University Press.
2. *American Heritage Desk Dictionary*. 1981. Boston: Houghton Mifflin Co., p. 341.
3. Josephson Institute on Ethics, 2002. http://josephsoninstitute.org.
4. American Heritage, Op. Cit.
5. Roberts, M. and E.G. DeRenzo. 2007. Ethical considerations in community disaster planning. In S.J. Phillips and A. Knebel, eds. *Mass Medical Care with Scarce Resources: A Community Planning Guide*. Rockville, MD: Agency for Healthcare Research and Quality, US Department of Health and Human Services (AHRQ Publication No. 07-0001). Accessed at: http://www.ahrq.gov/research/mce/mceguide.pdf.
6. Childress, J.F. 2004. Disaster triage. *American Medical Association Journal of Ethics: Virtual Mentor*. 6(5). Available from: http://virtualmentor.ama-assn.org/2004/05/ccas2-0405.html.
7. Eckenwiler, L.A. 2004. Ethical issues in emergency preparedness and response for health professionals. *American Medical Association Journal of Ethics: Virtual Mentor.* 6(5). Available from: http://virtualmentor.ama-assn.org/2004/05/msoc2-0405.html.

8. Ibid.
9. Quarantelli, E.L. 1991. *Lessons from Research: Findings on Mass Communications System Behavior in the Pre-, Trans- and Postimpact Periods.* Newark: Disaster Research Center.
10. Scanlon, T.J. 1992. *Disaster Preparedness: Some Myths and Misconceptions.* Easingwold: The Emergency Planning College.
11. Quarantelli, E.L. and R. Dynes. 1977. When disaster strikes. *Psychology Today.* 4:67–70.
12. Scanlon, Op. Cit.
13. Sutton, J. Social media and the democratic convention. *Natural Hazards Observer,* XXXIII(2):7–9. Available from http://www.colorado.edu/hazards/o/archives/2008/nov08/nov08_observerweb.pdf.
14. Hoffman, S. 2009. Preparing for disaster: Protecting the most vulnerable in emergencies. *University of California, Davis Law Review.* 42:1491.
15. Garrett, B.L. and T. Tetlow. 2006. Criminal justice collapse: The constitution after hurricane Katrina. *Duke Law Journal.* 56; Tulane Public Law Research Paper No. 06–09. Available at SSRN: http://ssrn.com/abstract=902640.
16. Hoffman, Op. Cit.
17. Garrett and Tetlow, Op. Cit.
18. Hoffman, Op. Cit.
19. www.usaid.gov.
20. MSNBC. 2008. *'Disaster Fatigue' Blamed for Drop in Giving: After Two Major Overseas Tragedies, Americans Are Less Generous.* http://www.msnbc.msn.com/id/24712998/.
21. Alexander, D. 2008. *Forty-Five Common Misconceptions about Disaster.* http://emergency-planning.blogspot.com/.
22. Hoffman, Op. Cit.
23. Cutter, S. 2006. *The Geography of Social Vulnerability: Race, Class and Catastrophe.* http://understandingkatrina.ssrc.org.

CHAPTER 4

Political and Legal Issues

John C. Pine

CONTENTS

Organizational Framework for Disaster Readiness and Response 78
   National Planning and Preparedness 78
      National Disaster Recovery Framework 78
      National Preparedness Guidelines 79
      National Incident Management System 80
   Structure of the U.S. Emergency Management System 81
      Federal 81
      State 82
      Roles and Use of the National Guard 83
      Local 84
Organizational Issues in Response to Catastrophic Events 85
   Federalism and the Role of States in Preparedness Response and Recovery 85
   Deployment of Federal Troops 87
   Governmental Powers 87
   Jurisdictional Collaborations 88
      Barriers to Inter-Jurisdictional Collaborations 91
      Implementing Inter-Organizational Partnerships 91
      Use of Private Resources in Response 92
   Communicating Warnings and Evacuation 93
      Limits on Population Return to Evacuation Zones 93
      Compelling an Evacuation 94
   Liability of Officials and Volunteers 94
      Negligence 94
      Immunity in Emergency Management 95
      Indemnification of Public Officials and Volunteers 95
Recovery from Catastrophe: Opportunities for Change 96
   Opportunity for Political and Legal Change 98

Emergency Management System Challenges and Vulnerabilities......................... 101
    Limitations to Department of Defense Response Authority............................ 102
    Key Organizational Issues 103
Conclusions 105
References 106

Disasters present dynamic challenges to communities, governmental units at all levels, businesses, and not-for-profit organizations. Disruptions from disasters have impacts within and between our social/political, economic, and environmental systems as well as our infrastructure from a local to international level, and catastrophes can be expected to provoke both more and different kinds of stresses. Coping strategies for our governmental, political, or public entities are essential if we are to mitigate the adverse impacts of large-scale extreme events or catastrophes. This chapter provides a base for examining our organizational framework for readiness and response of public agencies. We examine our structure for planning, preparedness and response from a national perspective as well as our state and local structures for emergency management.

Our organizational structures provide a foundation from which agencies can facilitate their programs and activities. Key issues, however, have a major influence on the success of agency programs and operations including the nature and extent of governmental powers, jurisdictional collaborations, and the liability of agencies and their officials, including volunteers.

Large-scale extreme events have not only widespread impacts but they also offer unique opportunities for change. We examine the nature of this opportunity for change and the organizational dynamics that make coping and adaptation possible. We also examine the challenges to the emergency management system from the use of military forces including the National Guard in response to a catastrophe and the unique barriers to effective decision making and more specifically changes in public policy in response to extreme events. We acknowledge the challenges presented by mixing rational decision making and organizational structures with political dynamics that impact levels of trust, organizational communication, and flexibility.

ORGANIZATIONAL FRAMEWORK FOR DISASTER READINESS AND RESPONSE

National Planning and Preparedness

National Disaster Recovery Framework

The National Disaster Recovery Framework was adopted in 2008 to enable all response partners to prepare for and provide a unified national response to disasters and emergencies—from the smallest incident to the largest catastrophe (FEMA 2011; DHS 2008). It establishes a comprehensive, national, all-hazards approach to domestic incident response. The Framework defines the key principles, roles, and structures that organize the way we respond as a nation and builds on the National Preparedness Guidelines (2007) described in the following section. The Framework describes how communities, tribes, states, the Federal Government, and private sector and nongovernmental partners apply these principles for a coordinated, effective national response. It also identifies special circumstances where the Federal Government exercises a larger role, including incidents where federal interests are involved and catastrophic incidents where a state would require significant support. The Framework enables first responders, decision makers, and supporting entities to provide a unified national response.

In recent years, the United States has faced an unprecedented series of disasters and emergencies, and as a result, national response structures have evolved and improved to meet these threats. The Framework reflects those improvements and replaces previous structures and represents a natural evolution of the national response architecture. It is intended to guide the integration of local, tribal, state, and federal response efforts. By adopting the term "framework" within the title, the 2010 document is now more accurately aligned with its intended purpose.

The Framework is written for senior elected and appointed leaders, such as federal department or agency heads, governors, mayors, tribal leaders, and city or county officials who have a responsibility to provide an effective response to preserve the safety and welfare of the community. It informs emergency management practitioners, explaining the operating structures and systems used routinely by first responders and emergency managers at all levels of government. It is also augmented with online access to supporting documents, further training, and an evolving resource for exchanging lessons learned.

National Preparedness Guidelines

The National Preparedness Guidelines were adopted by the Department of Homeland Security (2007) so that the nation would be prepared with coordinated capabilities to prevent, protect against, respond to, and recover from all hazards in a way that balances risk with resources and need. The guidelines provide a foundation for the National Disaster Recovery Framework (2008), which further clarifies our national response and recovery efforts. Specifically, the guidelines were intended to:

- Organize and synchronize national (including federal, state, local, tribal, and territorial) efforts to strengthen national preparedness; guide national investments in national preparedness;
- Incorporate lessons learned from past disasters into national preparedness priorities;
- Facilitate a capability-based and risk-based investment planning process; and establish readiness metrics to measure progress and a system for assessing the nation's overall preparedness capability to respond to major events, especially those involving acts of terrorism.

These preparedness guidelines reinforce the fact that preparedness is a shared responsibility. They were developed through an extensive process that involved more than 1,500 federal, state, and local officials and more than 120 national associations. They also integrate lessons learned following Hurricane Katrina and a 2006 review of states' and major cities' emergency operations and evacuation plans.

Included within the National Preparedness Guidelines are a National Preparedness Vision statement that provides a concise statement of the core preparedness goals for the nation; planning scenarios that identify a set of high-consequence threat scenarios of both potential terrorist attacks and natural disasters; a Universal Task List (UTL) which is a menu of some 1,600 unique tasks that can facilitate efforts to prevent, protect against, respond to, and recover from the major events that are within the National Planning Scenarios; and a Targeted Capabilities List (TCL) which defines 37 specific capabilities that communities, the private sector, and all levels of government should collectively possess in order to respond effectively to disasters. The Guidelines thus provide a range of readiness initiatives that are the umbrella for an all-hazards oriented, risk-based preparedness effort.

The Preparedness Guidelines establish a *capabilities-based approach* to preparedness. Simply put, a capability provides the means to accomplish a mission. They address preparedness for all homeland security mission areas: prevention, protection, response, and recovery.

The Preparedness Guidelines include a series of national priorities to guide preparedness efforts that meet the nation's most urgent needs. The priorities reflect major themes and recurring issues identified in national strategies, presidential directives, state and Urban Area Homeland Security Strategies, the Hurricane Katrina Reports, and other lessons-learned reports. The priorities will change over time as the Guidelines are implemented. The priorities include

1. Expand regional collaboration
2. Implement the National Incident Management System
3. Implement the National Infrastructure Protection Plan
4. Strengthen information sharing and collaboration capabilities
5. Strengthen interoperable and operable communications capabilities
6. Strengthen detection, response, and decontamination capabilities
7. Strengthen medical surge and mass prophylaxis capabilities
8. Enhance community preparedness by strengthening planning and citizen capabilities

National Incident Management System

The National Incident Management System (NIMS) provides a consistent nationwide template to enable federal, state, local, and tribal governments and private-sector and nongovernmental organizations to work together effectively and efficiently to prepare for, prevent, respond to, and recover from domestic incidents, regardless of the cause of the disaster.

It provides a set of standardized organizational structures such as the Incident Command Structure (ICS), multiagency coordination systems, and public information systems, as well as requirements for processes, procedures, and systems designed to improve interoperability among jurisdictions. NIMS specifically includes training requirements, structure for resource management, personnel qualification and certification requirements, equipment certification provisions, communications and information management elements, guidelines for managing technology support, and provisions for continuous system improvement. NIMS provides the structure and mechanisms for a national-level policy and operational direction for federal support to state, local, and tribal incident managers. Having a national structure that can be implemented at the local or regional level allows for a consistent process for emergency response. This common response structure allows response agencies to easily assist other jurisdictions as needed and supports mutual aid efforts. The structure also provides a basis for adapting organizational roles and processes that are needed to address unique communication, personnel, equipment resources, medical, or environmental needs. The structure provided by NIMS allows response agencies to organize response efforts in a constructive manner and overcome the chaos that could evolve from very large and complex disaster events.

Note: For an excellent discussion on the U.S. national response system, see Davis et al. (2007). Hurricane Katrina Lessons for Army Planning and Operations. Rand Corporation, Santa Monica, CA.

Structure of the U.S. Emergency Management System

Federal

The political system in the United States is a shared one among federal, state, and local governments. As a federalist system, emergency management is a decentralized function of many organizations that include many local and state agencies that play a critical part of our response and recovery efforts. As a result of this decentralized system, conflict evolves from the execution of state and local policies and actions. The federalist system has its advantages including flexibility, diversity and redundancy of operations, and local and regional focus on hazards and vulnerabilities (McEntire and Dawson 2007).

The emergency management system in the United States involves many stakeholders including federal agencies (executive, legislative, and judicial branches), state and local agencies, non-profit organizations (Red Cross and faith-based organizations), and private organizations from small businesses to large corporations. Although the federal government provides extensive resources for emergency management and especially support for response and recovery efforts, local governments have the greatest responsibility for emergency management activities and services.

A part of the federal system is a basic requirement that state and local levels of government comply with national legislation, regulations, and court decisions. Thus, state and local jurisdictions may be required under federal statutory or administrative programs to follow specific planning, mitigation, or response guidelines. Local and state compliance with federal programs and policies, however, is often the result of funding requirements that accompany financial resources for planning, mitigation, response, or recovery. Issues associated with control and direction have increased since the formation of the U.S. Department of Homeland Security (DHS) following the attacks of September 11, 2001.

The Robert T. Stafford Disaster Relief and Emergency Assistance Act (42 U.S.C. Section 5170) provides an orderly and continuing means of assistance by the Federal Government to state and local governments in carrying out their responsibilities to alleviate the suffering and damage which result from disaster. It supplements state and local resources in major disasters or emergencies where state and local resources have been overwhelmed. Thus, federal resources would automatically be involved in responding to a catastrophe. Except to the extent that an emergency involves primary federal interests, the declaration of a disaster must be triggered by a request to the president from the governor of a state. This legislation allows the president, in response to a state governor's request, to declare an "emergency" or "major disaster" in order to provide federal assistance. The law allows the federal government to support state, tribal and local government response efforts. Operational components that may be activated under authorization of the Stafford Act include the National Response Coordination Center (NRCC), Regional Response Coordination Center (RRCC), Joint Field Office (JFO), and Disaster Recovery Centers (DRCs).

The Department of Homeland Security (DHS) National Operations Center continually monitors potential major disasters and emergencies. When advance warning is received, DHS may deploy—and may request that other federal agencies deploy—liaison officers and personnel to a state emergency operations center to assess the emerging situation. An RRCC may be fully or partially activated. Facilities, such as mobilization centers, may be established to accommodate federal personnel, equipment, and supplies.

State

States have a major role in the U.S. emergency management system and one that complements federal agency roles and responsibilities. State legislatures adopt emergency management legislation, state agencies adopt program codes and administrative regulations; they provide funding for state and local governmental emergency management activities and serve as an interface with federal agencies and other groups who engage in the emergency management process from planning to response and recovery. Each state emergency management statute clarifies the role, authority and programs of emergency management in that state. State agencies develop integrated and comprehensive emergency management programs (preparedness, response, recovery, and mitigation). A key function that state agencies provide is to coordinate agency activities at the state level. They also assist local governments in providing guidance and support for emergency management activities. Further, states or federal agencies might assume direct control of the emergency response activities where special hazardous materials expertise is required and not available at the local level. Federal law might also designate a federal agency as the lead response agency, as in a terrorist incident or because the incident impacts shipping in a waterway.

State homeland security and emergency management statutes may include a provision that an all-hazard emergency response plan be developed. The state statutes may clearly outline the nature and extent of authority of the governor in a disaster as well as the role and functions of local governments in disasters.

State governors have a major role in the emergency management system. They serve as the senior state official in all matters related to disasters and emergencies and have the responsibility for emergency management activities within the state. The state emergency management statute outlines the governor's role and authority in declaring a state disaster; they direct the state's disaster response and are the commander of the State National Guard. A key role for the governor is to formally request federal aid as well as to implement interstate mutual aid agreements.

If effective response in a disaster is beyond the capability of the state, the governor may request a Presidential Declaration of Major Disaster or Emergency (The Stafford Disaster Relief & Emergency Assistance Act). This request for a national disaster declaration is founded on circumstances where the disaster is of such severity and magnitude that effective response is beyond the capabilities of the state and the affected local governments. Federal assistance is thus necessary (U.S.C. *Stafford Act*). The governor submits an official request to the president through the FEMA regional director asking for federal assistance under the Stafford Act.

In addition to declaring a state disaster, the governor has the authority to suspend state laws, mobilize the state National Guard, seize personal property, direct evacuations (the governor's powers may be limited to directing an evacuation rather than mandating an evacuation), and authorize emergency funding.

Local authorities request help from their state government, which, if warranted, activates the programs and activities of the state disaster response plan. Generally, governors have, or are granted, the power to use all available state resources needed to respond effectively and efficiently. In many states, governors can suspend state laws or local ordinances if it is determined that the law in question will restrict or prohibit efforts to relieve human suffering caused by the disaster. In some states, after a state emergency declaration, the governor may establish economic controls over such resources and services as food, wages, clothing, and shelter in affected areas.

Under a state emergency declaration, governors are empowered to mobilize the National Guard and direct its efforts. Most are also empowered to direct citizen evacuation, to order the control of movement into or out of disaster areas, to release emergency funds, and to reallocate state agency budgets for emergency work. States generally coordinate activities with private relief organizations and local communities.

Roles and Use of the National Guard

The National Guard has constitutional and statutory roles as both a state militia and as a federal military reserve force. As the state militia, the state National Guard is commanded by the governor. Each member of the National Guard has dual status as a member of the National Guard of one's state and of the Army or Air National Guard of the United States, the latter being a reserve component of the Army or the Air Force, respectively.

The National Guard may be activated under state law to deal with civil disturbances or natural disasters, maintain vital services (such as hospitals or prisons), conduct drug enforcement operations, and respond to other threats to the security of the state's citizens or violations of state laws. In addition, the president is authorized to activate the National Guard into federal service to deal with a wide range of domestic emergencies or disasters. These include suppressing insurrections if requested to do so by the state's governor or legislature or enforcing federal laws.

Normally a request to use the National Guard is made by local authorities through the State Office of Emergency Management. National Guard forces have been used locally for search and rescue, hazardous materials decontamination, communications equipment and personnel, transportation equipment and personnel, security and maintenance of order, mass feeding, the provision of potable water, housing, health and medical care, sanitation, temporary restoration of essential facilities, engineering services, and debris clearance (FEMA 1984).

Local

Local governments, whether cities, towns, boroughs, villages, counties, or a parish, are central organizations in emergency management since local government has the primary responsibility for public safety, including emergency response following a disaster. The local elected government official (county level) is usually the person in charge, unless another official has been designated through ordinance or legislation. In general terms, state law defines who will do what in preparing for, mitigating, responding to, or recovering from emergencies or disasters. The objective here is to establish a legal authority for the development and maintenance of an emergency management program and organization and to define the emergency powers, authorities, and responsibilities of the chief executive official and the emergency manager.

Local government units may be required under state homeland security and emergency management statutes to develop an all hazards emergency plan. Since these are state laws, they impose a statutory duty to plan for disasters. The statute may provide that the local government (county level) will forward the plan to the state office of emergency preparedness.

Emergency Planning and Community Right to Know legislation adopted at the state level requires that communities plan for extremely hazardous substances, which are a defined set of hazardous substances by U.S. Environmental Protection Regulations (United States Code. 42 U.S.C. §§ 11001–11050). Local jurisdictions are required to obtain inventory information from local chemical processors or users who store, process, use, or transport hazardous substances. If they have any extremely hazardous substances in their inventories, they are required to complete a plan.

Local planning requirements also are associated with state or federal funding programs. Rather than requiring mitigation planning in state emergency management statutes, the planning requirement is associated with qualifying and obtaining mitigation funds by local entities from state or federal agencies. If the local entity fails to complete the local mitigation plan, it does not qualify for consideration of mitigation funds. It should be noted that state statutory requirements to develop a local emergency response plan establish a legal duty "to plan" on the part of the local entity. Failure to comply with this statutory duty could lead to a claim of negligence on the part of the local entity.

ORGANIZATIONAL ISSUES IN RESPONSE TO CATASTROPHIC EVENTS

Federalism and the Role of States in Preparedness Response and Recovery

The federal system in the United States is one that is based on enumerated powers specifically granted to it in the U.S. Constitution and statues. The Tenth Amendment to the Constitution provides that powers not delegated to the federal government nor prohibited by it to the states are reserved to the states. Key federal powers include collection of taxes, duties, pay debts, and provide for the common defense and welfare. Others include regulating commerce with foreign nations and among multiple states, establishing a militia, and to protect civil rights and liberties.

Faber (2006) notes that Hurricane Katrina may have exposed a weakness in our federalist system. The power and authority to effectively prepare, respond, mitigate, and recover from disasters is shared between state, federal, and local governments. As a result of our federalism, FEMA and DHS are not in complete control.

Governors of states have designated authority in a declared emergency. Declaring an emergency activates the emergency response and disaster recovery powers of the state or political subdivisions. Additionally, it typically will activate specific powers for the governor or the designee to take a variety of actions for the duration of the declaration.

For most states, the governor may deploy and use any resources that the state emergency response plan provides. Governors may use or distribute any supplies, equipment, materials, and facilities assembled, stockpiled, or arranged to be made available under any law relating to disaster emergencies. As the state commander-in-chief they may use organized and unorganized militia and of all other forces available for emergency duty. They may suspend the provisions of any regulatory statute prescribing the procedures for conduct of government business, or the orders, rules, or regulations of any agency if strict compliance with any of these provisions would, in any way, prevent, hinder, or delay necessary action in coping with the emergency and use all available resources of state or local unit of government reasonably necessary to cope with the emergency.

State law may also allow the chief executive officer of the state to use state or local resources in an emergency response. This could include the direction of personnel or agency resources. Further the governor or chief executive officer may be allowed to take and use private property to cope with an emergency, subject to any applicable requirements for compensation.

The power to order or compel an evacuation varies by state, but provisions are made for assisting in each state the evacuation of all or part of the population from any stricken or threatened area in the jurisdiction if the head of the unit of government considers this action necessary for the preservation of life or other disaster mitigation, response, or recovery. The governor may prescribe routes, modes of transportation, and destinations in connection with evacuation as well as to control ingress to and egress from a disaster area, the movement of persons within the area, and the occupancy of premises in the area and make provision for the availability and use of temporary emergency housing. The governor may suspend or limit the sale, dispensing, or transportation of alcoholic beverages, firearms, explosives, and combustibles.

A critical power available to state governors is the authority to allow persons who hold a license to practice medicine, dentistry, pharmacy, nursing, engineering, and similar other professions as may be specified by the governor to practice their respective profession in the state during the period of the state of emergency if the state in which a person's license was issued has a mutual aid compact for emergency management with the state.

Question: What is the role of the federal government in disasters? What is the primary benefit for obtaining a federal declaration of a disaster?

The concept of federalism is based on the principle that our national government has specified powers and authority through the Constitution except for those not regulated to the states. State and local governments are provided the authority to protect public safety and the Stafford Act provides that the president may direct federal agency resources and utilize agency authorities and resources in support of state and local agencies in response to the disaster. The Stafford Act thus allows the federal government to assist state and local governments in disasters by providing a wide range of resources including financial resources. Authority and responsibility for responding to natural and technological disasters thus resides in the states, but the federal government may assume authority and responsibility for disasters that threaten national security or the very existence of the government. As a result, federal agencies can act directly and assume leadership in crisis situations related to war, terrorism, and certain types of criminal activities, such as bombings, kidnappings, and bank robberies. Operational control of the disaster is maintained by state and local officials under their powers to protect public safety.

The concept of federalism thus may change depending on the situation. For most disasters, states have the power to direct response operations as part of public safety and the federal government supports these activities. The federal government however, is able to maintain some indirect control by placing conditions on some resources provided to the states and local jurisdictions. Access to special disaster funds may be dependent on compliance with specific rules and processes established by the federal government.

Note that in Barry's (1997) analysis of the great Mississippi River flood of 1927, federal responsibility for flood control represented a great change in U.S. governance. The federal role in state, local, and individual affairs changed significantly following the 1927 flood and also as a result of the federal programs that were established as a result of the depression in the 1930s.

Deployment of Federal Troops

During the immediate aftermath of a disaster, a governor may request the president to send in the U.S. military and use the resources of the Department of Defense to preserve life and property. This emergency assistance is limited to 10 days.

The Stafford Act further provides for circumstances under which the president may deploy federal troops. The Stafford Act requires that the governor determines that the situation is of such great severity that the state is unable to deal with the situation without federal help. Prior to the deployment of federal troops, the governor must execute the state response plan and activate the state National Guard units under state control. Note that the governor may keep National Guard units under state control.

The Posse Comitatus Act (18 U.S.C. 1385), along with other related laws and administrative provisions, prohibits the use of the military to execute civilian laws unless expressly authorized by the Constitution or an act of Congress. This federal provision (18 U.S.C. Section 1835) provides that "Whoever, except in cases and under circumstances expressly authorized by the Constitution or Act of Congress, willfully uses any part of the Army or the Air Force as a posse comitatus or otherwise to execute the laws shall be fined under this title or imprisoned not more than two years, or both." The Posse Comitatus Act thus allows Congress to authorize the military to assist in disaster response.

Note: For more information on the Posse Comitatus Act, see Elsea, J. 2005, CRS Report RS20590, The Posse Comitatus Act & Related Matters: A Sketch, and Elsea and Mason 2008, CRS Report RS22266, The Use of Federal Troops for Disaster Assistance: Some Legal Issues. For an excellent discussion of the statutory role of the National Guard and their state or Federal status, see "Hurricane Katrina: DOD Disaster Response" prepared by S. Bowman, L. Kapp and A. Belasco. Congressional Research Service (2005).

Governmental Powers

Nicholson (2008) notes that one of the most challenging aspects of emergency response is the fact that often a decision must be made between options that are universally unattractive. Sometimes, citizens will view the same situation from a very different perspective than public officials.

Evacuation is a good example of this phenomenon. Legal authorities for declaring an evacuation are found in state statutes or local ordnances. The law may grant the head of government the authority to force people to evacuate their homes and businesses and may be the best protective step that can be taken. Unfortunately, evacuation can be very expensive and disruptive for households and businesses. Further, it may cause significant inconveniences for residents.

Providing the governor with the power to compel an evacuation addresses the need to protect individuals who may not agree or appreciate the need to leave the area. This authority may be provided at a cost to local business operations or to the inconvenience of residents. An evacuation order could disrupt local business operations especially for healthcare facilities. Local or state officials might be able to take steps to address the cost or disruption associated with a mandatory evacuation by providing free public transportation, housing, food, caring for pets, or relatives. Large-scale evacuations thus address the need to protect citizens in extreme events; unfortunately, long-term displacement may be more common in a large-scale catastrophic event.

For situations where public officials need to keep residents away from an area that poses danger to the public, local officials could explain in detail the nature and extent of local hazards and steps that address resident's concerns for safety and security of their property. The key is that state or local officials might have the legal right to impose mandates on citizens but realize that it is very unpopular and could cause negative political fallout.

Jurisdictional Collaborations

Catastrophic preparedness requires regional and potentially international collaboration between states, federal agency the response efforts or the international response community. Catastrophes by definition overwhelm response capacities. Under this view, it is critical that preparedness efforts should be regional in nature. Planning efforts should involve the federal agencies that have regulatory or monitoring responsibilities as well as the identification of procedures to allow for international response teams. Unfortunately, planning for a regional or international response is not mandated by federal statute but the process of involving international response efforts is controlled by federal law. Note that evacuation planning activities by Louisiana were resisted by neighboring states until 2005. The evacuation executed for Hurricane Katrina was a successful multi-state collaboration.

One of the key challenges in preparedness and response to disasters is the tendency of organizations to maintain their independence and autonomy while a broader community-wide focus and inter-organizational interdependence are needed (Tierney et al. 2001). Tierney et al. (2001) note that there are key problems and challenges that must be anticipated in catastrophic preparedness initiatives. First, the quality and timeliness of organizational decision making suffers in extreme events but with planning and organization, disruptions can be minimized. In a normal non-crisis time, people and organizations typically try to make rational choices. Anticipating what increased pressures will evolve in a disaster makes it possible to overcome any deviation from quality decision making. Second, in a crisis situation, a rational model to decision making and organizational functioning is not appropriate; what is needed are strategies for organizational adaptation and flexibility. Disasters rarely, if ever, allow for rational decision making. As a result, strategies need to be identified that allow the organization to cope with the many unexpected external and internal pressures. At best, decision making in disasters exhibits, "bounded rationality." Tierney et al. (2001) suggest that we stress primary organizational goals and organizational structures to support the resolution of unanticipated operational needs. Because of the constraints in a disaster, rational decision making can rarely be achieved.

Inter-organizational conflict and collaboration are a key force that impacts the development of sound public policy. Burby (1998) explains the key principles that offer a foundation for sound public policy and avoids the cycle of recurring disasters in vulnerable locations. First, public policy makers must limit the practice of subsidizing the risks associated with the use of vulnerable geographic areas. By offering flood insurance in high-risk areas, we end up facilitating development in areas that are vulnerable to hazards. Second, public agencies at all levels must enhance their capacity to share information about the nature of risks and sustainable ways of living with hazards. Risk communication thus becomes a high priority. Third, public agencies at all levels must identify alternative approaches in the way they manage the use of hazardous areas. Creative uses of vulnerable areas for public use such as parks, conservation uses, or natural areas allow areas to be available for use but not subject to damage from hazards. Fourth, governments must do a better job of coordinating policies for the management of exposures to hazards. Increased planning and coordination can provide a foundation for ensuring that public policies intended to mitigate disaster losses on any scale result in constructive economic, social, and environmental outcomes. Finally, governments at all levels must foster public policies especially in governance and land management to better match institutional systems and tools with the nature of the problems presented by short-term disasters or long-term catastrophic events.

May and Deyle agree with the fundamental issues noted by Burby and contend that public policies dealing with preparedness are fragmented and encourage resistance to change where integration and coordination of public policy is critical (1998, p. 57). Although their observations were made years ago and focused on hazard mitigation, one may see that their position is still accurate today. This is particularly true when considering catastrophes, given their relative infrequency. Public policies may fail to stress the value of investment in hazard mitigation and result in increasing property losses and more complex barriers to emergency response and recovery.

When we see problems associated with communications technology deployed by neighboring jurisdictions, allocation of resources in a response or actions by one agency conflicting with a neighboring one, what we observe may be a symptom of the problem rather than the primary issue. May and Deyle (1998) and Burby (1998) would likely contend that what you face in an emergency response is the result of our mitigation policies and programs. Failure to acknowledge our vulnerabilities only serves to increase the socio-cultural, economic, political and environmental impacts brought by disasters, and even more so by catastrophes.

Public agencies at the local, state, and national levels must collaborate both vertically and horizontally in preparedness efforts. Prior to the response to Hurricane Katrina in 2005, agencies at all levels attempted to integrate their plans, but response efforts, as examined in many national assessments, did not find that preparedness efforts were effective (U.S. House of Representatives 2006; The United States Senate 2006; and the Townsend 2006).

Many factors influence the effectiveness of preparedness efforts and are central to collaboration among and between all levels of government. First, disasters are not just physical events that involve property damage and personal injury. They are also political in nature and almost always involve inter-organizational conflict and blame. As a result, there is conflict between public organizations at all levels, and between them and non-profit agencies and the business community, all of which are part of response operations. Disagreements may evolve concerning who will be given authority over incident command; which organizations will be assigned seemingly menial or less visible tasks; which organizations will be given additional resources and responsibilities; or who will get credit or blame for the outcome of the event. Because of this conflict, some organizations restrict communication and coordination with others simply because inter-organizational rivalries exist and nobody wants to look bad.

Public policy choices and priorities evolve when disasters are declared and when resources begin to be distributed. There may be disagreement about who should get help first leaving open claims of favoring major supporters and ignoring those who have significantly less political power. To say the least, these choices may impact a community response to a disaster, and the strength of the impact may be even more notable in catastrophes when major decision-making is often in the hands of outsiders. Despite this, emergency managers can use politics to their advantage after a disaster. Disasters generate an incredible amount of interest on the part of the media, citizens, and politicians (i.e., no one cares about disasters until they happen, and this attention fades quickly soon after the event occurs). Further, disasters are unique "focusing events" that can determine the policy agenda in this issue area (Birkland 2006). Finally, emergency managers should harness the interest in disasters to improve the ongoing response, seek recovery aid, and promote additional mitigation and preparedness activities.

Given the structure of our political system, decision making is likely to be very difficult in a catastrophe. There are many factors that impact decision making and why it is problematic during disaster response operations. First, local officials may have very limited situational awareness as events in a catastrophe unfold and some organizations have inherent conflicts with others during response operations in a catastrophe.

Dror (1986) identified reasons why decision making under disaster conditions is difficult and, suggested strategies to address the difficulties (1988). He determined that the situations involve adversity and are characterized by injury, death, destruction and demand the immediate attention of decision makers. Time is critical in a disaster and because people's lives and well being are at stake in a disaster, there is incredible pressure for decision makers to act quickly and even prematurely. There are no easy decisions in disasters for they are often accompanied by situations where there are drawbacks to nearly every decision that needs to be made. Decision making during response operations is a challenge as uncertainty is an expected correlate of disasters, and even more so in catastrophes in which the extent of the needs overwhelms the ability to communicate and comprehend them. The physical and emotional demands placed on decision makers are great and they may impair effective decision-making.

Strategies for effective decision making in a disaster response include (Dror 1986) designing preferable models. This strategy is similar to the rational model as it entails studying the situation or problem in detail, determining the gap that exists between the goal and reality, and intervening to adapt the process to the desired outcome. Debugging the response process is also recommended. This method includes an acute observation of the decision process in order to correct potential weaknesses and mistakes as they become apparent. Finally, Dror encourages us to think critically and to "think outside the box."

Barriers to Inter-Jurisdictional Collaborations

Hurricane Katrina dispelled any illusion that the answer to inter-organization collaboration was systematic partnerships. The collaboration unfortunately needs more than just an inter-agency agreement. Katrina was an indictment of existing arrangements that were supposed to provide a basis for agency coordination and cooperation. One must acknowledge that we have not ever experienced a disaster in the scope, scale, and combination of effects that followed in the wake of Katrina. The question is what went wrong with our inter-jurisdictional collaborative arrangements. Some just classify Katrina as a "mega-catastrophe" (King 2005; Sylves 2005; Litan 2005). However, mounting evidence leads us to believe that Hurricane Katrina was only a precursor of catastrophic events to come.

Mitchell (2006) sees that we fail to see the "holistic" approach in dealing with disasters. As an example, federal, state, and local plans were not fully integrated leading to many of the failures observed in Katrina. Too often, we approach disaster management from a local scale not acknowledging our inter-dependency between local, regional, state, and national levels. Unfortunately, the response to Hurricane Katrina may be characterized as simply "muddling through."

Platt (2000) notes that the U.S. Congress has created a complex array of federal agencies based on laws, agency programs, policies, and strategies that are intended to operate on the basis of partnerships, with state and local agencies, non-governmental organizations, and the private sector. Unfortunately, Congress has provided over 50 different laws and executive orders to authorize this patchwork system. This complexity is antithetical to flexible operation in times of emergency.

Implementing Inter-Organizational Partnerships

Formal partnerships among organizations associated with the emergency management process provide a sound base from which successful operations form. These partnerships are a policy instrument for building collaborations between entities and provide us a more holistic strategy to deal with complex disaster response, mitigation, and recovery issues. These formal arrangements are based on mutual collaboration and shared responsibility among groups that have common goals. They require broad-based inter-jurisdictional thinking and decision making. Given that much of the public safety governmental role in the United States is locally driven, partnerships are at the heart of the U.S. hazards preparedness and response policies.

Most inter-jurisdictional partnerships are interest-centered and tend to last only as long as the groups that come together share those interests (Mitchell 2006). Once those shared interests change, the partnerships weaken or disappear. As a result, partnerships must be based on something more stable than just mutual interests.

Vertical collaborations between federal, state, and local entities, including nonprofits or businesses, as well as horizontal partnership such as between states, must be based on different incentives. For our federal-state alliances, these vertical linkages are centered on federal support and compensation that is beyond the capacity of local entities. Funding is intended to drive cooperation and collaboration.

Horizontal cooperation has a very different basis and is usually goal directed or need based. Local jurisdictions that adopt mutual aid agreements should be aware of potential legal claims that may arise from doing so. While agreements address liability for damage to third parties or for their employees, state law must be examined to ensure that each party in the agreement is protected from third-party claims. Most state disaster acts provide immunity for agencies with formal partnerships that are recognized under state law (Mitchell 2006).

Mutual aid agreements are a key part of formalizing partnerships between jurisdictions and agencies. They are mandated by a number of standards, including the National Fire Protection Association (NFPA 1600) and NIMS. The elements of these agreements include clarification of roles and responsibilities, operational procedures, allocation of costs, communications, and liability provisions. See http://www.emacweb.org for more details on the Emergency Management Assistance Compact (EMAC). Mutual aid agreements and joint international preparedness initiatives are critical to providing effective response and recovery processes in geographic regions where large-scale collaborations will be needed. States that border both Mexico and Canada should work with federal agencies and our international partners to identify and secure appropriate agreements or clearances that would support effective mutual aid in a disaster of any scale.

Mitchell (2006) notes that the European Union directed and implemented a continent-wide integrated hazards response strategy despite some of their membership who believed that there was no need to establish such partnerships. A critical part of this strategy is a comprehensive education and communication effort to acquaint agencies and nations with the benefits of such inter-institutional arrangements. The European Union approach illustrates a more holistic one in contrast to the U.S. effort that is more decentralized.

Broad-based collaborations can also be enhanced by adopting goals which are shared by many jurisdictions. Agreement to enhance community sustainability and sustainable development provide an example of common broad-based goals, which combine economic, social, and ecological outcomes and form the basis for a shared vision of the future for the region.

Use of Private Resources in Response

State emergency management acts provide for the acquisition of private property in a declared disaster. It should be noted that the provisions require the public entity to provide fair and adequate compensation to the property owner for the use of the property in a disaster response.

Public agencies should have a standard operating procedure for taking private property in a disaster response including consultation with agency legal counsel and notice to property owners when possible. In cases where time does not permit and that other property is in danger, documentation of the existing situation is advisable to provide for a strong justification for the public agency actions. Many disasters provide clear illustrations of when property can be taken to aid in the response or in order to remove barriers to an effective response.

Communicating Warnings and Evacuation

Many public officials are hesitant to issue clear warnings when they believe that the public is in danger. The law in each state provides "discretionary" immunity to public policy makers who are charged with executing the laws and protecting the property and lives of the public. Where public officials must determine public policy, they are protected by this form of governmental immunity. Issuing a warning would be an example of a public policy decision that falls under the protection of governmental discretionary immunity.

Many public officials rely on the expertise and experience of professional staff in providing background information for the determination of a public policy decision. Where state or local officials are specifically allowed to issue public hazard and evacuation warnings and rely on the information and recommendations of their staff, the discretionary immunity still applies. For the public employee, they are also acting in their official capacity and enjoy protection from civil liability suit. In this situation, the employer is responsible for the actions of the employee (vicarious liability) and will defend the employee along with the agency if a claim is filed in court.

The fact that the employees form their recommendation to public officials from computer hazard models, experience, or direct observation of a disaster scene does not impact the protections that they enjoy under state law. The final decision to issue a public warning or order an evacuation is made by the public official with input by a staff member. The public warning is thus an action of the public policy maker not that of the employee. The protection provided by discretionary immunity for public officials is intended to encourage sound public policy decisions and not to discourage public officials from making complex choices.

It might be noted that there are many factors that influence public policy decisions involving warnings. Economic, political, natural, and social factors all affect the determination to order an evacuation. The fact that a public official in hindsight might have made a different decision to issue a more timely warning does not remove the protections provided by state law. The impacts from a public official's decision associated with catastrophic events may result in changes in public policy well after the disaster but discretionary immunity still protects the public official's actions.

Limits on Population Return to Evacuation Zones

State emergency management acts provide the governor the authority to limit or exclude the public in entering an area impacted by a disaster. Protecting the public in an unsafe environment may also be viewed under local government police powers. The inconvenience on members of the public to gain access to disaster areas is well justified by the circumstances. The powers granted to the governor in limiting access to an area are very broad and may be defined as broad an area as needed. The discretion granted to the governor (or the governors of more than one state in a large-scale catastrophe) is intended to protect public safety of citizens and responders from the dangers presented by disaster. Even if citizens make a constitutional claim against local or state officials, the courts would likely see that protecting the public in an unsafe circumstance was a small price to pay in order to allow responders to perform their job without the distraction provided by the public who just want to know what is going on.

As with other situations, it is advisable for public officials and senior managers to document the situation that they face. Take photos of the area to show the area is unsafe and that their protective actions are in the public interest.

Compelling an Evacuation

Requiring the public to leave a high-risk area when a disaster is likely to occur is not always provided under state law. Public officials would be advised to check with legal counsel to confirm that they have the authority to remove citizens from a high-risk area. Knowing precisely what our legal authority includes is a wise approach and legal counsel will appreciate the opportunity to clarify any provisions in the law that could influence when and how an evacuation might be initiated.

Liability of Officials and Volunteers

A tort is an action that harms another and occurs when a person acts or fails to act, without right and as a result another is harmed. Torts involve civil actions for personal injuries or property damage rather than a criminal action or a contractual claim.

Tort law is defined at the state level by statutes, court decisions, and constitutional provisions; it applies to government entities, individual citizens, and businesses. The law protects individual and business interests from harm and provides a means for those harmed by another to seek compensation for their loss.

Tort claims provide a basis for distributing losses to those who are responsible for the harm and protecting both the interests of the person injured and the governmental jurisdiction. Torts encompass intentional acts that harm others (trespass, assault and battery, defamation, and invasion of privacy), claims of negligence (unintentional acts or omissions), as well as strict liability (products' liability and workers' compensation) (Oleck 1982).

Negligence

State common and statutory law provides that a person has a duty to exercise that degree of care, skill, and diligence where a reasonable or prudent person would exercise under similar circumstances. This rule, as applied to governmental entities, must be understood in terms of the essential elements of *negligence*. It requires that a duty must exist and a person's actions must conform to a reasonable standard of care provided by statute, defined by common law (based upon judicial decisions), or established by public policy. For a claim of negligence, the law requires that there be a breach of conduct or a failure to conform to that standard of care, or a failure to carry out the duty. Further, there must be some type of damage or actual loss. Finally, claims of negligence must demonstrate a connection between the act of the governmental employee, official, or agency body and injury to a third party(ies).

Immunity in Emergency Management

Given the critical nature of effective emergency response in disasters, state and local jurisdictions have been protected from threats posted by claims of negligence. This protection comes in the form of discretionary immunity protecting public officials and employees for their policy-making decisions, governmental immunity for actions carrying out critical public functions such as public safety activities, health and building inspections, as well as mandated actions (the collection of taxes). Statutory immunity is also recognized in each state for specific public activities such as response to hazardous materials spills, emergency preparedness, and response activities associated with hazards or disasters. There are exceptions to the immunity provided to public agencies and officials where there is willful misconduct.

Indemnification of Public Officials and Volunteers

A key part of the threat posted by liability claims against public officials and employees is that they are generally entitled to protection against personal financial loss or indemnification. This may apply to both attorney's fees and judgments that might be awarded against them. State statutes generally provide that the governmental unit is responsible (liable) for the negligent acts or omissions of its agents (including volunteers) or employees who are acting within the scope of their duties as public employees. This protection includes not only paid employees, but also elected officials who receive no pay and volunteers who act on behalf of the public agency. State immunity is in addition to the federal Volunteer Protection Act (42 U.S.C.A. §§ 14501–14505, 1997). The liability is thus passed on vicariously to the governmental unit as employer. It should be noted that this protection may not be passed on to the government entity if the employee acted outside the scope of one's duties, acted with an intent to harm (malice) or the intent to harm another, or if the actions were with reckless disregard for the rights of others.

In catastrophic events, many non-profit organizations will assist in the response and likely engage many volunteers. The protections provided public agencies in response efforts may be passed along to non-profit agencies, their staff and volunteers when these agencies act on behalf of the local or state government agency. In effect, the non-profit agencies and volunteers must be acknowledged as acting on behalf of the public agency. It should be stressed that these non-profit agencies coordinate their activities with local or state government entities.

RECOVERY FROM CATASTROPHE: OPPORTUNITIES FOR CHANGE

The challenges of rebuilding after catastrophes involve not only government officials but also residents, real-estate developers, business owners, and many professionals such as engineers, architects, and urban designers/planners. The debate that results is one that the entire community has at stake. Berke and Campanella (2006) pose several questions that are at the core of this debate.

Question: How can we plan for more resilient places that are socially just, economically vital, ecologically compatible, and less vulnerable to future disasters? How can the hundreds of thousands of displaced residents be given a voice in determining the future of their communities? What reforms are needed to federal and state policies that influence development of hazardous areas? *Berke and Campanella (2006) believe that pre-disaster recovery planning for resiliency is the key in dealing with these questions.*

Hurricane Katrina provided a "window" for effective recovery planning and building resilient and sustainable communities. Windows are moments of opportunity when a problem has become urgent enough to push for change of entrenched practices (Birkland 1997). Unfortunately, this opportunity is limited and local officials and community leaders need to take advantage of this opening for change. Pre-disaster planning allows the local community to have strategies to cope with temporary housing, damage assessment, debris removal, restoration of utilities, re-occupancy permitting, and reconstruction priorities. Long-term strategies in the pre-disaster recovery planning include: building moratoria, planning for stricken areas, and relocation of housing to safer sites. More importantly, pre-disaster recovery planning allows policy makers to envision the community outside of the distress and extreme emotions that come with disaster. Given the developments in hazard models, more accurate data and potential increasing threats brought on by climate change, communities should review their hazards analysis to determine if their conclusions should be altered to address a greater risk from hazards. Birkland recommends that long-term planning must be addressed in an integrated manner including transportation, housing, land use, the environmental issues and that planning must balance the social, cultural, economic, and ecological needs of the community.

Research has demonstrated that most communities have failed to develop effective pre-disaster recovery plans. What they have developed has been considered inadequate to address community problems after a disaster. The end result is that the community is then engulfed in conflicts over recovery policies and expenditure of limited resources (Burby and May 1997; Nelson and French 2002).

Question: Policy makers at the national, state, and local level have the opportunity to address long-term issues that involve resiliency and future vulnerability to hazards. However, many find it easier to be more concerned with dealing with immediate concerns (i.e., potholes, waste disposal, and crime) rather than long-term issues that will impact the community for an extended time. What have we learned from the recovery process following Hurricanes Katrina and Rita in 2005?

Smith (1996) observes that disasters provide opportunities for political change. He sees that recovery following disasters presents a chance for new alliances to emerge and mobilize. Disasters shape, maintain, destabilize, or destroy both political organizations and relations. Disasters thus create a context in which power arrangements may be articulated and challenged, which changes political perceptions, shapes individual intentions, and strengthens or dissolves institutional alliances. A catastrophic event may bring about new ideologies, activism, and power alliances and thus presents an opportunity for change.

The post-disaster time period also presents some critical issues that impact the results from the recovery process. Berke and Campanella (2006) identify key issues that must be addressed in shaping a resilient community that has suffered a catastrophe. They suggest that state and federal land use and development policies foster rebuilding or development in hazardous areas and impede sensible local pre-disaster planning. Gulf coast states, with the exception of Florida, fail to require comprehensive land use planning. As a result, local communities build back without consideration of future risks from hazards. The federal government also fails to require local planning to avoid development in high hazard areas.

Berke and Campanella (2006) further note that new urban models must be utilized to enhance resiliency and avoid risk from hazards. Sprawl rather than high-density new urbanism could result following a disaster. They suggest that compact urban form design should be considered as communities struggle to recover from disasters.

Engagement of community stakeholders in a meaningful manner is critical to the planning process (Berke and Campanella 2006). Citizen participation can be viewed as a means of restoring and repairing the social fabric of a community following a disaster. Engaging the entire community in a meaningful manner provides opportunities for the community to heal in many ways. Residents displaced for long periods following Hurricane Katrina struggled to engage in the community restoration process. The complex situation presented by Katrina will likely influence recovery efforts for many years. Future research will judge the results of these recovery efforts.

Research prior to Hurricane Katrina in 2005 suggests that when the community is not engaged, plans and implementation strategies do not benefit from local knowledge and capacities (Healy 1997; Zaferatos 1998). Too often policy discussions are dominated by external experts who lack an understanding of local conditions. The end result is that the planning that takes place actually creates opposition and conflict to the plans. This may be particularly true in catastrophes in which a large number of the original population of a community may not be able to return from evacuation within the time frame in which decisions are being made.

Restoring the community is more than rebuilding the infrastructure; it is preserving and restoring the torn social fabric that reconnects family, social and religious networks at the grassroots level, neighborhood by neighborhood. Reconstruction of the community's social fabric requires that citizens be engaged in planning for schools, childcare, shops, places of worship, and recreation opportunities.

Some argue that there is too much at stake for the federal government to stand by and wait for state and local governments to embrace strong land-use requirements in mitigating hazards. Some suggest that the federal government must take strong measures to require the following if they use federal funding in recovery: State and local governments must be required to adopt classic grass roots organizing to encourage citizen participation and the renewal of civic institutions that can participate in difficult recovery problems. Local governments must provide opportunities for local communities to acquire civic skills and ensure that all parts of the community are engaged. Finally, local entities must reinforce the value of collective action rather than a culture of quick action without the consideration of the broad networks of the community (Waugh and Sylves 1996).

Waugh (2006) notes that "Hurricanes Katrina and Rita will leave political scars, as well as social and economic scars, on the Gulf Coast. Politicians and administrators may pay a high price for failing to deal with the disasters adequately or simply for appearing ineffectual." He goes on to explain that "failure was evident from the city hall level to the White House. The assumptions upon which local, state, and federal disaster responses were based, were seriously flawed. A large percentage of the affected population was much more vulnerable than officials assumed. Finally poverty and racial distrust complicated the disaster and the response" (p. 20).

Note: For a discussion of local government organizational response issues and strategies, see Meeting the Challenge: organizational and governmental response in disasters—Chapter 4—Tierney, Kathleen J., Michael K. Lindell, and Ronald W. Perry. 2001. *Facing the Unexpected: Disaster Preparedness and Response in the United States*. Washington, DC: Joseph Henry Press.

Opportunity for Political and Legal Change

Hurricanes Katrina and Rita revealed many issues that needed to be addressed to reduce future vulnerability of structures to hurricane winds. The Louisiana Legislature was called into session following Katrina and Rita to establish a strong statewide building code. The consequences of failing to adopt strong building codes were viewed by public officials at the local and state level as unacceptable. The push for changes in the law was driven by lenders, insurers, and business interests who expressed that a sound recovery had to be based on safe construction guidelines from the new building code.

> December 2005—Louisiana Governor Kathleen Blanco signed a bill that calls for the state to adopt the International Building Code (IBC), International Existing Buildings Code (IEBC), International Residential Code (IRC), International Mechanical Code (IMC), and the International Fuel Gas Code (IFGC).
>
> The bill applies to buildings rebuilt in the wake of Hurricanes Katrina and Rita, and to all buildings built or rebuilt statewide starting in 2007. Under the legislation, the 11 parishes hit hardest by the hurricanes must put the new code into effect in 30 days if those parishes already have inspectors. If they do not, they have 90 days to begin enforcement. The bill also establishes a 19-member council to oversee enforcement of the codes by local governments.

While Hurricane Katrina devastated much of Louisiana, the state is poised to rebuild stronger and safer than ever using the International Codes (I-Codes) developed by the International Code Council.

The code requires homes and businesses built along the Gulf Coast to withstand winds of 130 to 150 miles per hour. The bill also establishes a 19-member council to oversee enforcement of the codes by local governments.

"The massive effort to rebuild Louisiana will be long and difficult. However, with the International Codes in place to help guide reconstruction, homes and businesses will be safer, stronger and more resistant to future natural disasters," said Sara Yerkes, International Code Council Senior Vice President of Government Relations. "As we have witnessed, in addition to the loss of life, there are many repercussions when natural disasters damage homes and businesses. Hurricane damage disrupts private industry and government services, puts people out of work, reduces disposable income and diminishes the tax base. By adopting and enforcing I-Codes, the state is helping to protect lives and property while limiting the far-reaching effects of hurricanes and other natural disasters."

Many states, including hurricane-prone states, enforce the I-Codes or state codes based on the I-Codes (such as the Florida Building Code), for residential and commercial buildings. I-Codes contain the latest technologies for building construction. They take into account valuable lessons learned over the years. I-Codes provide state-of-the-art requirements for hurricane resistance, based on wind speed data collected from previous hurricanes. In wind borne debris regions, I-Codes address window, garage and door protection, such as shutters and impact-resistant windows, to protect against flying debris. I-Codes also provide wind load criteria for the design of hurricane resistant roof tie-downs and exterior cladding.

"Though there may be a slightly higher initial cost, homes and commercial buildings constructed under the I-Codes are less likely to be destroyed during a natural disaster, greatly reducing costs to the property owner. The added level of protection for your home, your belongings, and, most importantly, your family will pay off in the long run," said Yerkes. "Properly constructed buildings and homes are more resistant to general deterioration as well." *From:* http://www.bookmarki.com/Blanco_Signs_Louisiana_Building_Code_Bill_s/190.htm.

During the months following Hurricane Katrina in 2005, efforts were initiated by the mayor's office of the City of New Orleans to ensure that the city had a sound and stable legal and administrative system. Changes were made in the state constitution to merge small assessor offices into a single parish unit. Prior to this change, individual property records needed for the recovery were located in offices throughout the city. In addition, initiatives to consolidate other local services were also undertaken.

The Louisiana Recovery Authority, the Governor of Louisiana and the Louisiana Congressional delegation proposed using funds provided by the U.S. Congress to establish the "Road Home Program." The funds enabled over 150,000 homeowners to obtain financial support to rebuild, relocate in the city, within the state or secure a buyout of their residence. Limited funds were provided for restoring or rebuilding rental property. Examine the "Road Home Program" at http://lra.louisiana.gov/.

The key to building and sustaining resilient communities is the establishment of a sound hazard mitigation policy that is reflected in local ordnances and mandated by state law. Strong building codes and land use planning laws provide the legal framework for ensuring that communities are resilient following a disaster. Priorities that include expenditures in retrofitting infrastructure reflect a political commitment to reducing the adverse economic and social impacts from disasters.

Quarantelli (2005) sees that catastrophes may require that we change our administrative or legal systems, for these events "... not only disrupt society, but may cause a total breakdown in day-to-day functioning. One aspect of a catastrophe, is that most community functions disappear; there is no immediate leadership, hospitals may be damaged or destroyed, and the damage may be so great and so extensive that survivors have nowhere to turn for help." Tobin and Montz (1997, p. 31) note that in disaster situations, it is not unusual for survivors to seek help from friends and neighbors, but this cannot happen in catastrophes. In a disaster, society continues to operate and it is common to see scheduled events continue, but this is not the case in catastrophes.

Disasters triggered by natural or human caused hazards do not cause political change, rather they act as catalysts that put into motion social processes at different social levels. The political change may thus be the result of the pre-disaster socio-political and cultural characteristics present at the local, state, or national scenes. Disasters occur in a social context where some social organizations flourish and where specific types of relationships with external power affect local and national conditions.

Stehr (2006) poses the question of whether it is really possible to reconcile the competing forces of economic development and political considerations with hazard mitigation policies. Given circumstances where local officials have few incentives to mitigate the adverse effects of hazards, local communities may be unwilling to adopt policies that support hazard mitigation, foster economic development and avoid the conflicts.

Media coverage of a catastrophe also drives major policy considerations and this attention promotes the consideration of possible policy changes. Focusing events such as Katrina tend to break up log-jams, which result from political stalemates. Positions that in the past are firmly held, may become suddenly more adaptable because of the event.

Opportunities for change following a disaster may be considered within the context of using the opportunity to learn from past mistakes. Pratt (2006) raises the question of whether the catastrophe resulting from Hurricane Katrina was the exception or if it is just an example of our failure to bring about constructive changes following a disaster. Was Katrina the exception? Was it an unforeseen catastrophe that exceeded our comprehension? He notes that Hurricane Betsy ravaged the city in 1965 and over the next 40 years the city grew into very vulnerable geography. Pratt suggests that we view this as an "event" that provides a framework for examining our social, economic, political, and environmental systems.

Vale and Campanella (2005) raise a similar issue in noting that most modern disasters that impact a large city result in rebuilding at the same location and have yet to see a city entirely relocate. One may view Katrina and New Orleans not from a single disaster but a cluster of traumatic episodes that include socioeconomic decay, diminishing investment in infrastructure and buildings, large-scale abandonment, population flight, and decay reflected in schools, water and sewer systems, transportation, and healthcare over an extended period. Political and legal systems are not isolated from the social, cultural, and economic elements of the city and thus are part of them.

Recommendations from the Urban Land Institute's report (2005) suggested a phased restoration of the city. This recommendation identified priority areas for immediate rebuilding while other areas of the city would not be included in immediate restoration efforts. "Rebuilding should happen in a strategic manner, encouraging those areas that sustained minimal damage to begin rebuilding immediately and those areas that have more extensive damage to evaluate the feasibility for reinvestment and proceed in a manner that will ensure the health and safety of the residents of each neighborhood and proceed expeditiously" (p. 8).

The mayor rejected this recommendation and then initiated a multi-year planning process that allowed residents to rebuild where they wished. In order to gain more insight into this dynamic, it may prove useful for the reader to review the Urban Land Institute report and examine why the recommendations for the restoration of the city had such a negative reaction by some members of the public. What appeared to be a window of opportunity to change the City of New Orleans was influenced by resident fears of how change might impact their neighborhood. Referring back to Quarantelli's list of characteristics of catastrophes from Chapter 1, you'll remember that catastrophes, more than disasters, result in outsiders having significant influence on how local response and recovery operations are implemented.

Birkland (2006) argues that "focusing events" such as Katrina elevate problems on the policy agenda thus gaining "mass and elite attention." He notes that disaster events may not lead to expected political outcomes or policy changes, for the event may overwhelm everyone so as to limit learning. The attention that is generated and the learning that results is a function of the consequences of the event. Political debate is generated by significant events so that policy change or legislation is triggered by events. New ideas are not necessarily developed in response to events, but that these events may reinvigorate attention to preexisting ideas and propositions.

EMERGENCY MANAGEMENT SYSTEM CHALLENGES AND VULNERABILITIES

The White House report *The Federal Response to Hurricane Katrina: Lessons Learned* (2006) noted the positive impact and use of the U.S. military in response operations. The military provided a great operational response resource but this was unfortunately not the military's primary mission.

The direct federal response to Hurricane Katrina demonstrates that the Department of Defense (DOD) has the capability to play a critical role in the nation's response to catastrophic events. During the Katrina response, DOD—both National Guard and active duty forces—demonstrated that along with the Coast Guard it was one of few federal departments that possessed real operational capabilities to translate presidential decisions into prompt, effective action on the ground. In addition to possessing operational personnel in large numbers that have been trained and equipped for their missions, DOD brought robust communications infrastructure, logistics, and planning capabilities. Since DOD, first and foremost, has its critical overseas mission, the solution to improving the federal response to future catastrophes cannot simply be "let the Department of Defense do it."

The federal response to Hurricane Katrina highlighted various challenges in the use of military capabilities during domestic incidents. For instance, limitations under federal law and DOD policy caused the active duty military to be dependent on requests for assistance. These limitations resulted in a slowed application of DOD resources during the initial response. Further, active duty military and National Guard operations were not coordinated and served two different bosses, one the president and the other the governor.

Limitations to Department of Defense Response Authority

For federal domestic disaster relief operations, DOD currently uses a "pull" system that provides support to civil authorities based upon specific requests from local, state, or federal authorities. This process can be slow and bureaucratic.... Assigning active duty military forces to support disaster relief efforts usually requires a request from FEMA, an assessment by DOD on whether the request can be supported, approval by the Secretary of Defense or his designated representative, and a mission assignment for the military forces or capabilities to provide the requested support. From the time a request is initiated until the military force or capability is delivered to the disaster site requires a 21-step process. While this overly bureaucratic approach has been adequate for most disasters, in a catastrophic event like Hurricane Katrina the delays inherent in this "pull" system of responding to requests resulted in critical needs not being met. One could imagine a situation in which a catastrophic event is of such a magnitude that it would require an even greater role for the Department of Defense.

The White House Katrina Report (2006) also discussed linkages between active duty military units and the state national guard. Note the potential political struggles that could emerge between the federal government and the state governor who controls the National Guard units.

> In the overall response to Hurricane Katrina, separate command structures for active duty military and the National Guard hindered their unity of effort. U.S. Northern Command (USNORTHCOM) commanded active duty forces, while each State government commanded its National Guard forces. For the first two days of Katrina response operations, USNORTHCOM did not have situational awareness of what forces the National Guard had on the ground. Joint Task Force Katrina (JTF-Katrina) simply could not operate at full efficiency when it lacked visibility of over half the military forces in the disaster area. Neither the Louisiana National Guard nor JTF-Katrina had a good sense for where each other's forces were located or what they were doing. For example, the JTF-Katrina Engineering Directorate had not been able to coordinate with National Guard forces in the New Orleans area. As a result, some units were not immediately assigned missions matched to on-the-ground requirements. Further, FEMA requested assistance from DOD without knowing what State National Guard forces had already deployed to fill the same needs. Also, the Commanding General of JTF-Katrina and the Adjutant Generals (TAGs) of Louisiana and Mississippi had only

a coordinating relationship, with no formal command relationship established. This resulted in confusion over roles and responsibilities. (p. 55)

Key Organizational Issues

Waters and Kettl determined that there was a lack of intergovernmental relationships between federal, state, and local agencies (2006). They determined that there was a lack of clear roles and responsibilities, decision making, and political infighting. Further there was an ever-increasing role of the federal government in disaster response and recovery along with an expectation that the federal government will help (bail everyone out). They noted that for the first 72 hours, all disasters are local and state, and the federal strategy should be to strengthen local and state capacity to deal with disasters. There were no alternative plans and no capacity to adapt existing plans and there was too much of a reliance on calling in the federal troops.

Perro's (1984) normal accidents approach and the analysis of high-reliability organizations has provided a good structure in understanding organizations that deal with complex technologies. Perro contends that organizations that are prone to catastrophic failure have similar operational processes and organizational cultures including the way the organization is managed. He determined that the structure provided within an organization determines how well adaptation is made in times of crisis. Unfortunately, he saw that too many organizational systems were unable to correct or adapt when needed (see Tierney 2005).

Ward and Wamsley (2007) contend that ICS has been, in effect, a standardized coordinating system for fighting forest fires and brush fires, but that it is not sufficiently flexible to deal with the diverse disasters or the variety of unexpected issues that typically arise during a disaster response operation. While ICS creates a centralized coordinating structure, it also creates an artificial barrier between formal response systems and the informal networks that form at the local level in response to disasters. They contended that the National Response Plan had not been fully integrated at the state and local levels negating potential benefits of this approach to organizing for disaster response. Flexibility and adaptation were needed rather than rigid organizational frameworks (DHS 2004). Finally, coordination was unclear and command structure was confusing; what was needed was fluid lines of authority and discretion.

Hurricane Katrina demonstrated that we remain in a reactive policy-making position and that we fail to effectively learn from disasters and make constructive adjustments. Kingdon (1984) sees that policy making is a three-stage process including problem recognition, problem definition, and policy adoption.

Problem recognition includes the acknowledgement of a situation by policy makers that requires their collective action in the form of new programs, adaptation of existing ones or the elimination of barriers to a situation. Two situations requiring policy attention would be: Non-existing building codes and victims of disasters required to remain in unsatisfactory housing or public shelters. A sufficient number of policy makers must agree on the nature of the problem for action to be taken to develop a satisfactory solution to address it.

Problem definition includes the agreement by policy makers on a common framework for the issues that have been identified and consensus that action must be made. Unless a consensus is reached on the nature of the problem, no adequate resolution to it will be made.

Policy adoption is formal law making which can be at the federal, state, or local levels. Open debate in council meetings, commission hearings, or full assembly environments provides a basis for adopting measures that will address the problem(s).

Ward and Wamsley (2007) reflect on the contribution of Baumgartner and Jones (1993) in the concept of "punctuated equilibrium." This theory contends that policy making is an inherently unstable process that is reflected in continued disagreement even following formal approval of a public policy (i.e., critics remain unconvinced of the adopted solution). Events over time will erode public confidence in the adopted solution allowing the opposition to overturn the previously adopted measures and replace these measures with alternative ones. Events such as the response to Hurricane Katrina open the problem and debate, allowing the equilibrium within the policy to become unsettled. This instability provides the opportunity for an alternative policy to be adopted. Ward and Wamsley (2007) note that the U.S. emergency management system is diverse and different problem definitions and contradictory solutions by those in the system contribute to an unstable environment. "In the unstable environment of disaster response, in which unprecedented and unanticipated events of national magnitude can exceed the capacity of any given solution, change may be the only constant" (p. 218).

Government decision makers pursue political agendas suggesting that agencies can and will use rational methods of policy making in an efficient manner. This is in contrast to an approach that distinguishes between political and administrative roles. In an unstable environment, agency heads and their staff may attempt to deal with their environment by quickly and efficiently adopting new policies that allow the institution to adapt to existing instabilities (within current legislative/policy frameworks).

Lack of effective response may lead to political blame games and organizational change that over steps current authorities and separation of powers. Unfortunately, the result is still confusion in a very complex environment. The issue remains in how to deal with the confusion in a rational manner that does not lead to conflicts in political and administrative roles. Ward and Wamsley (2007) suggest that:

> The myth of an efficient, effective and organized bureaucracy overlooks the complexity, difficulties and near failures involved in achieving our national goals, enabling us to maintain a profound faith in the application of rational governance in pursuit of organizational efficiency. We reject excuses for failure. It is precisely this national consciousness—this myth—that allows the blame game to be so effective. In our rush to find out who or what is responsible for failure, we ignore the complexity of the system and the role that this complexity has played. We substitute simplistic and convenient answers that are grounded on faulty analysis. By identifying the wrong problem, or incomplete one—at best—we formulate a misguided solution. This inevitably results in future and organizational failures. (p. 219)

They go further to suggest that in a centralized hierarchical system a network approach can acknowledge the contribution of many players at various levels of response. The network approach thus provides a means of acknowledging the contribution of different organizational cultures that can work toward a common set of goals and priorities. Despite the complexity of the networks and differences, what is needed is high levels of trust, communication, and organizational flexibility in the emergency management system.

CONCLUSIONS

The structure of the United States emergency management system has been fine-tuned since 2001 as an acknowledgement of the unique challenges presented by large-scale extreme events. We observed from the unique problems and dynamics that surfaced from the 9/11 terrorist events that our current system needed realignment. The adoption of the National Disaster Recovery Framework, our National Preparedness Guidelines, and continued use of the National Incident Management System were all initiatives to allow our emergency management system to deal with large-scale extreme events. The intent of these changes at our national level was intended to provide state and local emergency management structures to function more effectively and cope with disasters that impacted larger geographic areas, larger population centers, and the cascading disruptions within our social, economic, and natural systems as a result of a catastrophe.

The threat of large-scale extreme events moves us to consider the use of military forces including the National Guard in response and recovery operations. The circumstances surrounding a catastrophe also require us to re-examine the powers and authorities of our public agencies at all levels and examine the impacts of these authorities and responsibilities in light of the operational response requirements of extreme events. We are encouraged to take a second look at the nature and extent of governmental powers and structures at all levels to ensure that our organizational and political system provides the appropriate foundation for emergency response and recovery to a catastrophe. The concept of "hypercomplexity" and the need to embrace organized networking in the response to catastrophes, as voiced by Lagadec and others, provides one pathway to envisioning a more flexible approach to recognizing and addressing the hugely complex intertwined demands that result from catastrophes.

Despite the many complex challenges presented by a catastrophe, we acknowledge that they present a unique opportunity for change. We do observe that this opportunity for change does not always meet our expectations but that within our political system, the chance to address fundamental community or regional problems is provided. This opportunity for unique adaptation occurs at a time when rational decision making at the national, regional, or local level faces off with complex agendas which make organizational collaborations more difficult to implement and maintain.

Despite the challenges presented by a more complex organizational and political environment, we continue to search for organizational structures at all levels that build valuable collaborations that provide the necessary trust, communication, and flexibility for coping with catastrophe.

REFERENCES

Barry, J. M. 1997. *Rising Tide: The Great Mississippi Flood of 1927 and How It Changed America.* New York, NY: Simon & Schuster.
Baumgartner, F. and B. Jones. 1993. *Agendas and Instability in American Politics.* Chicago: University of Chicago Press.
Berke, P. R. and T. J. Campanella. 2006. Planning for post-disaster resiliency. *The Annals of the American Academy of Political and Social Science* 604: 192.
Birkland, T. 1997. *After Disaster: Agenda Setting, Public Policy and Focusing Events.* Washington, DC: Georgetown University Press.
Birkland, T. A. 2006. *Lessons of Disaster: Policy Change After Catastrophic Events.* Washington, DC: Georgetown University Press.
Bowman, S., L. Kapp, and A. Belasco. 2005. *Hurricane Katrina: DOD Disaster Response.* Library of Congress. Washington, DC: Congressional Research Service, RL33095.
Burby, R. 1998. *Cooperating with Nature: Confronting Natural Hazards with Land-Use Planning for Sustainable Communities.* Washington, DC: Joseph Henry Press.
Burby, R. and P. May. 1997. *Making Governments Plan: State Experiments in Managing Land Use.* With Philip Berke, Linda Dalton, Steven French, and Edward Kaiser. Baltimore: Johns Hopkins University Press.
Davis, L. E., J. Rough, G. Cecchine, A. Gereben Schaefer, and L. L. Zeman. 2007. *Hurricane Katrina: Lessons from Army Planning and Operations.* Santa Monica, CA: Rand Corporation.
Department of Homeland Security (DHS). 2004. *National Response Plan.* Washington, DC: DHS.
Department of Homeland Security (DHS). 2007. *National Preparedness Guidelines.* Washington, DC: DHS.
Department of Homeland Security (DHS). 2008. *The National Response Framework.* Washington, DC.
Dror, Y. 1986. *Policy-Making Under Adversity.* New Brunswick, NJ: Transaction Books.
Elsea, J. 2005. *The Posse Comitatus Act and Related Matters: A Sketch.* Library of Congress. Washington, DC: Congressional Research Service. RS20590.
Elsea, J. K. and R. C. Mason. 2008. *The Use of Federal Troops for Disaster Assistance: Legal Issues.* Library of Congress. Washington, DC: Congressional Research Service. ADA492865.
Emergency Management Assistance Compact (EMAC) Web site: www.emacweb.org.
Federal Emergency Management Agency. 2011. *National Disaster Recovery Framework: Strengthening Disaster Recovery for the Nation.* Washington, DC: Federal Emergency Management Agency.
Healy, P. 1997. *Collaborative Planning: Shaping Paces in Fragmented Societies.* London: Macmillan.
King, R. O. 2005. *Hurricane Katrina: Insuring Losses and National Capacities for Financing Disaster Risk.* September 15. CRS Report for Congress no. RL 33086. Washington, DC: Congressional Research Service, Library of Congress.

Kingdon, J. 1984. *Agendas, Alternatives and Public Policy Politics.* New York: Harper Collins.
Litan, R. E. 2005. *Sharing and Reducing the Financial Risks of Future Mega-Catastrophes.* Economic Studies Working Paper, November 11, Brookings Institution, Washington, DC.
Louisiana Recovery Authority. The Road Home Program. See: http://lra.louisiana.gov/
Louisiana Revised Statutes. 2008. *Louisiana Homeland Security and Emergency Assistance and Disaster Act.* 29: 726.
McEntire, D., and G. Dawson. 2007. The intergovernmental context. In *Emergency Management: Principles and Practice for Local Government*, 2nd ed., edited by W. Waugh and K. Tierney. Washington, DC: ICMA Press.
May, P. J. and R. E. Deyle. 1998. Governing land use in hazardous areas with a patchwork system. In *Cooperating with Nature*, edited by Raymond J. Burby. Washington, DC: Joseph Henry Press.
Mitchell, J. K. 2006. The primacy of partnership: Scoping a new national disaster recovery policy. *The ANNALS of the American Academy of Political and Social Science* 604: 228.
Nelson, A. and S. French. 2002. Plan quality and mitigating damage from natural disasters: A case study of the Northridge earthquake with planning policy considerations. *Journal of the American Planning Association* 68: 194–207.
Nicholson, W. C. 2008. Legal issues in emergency management. In *Introduction to Emergency Management*, edited by M. Lindell. Emmitsburg, MD: Fema Higher Education Project.
Oleck, H. L. 1982. *Tort Law Practice Manual.* Englewood Cliffs, NJ: Prentice-Hall.
Pelling, M. and K. Dill. 2006. *Natural Disasters as Catalysis of Political Action.* Chatham House. ISP/NSC Briefing Paper 06/01. pp. 4–6.
Perro, C. 1984. *Normal Accidents: Living with High Risk Technologies.* New Your: Basic Books.
Platt, R. 2000. Extreme natural events: Some issues for public policy. Presented at Extreme Events Workshop, Boulder, CO.
Quarantelli, E. L. 2005. Catastrophes are different from disasters: Some implications for crisis planning and managing drawn from Katrina. Katrina: Perspectives from the social sciences. Disaster Research Center, University of Delaware.
Stehr, S. D. 2006. The political economy of urban disaster assistance. *Urban Affairs Review.* 41: 492.
Sylves, R. T. 2005. Revolution needed in U.S. emergency management, EIIP (Emergency Information Infrastructure Project) Virtual Forum Presentation.
Tierney, K. 2005. Social inequality, hazards, and disasters. In *On Risk and Disaster: Lessons from Hurricane Katrina*, edited by R. J. Daniels, D. F. Kettl, H. Kunreuther, pp. 109–28. Philadelphia: Univ. Penn. Press.
Tierney, K., M. Lindell, and R. Perry. 2001. *Facing the Unexpected: Disaster Preparedness and Response in the U.S.* Washington, DC: Joseph Henry Press.
Townsend, F. F. 2006. *The Federal Response to Hurricane Katrina: Lessons Learned.* Washington, DC: The White House.
Tobin, G. A. and B. E. Montz. 1997. *Natural Hazards: Explanation and Integration.* New York: Guilford Press.
United States Code. Emergency Planning and Community Right to Know Act. 42 U.S.C. §§ 11001–11050.
United States Code. The Volunteer Protection Act. 42 U.S.C.A. §§ 14501–14505.
United States Code. The Stafford Disaster Relief and Emergency Assistance Act. 42 U.S.C. 5121.
United States Code. The Posse Comitatus Act. 18 U.S.C. 1385.
United States House of Representatives. 2006. Select Bipartisan Committee to Investigate the Preparation for the Response to Hurricane Katrina. *A Failure of Initiative.* 109th Congress 2nd Session.

United States Senate. 2006. *Hurricane Katrina: A Nation Still Unprepared.* (S. Rept. 109-322). Washington, DC: U.S. Government Printing Office.

Urban Land Institute. 2005. *A Strategy for Rebuilding New Orleans.* Washington, DC: Urban Land Institute.

Vale, L. and T. Campanella eds. 2005. *The Resilient City: How Modern Cities Recover from Disaster.* Oxford: Oxford University Press.

Walters, J. and D. Kettl. The Katrina Breakdown. 2006. *On Risk and Disaster: Lessons from Hurricane Katrina,* edited by R. J. Daniels, D. F. Kettl, and H. Kunreuther. Philadelphia, PA: The University of Pennsylvania Press.

Ward, R. and G. Wamsley. 2007. From a painful past to an uncertain future. In *Emergency Management: The American Experience 1900–2005*, edited by C. B. Rubin. Fairfax, VA: Public Entity Risk Institute.

Waugh, W. L. Jr. and R. T. Sylves. 1996. The intergovernmental relations of emergency management. In *Disaster Management in the U.S. and Canada: The Politics, Policymaking, Administration, and Analysis of Emergency Management,* 2nd ed., edited by R. T. Sylves and W. L. Waugh, Jr. Springfield, IL: Charles C. Thomas Publisher, Ltd, pp. 46–68.

Waugh, W. L. Jr. 2006. The political costs of failure in the Katrina and Rita disasters. *The ANNALS of the American Academy of Political and Social Science* (AAPSS) 604: 10.

Zaferatos, N. 1998. Planning the native American tribal community: Understanding the basis of power controlling the reservation territory. *Journal of the American Planning Association* 64(4): 395–410.

CHAPTER 5

Economics of Catastrophes and Disasters

Kevin M. Simmons

CONTENTS

Introduction 110
Social Vulnerability 111
Natural Hazard Issues for Social Scientists 112
    Risk 112
    Microeconomic Questions 112
    Mitigation 112
    Private Mitigation 113
    Public Mitigation 114
        Land Use Restrictions 114
        Building Codes 115
    Evacuation 116
    Tax Incentives 117
    Direct Subsidies 117
    Warning Systems 118
    Macroeconomic Questions 118
    Inflation 119
        Gross Domestic Product 121
    Unemployment 122
    Migration 123
Financial Markets 124
    Insurance 124
    Banking 125
    Real Estate 126
Conclusion 127
Discussion Questions 127
    Land Restrictions 127
    Building Codes 127
    General Public Mitigation 127

Migration 128
Macro-Effects 128
References 128

INTRODUCTION

Disasters can grab the attention of the public for days and in some cases weeks. Pictures of the devastation fill the airwaves as the horrifying sight of tornadoes, hurricanes, and other events show the world how powerful nature can be. But a natural disaster has impacts that extend well beyond the onset of the event. Cities can be severely damaged. Homes can be destroyed. Families can be left without a place to live or a job to sustain them. By the time the long term extent of the disaster's impact can be assessed, the cameras may be gone and residents have to put their lives and their community back together without the larger public aware of what that effort requires. It is in this area that social scientists can make a contribution to the understanding of these awful events.

The first priority after any disaster is to ensure that all victims of the event have been accounted for. For those injured by the event, great stress is placed on the local medical community to care for their injuries. Many of the injuries are minor and those victims are quickly treated and returned to their families. Some injuries, however, are life threatening. For people suffering from those, the road to recovery may be long. But regarding those unfortunate souls who perished in the disaster, there are families and loved ones grieving the loss and trying to make sense of what is seemingly so senseless. For days after the disaster, the community will endure one memorial after another as families mourn their loss.

The next priority is to take stock of the economic losses. Obviously, there are insurance companies who quickly arrive with scores of adjusters to work with their customers who were impacted by the event. Insurance is based on a simple premise. If the long-term risk of a particular event is known, an insurance company can collect sufficient premiums to ensure that when the event does occur, those affected will be compensated for their financial losses. But even for people who are fully insured, there are challenges as they may need a place to live while repairs are being made to their home. Additionally, there are deductibles to pay and there are some things that may be financially insured but the true value lies in the sentiment attached to an item that is now gone forever.

Local officials also need to perform an accounting of the damage in order to determine what effect the disaster has had on the property values that are the basis for many local tax revenues. These efforts are often out of the public eye, but it is not until this phase of the event occurs that we know how large the overall impact will be. Questions about the longer term viability of the community also are relevant. What will happen to the businesses impacted by the disaster? Will they pick up the pieces and re-open or close up shop taking with it the jobs and services provided by this enterprise? This chapter will explore these economic aspects of a disaster and the attending social issues that accompany those losses.

Please note that most of the information discussed in this chapter is based on research and experience related to disasters rather than catastrophes. We demonstrate in other chapters of this book that catastrophes differ from disasters in some fundamental ways, but we lack sufficient research into the economics of catastrophes to make many definitive statements. Thus, in this *chapter we summarize what we have learned about the economics of disasters and expect that* much of this information can be transferred to some kinds of catastrophes ... but in significantly expanded mode. Remember that in catastrophes, response and recovery resources are much less likely to come from local authorities or organizations, many major decisions are more likely to be made by outsiders, and directly affected local populations are likely to have to wait much longer to receive outside assistance, maybe weeks or longer. Furthermore, if we look at the economic impact of catastrophes, as compared to disasters, in catastrophes they are more likely to be felt internationally.

SOCIAL VULNERABILITY

As we examine the potential societal impacts of a major catastrophe, we quickly see that the consequences do not fall on people and/or groups uniformly. It may be a tragic way to view a disaster but a catastrophic event highlights the disparate vulnerabilities in a way that normal life cannot. Policymakers who can identify the vulnerabilities in such a way that they anticipate the consequences go a long way toward minimizing the effects.

Traditionally, emergency management has focused on the needs and potential vulnerabilities of the community in aggregate. This approach misses the fact that the vulnerability of certain groups may vary widely across the community. Recently, attention has been focused on the fact that the potential negative consequences of a disaster do not fall evenly across all groups.[1] Differences in vulnerability can cut across obvious criteria such as living in a flood plain versus living on higher ground but the differences also cut across socioeconomic and demographic criteria as well. One lasting lesson from Hurricane Katrina was the disproportionate number of casualties suffered by people from lower income neighborhoods. This event combined the effects of many different vulnerabilities that lower income families in New Orleans faced. First, lower income neighborhoods are often located in the worst locations. In the case of New Orleans, this meant well below sea level, protected by aging levees. Second, lower income families were less likely to own personal vehicles which would have enabled them to evacuate. The economic aftermath is harder on lower income families also, since finding new employment after a disaster is more difficult when you have fewer marketable skills and you may be removed from a support network. Another vulnerability is age. Even well to do elderly residents are at a disadvantage when disaster strikes. Evacuation is harder and many are reluctant to leave their homes. Combine advancing age with the problems of the poor and you have a group that is perhaps at the greatest risk. The point is simply that every community is really a set of smaller communities, each with particular issues that make them more or less likely to survive a disaster.

Emergency managers must include the particular needs of each of these smaller communities in their plans when contemplating a disaster.

NATURAL HAZARD ISSUES FOR SOCIAL SCIENTISTS

Risk

Generally, disasters fall into the sub-discipline of Environmental Economics but they have topics that are of great interest to social scientists who study risk. We make risky choices every day. Most involve little risk of actual harm but the decisions we make reveal something about how we deal with risk. Living in a community that may be prone to a natural disaster exposes its residents to the risk that hazard poses and it is helpful to policy makers to understand how residents view the chance of the hazard occurring. Do they underestimate the chance that the disaster will occur or do they fully understand how likely it is to happen? Further, once told that an event is imminent, how will they react? This became an interest after the Joplin tornado in May of 2011. In an assessment performed by the National Weather Service, some residents claimed that they believed tornadoes "never" happened in Joplin.[2] The report continues to describe resident's reactions to the tornado warnings as a multi-step, non-linear process that required many residents to verify the threat before they heeded the warnings. Such a process costs people time and could have increased the casualties. And it is worth noting that the Joplin tornado occurred 3 weeks after hundreds were killed in Alabama by a string of violent tornadoes.

Perhaps the leading economic voice on how people respond to the risk of natural hazards is Howard Kunreuther of the Wharton School. In the 1970s, he developed a theory on how people treat disasters and classified these events as "Low Probability, High Consequence." It has been assumed that people tend to ignore risks of this type and human behavior, in the aggregate, tends to support this assumption.[3] The interviews with Joplin residents certainly confirm that many did not fully appreciate the risk they faced and as a result were not prepared for the monster tornado that claimed 158 lives that day. With this in mind, we next examine some of the ways that communities can prepare for eventual disasters with the goal of preventing as many casualties as possible.

Microeconomic Questions

As a social science, economics can be broken down into two large categories, microeconomics or decisions made by individual people or individual entities such as a firm or community and macroeconomics, decisions made by society. We first look at how individual people or communities plan for disasters through the actions they take prior to an event.

Mitigation

One of the most beloved children's stories is that of the three pigs and how they plan for the potential encounter with the big bad wolf.[4] For hazards researchers this story serves as a perfect allegory for mitigation: the actions that are taken before the onset of a disastrous event that will limit or avoid entirely the consequences the potential event poses. In the story, the first two pigs choose expediency over protection in building their homes and when the disaster occurs, the arrival of the wolf, they find that they are not protected. Their older brother, on the other hand, plans carefully and takes his time in building his brick home, which serves as good protection from the eventual visit from the wolf.

A more formal look at mitigation is done by Isaac Ehrlich and Gary Becker[5] where they break mitigation down into two types, self-insurance and self-protection. Self-insurance reduces the loss when an event occurs much as a sprinkler system reduces the loss from a fire. Self-protection reduces the probability of a loss in the first place. The actions taken by the third pig fall into the category of self-protection since a hardened home would protect him from the huffing and puffing of the wolf. But viable mitigation from disasters would include both types.

How people or communities prepare for potential disasters begins with how much they believe the risk of the hazard to be real. If they do not believe the disaster may affect them, as was evident in some of the answers by residents in Joplin, then preparing for the event makes no sense. However, if they recognize the hazard as one that can affect them, then preparing for it comes quite naturally. In reality, it is a little more complicated than that because most people weigh the benefits of preparing for the disaster against the costs of the preparations to make their decision. It is here that economists can contribute to the analysis about what, if any, preparations for disasters make sense for the individual resident and for the community. Further, the effect these decisions have on other related issues, so called secondary effects, can be understood better when viewed through the lens of the economist.

Private Mitigation

One way to examine how real residents view a particular threat is to conduct studies using surveys designed to gauge how likely they believe a hazard may or may not occur. In some instances this is the only available way to elicit this kind of information. Another approach, often favored by economists, is to see if market signals exist, which suggest how residents feel about the likelihood of a potential disaster. Are residents willing to pay a premium for features on their home that would protect them from the hazard in question? If people are willing to pay more for homes that provide better protection than other homes, then hazard mitigation is not being ignored. Several studies have been conducted that looked at individual decisions made by people who live with the threat of a particular hazard and found that mitigation for that hazard has market value.[6] This study found that hurricane mitigation on a barrier island in the Gulf of Mexico added about 5% to the sales price of the home. Secondly, residents in an area respond more when the perceived probability of a hazard increases. Using the same data as the 2002 study, the authors found that increased national hurricane activity affected the premium people paid for hurricane mitigation. For example, immediately after Hurricane Andrew, hurricane mitigation premiums increased but began to decline as the event faded from memory.[7] A similar study was conducted in Oklahoma testing for the value added to a home, which contained a tornado shelter[8] and found similar results. A tornado shelter in a part of the country known for violent tornadoes added about 3½% to the sales price of the home. In areas where mitigation has value, the increased "demand" for mitigation causes the price of mitigation to increase. If officials assume that mitigation has no value, and some do, a market would not exist and the price of mitigation would essentially be zero. These studies question that assumption and establish that mitigation does have value in some areas. This knowledge assists local officials in designing programs to prepare the community for an eventual disaster. For instance, if a threat is real but ignored by the public, aggressive programs may be called for whereas if the public does exhibit an understanding that a threat is real, programs that supplement existing market-based actions may be more appropriate.

Public Mitigation

As a discipline, economics alone cannot establish whether or not a public policy should be undertaken. Decisions made for the benefit for an entire community require input from a variety of experts. But anytime a decision is made that requires people to do, or refrain from doing, a particular action, the possibility exists for unintended consequences that could offset the benefit expected for the community. The concern that most economists have is that policies should undertake a cost/benefit analysis to determine if the cost of the action is justified by the benefits. This is not to say that benefits relate to actual dollar transactions. A great deal of effort has been made to place monetary values on non-monetary issues. For example, the 1990 Clean Air Act used a procedure to estimate a "Value of Life" in deciding whether or not the actions were justified.

Land Use Restrictions

One obvious public policy regarding a possible hazard is land use restrictions. Communities have the power to determine what type of development is allowed for a given piece of land. If the property, for instance, is in a 100-year flood plain, residential development can be restricted. Similarly, in California some areas are deemed a Seismic Zone where damage from earthquakes is expected to be higher than elsewhere.

Land use restrictions create a situation where the government has established a "quota" on marketable land. By definition this reduces the quantity of land that can be used for development and could make the land that is available for development more expensive. In regions where the demand for land is very high, real estate developers petition local communities to relax those restrictions and allow more land to be developed. Often the pressure from developers can be intense. This is particularly true when there are neighboring communities willing to allow development in risky areas and developers can be quick to remind one town that others are waiting for this growth if they do not comply. Communities want to grow as growth brings with it new amenities for their population, not to mention the tax revenue from new residents and new businesses. Allowing the development to occur in a different community would mean that one town gains economically at the expense of another. Further, it drives up the price of the remaining homes in the town making it difficult for some families to move there.

QUOTA

When an artificial quota is imposed below the equilibrium market quantity, consumers are forced to pay a higher price than would prevail if no quota were established.

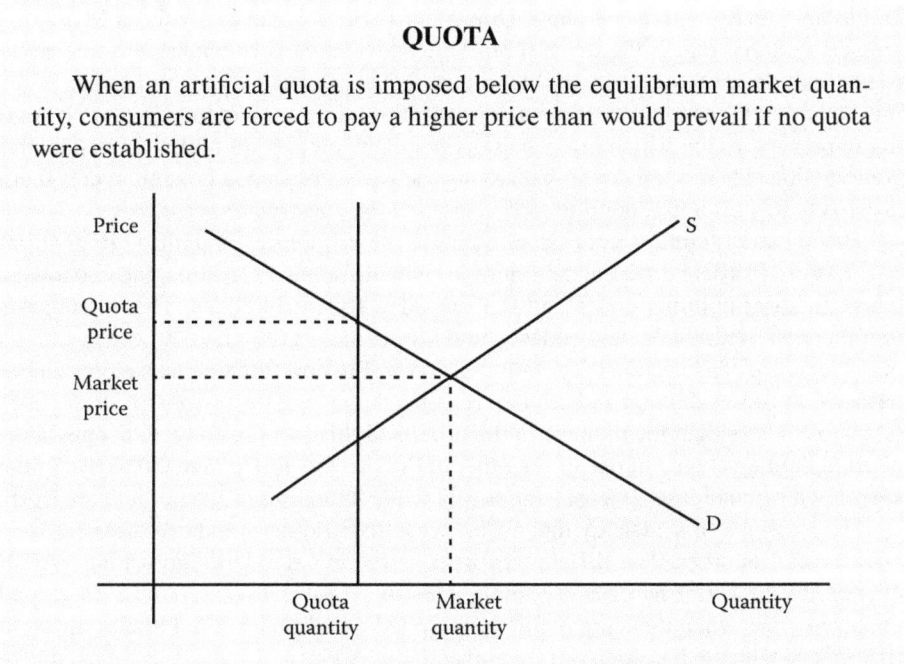

Building Codes

Another common policy is the adoption of building codes. Florida began a process after Hurricane Andrew of enacting stricter building codes, particularly in coastal counties. These codes were put to a test during the hurricane seasons of 2004 and 2005. Empirical evidence suggests that homes built to the newer codes suffered less damage than homes built in the period prior to Hurricane Andrew.

Few would argue with some level of minimum building codes for new construction. But how stringent should they be? The case of Florida is obvious because of the high risk of hurricanes in that state. Yet, it is possible to overshoot, even in Florida. For instance, if asked, a structural engineer could probably design a home that could withstand the strongest winds likely to occur. And if each home were constructed to these standards, damage from wind storms would be minimal. But how many families could afford the home? This action decreases the supply of available homes while limiting the number of families that are able to afford them. Price pressures will either force only wealthy families to move there or diminish the market to the point that no homes will be built. There must be some type of balance between a restrictive code and affordability.

Some communities have made the decision that the building codes will be strict regardless with public safety as the justification. But the ones that are most successful are those where the demand for living in that town is so high that residents are willing to pay a large premium for the privilege of living there. One example in the Dallas area is Highland Park. This town is located just north of downtown Dallas and, along with its neighbor University Park, is home to Southern Methodist University. It has one of the strictest building codes in the area but can enforce it due to the high demand to live in Highland Park.[9] One example is that all electric wires must be in metal conduit, even though residential wires are wrapped in a vinyl coating to prevent arcing which often causes fires. Few towns require this for residential construction. There is no doubt that having the wires encased in conduit makes them less likely to start a fire, but it greatly increases the construction cost.

Having strict building codes can highlight the differences in damage if a natural hazard were to affect different communities with different codes. Imagine two towns, one with strict building codes and the second with lenient codes. Theory suggests that the town with the lenient codes would attract more growth, at the expense of its neighbor since construction costs would be lower. But now imagine that a tornado has a track that causes damage in both towns. If the damage in the town with strict codes is obviously less than the damage in the other and this fact is known to people interested in buying a home in one or the other of the two towns, the demand to live in the safer town can increase, at least temporarily while memories of the tornado are fresh.

Now extend this idea to the differences in building standards between one country and another. The differences in construction standards go a long way in explaining the differing casualty totals when a catastrophe occurs in a developed country versus when it occurs in an undeveloped one. In the United States, an event that kills dozens is considered a "big event." In 1989, the Loma Prieta earthquake that hit San Francisco measured 6.9 on the Richter scale and killed 62 people.[10] But compare that earthquake to the January, 2010 quake in Haiti. It registered 7.0 on the Richter scale but killed over 300,000 souls.[11] The difference in casualty totals reflects the differences in construction practices. As Susan Hough and Lucille Jones of the U.S. Geological Survey state in an Op-Ed to the San Francisco Chronicle, "Earthquakes Don't Kill People, Buildings Kill People."[12]

Evacuation

For hazards that allow communities time to prepare before the advent of the event, it is possible to have people evacuate the area. Hazards that fall into this category are hurricanes, wildfires, floods, and to a lesser degree, some geo-hazards (earthquakes, volcanoes). Evacuations can be costly so officials that must decide whether or not to evacuate an area must be mindful of potential consequences. An example is the evacuation of the Houston area prior to Hurricane Rita. Devastation in New Orleans from Katrina was fresh on the minds of the population and local officials. However, the resulting evacuations for Rita caused dramatic traffic blockages whereby many motorists were unable to get fuel and were left stranded on the interstate.[13]

Further, evacuations are costly for those who evacuate since they have to find a place to stay, may miss work and thus their pay for an undetermined amount of time. A rule of thumb for hurricane evacuations is that it costs 1 million dollars per mile. However, a study after Hurricane Bonnie calls this assumption into question.[14] Regardless, it costs money to leave home, school, and jobs to respond to the evacuation order. If officials want to maintain their credibility with the public, they must be very sure that they are asking the public to do something that enhances their safety.

Evacuations create a disruption in business activity that cannot be reclaimed, so many residents and business owners are reluctant to leave until the very last minute. As a result mandatory evacuations are a tough call for officials. Hurricanes do not always follow a predicted path and the population of an evacuated area may find that they left their homes and businesses for a hurricane that veered in a different direction. Hurricane Charley is a good example. It was predicted to hit the Tampa Bay area but veered south, at the last minute, and struck Charlotte County.

Tax Incentives

Some hazards require that individuals take action to protect themselves. Examples include the installation of hurricane shutters to protect vulnerable portions of a home (windows and doors) or saferooms to protect inhabitants who live with the threat of a tornado. But private mitigation can be encouraged by the public sector. In the fall of 2002, the state of Oklahoma passed a measure to provide a property tax discount for homeowners who install a saferoom in their home. The measure exempts up to 100 square feet of a home constructed to the Federal Emergency Management Agency (FEMA) standard for a tornado saferoom. Economists typically find these incentives to be one of the most efficient ways that government can encourage residents to take protective actions for themselves. The benefit is difficult to quantify since these saferooms will not reduce property damage but do save lives. However, the cost is not borne by the public directly, as a subsidy would, but will lower the effective cost of the saferoom thereby increasing demand.

Direct Subsidies

After the Oklahoma City tornado of 1999, FEMA and the state of Oklahoma created a program to provide subsidies of $2,000 to residents of the state for the installation of a shelter in their home. The plan had three phases with the first phase being residents directly impacted by the tornado, the second phase was for residents who lived in a county affected by the tornado and finally the third phase provided for any resident of Oklahoma to apply for the subsidy if funds were still available. A study of this program was critical of the plan as the benefit of reducing tornado casualties from this subsidy exceeded the estimated benefits using the "value of life" approach.[15] For instance, the state of Oklahoma has an average of four fatalities a year from tornadoes. To ensure that all fatalities are prevented, a shelter would need to be installed in all homes at a cost of more than $2 billion. Even at a life of the shelter of 50 years, the cost per life saved exceeds $35 million. This is more than most experts would suggest being spent by a public entity for life-saving programs. There are competing uses for public funds and $2 billion would likely be better spent on programs where more lives could be saved.

A second criticism of programs like the Oklahoma Saferoom Initiative is that it treats all residents the same. There is evidence that tornado shelters have market value without the subsidy, so the money may have been better spent on other programs. Also, the benefit of reduced casualties depends on the type of housing. People who live in mobile homes are many times more likely to die or be injured from a tornado than those living in permanent structures.[16] Perhaps the subsidy could have been directed at that portion of the housing stock using underground shelters or community shelters for mobile home parks.

Warning Systems

One area of public mitigation that has shown great improvements in recent years is warning systems. Warnings for hurricanes and tornados have become very reliable and ever more precise. This reduces the need for hasty evacuations for hurricanes which reduces the business disruption that occurs when people are asked to leave an area. Tornado warning systems, with the advent of Doppler radar have improved dramatically.[17] Combined with on ground spotters, forecasters can warn residents with more lead time, which gives people the chance to take cover.

Radar was first used to track tornadoes in the 1950s. Afterwards, a sharp drop in casualties was noticed. As the skill of forecasters increased, casualties continued to decline. The next step in technology was the use of Doppler radar which began to be installed in Weather Field Offices in the 1990s. Another drop in casualties was noted as this system increased the amount of warning time to communities of a possible tornado.

Now that lead time for tornadoes has increased to the point where most people have sufficient time to take whatever shelter is available to them, the focus should be on increasing the accuracy of the warnings. This brings up a topic that is receiving more attention after the tornadoes of 2011 and that is false alarms. Referring again to the National Weather Service (NWS) report after the Joplin tornado, many residents reported that the initial warnings (by local sirens) were ignored because they did not believe that a tornado was imminent even with the warnings.[18] The national false alarm rate for tornadoes is 75%, so it is not unreasonable for people to think twice before responding. For researchers an obvious question regards the effect, if any, this false alarm rate has on casualties. While the national rate is 75%, it varies from 50% to 90% in some areas of the country. Several researchers have tried to document a "cry wolf" effect using survey data but have found little evidence that such an effect exists.[19] However, one study did document a "cry wolf" effect.[20] But this study evaluated the effect of false alarms on casualties rather than on response. It found that as the false alarm rate increased, casualties increased as well. It is not clear what the ideal false alarm rate should be, but if evidence suggests that false alarms matter to people who receive warnings then we have identified a starting point for refining the warning process.

Macroeconomic Questions

Macroeconomics looks at issues that affect society as a whole and cannot be changed by the actions of one individual or one firm. But large economic shocks can make a big difference to how an economy functions and may result in the loss of jobs, businesses, or could affect the prices of the goods and services that people buy. If a natural disaster is large enough, the potential is there for the aftermath of the event to have this type of effect and in this section those impacts are considered.

Inflation

Inflation is a general rise in the price level of an economy and simply understood can be caused by two forces: increase in aggregate demand or decrease in aggregate supply. For instance, demand pull inflation can be exacerbated by large inflows of cash to help rebuild a community after a disaster has destroyed much of the community. Cost push inflation occurs when supplies of necessary commodities are in short supply.

If a disaster occurs that damages a large number of buildings and infrastructure, rebuilding will create a temporary demand for lumber, concrete, and the other materials needed for construction. But it also brings construction workers into the community who may not live there permanently. These workers will need somewhere to live and they will be purchasing groceries, using utilities, and so forth. This increased demand can increase the prices on goods and services in this community, at least while the rebuilding is happening.

Some disasters, such as catastrophes, are so large that the supply of building materials that can be purchased locally is not sufficient. When this happens, supplies are rerouted from other parts of the country or world to keep up with demand. For some period of time, communities unaffected by the disaster can see an increase in the prices of those materials, not because their community has increased its demand but because their local supply has been diminished to serve the demand created by the catastrophe. As an example, consider the price of cement after the Haiti earthquake which occurred in January of 2010.

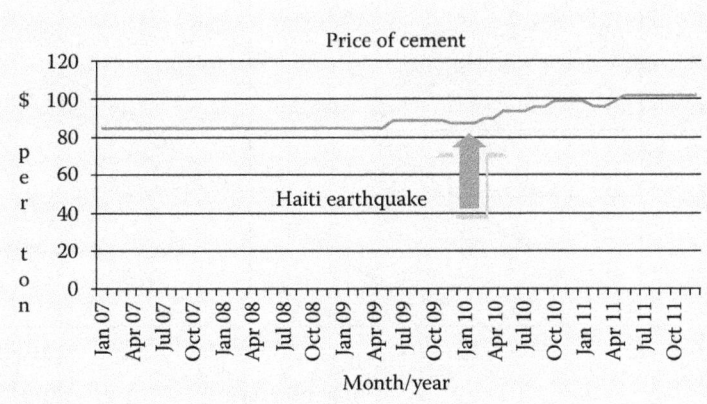

The scale of the catastrophe in Haiti was such that thousands of buildings were destroyed and to rebuild them required a large amount of concrete. While this one event is not the only factor in the price of concrete, such a large shift in demand can be seen in the price after the quake.[21]

INFLATION

Prices can increase if Aggregate Demand increases beyond a sustainable level of output. This is called "demand-pull inflation."

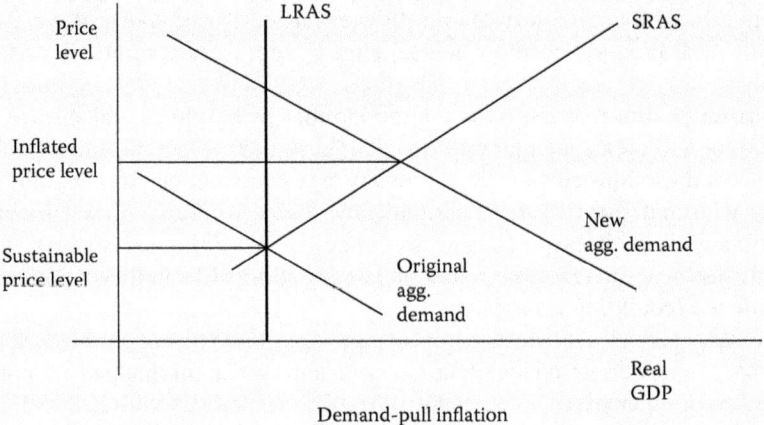

Demand-pull inflation

Inflation can also be caused by a decrease in the supply of goods and services. This is called "cost-push inflation."

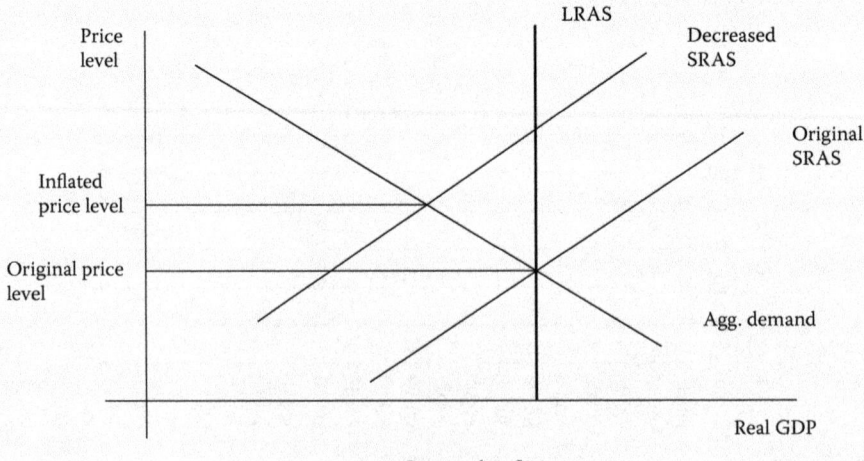

Cost-push inflation

Regardless of how inflation begins, it can have very harmful effects on an economy. Higher prices make rebuilding more expensive and can send false signals to people in the economy. For instance, higher prices may obscure fundamental changes that are occurring in the region which have little to do with the disaster.

Gross Domestic Product

Economists measure economic activity with a concept known as gross domestic product (GDP). GDP is the sum of all goods and services bought and sold in a specific economy. The effect of a disaster on local GDP is somewhat ambiguous and depends on the nature of the event. While normal economic activity is suspended, rebuilding of the community can actually increase local GDP. On the other hand, if the nature of the event causes a slow rebuilding process, local GDP can decrease for an extended time frame. If the community has an economic reason to exist, then rebuilding can be expected to occur and quickly gets the area back up and running, assuming that the size of the event is not so large that reconstruction cannot get rapidly underway. There are also cases, when the economy was fragile before the disaster. In situations like that, it is possible that the area never recovers from the disaster. One recent study that uses U.S. hurricane data from 1970 through 2005 concludes that local economies suffer an initial drop in the economic growth rate of 0.8%. On average, however, the growth rate recovers 0.2%. The author of this study concludes that the long run effect on economic growth is small.[22] But as mentioned earlier, effects differ in non-developed countries. A catastrophe can destroy enough infrastructure to make recovery difficult or in some cases impossible. For instance, consider a country which relies on agricultural products that take several years to begin producing like a vineyard or orchard. A large event such as a flood can destroy the vines and trees and would require years for production to begin again. People living in such an environment would not be able to quickly go back to the life they knew.

Perhaps the scenario that troubles economists the most is when a disaster occurs in a region that provides a strategic commodity used by the entire nation. Such an event could cause large GDP effects felt not only locally but nationally as well. For example, offshore oil rigs in the Gulf of Mexico can be affected by hurricanes. And many of the refineries that process the oil into gasoline are located on the Gulf coastline. A disruption to these supplies can have effects that are felt well beyond the region.

DECREASED GDP

If aggregate demand decreases from its sustainable level, the resulting equilibrium between AD and SRAS will cause the local GDP to decrease. If this condition is sustained for an extended period of time, it is called a recession.

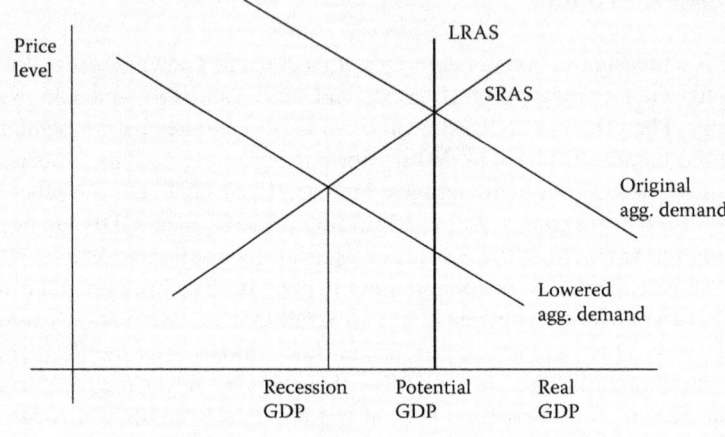

Unemployment

In a similar way to the possible effects of how a disaster impacts GDP, employment effects can be ambiguous. Short-term aggregate employment can actually increase if rebuilding efforts are substantial.[23] The rub is that those employed in the rebuilding may come from outside the community and displace jobs for those who lived in the area prior to the event.

Employment in industries that were operating prior to the disaster may suffer, at least in the short run. If the event was large, the short run may end up being quite a long time as some industries will not return if damage to needed infrastructure makes it difficult to operate. This certainly occurred for some industries that left southern Louisiana after Katrina. One noted example was Oreck Vacuum Cleaners,[24] which moved their Louisiana manufacturing facility out of the area after Hurricane Katrina. The reasons for a business departing a region are varied. It can be the case that the business was not doing well and the disaster provided the impetus to make a decision about where to locate. Another reason is that the event was large enough to spark an exodus of the population from the area, thus costing the business the necessary workforce and customers. Additionally, businesses depend on transportation, communication, power supply, and water infrastructures; where these are a long time being rebuilt, businesses may simply fold, or exit for a better infrastructure environment.

EMPLOYMENT

To determine the equilibrium level of employment we need to know the demand for labor, which comes from local businesses and the supply of labor which is determined by the local labor supply. The intersection of demand and supply of labor will give the equilibrium wage and quantity of labor employed in the community. If the demand for labor decreases while the supply is constant, unemployment results.

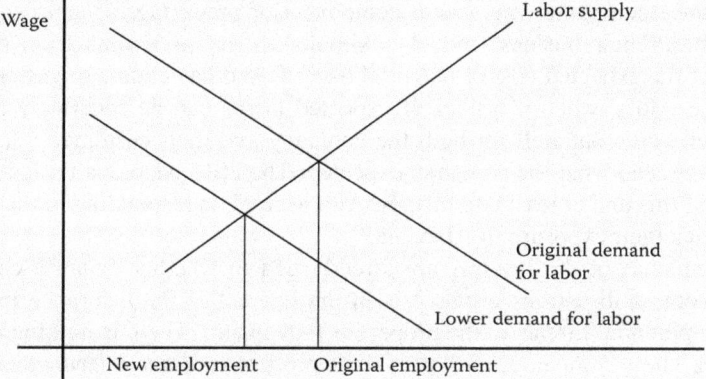

This graph shows what happens to employment if demand for labor decreases due to business disruption after a disaster.

Migration

It is rare, but sometimes a disaster can prompt relocation of residents affected by the event. Such migration is much more likely in catastrophes than disasters. Migration can be very small in size, to population shifts of a massive scale depending on the event and the resilience of the community. Some communities may choose not to rebuild certain sections of a town but, overall, population is not affected. Disasters may reveal vulnerabilities that were either unknown or overlooked by the community. Rebuilding the affected portion of the town may not occur but other areas in the community will simply absorb the displaced residents.[25]

On the other hand, large changes in population can occur if residents see no economic future for them. Such was the case during the Dust Bowl of the 1930s and for many after Hurricane Katrina. If this is the case, the economy of the region will feel deep impacts. Some industries may never return which will force workers to retrain themselves for different occupations, if they wish to stay. Both the stricken community and destination communities will be affected. For the stricken community, labor supply will diminish and the reverse will be true for the destination community. One interesting finding from research conducted after Hurricane Katrina was that affluent residents are more likely to return than lower income residents. Two observations to draw from this finding: First, affluent residents are more likely to have property that is worth rebuilding. Second, they are also more likely to have the resources to conduct the rebuilding.[26]

FINANCIAL MARKETS

Insurance

Insurance companies are a vital component of preparing for and dealing with catastrophes. Their business model is simple; collect premiums from customers that reflect the expected cost of potential hazards and pay claims to customers who experience a loss, when it occurs. If expected losses can be accurately predicted, this model works out well for both the company and their customers. Sometimes, the losses exceed what the company expected. The 2011 Alabama tornadoes is one example of this and at least one insurer, Alfa Mutual, is responding to the losses by pulling back their exposure in Alabama.[27]

The interests of the insurers are directly tied to whether or not a community can overcome a disastrous event. It is in the interest of the insurance industry to minimize potential threats to the properties they insure. There is nothing malicious about this. These companies must earn some profit to continue offering their product to the public. As a result, the insurance industry lobbies local governments to enact adequate building codes for the area and may offer incentives to their customers to lessen the effect of a potential hazard. Examples of these incentives are discounts for hail resistant roof materials and in Florida, incentives to create a wind-resistant structure.

After Hurricane Katrina, the industry received a great deal of negative press for their refusal to pay for damage caused by flood waters. In fact, flood insurance is available and subsidized by the federal government. Most homes damaged in the hurricane did not have this type of insurance and the industry, rightfully, refused to pay those claims. In some cases, it became a political issue and some of the companies settled with their customers. Other companies simply refused to sell insurance in these locations which makes redevelopment even more difficult.

Since flood insurance was brought to the public glare as a result of Katrina it deserves some discussion for this book. It is available to the public through local insurance agents but the policy itself is guaranteed by the federal government.[28] Homeowners can purchase policies up to $250,000 which should cover most homes. The rates are lower than would otherwise be the case if an insurance company were to take on this risk. Ultimately, it is the taxpayer who subsidizes this risk and it is this fact that has created some concern among economists. Anytime risk is shifted from the entity that faces the risk to a third party, it causes people to do things they otherwise would not do if they were responsible for the consequences. Economists call this "moral hazard." The demand for housing in a disaster-prone area is greater than it would have been if the homeowner bore the entire risk. This drives up insurance costs for non-flood insurance as these homes are more likely to be damaged by the winds of hurricanes, which is covered by a homeowners policy.

Despite the fact that flood insurance is available and subsidized, many residents choose not to purchase it. In the event of a flood, this leaves un-insured residents in a very vulnerable position. A house destroyed by flood will likely need to be completely rebuilt and if the homeowner only has standard homeowners insurance, the cost of that rebuilding falls on him/her. Meanwhile, the existing mortgage on the house is still a liability of the homeowner which leads many to have no choice but allow the property to be foreclosed on by the bank. There are no winners here. The homeowner has lost a home and is now stigmatized with a foreclosure. The bank has a property that is worth almost nothing. It is with the motivation to avoid this scenario that flood insurance is subsidized. Hurricane Katrina and the 2011 floods have highlighted the issue on a national scale.

The market value of insurance companies is, to some degree, tied to events that will increase claims. One study evaluated the change in the price of stock-owned insurance companies. The finding suggests that as news of the pending hurricane suggested claims would be high, the price of the stock fell. Conversely, as better news about the approaching storm was made known, the stock price rose.[29,30]

Banking

Banking systems are quite resilient and can respond to most events. Exceptions may exist particularly if the community is only served by local banks and not state/national banking firms. Worst-case scenario may cause a local bank to go out of business which would make recovery more difficult. In this case, depositors would be protected by Federal Deposit Insurance Corporation (FDIC) but unless loan activity can be replaced, economic growth for the community would be handicapped.[31] For individuals in these communities, some banking services may be difficult to use, at least until supporting infrastructure can be repaired. For instance, ATM systems rely on electronic networks, to access distant accounts. If the infrastructure that supports this network is disabled, the ATMs would be unable to dispense cash and other transactions. In a similar way, electronic networks are necessary for credit card transactions. Remaining businesses may be unable to access their networks making use of credit cards difficult.

An extreme example would be if an entire region is affected by the catastrophe to the point that basic infrastructure, like electricity and communications networks, was unusable for weeks and perhaps months. Given the redundancy in these networks, such a scenario is unlikely but certainly could occur. Financial firms would be in a perilous condition since the movement of money is now almost exclusively done electronically. This would make normal business almost impossible. One important role played by financial intermediaries is to smooth out daily cash flow for a company. Some days the receipt of cash from sales does not match outgoing expenses. On these days, it is necessary for a firm to have bank extended line of credit. Days where cash receipts exceed expenses, the credit line is repaid. Additionally, without the ability to process transactions electronically, payment systems would be useless. Functionally, firms and individuals would be reduced to the use of cash, which would now have to be supplied to the community manually. Even if the demand for services and goods was still present, the pace of activity would slow to a grind, thus decreasing the overall economic activity of the area.

One possible and much more likely outcome in the aftermath of a large disaster would be that banks would be more careful about loans for business or homes in areas affected by the disaster. These areas may reveal a vulnerability not known before and as a result, banks would not want to have loan assets there. Even if banks are willing to make loans for homes and businesses, the cost of those loans may increase since there is now some uncertainty regarding the area that was not previously known.

Real Estate

Real estate markets are derived from the economic activity of the area. Demand for homes will rise or fall as economic activity in the community changes. Therefore, the impact on real estate values depends on how the disaster affected the GDP of the community. One possible effect is a temporary shift from residents buying homes to temporary reconstruction workers seeking rental property as well as displaced permanent residents seeking temporary housing. The workers only plan to stay in the area while their services are needed to rebuild. Once rebuilding is complete, they will leave and have little incentive to put down roots thus purchasing real estate. If we assume that the market for rental property is a separate market from purchased property, it would be necessary to show the opposite effects on the graph for each. For rental properties, demand would increase (shift to the right) while for purchased property the demand may decline (shift to the left). In reality, permanent real estate properties are linked to what is happening in the rental market. As demand for rental property increases, it is expected that demand for permanent real estate will follow. However, in the case of a community rebuilding from a disaster, there is an expectation that some of the demand for temporary housing will decline once the community has recovered.

Effects of disasters can be limited to local markets as redevelopment of affected areas may avoid land that was previously considered usable for residential/commercial purposes. For instance, a neighborhood may experience flooding when previously such an event was considered very unlikely. The fact that the area was flooded will change perceptions on the future use of that particular land. Even residents who want to return may find that rebuilding in such a way as to prepare for the next flood makes housing unaffordable. Likewise, banks may be unwilling to provide financing without flood insurance, which increases the costs even more.

Larger effects can occur if the event prompts massive population relocations. As mentioned previously, if industries such as Oreck Vacuum in Louisiana leave the region, real estate markets will respond to this loss of jobs. The most extreme recent example of this was the tornado that destroyed Picher, OK in the spring of 2008. Picher was already identified as a Superfund site and has no chance of rebuilding.

Short of a massive catastrophe, real estate markets begin to function normally not long after the reconstruction has been completed. Studies conducted after several notable tornadoes indicate that real estate markets in those towns show resilience, which suggests that the markets are functioning efficiently.[32,33] Even in smaller towns such as Tulia, TX, economic activity begins to return fairly quickly. Resilience is strong in most markets and was noted as far back as the nineteenth century when the classical economist John Stuart Mill noted: "... What has so often excited wonder [is] the great rapidity with which countries recover from a state of devastation; the disappearance, in a short time, of all traces of the mischiefs done by earthquakes, floods, hurricanes, and the ravages of war (pp. 94–95)."[34]

CONCLUSION

Natural disasters have an immediate effect that is often broadcast across the nation and the world as casualty tolls mount. But the impacts extend well beyond the fatalities and the injuries sustained by their unfortunate victims. They can disturb the normal economic activity of an affected community. This chapter has reviewed some of the economic and related social consequences left by disasters. With few exceptions, most communities return to their pre-disaster state quickly as they rebuild from the losses, wiser perhaps, but resilient in the face of nature's worst. In catastrophes, the extent and breadth of damages is expected to be much more extreme, deepening the economic consequences of the event, and slowing the recovery process.

DISCUSSION QUESTIONS

Land Restrictions

A good discussion may be to ask the students how they would approach the issue of land restrictions. Should developers be allowed to build residential properties in flood plains? Who should pay for levees? Quotas push the price up making homes more expensive. Is this in the best interests of the community?

Building Codes

Again, this is a good opportunity to ask the students their opinions on this policy. Stringent building codes increase the cost to construct residential homes making them more expensive. As costs to produce a home goes up, the supply of homes decreases. What is more important: having fewer but safer homes or more affordable homes?

General Public Mitigation

Attempts for a local government to enact regulations intended to mitigate the effects of a potential disaster sometimes run into political hurdles. Choose one type of public mitigation policy and describe the political tensions that can be anticipated. Should public welfare be more important than private interests? Defend your position either way.

Migration

Describe some of the factors that can amplify migration away from a disaster site. What conditions must be met for affected residents to return? Who is most likely to return? Why?

Macro-Effects

Assume that a disaster strikes the Gulf Coast and destroys several oil refineries. Outline the macro effects of this event on the national economy.

REFERENCES

1. Cutter, S. and Finch, C. 2008, Temporal and spatial changes in social vulnerability to natural hazards, *National Academy of Sciences, Proceedings of the National Academy of Science, USA* 105(7), 2301–2306.
2. NWS Central Region Service Assessment, Joplin Missouri Tornado—May 22, 2011, U.S. Dept of Commerce, NOAA, NWS Central Region Headquarters, Kansas City, MO, July 2011.
3. Camerer, C. F. and Kunreuther, H. 1989, Decision processes for low probability events: Policy implications, *Journal of Policy Analysis and Management*, 8(4), 565–592.
4. Jacobs, J. 1890, *English Fairy Tales*. Oxford, England: Oxford University. pp. 68–72.
5. Ehrlich, I. and Becker, G. S. 1972, Market insurance, self-insurance, and self-protection, *Journal of Political Economy*, 80(4), 623–648.
6. Simmons, K. M., Kruse, J. B., and Smith, D. 2002, Valuing mitigation: Real estate market response to Hurricane loss reduction measures, *Southern Economic Journal*, 67(3), 660–671.
7. Simmons, K. M. and Willner, J. 2002, Hurricane mitigation: An examination of the effect of previous events on the value of mitigation, *Journal of Economics and Business Studies*, 1(1), 54–62.
8. Simmons, K. M. and Sutter, D. 2007, Tornado shelters and the housing market, *Construction Management and Economics*, 25(11), 1117–1124.
9. http://www.hptx.org/index.aspx?page=28.
10. http://pubs.usgs.gov/dds/dds-29/.
11. http://earthquake.usgs.gov/earthquakes/recenteqsww/Quakes/us2010rja6.php#summary.
12. http://pasadena.wr.usgs.gov/office/hough/oped-sf.html.
13. Litman, T. 2006, Lessons from Katrina and Rita: What major disasters can teach transportation planners, *Journal of Transportation Engineering*, 132(1), 11–18.
14. Whitehead, J. C. 2003, One million dollars per mile? The opportunity costs of Hurricane evacuation, *Ocean and Coastal Management*, 46(11–12), 1069–1083.
15. Merrell, D., Simmons, K. M., and Sutter, D. 2002, Taking shelter: Estimating the safety benefits of tornado saferooms, *Weather and Forecasting*, 17(3), 619–625.
16. Simmons, K. M. and Sutter, D. 2005, WSR-88D radar, tornado warnings, and tornado casualties, *Weather and Forecasting*, 20(3), 301–310.
17. Simmons and Sutter 2005, ibid.
18. NWS, Op. Cit.

19. Barnes, L. R., Gruntfest, E. C., Hayden, M. H., Schultz, D. M., and Benight, C. 2007, False alarms and close calls: A conceptual model of warning accuracy, *Weather and Forecasting*, 22, 1140–1147.
20. Simmons, K. M. and Sutter, D. 2009, False alarms, tornado warnings and tornado casualties, *Weather, Climate and Society,* 1(1), 38–53.
21. Data acquired from http://www.ct.gov/dot/lib/dot/documents/dconstruction/cement_hist.pdf.
22. Strobl, E. 2008, The Economic Growth Impact of Hurricanes: Evidence from US Coastal Counties, Working Paper, Ecole Polytechnique Paris.
23. Ewing, B. T., Hein, S. E., and Kruse, J. B. 2008, *Natural Disasters and Bank Performance: Preliminary Report*, Texas Tech University.
24. http://www.nytimes.com/2007/01/15/us/nationalspecial/15oreck.html.
25. McCain, B., Simmons, K. M., and Willner, J. 2003, Tornadoes, stress and migration decisions: Evidence from Oklahoma city, *Southwestern Journal of Economics,* 5(2), 1–19.
26. Landry, C. E., Bin, O., Hindsley, P., and Whitehead, J. C. 2007, Going home: Evacuation-migration decisions of Hurricane Katrina survivors, *Southern Economic Journal*, 74(2), 326–343.
27. http://blog.al.com/live/2011/06/alfa_cuts_alabama_policies_tornadoes.html.
28. Kunreuther, H. 1974, Disaster insurance: A tool for hazard mitigation, *Journal of Risk and Insurance,* 41(2), 287–303.
29. Ewing, B. T., Hein, S. E., and Kruse, J. B. 2006, The response of insurer stock prices to natural hazards, *Weather and Forecasting*, 21(3), 395–407.
30. Covarrubias, G. and Ewing, B. T. 2005, Weather and shocks to insurance stock prices: Volatility and persistence, *Economics and Wind*, New York, NY: Nova Science Publishing, pp. 63–72.
31. Ewing, B. T., Kruse, J. B., and Thompson, M. A. 2005, An empirical examination of the Corpus Christi unemployment rate and hurricane Bret, *Natural Hazards Review*, 6(4), 191–196.
32. Wang, Y., Ewing, B. T., and Kruse, J. B. 2007, Local housing price index analysis in wind-disaster prone areas, *Natural Hazards*, 40(2), 463–483.
33. Ewing, et al. 2005, Op. Cit.
34. Mill, J. 1848. *Principles of Political Economy,* New York: A. M. Kelley Publishers.

CHAPTER 6

Logistics and the Management of Critical Supplies Following Catastrophes

José Holguín-Veras, Tricia Wachtendorf, Miguel Jaller, and Theresa Jefferson

CONTENTS

Introduction 131
Post-Disaster Humanitarian Logistics 134
Materiel Convergence 137
Characteristics of Catastrophes and Their Effects on Emergency Supply Chains 138
Suggestions for Improvement 143
    Disaster Response Planning 144
    Distribution of Critical Supplies 144
    Knowledge of Demand 145
    Contending with Materiel Convergence 146
Supporting Systems 146
Conclusion 146
Acknowledgments 147
References 147

INTRODUCTION

As recent events such as Hurricane Katrina (2005), the Haitian (2010) earthquake, and the Japanese (2011) earthquake/tsunami have shown, catastrophic disasters can produce unfathomable death and devastation. Following such events, we often see generous acts of compassion and charity. Unfortunately, the tremendous outpouring of support may prove chaotic, disordered, and present its own logistical challenges. Providing the huge quantities of resources (be they from formal or informal sources) required for the relief and recovery activities can initially become complicated by the inability to have a "clear picture" of the event, specific resource and supply requirements, and areas in need. When physical destruction accompanies the event—as it is so often, but not necessarily does—this task becomes even more difficult due to the severe loss of infrastructure and lifelines. Moreover, when promised resources fail to arrive or are delayed in their arrival and distribution, affected populations may be unable to obtain what they require for survival and rebuilding.[1]

This is exacerbated after catastrophic events when response operations are in a race against the clock to save lives, minimize human suffering, protect property, and restore community functioning. In general, the aid response effort requires the transport of large volumes of critical supplies and personnel into the disaster site(s) to be distributed internally in a short time frame, under conditions where those charged with such tasks are normally unaware or uncertain regarding what is actually needed, and when and where it is required. In addition, the coordination, collaboration, and decision making required for the response process are very difficult, as evidenced in the cases of Haiti and Japan.[2,3] Despite the fact that extreme events occur infrequently and that no two are exactly the same, their characteristics and impacts on people, infrastructure and the environment do show some commonalities. The differences relate to the extent of the event's impacts, whether it is a small localized disaster or a widespread catastrophe, which in turn imposes new requirements to the logistical response process. In a catastrophic event "most or all of the community-built structure is heavily impacted ... [and] facilities and operational bases of most emergency organizations are themselves usually hit;" "local officials are unable to undertake their usual work role;" "help from nearby communities cannot be provided;" "most, if not all, of the everyday community functions are sharply and concurrently interrupted;" "the mass media system especially in recent times socially constructs catastrophes even more than they do disasters;" there are "mass out-migrations for protracted periods of time;" and "because of the previous six impacts, the political arena becomes even more important."[4-6] However, not all characteristics need to be present to be considered a catastrophe, but their prevalence is an indication of how catastrophic the event is.[7,8] Yet, the identification and understanding of the differences and similarities among events allows for the development of comprehensive response plans that should consider a wide range of scenarios.[9]

As we reflect on recent catastrophes, similar patterns to what occurs after a more moderate disaster are evident. One such commonality is the large influx of personnel, materiel, and information to the impacted area, as well as other areas associated with the response.[10] This process, formally defined as convergence,[11] can originate from local, national, or international governments, non-governmental organizations, private sector organizations, and the general public. Although convergence is and should be expected after any type of event, still local governments and organizations are rarely able to contend with it. The lack of resources to deal with convergence coupled with its usually large proportion of unsuitable aid (e.g., non- and low-priority donations) creates a logistical nightmare. This is in part one of the reasons why relief operations are normally perceived as ineffective and inefficient. Other considerations include the fact that after disaster or catastrophic events: (1) the transportation, communication, social, and built-structures may be severely impacted; (2) there are complex interactions between the dozens and even thousands of supply chains that arise hampering a coordination process; (3) the needs for life-sustaining items increase tremendously as large proportions of local inventories may be destroyed; (4) there is often a lack of established procedures to expedite the flow of high-priority supplies; (5) there is a lack of empirical studies or methodologies to quantify and assess the immediate resource requirements; and (6) the humanitarian logistics structures performing the response operations may lack integration with the social fabric of the impacted area.[12–17]

An assessment of the response to Hurricane Katrina conducted by Holguín-Veras et al.[18] identified several issues affecting the logistical operations: the communications infrastructure was severely damaged, assets were not visible—including trucks with supplies that went untracked; organizations were understaffed with people trained in logistics; logistics systems between agencies were incompatible; pre-positioned resources were used inefficiently while procurement delays ensued; and planning for the handling and distribution of the influx of spontaneous donations was inadequate. As one of Holguín et al.'s interviewees stated, "... [Our] disaster preparation plan is a great checklist of everything that you have to do and it covers almost every type of emergency, except the one we had."[19]

As shown, the logistics processes in motion in the aftermath of a disaster or Post-Disaster Humanitarian Logistics (PD-HL) are extremely complex. The remainder of this chapter discusses the issues affecting PD-HL, emphasizing the impacts of catastrophes on the logistics process and the difficulties of contending with materiel convergence. This chapter ends with a set of recommendations for improvements and conclusions (see Figure 6.1).

Figure 6.1 Cedar Rapids, Iowa. Flooding causes disruption of normal supply chain where roads and railroads become unavailable. (http://www.ng.mil/resources/photo_gallery/emergency_response/disaster/images/full/080613-F-4218S--161.jpg.)

POST-DISASTER HUMANITARIAN LOGISTICS

Logistics systems are concerned with managing the flow of supplies and personnel from their point of origin to the appropriate places at the correct time. These supply chains require collaboration and communication to successfully integrate inventory, warehousing, transportation, distribution, and security. However, under extreme events, these systems must function in an environment that is constantly changing, where damage to communication systems impedes the sharing of information, damage to infrastructure and lifelines delays the delivery of resources, and disparate organizations inhibit collaboration. Furthermore, the logistic process required to immediately respond to an extreme event or PD-HL faces many challenges not shared by its commercial counterparts.[20] There are radical differences between humanitarian and commercial logistics[21–23] in terms of the: (1) objectives pursued; (2) origination of the commodity flows; (3) knowledge of demand; (4) decision-making structure; (5) periodicity and volume of logistic activities; (6) state of social fabric and networks; and (7) state of the supporting systems.[24]

In addition, these systems are faced with the challenge of identifying: (1) population needs, operational needs, and the needs of the organizations involved in disaster relief efforts (i.e., what is needed?, how much is needed?, when is it needed?, where is it needed?); (2) the available capacity of local infrastructure; (3) the available resources (i.e., material, human, information); (4) the factors that hinder or facilitate relief efforts; and (5) the social, cultural, and environmental characteristics of the potential disaster area that may have a bearing on the effectiveness of the relief efforts.[25] These challenges are magnified by the impact and type of event. For example, the sheer volume, size, and geographic coverage of catastrophes create a level of complexity that makes it extremely difficult to coordinate the delivery of the correct resources to the right place in a timely manner.

According to Holguín-Veras et al.[26] in the United States, the federal disaster logistics system functions as a pull system. This means that a state will send requests for supplies to FEMA, and FEMA tasks other federal entities to fulfill the request. Once the federal government provides the assistance, the state is responsible for making it available to those in need. During a catastrophe, state and local officials rapidly become overwhelmed by response activities and this pull system is not effective. At this point, the supply chain becomes a push system as resources are sent to the impacted area without waiting for state requests.[27]

Central to the problem of provisioning critical supplies is the demand estimation process. According to Dynes et al.[28] and Taylor and Quarantelli,[29] after disasters, there are two types of demands: agent- and response-generated. Agent-generated demands are those generated by the disaster agent itself as it impacts the community, while response-generated results are from the activities performed in response to the disaster agent. In terms of agent-generated demands, there are different guidelines that provide an indication of the amount of supplies that should be handed out to the beneficiaries.[30,31] However, there is no quantification of the magnitude of the response-generated demands; estimates from the Hurricane Katrina response suggest that these demands are about three times the size of the agent-generated demands.[32] As a result, it could be expected that the total amount of supplies required for an event such as the Port-au-Prince earthquake translates into a daily requirement of 60,000–240,000 tons/day. Responses to recent catastrophes have clearly shown the magnitude of the resources that are needed, such as manpower, trucks, fuel, replacement parts, and myriad points of distribution for each, in order to be able to transport, manage, and deliver crucial materiel to the many different simultaneous operations on-going in the response.[33] This is undoubtedly, a major challenge. Another important aspect to be considered is the impact of the type of event on the local inventories in households or businesses. For instance, while after a disaster local inventories, especially those in the vicinity of the impacted area, may suffer minor damage, after a catastrophic event, they are likely to be severely impacted or even completely wiped out. In these cases, almost all supplies need to be brought from the outside and time is of the essence. Consequently, pre-positioning strategies should be analyzed and put in place so as to reduce the reaction time and provide the first wave of critical and life-sustaining supplies.

What is even more striking is that the efforts and resources required to do the local distribution may be of an order of magnitude larger than those required to transport supplies, equipment, and personnel to a disaster area. In essence, local distribution becomes the bottleneck of the relief effort. This was clearly demonstrated in the Haiti experience, where large quantities of supplies piled up at the airport due to the inability of the agencies (e.g., United Nations) to distribute them. In a similar situation, the response plans put in place by the governmental organizations after Japan's earthquake, tsunami, and nuclear crisis only accounted for the transport of supplies to the distribution centers, but did not define the local distribution to the anticipated and emergent shelters or other points of distribution. In essence, local distribution requires a logistical structure, assets, and manpower that are able to operate throughout a large geographic area in a timely manner. However, there is no single organization with sufficient capacity to achieve an efficient distribution of supplies.

In this sense, it is important to define the humanitarian logistics structures of the organizations involved in the response efforts on the basis of their level of integration with the social fabric of the impacted area. According to Holguín-Veras et al.,[34] three cases exemplify the relevant operations: (1) Agency Centric Effort (ACE) or a foreign agency with little or no integration with the locals that operates based on its internal capacity (has to bring and setup the entire logistical structure from the outside); (2) Collaborative Aid Network (CAN) that is the case of a network of individuals or groups that are part of both the local impacted community and a larger network that covers other communities; and in between these two cases, depending to what extent and on how an organization integrates with the locals, there is a (3) Partially Integrated Effort (PIE). Each of these types of structures has its strengths and weaknesses for conducting relief efforts. It suffices to say that, PIEs and CANs are likely to perform better than ACEs, as their integration with the local networks provides them with the resilience, knowledge, and human and technical resources to operate. Moreover, often these local resources can be assembled in a timely manner to start the local distribution. The advantage of having a foreign partner, as in the case of the PIEs, resides in its ability and resource capacity to bring large volumes of supplies and equipment to the disaster site, while the CANs are engaged in the local distribution.[35]

CANs can be considered as part of a holistic approach for the PD-HL process. Likewise, the private sector can be considered as playing a role in this approach as well, as it may be able to help transport and distribute emergency supplies in the aftermath of extreme events. This was recently demonstrated by the experience in Japan, where the local distribution was performed by private companies, though they faced numerous challenges in spite of their experience.[36] Other examples include the case of Home Depot and Walmart after Hurricane Katrina. Home Depot, for instance, delivered 800 truckloads of supplies such as bottled water, bug spray, and tarps.

However, as previously noted, commercial and humanitarian logistics are rather different and the expertise of the private sector may be highly limited when faced with disaster and catastrophic conditions. On the other hand, these companies have existing, efficient, nationwide distribution systems to transport materials with the existing relationships in the impacted community and knowledge of the local landscape which can be instrumental in providing assistance to those in need. They have recognized the need to plan for contingencies, such as transportation strikes, and can react to disruptions, such as road closures. In some instances, for example, Walmart, they have put in place emergency management departments responsible for preparedness, emergency operations, and recovery from a broad spectrum of events ranging from blizzards to man-made disasters.[37]

If partnerships are formed before an event occurs, the private sector could leverage the effort of governmental and non-governmental organizations in the PD-HL efforts. One of the principles of FEMA's current Whole of Community approach to emergency management involves utilizing the private sector. Stating "... we must leverage all of the resources of our collective team in preparing for, protecting against, responding to, recovering from, and mitigating against all hazards; and that collectively we must meet the needs of the entire community in each of these areas. This larger collective emergency management team includes, not only FEMA and its partners at the federal level, but also local, tribal, state and territorial partners; non-governmental organizations like faith-based and non-profit groups and private sector industry; to individuals, families, and communities, who continue to be the nation's most important assets as first responders during a disaster."[38]

A successful example of these partnerships is the case of the construction operations in terms of repairs, road openings, debris removal, and so on, pre-arranged by the Japanese government with the private sector.[39] These operations were conducted efficiently, even in cases where only a small disaster was considered in the arrangements. An analysis of the factors that explain the success in the implementation of these partnerships, sheds light on the types of considerations that need to be taken into account when designing future policies and response plans. One of these characteristics is in terms of the scalability of the operations to be performed whether it is a small disaster or a large catastrophe. For instance, road opening and construction repair operations are practically the same for a small or large event, and only the amount and criticality of the work differs. This is in contrast with PD-HL operations, where for small disasters, the local distribution of critical supplies does not require sophisticated planning and execution, whereas, in catastrophes, the PD-HL operations need to cover large areas to satisfy the needs of hundreds of thousands of individuals.[40] In essence, a response plan designed for a disaster, when scaled up to a catastrophe, may only increase the flow of supplies, which would be able to arrive to the entry points or distribution centers, but most likely will encounter severe obstacles to be locally distributed.

MATERIEL CONVERGENCE

Materiel convergence includes the influx of supplies, equipment, and physical resources to sites associated with a disaster, and there is evidence of this phenomenon in all major disasters.[41–48] Convergence also involves an influx of information and people. According to Fritz and Mathewson,[49] personal, or people convergence, can include those individuals who come to help (both formal and spontaneous responders); those who return to the area (such as residents or business owners); those who anxiously look for loved ones; those who are curious about the event (including the general public or the media); and those who hope to exploit the situation to their advantage. In some responses, we may also see the convergence of people who want to encourage or support the response efforts and those who have come to mourn or memorialize the victims.[50] As other chapters cover the question of emergent organizations and networks, our focus here is on materiel convergence.

The physical goods that arrive to response-related sites include supplies that are both gravely needed, as well as those which are unnecessary and overburden the system. Here, convergence is a social/behavioral phenomenon that possesses both positive and negative features that must be contended with. Consider specifically, materiel convergence, or the movement of supplies and equipment. The fundamental problem with materiel convergence is that empirical evidence and experiences at recent disasters have shown that it is composed of a large proportion of non- and low-priority goods (empirical evidence and direct observations at recent major disasters estimate this proportion in excess of 60%), which distract mission-critical resources that could be used for other more critical tasks.[51,52] These goods need to be identified, analyzed, sorted, labeled, inventoried, or even discarded if found not appropriate (e.g., expired, culturally offensive, unsuitable to the climate, not needed due to local availability of supplies) for the impacted population.[53] Besides the direct impact on the resources required to contend with the flow of these goods, materiel convergence also creates congestion by the vehicular traffic carrying these flows, as it happens at a time where infrastructure is severely impacted or its original capacity is not commensurate to the sudden increase in demand. Furthermore, a great percentage of the flows are likely to require additional processing and inspection times as they lack proper documentation, arrive without a consignee, or are inadequately packaged.[54,55]

Empirical evidence suggests that the magnitude of these flows is affected by the type of event, as large disasters and catastrophes are bound to attract a massive global response which is accompanied by broad media coverage. Lack of proper assessment or dissemination of the affected population's needs renders this massive international convergence ineffective. Moreover, the profusion of organizations that converge on an impacted area following an extreme event, impacts the overall effectiveness and increases the costs associated with coordinating response operations. For example, there is general consensus from those involved in the Indian Ocean Tsunami response that there were far too many agencies of all types in Indonesia and Sri Lanka.[56] There were over 500 organizations involved in the response to Hurricane Katrina. The influx of international agencies often grows unabated due to the ease of entry of competent personnel as well as those who are inexperienced and ineffectual. The risk associated with the quality of the response and the reputation of the humanitarian community increases as the number of inexperienced or irresponsible agencies increases. The proliferation of personnel caused by international convergence results in an increased burden on the local population and authorities as they try to navigate between organizations to determine who is the best resource for various supplies, services, and information.

A lack of standard operating procedure for coordination, as well as a frequent weakness in general coordination skill by the individuals involved, complicate the overall effort and lead to duplication of efforts along with a lack of operational clarity concerning organizational roles. In addition to the issues with coordination, the assessment process also poses challenges. Along with the multitude of agencies, comes a multitude of assessments. Often conducted by individual agencies for their own requirements, these assessments do not consider other participants, and with few exceptions tend to be shared only within their own organizations. During the first 3 weeks following the 2004 Indian Ocean event, 17 bilateral assessment teams are reported to have arrived on the scene. A single, collaborative, authoritative assessment for the Indian Ocean Tsunami was not conducted. A joint assessment performed by the United Nations and the Red Crescent Societies would have helped in determining requirements.[57] Assessments by the media tend to have a tremendous sway on donor policy, negating more formal assessments.[58]

This section provided a general description of the PD-HL systems and its challenges. The next section briefly discusses the direct impact of catastrophes on the logistics response.

CHARACTERISTICS OF CATASTROPHES AND THEIR EFFECTS ON EMERGENCY SUPPLY CHAINS

Chapter 1 provided an in-depth discussion on the ways in which catastrophes differ from disasters. These differences have implications for the logistical considerations of critical resource provision. Wachtendorf et al.[59] closely examined the emergency relief operations after Hurricane Irene struck the U.S. Gulf Coast in 2005. Using the characteristics of catastrophe offered by Quarantelli[60] and adding an additional characteristic based on their own research, the authors detailed ways in which the characteristics generate specific challenges for logistics and emergency supply chain management. These challenges are noted in the section below. Of course, as we will discuss, the consequences of catastrophe in this domain reach well beyond Hurricane Katrina and have consequences in other events of a catastrophic nature.

Quarantelli[61] noted that catastrophes can leave much of a community's built structure destroyed or incapacitated, including those relied upon by emergency organizations (see Figure 6.2).

Following the 2010 Haiti earthquake, for example, Port-au-Prince was described as the "flattened" capital.[62] Hospitals were badly damaged, and destruction of sometimes limited lifeline infrastructure left basic services such as water and electricity unavailable. Roads were blocked by debris and the seaport was badly damaged. Similarly, the 9.0-magnitude earthquake that struck Japan in 2011 caused the formation of 30-foot walls of water that swept across rice fields, smashed towns, dragged houses onto highways, and tossed cars and boats, turning much of the inundated areas into swampy wastelands. During Hurricane Katrina, high winds, storm surge, and flooding generated by levee breeches in New Orleans also led to significant damage to the built environment, including structures and infrastructure. Homes, businesses, schools, hospitals, and emergency management facilities were largely unusable. The region experienced widespread damage to transportation, power, and communication infrastructure.[63]

As Wachtendorf et al.[64] explain, such widespread devastation presents a daunting challenge for those attempting to navigate the impact zone. Damage to roads, bridges, airports, and seaports results in significant time delays in supply delivery. With critical infrastructure damaged, including electrical grids and lines, telephone systems, and mobile and Internet technology, the difficulty to communicate resource needs—particularly as circumstances evolve—becomes immensely challenging. Even if a community was proactive in its planning and pre-positioned supplies throughout the area, those supplies and their facilities may have suffered damage during the event. What's more, as logistics personnel and emergency managers look for space to store and distribute incoming aid, alternative space is likely to have been destroyed as well. Finally, with such widespread and comprehensive damage to an area, the response and short-term recovery period may be significantly protracted compared to that of a more routine disaster event. As a result, the incoming flow of supplies related to the

1. Damage to roads and bridges creates difficulties navigating the impact zone, resulting in significant time delays in supply delivery.
2. Damage to communication infrastructure leads to inadequate communications.
3. Prepositioned supplies may be damaged.
4. Alternative space for supply warehousing and distribution may be difficult to identify.
5. The response and short-term recovery period may be protracted. A quick influx of long-term recovery-related supplies may unnecessarily clog the system.

Figure 6.2 Consequences for the emergency supply chain as a result of widespread damage to built environment. (Adapted from Wachtendorf et al. 2010.)

long-term recovery could over-run the system. These long-term recovery resources may be high-priority items at a particular phase of the recovery, but if they arrive too soon after a catastrophic event, they will add to the already large flow of low-priority items that must be sorted, transported, inventoried, and stored in limited space.

Quarantelli's[65] second catastrophe characteristic describes how such events can leave local officials in a position where they are unable to undertake their more routine professional roles. What local residents might usually be able to count on officials to do—be it sanitation, processing permits, providing education, providing security, operating communication systems, or other tasks—is suddenly unavailable. Unlike a short-term emergency, where a few officials might be otherwise preoccupied for a few days, this community impact touches many domains and officials are unable to resume routine operations for well into the recovery period.

It is important to remember that local officials are often themselves victims of the event. In Haiti, the earthquake killed the leadership of the United Nations Mission for the Stabilization of Haiti (known by its Spanish acronym, MINUSTAH), the leadership of the Catholic Church, destroyed 14 out of the 16 buildings that housed government ministries, and killed numerous government workers.[66] After Katrina, some local officials evacuated the city with their families, and the many who were left behind to contend with the storm's aftermath were relocated to other response facilities. Following the 2011 Japan tsunami, many communities along the country's coast lost key local officials to the tsunami waves. With the widespread destruction to coastal communities, local officials were displaced alongside other residents, and were challenged to contend with the tsunami's destruction, let alone routine needs that persisted.

Consequently, Wachtendorf et al.[67] found that the local system can become overburdened in the catastrophe aftermath. A community may be able to absorb some of the materiel for emergent needs after a disaster. Even after a high consequence event such as the 2001 World Trade Center disaster, local officials in New York City were able to continue to engage in routine fire suppression, crime control, healthcare, and sanitation services while contending with the destruction at Ground Zero. The same was not so for many of the local communities after Hurricane Katrina, the 2010 Haiti earthquake, and the 2011 events in Japan. At times, even connecting to a local official who could make a decision on a pressing matter related to aid delivery was a harrowing experience for survivors (see Figure 6.3).

1. Overburden on the local system and difficulties contacting those who would normally communicate needs in a disaster.
2. Additional personnel from outside the area are especially needed for the emergency supply chain, even though integrating outside personnel can bring coordination challenges.

Figure 6.3 Consequences on the emergency supply chain as a result of local officials being unable to undertake routine work roles in the recovery period. (Adapted from Wachtendorf et al. 2010.)

Moreover, with this added burden on local officials, personnel from outside the local jurisdiction found it necessary to help with the logistic operations. Unfamiliar with local culture, geography, and politics, even those with extensive logistics skills experience a learning curve to their new operational environment. The converging personnel also present their own logistical requirements including clothes, food, supplies, equipment, and shelter.

According to Quarantelli,[68] one of the common characteristics of catastrophe is that help from neighboring cities and counties cannot be provided, simply because they, too, suffer the effects of the event. Catastrophes are regional events, and those neighboring jurisdictions that would usually be expected to provide mutual aid are themselves left seeking assistance. Consequently, communities must rely more heavily on supplies coming from a great distance. The impact on the emergency supply chain is clear. Greater distance requires greater time devoted to travel. In a catastrophe, the task of coordinating the delivery of goods coming from far away requires much more work using adaptive logistics, than would be the case of bringing in goods from nearby with pre-established memoranda of understanding, as is the case in many disasters. Indeed, rather than serving as potential supply resources, catastrophes can generate competition as affected communities vie for the same limited goods (see Figure 6.4).[69]

Another challenging characteristic of catastrophe is the sudden, widespread, and concurrent interruption of most, if not all community functions (see Figure 6.5).[70] As Wachtendorf et al.[71] state, without the operation of everyday functions such as healthcare, education, mail service, transportation, utility service, community-based, and

1. Competition between communities for scarce resources rather than mutual aid provision.
2. Greater need for external convergence equals:
    a. Greater time delays in reaching impacted areas, and
    b. Increased challenges in coordinating what is coming in.

Figure 6.4 Consequences on the emergency supply chain as a result of the inability of nearby communities to provide help. (Adapted from Wachtendorf et al. 2010.)

1. Some community-based organizations that would normally play a role in distribution (e.g., some local food banks or churches) are themselves significantly impacted or not allowed back into impacted areas.
2. Local commerce is impacted, making it more difficult to acquire large amounts of resources locally or to identify local suppliers still in operation.

Figure 6.5 Consequences on the emergency supply chain as a result of sharp and concurrent interruption of most everyday community functions. (Adapted from Wachtendorf et al. 2010.)

faith-based organizations that would normally provide assistance during a disaster may remain evacuated well after the response period has subsided. Indeed, those returning to the area to help may be turned away because local officials know that community functions remain disrupted. Without activity related to local commerce, the ability to acquire large amounts of resources locally or to identify local suppliers still in operation may prove next to impossible.

Quarantelli[72] notes the importance of two other characteristics. First, the mass media socially construct elements of the catastrophe to a greater extent than they do following disasters (see Figure 6.6). Second, the political arena becomes particularly important. These too, have important consequences for emergency supply chains. Catastrophe receives national, if not worldwide, media attention. With that international spotlight comes a greater likelihood of goods converging from across the globe. Transportation costs increase. Challenges related to incompatible logistics systems—when they are even present—increase. More so than in a disaster, where many people may still be relatively able to communicate their emergent needs, the mass news media are frequently among the first to be able to gain access to locations and report their narrative out to the world.[73] How they frame the events, therefore, have direct implications for interpretations of what goods are needed. With respect to the political arena, the stakes are raised for the many levels of government actors. When supplies are not readily available to victims, the blame game can emerge quite quickly (see Figure 6.7). Goods may be directed to some areas given what has transpired in the political arena rather than solely related to needs articulated from the front lines. Equally important for the emergency supply chain, delays can ensue as the blame-game unfolds without resolution.

1. Convergence of donated goods from across the county and around the world occurs on a larger scale.
2. As a result, logistics operators encounter additional challenges (more than the "typical disaster") in sorting perishable or low-priority goods from high-priority items.
3. Media may, more so than in a disaster, serve a role in providing the first picture of critical needs, thereby impacting the flow of supplies through their particular framing of the event.

Figure 6.6 Consequences on the emergency supply chain as a result of heightened social construction of the event by mass media. (Adapted from Wachtendorf et al. 2010.)

1. Heightened discourse of who is at fault as different levels of government blame one another for inadequacies in supply distribution.

Figure 6.7 Consequences on the emergency supply chain as a result of increased importance of the political arena. (Adapted from Wachtendorf et al. 2010.)

1. Competing demands for emergency resources spread over a wider area, adding further complexity in the flow of goods as the location of those in need changes.

Figure 6.8 Consequences on the emergency supply chain as a result of mass and extended out-migration of residents. (Adapted from Wachtendorf et al. 2010.)

Imagine that a catastrophic event struck your community and the surrounding areas. Take a few minutes to brainstorm the kinds of material resources you would need to consider were you to serve as logistics coordinator for a catastrophic event. For example, you might be concerned with providing subsistence (e.g., food, water); energy (e.g., heating oil, gasoline, generators for electricity); administrative supplies; or engineering and construction material. These are just a few ideas to get you started. What other resources would be needed, and what may prevent the timely delivery of any or all of these goods given the catastrophic nature of the event?

Figure 6.9 Brainstorming activity.

Finally, Wachtendorf et al.[74] pointed to a sixth catastrophe characteristic. The events of Hurricane Katrina and the 2011 Japanese earthquake suggest that extensive and extended out-migration are common occurrences in catastrophes. With the built environment destroyed and community functions almost entirely disrupted, it is likely that a large portion of the population will leave for a lengthy time period (see Figure 6.8). Following Hurricane Katrina, residents fled to nearby communities in Gulf Coast states, but they also evacuated to almost every state in the nation. Some opted—by choice or lack of available options—to continue to reside in their new home communities. Others returned after weeks, months or even a few years. Consequently, demands for emergency supplies spread far beyond the confines of the impact zone. Certainly one strategy could have been to send all available supplies to devastated areas of Louisiana, Mississippi, and Alabama in 2005, but with many survivors eventually leaving for elsewhere, goods needed to be redirected as well. After communities surrounding the Fukushima nuclear power plant evacuated, most emergency supplies were less useful if they were sent to the affected area than to communities hosting internally displaced populations.

Clearly, the characteristics of the event point to more than a simple dichotomy between event types. Despite the many similarities between events traditionally defined as disasters and those more recently defined as catastrophes, the consequences of the difference between the two affect the social and physical environments in which emergency supply chains must operate (see Figure 6.9).

SUGGESTIONS FOR IMPROVEMENT

Following, a set of suggestions for improvement are recommended. These suggestions build upon the descriptions provided in previous sections and experiences from recent disasters and catastrophes. These recommendations are analyzed in terms of their contribution to disaster response planning, distribution efforts for critical supplies, strategies to estimate resource requirements, and to contend with materiel convergence.

Disaster Response Planning

Recent disaster experiences have demonstrated the need to proactively plan for disaster response operations. Furthermore, these plans should be designed to account for a wide range of events, as to be able to consider and prepare for the worst-case scenario. These plans should be robust enough so that they can be applied to any scenario. It is important to consider the scalability of the operations. In essence, disaster plans should be able to adjust either upwards or downwards in order to satisfy the needs. Detail must be provided to allow for all aspects of PD-HL, including technical, economic, and social considerations. The specific roles of the different organizations must be established. A set of actions to conduct and foster formal training in humanitarian logistics and realistic exercises should be developed. The plan designs should *engage all segments of society in the response*, establishing their specific functions and roles. As part of the planning efforts, the different organizations and social networks should be identified, and proactive action should be implemented in order to improve the level of interoperability between the systems. Furthermore, the synergies should be identified to take advantage of the knowledge, resources, connections, and access to the communities, which would improve the local distribution of critical supplies.[75] In addition, the response plans must be flexible enough to contend with the number of emergent organizations.

During the planning phase, efforts should be made to support and foster partnerships with the private sector, through a set of pre-arranged contracts being designed to assist in securing services, material resources, equipment, or personnel. These arrangements should be designed to take into consideration the scalability of operations and a wide range of event conditions.

Distribution of Critical Supplies

The evidence from recent disasters has shown that the local distribution is the most challenging part of, PD-HL process. Long-haul transportation, even in the aftermath of a catastrophe, resembles traditional logistics operations, where long standing tradition and experience of aid organizations provide a key advantage for this stage of the distribution process. However, during extreme events, the amount of resources required to manage, transport, and distribute critical supplies inside the impacted area is extremely large, and unfortunately proportionally scarce. In these events, understaffing of key response agencies and lack of training in logistics management can generate substantial logistical problems. Thus, it is imperative that PD-HL efforts integrate the local communities and social networks. Furthermore,

Figure 6.10 A Paratrooper assigned to A Co., 2nd Brigade Special Troops Battalion, 2nd Brigade Combat Team, removes rubble from the streets of Port-au-Prince, Haiti, making it easier to distribute aid to the Haitian people. (http://www.army.mil/media/105507.)

these communities and networks must be standardized to the extent possible during the pre-event planning period, and trained so as to be able to extend their routine functions and operations to disaster response activities[76,77] (see Figure 6.10).

Knowledge of Demand

As previously discussed, there are two distinct demands associated with a specific event: disaster agent-generated and response-generated demands. It is important to develop strategies to estimate the immediate resource requirements for both of these demands. In addition, methodologies to produce forecasts that can support procurement policies and to use sensing technologies to conduct assessments must be developed. Furthermore, given the impact of catastrophic events on the availability of local inventories, the distribution network, the disruptions in the private supply chains, and the fact that most of the supplies need to be brought in from the outside, strategies must be developed to ensure a timely response and fast provisioning of critical and life-sustaining items. These strategies entail a combination of pre-positioning or blanket purchase agreements of critical items,[78,79] or other methodologies that should integrate the public and private sector, the general public and other organizations.

In addition, the strategies should be able to contend with the phenomenon of precautionary/opportunistic buying. This is the process characterized by individuals, especially in the periphery of the disaster area, acquiring large amounts of critical supplies in fear or concern for shortages. This imposes an extra challenge to PD-HL as it prevents or decreases the amount of supplies available to benefit the directly impacted population.[80]

Contending with Materiel Convergence

Despite the much-needed supplies, equipment, and personnel brought in as part of the convergence process, there is a large proportion (>60%) of non- and low-priority goods that reach the impacted area as part of these flows. This non- and low-priority component requires large amounts of scarce resources that are needed for other more critical tasks, which in turn negatively impact the flow of high-priority goods. Thus, it is important that organizations develop proper dynamic access control procedures to ensure that only high-priority content enters the impacted area, and that the non- and low-priority goods are adequately dealt with outside; that donation management plans are put in place so as to provide guidelines on how, what, when and where to donate and provide information that allows a match between needs and potential donors; that efforts are made to understand the dynamics of the priority of the goods; and understand the role of the media in influencing materiel convergence.[81–83]

SUPPORTING SYSTEMS

Another important aspect focuses on the assessment and development of supporting systems. Supporting systems include the transportation and communications infrastructure required for PD-HL operations as well as the technologies and systems that are required for the assessment of the conditions of the previous systems. In essence, it is important to develop and put in place technologies that allow for the quick assessment of the state of the transportation network and other critical infrastructures in a timely manner. This will allow updating procedures and response plans. In addition, it will contribute to the efficient and effective allocation of resources.[84,85]

It is important, however, that any supporting system is designed considering the interoperability with other systems and with the systems of other organizations, be they local or foreign. This is more important in terms of communication systems, and the development of self-contained systems that do not rely on the infrastructure of the impacted area, which may be severely damaged.[86,87]

CONCLUSION

This chapter focused on the specific characteristics of PD-HL. Specifically, the discussion briefly explained the challenges faced by PD-HL compared to its commercial counterpart. These challenges are exacerbated by the type of extreme event (i.e., disaster, catastrophes). In general, PD-HL operations are a complex process that must: (1) identify the needs of the impacted population and the needs of the response process itself; (2) cope with an extremely difficult local distribution process; (3)

account for a large number of intervening organizations; and (4) contend with a large flow of non- and low-priority supplies.

In order to improve the state of PD-HL, the chapter discusses a set of suggestions for improvement. As part of these, we argue that disaster response plans must be developed to account for a wide range of disasters and be robust enough to be scaled up or down depending on the actual need; that emphasis must be paid to the local distribution process and proactive plans be developed as to guarantee an efficient and effective process; that in order to achieve the PD-HL goals, an assessment of the needs and the development of strategies to secure the needed supplies is required; that the PD-HL process is severely impacted by the large influx of non- and low-priority goods which need to be dynamically contended with, by putting in place access control systems and understanding the role of the media; and, the development and implementation of supporting systems that allow for a rapid assessment of the infrastructure or other required systems.

ACKNOWLEDGMENTS

The material in this chapter is also in part based upon work supported by the authors under the following grant numbers. Multidisciplinary Center for Earthquake and Engineering Research (MCEER), New Technologies in Emergency Management, No. 00-10-81 and Measure of Resilience, No. 99-32-01; by special supplemental funding provided by the National Science Foundation, Public Entity Risk Institute No. 2001-70; University of Delaware Research Foundation; National Science Foundation 1123924, 1034627, 0624083, 0554949, 0510188, 1138643; and funding provided by the Disaster Research Center and the Earthquake Engineering Research Institute for quick response fieldwork. Any opinions, findings, and conclusions or recommendations expressed in this material are those of the authors and do not necessarily reflect the views of the funding agencies.

REFERENCES

1. Boin, A. 2009. The new world of crises and crisis management: Implications for policy-making and research. *Review of Policy Research*, 26(4), 367–377.
2. Holguín-Veras, J., Jaller, M., Wachtendorf, T. 2012. Comparative performance of alternative humanitarian logistic structures after the Port au Prince earthquake: ACEs, PIEs, and CANs. *Journal of Transportation Research Part A: Policy and Practice*. (In Print.)
3. Holguín-Veras, J., Taniguchi, E., Ferreira, F., Jaller, M., Thompson, R. 2012. The Tohoku disasters: Chief findings concerning the post-disaster humanitarian logistics response. *Journal of Transportation Research Part A: Policy and Practice*. (Under Review.)
4. Quarantelli, E.L. 2006. Catastrophes are different from disasters: Implications for crisis planning and managing drawn from Katrina. Understanding Katrina: Perspectives from the social sciences. *Social Science Research Council*. Retrieved from: http://understandingkatrina.ssrc.org/Quarantelli/.

5. Wachtendorf, T., Brown, B., Holguin-Veras, J. (Under Review). Catastrophe characteristics and their impact on critical supply chains: Problematizing materiel convergence and management following Hurricane Katrina.
6. Holguín-Veras, J., Jaller, M., Wassenhove, L.N.V., Pérez, N., Wachtendorf, T. 2012. On the unique features of humanitarian logistics. *Journal of Operations Management*. (In Print.)
7. Wachtendorf et al., under review, op. cit.
8. Holguín-Veras et al., 2012a, op. cit.
9. Holguín-Veras et al., 2012c, op. cit.
10. Kendra, J., Wachtendorf, T. 2003. Reconsidering convergence and converger legitimacy in response to the World Trade Center disaster, in L. Clarke (ed.) *Terrorism and Disaster: New Threats, New Ideas* (Research in Social Problems and Public Policy, Vol. 11). New York: Elsevier, pp. 97–122.
11. Fritz, C.E., Mathewson, J.H. 1957. *Convergent behavior: A disaster control problem*. Special Report for the Committee on Disaster Studies: Disaster Research Group. Washington, DC: National Academy of Sciences–National Research Council. Issue 9.
12. Holguín-Veras, J., Pérez, N., Ukkusuri, S., Wachtendorf, T., Brown, B. 2007. Emergency logistics issues affecting the response to Katrina: A Synthesis and Preliminary Suggestions for Improvement. *Transportation Research Record*. Washington, DC, 2022/2007: 76–82. DOI: 10.3141/2022-09.
13. Holguín-Veras, J., Jaller M. 2011. *Immediate Resource Requirements after Hurricane Katrina*, Natural Hazards Review (in press). http://dx.doi.org/10.1061/(ASCE)NH.1527-6996.0000068.
14. Holguín-Veras et al., 2012a, op. cit.
15. Holguín-Veras et al., 2012b, op. cit.
16. Holguín-Veras et al., 2012c, op. cit.
17. Jaller, M. 2011. *Resource Allocation Problems during Disasters: The Cases of Points of Distribution Planning and Material Convergence Control*. Civil and Environmental Engineering. Troy, Rensselaer Polytechnic Institute. PhD.
18. Holguín-Veras et al., 2007, op. cit.
19. Ibid.
20. Holguín-Veras, 2012a, op. cit.
21. Beamon, B. M. Humanitarian relief chains: Issues and challenges. *34th International Conference on Computers and Industrial Engineering*, November, 2004. San Francisco, CA, pp. 1–6.
22. Van Wassenhove, L. N. 2006. Humanitarian aid logistics: Supply chain management in high gear. *Journal of Operations Research Society*, 47, 475–489.
23. Holguín-Veras et al., 2012a, op. cit.
24. Ibid.
25. Pan American Health Organization 2001. *Humanitarian Supply Management and Logistics in the Health Sector*. Claude de Ville de Goyet (ed.). Washington, DC: Pan American Health Organization, 189p.
26. Holguín-Veras et al., 2007, op. cit.
27. Ibid.
28. Dynes, R., Quarantelli, E., Kreps, G. 1972. *A Perspective on Disaster Planning*. Report Series #11. Columbus: Columbus: Disaster Research Center, The Ohio State University.
29. Taylor, V., Quarantelli, E. 1976. *Some Needed Cross-Cultural Studies of Disaster Behavior*. Preliminary Paper # 28. Natural Hazards Symposium, Canberra, Australia. University of Delaware, Disaster Research Center, 5.

30. The Sphere Project 2011. 2011 *Sphere Handbook: Humanitarian Charter and Minimum Standards in Disaster Response*. Retrieved July 10, 2011, from www.sphereproject.org/
31. U.S. Army Corps of Engineers. 2010. *Florida POD Forecast Model*. Retrieved February 25, 2010, from http://www.swf.usace.army.mil/pubdata/ppmd/EmerMgt/PDF/FLPODFORECASTMODEL.pdf
32. Holguín-Veras, Jaller, 2011, op. cit.
33. Holguïn-Veras et al., 2012b, op. cit.
34. Holguín-Veras et al., 2012c, op. cit.
35. Ibid.
36. Holguín-Veras et al., 2012b, op. cit.
37. Suburban Emergency Management Project. 2008. *Wal-Mart Way in Disaster Preparedness/Response: Policy Implications*. Retrieved from: http://www.semp.us/publications/biot_reader.php?BiotID=569
38. The Federal Emergency Management Agency (FEMA). 2011. *Whole Community*. Retrieved from: http://www.fema.gov/about/wholecommunity.shtm
39. Holguín-Veras et al., 2012b, op. cit.
40. Ibid.
41. Fritz and Mathewson, op. cit.
42. Holguín-Veras et al., 2007, op. cit.
43. Hoguín-Veras et al., 2011, op. cit.
44. Holguín-Veras et al., 2012a, op. cit.
45. Holguín-Veras et al., 2012b, op. cit.
46. Holguín-Veras et al., 2012c, op. cit.
47. Jaller, 2011, op. cit.
48. Scanlon, T.J. 1991. *Convergence Revisited: A New Perspective on a Little Studied Topic*. Boulder, CO: Institute of Behavior Sciences, University of Colorado.
49. Fritz and Mathewson, op. cit.
50. Kendra and Wachtendorf, op. cit.
51. Jaller, 2011, op. cit.
52. Holguín-Veras et al., 2012a, op. cit.
53. Jaller, 2011, op. cit.
54. Ibid.
55. Holguín-Veras et al., 2012a, op. cit.
56. Telford, J., Cosgrave, J., Houghton, R. 2006. *Joint Evaluation of the International Response to the Indian Ocean Tsunami Synthesis Report*. Tsunami Evaluation Committee (TEC).
57. Ibid.
58. Wachtendorf, T. 2010. *When Push Comes to Shove: The Framing of Need in Disaster Relief Efforts*. International Research Committee on Disasters meeting, XVII World Congress of Sociology, International Sociological Association, Göteborg, Sweden.
59. Ibid.
60. Quarantelli, 2006, op. cit.
61. Ibid.
62. Cooper, A. 2010. *Haiti Appeals for Aid; Official Fears 100,000 Dead After Earthquake*. CNN World, January 13. Retrieved from: http://articles.cnn.com/2010-01-13/world/haiti.earthquake_1_haitian-president-rene-preval-earthquake-rubble?_s=PM:WORLD
63. U.S. Executive Office of the President. 2006. *The Federal Response to Hurricane Katrina: Lessons Learned*. Retrieved from: http://georgewbush-whitehouse.archives.gov/reports/katrina-lessons-learned/

64. Wachtendorf et al., 2010, op. cit.
65. Quarantelli, 2006, op. cit.
66. New York Times 2010a. Haiti lies in ruins; Grim search for untold dead. *New York Times*. Issue: January 13, 2010. Retrieved from: http://query.nytimes.com/gst/fullpage.html?res=9B01E7DC173BF937A25752C0A9669D8B63&scp=2&sq=haiti+earthquake+preval&st=nyt.
67. Wachtendorf et al. (under review), op. cit.
68. Quarantelli, 2006, op. cit.
69. Wachtendorf et al. (under review), op. cit.
70. Quarantelli, 2006, op. cit.
71. Wachtendorf et al. (under review), op. cit.
72. Quarantelli, 2006, op. cit.
73. Wachtendorf, 2010, op. cit.
74. Wachtendorf et al., (under review), op. cit.
75. Holguín-Veras et al., 2012b, op. cit.
76. Ibid.
77. Holguín-Veras, 2012c, op. cit.
78. Holguín-Veras and Jaller, 2011, op. cit.
79. Holguín-Veras et al., 2012a, op. cit.
80. Holguín-Veras et al., 2012b, op. cit.
81. Holguín-Veras et al., 2012a, op. cit.
82. Holguín-Veras et al., 2012b, op. cit.
83. Jaller, 2011, op. cit.
84. Holguín-Veras et al., 2012a, op. cit.
85. Holguín-Veras et al., 2012b, op. cit.
86. Holguín-Veras et al., 2012a, op. cit.
87. Holguín-Veras et al., 2012b, op. cit.

CHAPTER 7

Overview of Critical Infrastructure in Catastrophes

Matthew J. Levy and Rick Bissell

CONTENTS

Definitions 152
    Food, Water, and Shelter 153
    Logistics, Transportation, Communications, and Electricity 154
    Government and Finance 155
    Goods and Services 155
    Education and Research 156
    Public Health and Healthcare 156
Priorities 157
    First Echelon 157
    Second Echelon 158
    Third Echelon 159
    Fourth Echelon 160
Effects of Catastrophes on CI 160
    Resilience or Vulnerability: Socioeconomic and Cultural Impacts 161
    Two Cases: Infrastructure Collapse in Poor Haiti and Wealthy Japan 163
Strategies for Minimizing and Intervening in CI Failures in Catastrophes 164
    Mitigation 164
    Recognize Hypercomplexity 165
    Focus on Inviting Private Owners 166
    Recognize Professional Organizations 167
    Work with Non-Traditional Assets 167
    Recognize the Crucial Roles of Second-Echelon CI 167
Conclusions 168
References 168

It was not Hurricane Katrina that nearly decimated New Orleans, but rather a failure of the city's system of levees and dikes designed to protect the low-lying city from flooding. Likewise, the 2010, 7.0 magnitude earthquake in Haiti became a catastrophe because of the massive failure of housing, government ministry buildings, bridges, the Port-au-Prince port, and hospitals. The 2011, 9.0 magnitude earthquake and tsunami in Japan went from being a large disaster to a hypercomplex catastrophe when a series of nuclear power plants, an important part of the Japanese electrical power supply, failed and melted down, drawing away precious response resources and brain power from the needs of tsunami victims, and at the same time throwing regional power supplies into a tailspin. By contrast, the 8.8 magnitude earthquake and tsunami that hit Chile in 2010 only damaged some of the CI (critical infrastructure) Chileans depend on, and as a result the resources required for response were manageable within the country's skills and resources.

This chapter is about the effects of earthquakes, hurricanes, or other hazards on CI, and how the magnitude, scope, and severity of these effects, in turn, determine what is considered a disaster, and what becomes a catastrophe. Kirsch et al.[1] document how crucial hospitals in Chile were able to keep operating, even though sustaining significant damage by using their backup systems. In Chapter 15 of this book, Kirsch shows how the massive failure of hospitals in Haiti threw the medical and health portion of the response to that earthquake into the tragic reality in which, even with significant international assistance, the disaster-affected population did not receive the medical care they needed. This was a catastrophe. In this chapter, we define what CI is, the roles it plays in resisting or responding to disasters, and how catastrophes affect CI. We conclude the chapter with a discussion of some strategies for improving CI's resilience to disasters, as well as some strategies for responding to lost infrastructure in catastrophes. However, please note that entire books and considerable government planning documents have been written about managing CI in disasters. The role of this chapter is not to repeat or argue with conceptual or "how-to" publications related to CI in disasters, but rather to consider CI within the catastrophe scenario, and suggest adjustments or strategy changes that may contribute to improving the CI response to catastrophes. You will find that this chapter and Chapter 6 on logistics, while not overlapping, are closely related to each other.

DEFINITIONS

The concept of Critical Infrastructure (often referred to as CI) represents those elemental functions and services of a society that are essential for modern life as we know it. CI is often viewed as the virtual or physical systems and assets that are so vital that their incapacitation, destruction, or failure would be debilitating to a region or nation. Perhaps a more effective way to define CI would be as the vital services and systems necessary for society to function. Key Resources can be thought as those central resources (public or private) that are essential to the minimal operation of a government. At face value, it would appear that there is some ambiguity in conceptualizing "what" would be "critical" or "key" and to "whom." This largely depends on pre-disaster states of infrastructure and society's level of dependence on these resources. In addition, to their vulnerability to natural and human made disasters, the very nature of CIs make them high profile targets for intentional acts of destruction and terrorism.

Basic examples of CI are described in the following paragraphs. Of note, an underdeveloped region's paucity of a pre-event CI does not preclude it from suffering the sequela of not having specific CI following a catastrophic event. For example, a developing nation's pre-event lack of a safe drinking water supply system does not make that nation any less susceptible the consequences of not having clean drinking water (hepatitis, cholera, chemical contamination) following a catastrophic event.

Food, Water, and Shelter

Often considered to be core elements of any human society, food, water, and shelter are considered to be of the most basic needs of all human beings. As such, critical shortages of these resources have long been associated with being the genesis of complex humanitarian emergencies. Access to clean water goes hand in hand with a system to eliminate dirty water. An intact water supply system capable of producing potable water fit for consumption, combined with an effective sanitary wastewater management system that isolates sewage and contaminants from the freshwater sources is often heralded as cornerstone of any effective public health infrastructure.[2] Frequent monitoring of the water supply network to ensure the safety of drinking water is paramount. Alternative strategies for the acquisition of fresh drinking water in catastrophic situations include rain water collection, desalination capabilities, and point of consumption multistage filtration devices. Management of wastewater includes having redundancies in the ability to channel and divert sewage. Such examples include gravity-based systems as well as pumping facilities with intrinsic failsafes including one-way and automatic shutoff valves and redundant fuel sources. Another consideration for sanitation is the porosity of the soil upon which "camps" might be set up. The Goma camps that were set up for refugees from the Rwandan genocide were placed on non-porous volcanic soils, resulting in massive outbreaks of cholera and other gastrointestinal diseases as soon as population size and contamination loads increased, claiming thousands of lives.[3,4]

A sustainable food supply system must have redundancies in ability to both produce and distribute foods. Fundamental issues surrounding food supply include mills able to process and store sufficient quantities of grains, epidemiologic surveillance of livestock and alternative means of distributing food throughout the population.

Dwelling structures vary largely throughout the world and are directly related to availability of construction materials, building codes and geophysical limitations of the land itself. There is a well-established link between these factors and the subsequent failures of structures following a catastrophic event. The clearest examples of this include the widespread collapse of structures following the earthquakes in Haiti and Pakistan. Once rendered homeless, short- and long-term provisions to shelter the displaced must account for a variety of issues including individuals with chronic health conditions, multigenerational families, pets, and domestic animals as well as the special needs of the very young and very old.

Logistics, Transportation, Communications, and Electricity

Everyday logistics resources are easily taken for granted in industrialized nations and include those that allow for the facilitation of transportation, telecommunications and a stable, reliable electrical power grid. Transportation includes the movement of both persons and goods and encompasses modalities of land, sea, and air transport. Ground-based transportation includes both rail and roadway-based systems (railways, highways, bridges, tunnels, and pipelines). In addition, mass transit systems native to most major metropolitan areas around the world are the primary means of movement for a large numbers of people. Failures effecting ground-based transportation systems include but are not limited to structural failures, fuel shortages, and mechanical failures. Sea-based modes of transportation remain the method of choice for the intercontinental movement of goods and bulk resources. Ports and harbors serve as the functional interface for the movement of these goods in and out of a region and are equally vulnerable to the failures of other ground-based resources. Air-based movement of people has revolutionized global transport over the last 100 years. Air-based movement of people and resources remains the most costly, however, it is also often the fastest means of moving victims and refugees out of a disaster area and essential goods and personnel into a region struck by catastrophe. Aviation resources themselves pose their own challenges and require significant logistical support for safe and effective operations. Large aircrafts require significant runway space for takeoff and landings, quantities of fuel are needed to sustain operations, as well as other aviation support resources to ensure the safe operation of aircraft.

A reliable and stable electrical power grid is a functional cornerstone in modern society. Power grids themselves are subject to overload and failure. The large, highly specialized switches, transformers, and high tension transmission lines that comprise a power grid are intrinsically vulnerable to failure. Replacement parts and resources are of limited supply and require specialized manufacturing techniques. Electricity generation itself is a source of much consternation. Fossil fuels and other finite resources will be limited and replenishment a challenge, particularly if the transportation infrastructure fails. Experts agree that diversification of electrical power production resources is the most robust way to avoid this problem. Nuclear power has long been an area of debate and discourse. Proponents of nuclear power maintain that it is a reliable means of effectively producing large quantities of sustainable electricity without the use of fossil fuels. Opponents of nuclear power have long emphasized its potential for disaster as a result of uncontrolled reactions or "melt downs," environmental contamination and ecosystem destruction, and the ever-present concern of an intentional attack or isotope theft. Indeed, recent history has validated some of these concerns. In the wake of a natural disaster—an earthquake and tsunami in Japan that led to a cooling system failure and structural compromise of several nuclear reactors, resulting in one of modern history's worst engineering catastrophes.

Telecommunications and information technology present another aspect of the infrastructure of modern life and provide many direct and indirect benefits to society. Directly, telecommunications (wired or wireless) and information technology infrastructures including optical fiber backbones and data switching centers serve as the conduit for routing vital voice and data traffic. Indirectly, a salient benefit of having advanced data and information systems is the revolution of social networks. Social networks represent the ultimate nexus of information systems and human behavior and have already proven their worth in time of disaster and crisis, allowing those in affected areas to provide real-time "status" updates to the rest of the world. However, the more dependent we have become on having continuous connectivity and broadband services, the more vulnerable we are service interruptions due to network outages, power failures, and intentional denial of service attacks and system overload.

Government and Finance

The continuity of government (COG) services and leadership positions at all levels is essential to ensuring that resources under the command and control of the government can be swiftly mobilized and effectively utilized to maximize aid to those affected most by a catastrophic disaster. To accomplish this, COG and Continuity of Operations (COOP) must include a variety of factors. Strategies to maintain law and order and emergency services start with local emergency response elements but quickly cascade into complex often hard to navigate issues including use of military personnel and resources in noncombat domestic situations, specific plans for the corrections system management of the incarcerated and the institution of martial law. Key government leaders themselves are sometimes considered a part of the CI and require designation of alternate personnel and succession plans. Government buildings and structures should have necessary engineering features (seismic design features, wind ratings, blast energy dispersal) to help minimize the potential for structural failure. In addition, these structures should possess the flexibility to allow for multipurpose use including sheltering of personnel and as alternate command and control sites. The financial system of a nation itself is considered a CI. Banks, reserves, and stock and securities exchanges must maintain redundancies in transaction systems. Adequate reserves of cash and precious metals represent some of the necessary physical components to ensure an effective monetary system, whereas the ability to enact public policy in the form of economic instruments (subsidies, etc.) can aid in mitigation efforts of CIs and ultimately serve to decrease the financial burden of a catastrophe.

Goods and Services

Goods, services, and manufacturing represent another consideration to not only a financial system's sustainability following a catastrophic event, but themselves can have direct roles in recovery by being able to provide needed essential items. Illustrating a true public/private partnership, one example of this would be a brewery modifying its canning and distribution system to package and distribute clean, potable water to those in need. The pharmaceutical industry's ability to produce essential life-saving medications makes it too an element of CI.

Education and Research

Both public and private educational and research facilities are often overlooked as CI. Schools can be used as shelters for displaced populations. In addition, the reopening of schools following a major event has been well documented as key to a region's successful recovery. Institutions of higher education and applied research possess equipment and personnel with specialty knowledge in the sciences and engineering (see Figure 7.1).

Public Health and Healthcare

The very nature of the healthcare and public health systems make them perhaps one of the best examples of CI. Although healthcare delivery models vary around the world, the ability to deliver organized and coordinated healthcare to a population is essential to response and recovery from catastrophic events. Providing healthcare requires appropriate facilities including acute care hospitals, long-term care facilities, psychiatric facilities, primary care clinics, and offices as well as laboratories and imaging facilities with necessary logistics and support infrastructure (water, generators, information technology, etc.). Healthcare personnel who are able to render care, possibly under austere conditions for extended periods of time, as well as the ample support assets (supplies,

Figure 7.1 Chemistry Department Building, University of Concepción, Chile after 27 February 2010 earthquake. The building's antiseismic frame was designed to withstand large earthquakes, and did. However, internal storage of chemicals was not secured, some fell and mixed, and the building was gutted by flames. (Photo courtesy of Rick Bissell.)

medications, vaccinations) are needed to ensure the delivery of healthcare following a catastrophe. A public health system with ongoing prevention programs (TB, malaria, cholera, HIV, etc.), as well as epidemiologic surveillance mechanisms in place capable of identifying emerging infectious diseases and prevention of epidemics, is central toward a population's long-term health and recovery following a catastrophe.

PRIORITIES

Each nation, and for that matter, jurisdictions within nations, may develop their own set of priorities for infrastructure protection and response. In the United States, much of the federal government's priority setting has been focused on assets that could be targeted by terrorists, or which are needed for continued government functioning after an attack.[5] Since the release of the newer Presidential Policy Directive-8, the federal government is moving toward a more flexible emphasis on the most likely disasters (i.e., hurricanes, tornadoes, earthquakes) or catastrophes. Not every country or jurisdiction is likely to have the same concern about terrorism, so to a certain extent, their CI protection and priorities will reflect local circumstances. For example, it is not unusual for a country that depends heavily on tourism for income to consider the infrastructure that supports tourism, that is, transportation, lodging, food services, and security to be extremely high priorities. For the sake of this discussion, we will focus on priorities that keep people alive and reduce suffering, and provide the tools and materiel necessary for rapid and effective response and recovery operations. We do not assume in this discussion of priorities that government is always the predominant provider of direct services to survivors.

Because survivors of a catastrophe have many needs simultaneously, it does not make sense to list all CI priorities in a single numerical progression of priorities from first to last, but rather we think of priorities as occupying four groupings or echelons. Each echelon represents a relative level of priority, recognizing that within each echelon the priorities change in time, and according to circumstances. Here are the generic catastrophe-related priority echelons, as we see them. Specific positions within each echelon will vary widely by circumstances. They are also meant as models, not all-inclusive listings.

   a. First echelon: water, food, shelter, healthcare
   b. Second echelon: transportation, communications, energy, law enforcement, monetary system
   c. Third echelon: government structures, IT, pharmaceuticals
   d. Fourth echelon: education, industry, research, and so on

First Echelon

Water, food, shelter, and healthcare are all undisputed priorities for basic survival. However, in many kinds of catastrophes, as compared to disasters, they become *even more important* because of the reality that survivors of a catastrophe are far less likely to have access to organized services that will provide them with basic necessities within the conventionally planned for 72–96 hours following an event. The relative importance of each item within this echelon is completely context-specific. For example, in an earthquake in a cold environment in which there is massive shelter loss, but in which there is still retrievable water and food, the provision of warm shelter and healthcare might be highest in the first 36–48 hours, and then the priority of water and food may rise as shelter needs become fulfilled ... or people expire from the cold. The same earthquake in a desert community, however, might prioritize water over food and shelter.

Because the context of a specific event is so important in catastrophe response planning, a general plan done at a high level of governance (i.e., state, province or nation) will not meet the needs of localities. This means that a core component of catastrophic disaster preparedness is the concentration on the need for local jurisdictions to participate by drawing up their own plans, which should include two components: a plan for self-sufficiency for at least a week, and a plan for rapidly integrating whatever kind of assistance can come in from the outside (volunteers, private voluntary organizations, commercial companies, and government). Likewise, the medium to higher levels of government (state, province, nation) need to develop into their plans specific variations that are in consonance with the plans and realities at the lower levels. In Chapter 11 (Planning) of this book, there is a description of the Catastrophic Planning Program in the United States, which is an attempt to try to take this "bottom-up" approach. The experience with this approach to date in the United States, focusing mostly notably on the New Madrid Seismic Zone, shows that this process is time-consuming and can be expensive, but it rewards all levels of government with a much clearer understanding of what their requirements will be, and fosters considerable development of local coordination and interdependencies.[6] The problem with traditional "top-down" planning, which is less expensive and easier, is that it is essentially incapable of capturing the context-related information that is really needed to meet the needs of survivors of catastrophes. Note also that "top-down" approaches intrinsically limit the autonomy (and perhaps even responsibility) of localities. This is in direct contrast to the needs of localities for survival on their own for a longer periods of time than is typically the case of disasters. Water, food, shelter, and healthcare all consist of, or are supplied, in normal times, by infrastructure that can be destroyed or interrupted by catastrophes.

Second Echelon

The second echelon includes such assets and functions as transportation, communications, energy, law enforcement (security), and the monetary system. All of these are aspects of the CI that are commonly hard-hit in catastrophes. This poses a major challenge, because these very same assets/functions are necessary for a successful response to meeting the needs represented in the first echelon. All of these functions are of crucial importance, but, as is the case in the first echelon, their relative importance within the echelon is related to the local realities of the community or jurisdiction in need of assistance. For example, transportation resources are always a high priority, yet communities that have a robust transportation system with few bridges or other vulnerabilities may need less attention to the transportation component of the response, whereas communities with a high transportation vulnerability index will require that finding solutions to transportation assets and organizations needs to be a top priority in meeting the first echelon needs of the population. In populations with a history of criminal activity or violence, security will need to be a top priority in order to ensure that supplies and services safely reach their destinations and can operate freely. Likewise, the type of event has an impact on the need for security. For example, while it is a given that a terrorism-based catastrophe would have security as a high priority, it is also true for a catastrophe in which a specific kind of life-saving or live-sustaining resource is available, but only in limited supply. This could be the case in a pandemic catastrophe when a vaccine or effective antimicrobial drug becomes available but in insufficient quantity to meet all of the need. In such a case, police protection of drug storage, transportation, and distribution sites would be urgent. Communications resources underlie the coordination of the application of all the other resources, yet, their relative priority within the second echelon would depend much on the type of event and the resilience of the local communications infrastructure. For example, a pandemic would be unlikely to seriously undermine communications assets. Access to the monetary system may not be something that is needed on day one, but it would not be long before people would need to obtain access to their funds. Planning for the use of the second echelon assets, as in the case of the first, will need to be context-specific and flexible. It is particularly important to realize that all such resources will be in short supply in a catastrophe, making it all the more important that resources be matched to expected needs so that they stretch out as far as possible.

Third Echelon

The third echelon includes assets that enable the second echelon's assets and infrastructure to be successful. They may not be needed on day one, but will become very important shortly thereafter, particularly because the response to a catastrophe requires so much more coordination than is typically the case of disasters. One of the major impediments to a coordinated local response to the 2010 earthquake in Haiti (see Chapter 15 for more details) was the fact that the major government ministry buildings collapsed, taking with them many of the government employees who would have been expected to help direct the emergency operations. And ... it did not stop there. The headquarters of the United Nations development assistance operations building also collapsed, killing the same UN experts who would be expected to conduct a needs assessment, communicate those needs, and coordinate the incoming international assistance.[7] There was no existing COG or COOP plan for functioning without either the Haitian national government or the UN personnel. As the response went forward, it became obvious, as would be the case in any modern catastrophe response, that computerized data (IT) storage and retrieval services would be needed. This is a third echelon asset that should be a part of all catastrophe preparedness planning, including the potential for specialized resources to construct or design new applications to meet needs specific to the particular catastrophe. Procurement and acquisition of these resources in a just-in-time manner is less than optimal and guarantees inefficient practice. There are a number of other third echelon assets that need to be considered, represented here by pharmaceuticals as an example. These are assets/functions/supplies or institutions that will be needed for the response to be effective, and which rise in importance after the first day or two of the response.

Fourth Echelon

The fourth echelon contains resources that are not necessarily needed in the first few days, or maybe even weeks of a response, but which underpin both the ability to construct a good pre-event plan, and which are important for the recovery period. Many national response plans may not directly mention the need for research and education, but they play an important role in guiding the development of effective response and recovery programs, and, as institutions, schools have been shown to have a stabilizing effect in the recovery of disaster-affected communities.[8,9] As such, schools are part of a community's infrastructure, and should be included in recovery plans as a key component of resettling the community. This is particularly important in catastrophes, in which a community needs to restore infrastructure that meets the population's basic needs, if the community is to avoid the massive outmigration that is common in catastrophes (see Chapter 12).

The reality of all four of these infrastructure priority echelons is that, in the case of catastrophes, there is no "one size fits all" formula that will work, as is assumed in some disaster plans. Catastrophes result in a higher level of complexity, a higher level of needs, and longer dependency periods than is typically the case in "regular" disasters, and the configuration of those needs is tightly related to the peculiarities of the event and the communities involved. The planning process must take into account these peculiarities and prepare for the utilization of and replacement of CI that protects the lives and well-being of survivors. Because catastrophes severely damage or destroy so much of our physical and/or non-physical infrastructure, survivors are likely to find themselves forced to live in an austere environment in which one has to care for one's own basic requirements: food, water, shelter, sanitation, protection from others, and healthcare ... or at least some portion of these things. And, for much longer than would be the case in disasters.

EFFECTS OF CATASTROPHES ON CI

Let us look for a few moments at a couple of the more likely types of catastrophes and see how they affect CI.

Earthquakes are fairly common and the infrastructure effects are well known. Human-made structures collapse, including housing, business, educational, manufacturing, and healthcare structures; transportation resources such as bridges, roads, railroads, airports, and maritime ports; communications resources such as hard-wired telephones as well as wireless communications that depend on transmitters and receivers; power supplies such as electricity, natural gas, and other piped hydrocarbons; and water supplies for consumption, sanitation, and industry. Potable water can also be contaminated when adjacent underground water and sewage pipes break. As is the case in most disasters, the infrastructure resources just mentioned do not stand alone. The availability of electrical and hydrocarbon-based power supplies, for example, is key to the functioning of other components of infrastructure such as communications, water pumping, transportation, heating/air conditioning of shelters, food preparation, and many aspects of healthcare. In disasters, it is fairly common to overcome many of these deficits fairly quickly by way of bringing in working replacements from outside of the disaster zone. The problem with catastrophes is that we cannot depend on quickly obtaining replacements, due to the size and complexity of the event. For example, the New Madrid earthquake scenario in the United States foresees destruction in a 5–8 state region, with extensive loss of key transportation and communications infrastructure. If the bridges crossing the Mississippi River are down for 200 miles of the river, there is no easy or quick work-around ... especially because many of the major roads' land-based bridges are also likely to be damaged or destroyed. A key point is that you *need infrastructure in order to repair infrastructure*; without transportation of construction materials and without communications for coordination and reporting, it is extremely difficult to repair the very infrastructural components that everything else depends on.

A high-mortality *pandemic* would not destroy the physical infrastructure, but rather would (or could) severely damage or limit the human infrastructure upon which almost all of us depend. By this we mean institutions such as security, healthcare, banking services, energy provision, transportation services, maintenance of water and sanitation services, food distribution, and so on. Chapter 13 provides more information on the pandemic scenario. For this present discussion, let us assume that a certain significant percentage of workers will not show up for work for fear of becoming exposed, or transmitting exposure to their families.[10,11] In addition, jurisdictions may enforce extreme isolation policies that prohibit crossing jurisdictional boundaries in order to limit opportunities for microbial transmission. The lack of workers then leads to a lack of services, which could conceivably lead to loss of law and order, loss of food delivery, and the conversion of a microbiological disaster into a full multi-system catastrophe.

When dealing with the effects of catastrophes on CI, the effects themselves are more important than the type of event. To help summarize some of the types of effects that responders and survivors will need to contend with, please see Table 7.1.

Resilience or Vulnerability: Socioeconomic and Cultural Impacts

Of course most events that reach catastrophe proportions affect both the physical and non-physical (or institutional) infrastructures. The challenge is vastly more complicated than in a disaster in which new supplies and new personnel can be relatively easily brought into the disaster zone. The wide geographic area affected and the lack of local human resources to fulfill institutional needs place

Table 7.1 Some Effects of Catastrophes on CI

Item	Effects
Energy supply	Loss of power plants, loss of electrical transmission lines and transformers, loss of refineries and pipelines, loss of transportation for delivery of energy products, loss of energy distribution control centers.
Potable water	Loss of above-ground and below-ground piping, loss of pumping capacity, loss of water treatment plants, contamination of water supplies, loss of primary sources (in flooding or dam breaks), inability to deliver by truck if road/bridges are blocked.
Shelter	Loss of housing and alternative shelters. Loss of retrievable construction materials. Inability to obtain supplies and construction crews with tools. Inability to shelter large populations safely for very long in large open facilities.
Transportation	Loss of bridges, roads, railroads, ports/docking, and airports. Blockage of transportation waterways. Loss of transportation personnel. Blockage of boundary crossing by quarantine or social distancing.
Healthcare	Loss of hospitals to damage, or to lack of energy, water, supplies, or personnel. Loss of labs and inability to transport specimens. Loss of electronic medical records. Loss of primary care sites and/or their providers. Inability to transport medications and other medical supplies. Inability to conduct useful needs assessments due to lack of communications, transportation, and energy.
Food supply	Major difficulties in delivering food due to loss of transportation or travel restrictions. Loss of refrigeration/food spoilage.
Monetary system	Loss of electricity means widespread loss of electronic transfers, which are the base of fund distribution, loss of ATM services for consumers, loss of personnel and facilities.
Security/law enforcement	Loss of personnel, mobility, and some communications. Loss of confidence.
Information	Loss of access to electronically stored or transmitted information, and/or lack of ability to transmit or receive the same.

the survivors in a position in which they cannot expect significant outside assistance for much longer than the 3 days that the U.S. emergency management system has traditionally told its population to be prepared to survive on their own. In many Western societies, many members of the population have not learned how to improvise shelter, seek and purify water, provide first aid, obtain and utilize alternative sources of food, and set up sanitation such that disease is kept to a minimum. Populations living in largely rural self-sufficiency environments in some of the poorer countries of the world would be more likely to adjust well to post-catastrophe conditions than many from wealthier countries, who have lost or never developed certain survival skills. Vulnerability is not always what would be calculated for disasters!

The issue of socially determined resilience and vulnerability is big in catastrophes, and hard to generalize because of peculiarities in the way resources are distributed in different societies. In much of the industrialized "Western" world, those who have higher levels of education and money may be less likely to be badly hit than those with lower levels of education and income, because of their increased awareness of how to escape danger,[12] their superior access to transportation, and their probability of living and working in structurally secure buildings. Within the richer countries, the wealthy portion of the population may represent resilience, at least until such time that they no longer have access to their resources. The *urban* poor may represent vulnerability, due to their relative inability to rapidly evacuate, their comparatively poor access to information, and their lack of the kinds of self-sufficiency skills that the rural poor are more likely to have.

Infrastructure has a role in this vulnerability/resiliency pattern, in that the wealthier portion of the population is more likely to live and work in areas in which there are good roads, sturdy buildings, and access to medical and security resources, whereas the opposite is more likely to be true of the poorer areas, with infrastructure that is less sturdy, less available, and less protected. Recognizing this, responders to catastrophes should consider first focusing on the more vulnerable communities.

Two Cases: Infrastructure Collapse in Poor Haiti and Wealthy Japan

Infrastructure collapse is a significant danger in both wealthy and poor countries, and can constitute the difference between a disaster and a catastrophe. The 2010 earthquake that struck Haiti near its capital and principle urban area is an example of almost total infrastructure collapse. In a country in which "substantial" buildings were designed to withstand hurricanes and not earthquakes, and the buildings of the poor were cobbled together as best as each family could afford with no construction standards or building inspectors, a huge percentage of the regional buildings collapsed.[13] This included everything from national government buildings, to commercial buildings, hospitals, police stations, prisons, the docks in the harbor, and vast numbers of private homes. Bridges also fell or were badly damaged, but the largest impediment to the transportation system was that roads were covered with debris from collapsed buildings and hillsides.[14] What piped water supply existed prior to the earthquake was destroyed. Electrical power transmission lines were damaged or destroyed in many localities. The buildings that fell, killing an estimated 230,000 people,[15] made the earthquake a catastrophe, before even considering the other infrastructure failures. The lack of passable roads, electricity, water, health-care facilities, delivery of food and security made the response to this catastrophe extremely difficult and far from adequate, despite the inputs of more than 50 countries and more than 100 non-governmental organizations. At the time that this chapter is being completed, 2 years after the earthquake in Haiti, much of the infrastructure that was damaged or destroyed has been only partially replaced, at best. Without real infrastructure improvement in the reconstruction process, Haiti will remain as vulnerable as before.

Japan is one of the wealthiest countries in the world with superb modern infrastructure that would be the dream of many countries. Its roads and bridges are of modern anti-seismic design and are well kept. Most private and public buildings are built to high-level earthquake-resistant standards. The subways and "Bullet trains" are reliable, clean, and attractive. The country has excellent communications and data connections, both wired and wireless, all powered up by an elaborate system of power plants, many of which are nuclear. In many low-lying coastal areas, significant tsunami barriers are constructed, and both earthquake and tsunami alert systems are present throughout Japan. As you will read in Chapter 15, even with all the care invested in Japan's infrastructure, the 2011 earthquake and tsunami surpassed design standards, resulting in massive coastal tsunami-driven flooding and the loss of nearly 20,000 lives. What converted this already difficult disaster into a catastrophe, as described by Kiriu (Chapter 15), was the insufficient protection of a key piece of infrastructure, the nuclear power plants at Fukushima Daiichi. The tsunami cut off fuel supplies to the emergency generators needed to keep cooling water flowing over the nuclear fuel rods, eventually leading to meltdowns, hydrogen explosions, and radiological contamination of surrounding air, land, and water. This nuclear plant emergency drew critical attention and resources away from the emergency response for several hundred thousand survivors, and put the overall combined situation into catastrophe dynamics. In both the Haitian and Japanese examples portrayed in these short descriptions, we see that infrastructure collapse led to a catastrophe, regardless of the wealth of the country, and contributed significantly to the barriers that interfered with the processes of emergency response: coordinated search and rescue, provision of first aid and trauma care, provision of safe shelter, water, and food, and evacuation to safer places.

STRATEGIES FOR MINIMIZING AND INTERVENING IN CI FAILURES IN CATASTROPHES

Mitigation

Insurance companies, engineers, scholars, and countless government guidance documents throughout the world point out that mitigation is effective, cost-effective, and a primary method of minimizing massive human suffering and financial losses when the earth shakes, the winds roar, waters flood previously dry land, and wildfires burn.[16–18] And yet, we persist in short-term thinking and short-term cost-cutting. The most important strategy for minimizing the contribution of CI failures to the actual destruction in a disaster (i.e., building and bridge collapses) as well as complicating the dynamics of response (i.e., communications outages, widespread loss of electricity, and other power sources, transportation blockages, loss of healthcare facilities) is to no longer turn a blind eye to mitigation as a primary strategy (see Figure 7.2). The benefits of this strategy will serve the public even if a given area is never subjected to catastrophic disasters. In the United States, core aspects of our transportation, water supply and communications grids are judged by engineers to be at high risk of failure *even without the external forces of an earthquake or hurricane.*[19] At its core, this is not an emergency management issue, but one of societal priorities, but it is extremely important to the attempt to minimize the occurrence of catastrophes as well as the difficulties of dealing with them when they do occur. As Gilbert White was fond of pointing out, emergency managers and disaster responders are more familiar with

Figure 7.2 Value of mitigation. This photo, taken in Concepción, Chile after the 27 February 2010 earthquake shows an older, unmitigated bridge in the foreground, with collapsed sections. The newer bridge in the background survived the giant earthquake undamaged and served as a vital transportation link for the response. (Photo courtesy of Rick Bissell.)

the consequences of poor mitigation than is the general public, and thus need to play an important role in raising societal consciousness of the priority of mitigation.[20]

At the time that this book is being written, the United States is investing millions of dollars in catastrophe preparedness programs, yet very little attention is paid, in terms of policy, funding or activity, to the need to substantially reinforce CI facilities as part of a coordinated national policy to reduce our vulnerability to catastrophes.[21] Likewise, Japan let decades of low tsunami occurrence lull them into thinking that coastal nuclear power plants had sufficient back-up systems, and this is in a country that has a very high degree of investment into general anti-seismic design. The strategy of prioritizing mitigation efforts for CI must be multi-disciplinary, covering (at a minimum) engineers, emergency managers, earth scientists (geography, geology, seismology, meteorology), health scientists, insurance organizations, and policy specialists. Even for countries as poor as Haiti is, when infrastructure is replaced, it should be done so in such a way that reflects a strong priority for mitigating future catastrophes. Mitigation research should also be a strong priority; the example of the U.S. National Science Foundation's long-term funding of the Earthquake Engineering Research Institute to conduct infrastructure failure research around the world sets a standard for other nations to follow.

Recognize Hypercomplexity

Hypercomplexity is one of the defining characteristics of catastrophes, and a key element of the massive difficulty in responding effectively to the needs of survivors.

And yet, it is barely recognized in the planning documents of many leading countries. The United Nations is working with the phenomenon of hypercomplexity in its cluster response design, which needs refining based on feedback from its use in Haiti and other places. However, the UN version is probably not exactly what individual countries need.

Hypercomplexity derives from the multitude of organizations, agencies, and individuals who all together create the highly networked system of services and goods that provide for the needs of all of us in twenty-first century societies. Because our societies are so networked, that is to say, that almost all the providers of our basic services of energy, hydrocarbon fuels, communications, data storage and retrieval, potable water, transportation, security, and food delivery depend on other organizations to deliver goods and services that enable their own work, it is fallacious to think that a single hierarchical decision-making mechanism will be able to conceive of all that needs to be done, nor know who does it. In a period of catastrophe response, there is insufficient time to start data gathering to figure out who can provide what necessary inputs to meet basic needs in a damaged infrastructure, or perhaps, even to figure out how damaged the infrastructure is. After all, the reality of multiple players in the provision of services and goods is mirrored by the reality of the multiplicity of players whose capabilities may be damaged by the catastrophe.

For these reasons, we think that a primary focus in the process of catastrophe preparedness needs to be re-thinking and reorganizing the way information is gathered, decisions are made, and functions are distributed in the response period. Most of the providers of goods and services in countries that have market-based economies are not government agencies, but rather private entities or private–public partnerships (i.e., utility service providers). Catastrophe planning needs to begin with a design for full integration of public, private, and scientific entities into the planning process as well as the response process. This may be some kind of "cloud" system, but it must include flexibility as one of its main attributes, because of the impossibility of predicting exactly what the needs and circumstances will be in the next mass emergency. The French use what they call the "rapid reflection force."[22] The complexity of catastrophes can only be tamed if it is recognized in the response design.

Focus on Inviting Private Owners

In line with the previous strategy, recognizing that a large percentage of CI is privately owned, emergency managers need to develop effective and consistent ways of involving private infrastructure owners in the planning process, as well as in drills and other evaluations. Some of the potential barriers to doing this successfully are the fears private owners may have over loss of control, or liability issues. These issues may be addressed, with legal counsel, by the development of memoranda of understanding between government and private entities. Another tactic is to develop legislation that serves to protect private owners who participate in disaster and catastrophe preparedness and response activities.

Recognize Professional Organizations

Many countries have professional organizations that have in their membership experts on a variety of issues that come to the surface in disasters and catastrophes. Government emergency management agencies cannot begin to have the level or variety of expertise that can be found in such professional organizations. It is too late to begin looking for expertise during a response; such relationships and operating agreements should be developed in the planning phase, and where possible the relevant professional organizations should be encouraged to participate in planning for catastrophe response. Such organization may provide key members for the "rapid reflection force" (to use the French term). In Chapter 15, we will see that one of the Japanese professional organizations, the Japanese Medical Association, formed a nationwide Japan Medical Assistance Team that in the aftermath of the 2011 earthquake and tsunami, provided key healthcare services needed by survivors after the Disaster Medical Assistance Teams left, and before regular healthcare services could be reinstated.

Work with Non-Traditional Assets

There are numerous stories of WalMart and other commercial powerhouses with excellent logistics capabilities, being stopped from delivering needed supplies to people affected by Hurricane Katrina because they did not have needed permits or government recognition. There are also stories of successful deliveries of water by Anheuser Busch and other drink producers to hurricane disaster sites in Florida. The truth is that many high-volume commercial organizations are far more agile and effective with complex delivery logistics than governments are, and they own their own resources. Catastrophe planning needs to focus on the goals of getting the right materiel and personnel to the right place at the right time, and if commercial organizations can do a better job than government, they should become invited partners who have specified roles, responsibilities, and liabilities. Government roads and transportation emergency managers might work with commercial service providers to make sure that roads these providers would use would receive priority status. Major privately owned IT and communications businesses represent a huge available cadre of expertise with the kind of flexibility to reach far beyond any "fixes" government-based agencies could provide.

Recognize the Crucial Roles of Second-Echelon CI

Earlier in this chapter we identified echelons of CI. In the second echelon are transportation, communications, energy, law enforcement, and the monetary system. The reality in catastrophe response is that the first echelon (water supply, food supply, shelter, and healthcare) cannot be addressed without addressing the second echelon, because these components of CI provide the services and logistical wherewithal that enables the provision of those services and supplies that meet survivors' most basic needs.

CONCLUSIONS

CI is comprised of a large number of often-interrelated physical assets and human institutions/services that provide for the basic needs of the population of any civilization, and which are thus of critical importance in responding to, and recovering from disasters and catastrophes. Poor design and maintenance of physical infrastructure can conspire to convert some disasters into catastrophes.

Knowing how to repair or replace infrastructure is covered in other literature. Knowing how to apply that knowledge in a catastrophe is the concentration here, and it is clear that catastrophes present a different constellation of challenges than is typically the case in disasters. The priorities and planning parameters may be quite different from disasters, requiring more attention to the specific conditions of the populations and communities that are being planned for. There may be a variety of ways of doing this kind of planning, but the "bottom-up" approach being tried out in the New Madrid Seismic Zone of the United States is one model worth looking at.

As is also the case in disasters, the mitigation of infrastructure damage should be a primary focus in the pre-event period. This is particularly important when considering catastrophes and the longer expected replacement time for CI. In the United States, a significant proportion of the nation's physical CI has been assessed by engineering specialists as being defective or at risk of failure, which increases the potential for disasters to convert into catastrophes. Similar conditions may exist in other countries.

One important message that emergency managers can take away from this discussion of CI and catastrophes is that they need to estimate how vulnerable their jurisdiction is to failures in a catastrophe. With that in mind, they then may need to re-orient public training so that people are urged to prepare themselves for a potentially long interval before outside help arrives, during which time they would need to provide for their own survival in an austere environment.

REFERENCES

1. Kirsch TD, Mitrani-Reiser J, Bissell RA, Sauer LM, Mahoney M, Holmes WT, Santa Cruz N, de la Maza F. 2010. Impact on hospital functions following the 2010 Chilean Earthquake. *Disaster Medicine and Public Health Preparedness*, 4(2), 122–128.
2. Nappier SP, Lawrence RS, Schwab KJ. 2007. Dangerous waters. *Natural History*, November 2007, 47–49. Available at www.jhsph.edu/water_health/_pdf/DangerousWaters.pdf. Accessed 1 May 2012.
3. Roberts L, Toole MJ. 1995. Cholera deaths in Goma. *Lancet*, 346(8987), 1431.
4. Siddique AK, Salam A, Islam MS et al. 1995. Why treatment centres failed to prevent Cholera deaths among Rwandan Refugees in Goma, Zaire. *Lancet*, 345, 359–361.
5. US Department of Homeland Security. Homeland Security Presidential Directive 7: Critical Infrastructure Identification, Prioritization, and Protection. Available at: http://www.dhs.gov/xabout/laws/gc_1214597989952.shtm#0. Accessed 30 April 2012.
6. Wells SA. Personal communication, 22 February 2012.

7. FEMA Haiti Earthquake Response, Quick Look Report 2010. Available from: http://info.publicintelligence.net/FEMAHaitiQuickLookReport.pdf. Accessed on 30 March, 2012.
8. UNOPS: Post-disaster Recovery: Building Schools and Health Centres in Indonesia. Available at www.unops.org/english/whatwedo/UNOPSinaction/Pages/UNOPS-buildings-chools-in-Indonesia.aspx. Accessed 30 April 2012.
9. Farrell T. 2008. *"New Orleans" Broadmoor Is Model for Disaster Recovery*. Belfer Center for Science and International Affairs, Harvard University John F. Kennedy School of Government. Available at: http://belfercenter.ksg.harvard.edu/publication/18305/new_orleans_broadmoor_is_model_for_disaster_recovery.html. Accessed 30 April 2012.
10. Schanzer DL, Zheng H, Gilmore J. 2011. Statistical estimates of absenteeism attributable to seasonal and pandemic influenza from the Canadian Labour Force Survey. *BMC Infectious Diseases*, 11:90. Doi:10.1186/1471-2334-11-90.
11. Jones DA, Nozick LK, Turnquist MA, Sawaya WJ. 2008. Pandemic influenza, worker absenteeism and impacts on freight. *Proceedings of the 41st Hawaii International Conference on System Sciences Transportation*. Available at http://csdl2.computer.org/comp/proceedings/hicss/2008/3075/00/30750206.pdf. Accessed 29 April 2012.
12. Russell LA, Goltz JD, Bourque LB. 1995. Preparedness and hazard mitigation actions before and after two earthquakes. *Environment and Behavior*, 27, 744–770.
13. FEMA Haiti Earthquake Response, Quick Look Report 2010. Available from: http://info.publicintelligence.net/FEMAHaitiQuickLookReport.pdf. Accessed on 30 March, 2012.
14. Sawer P. 2010. Haiti earthquake: Rescuers still struggling without working airport, port or roads. *The Telegraph*, 16 January 2010. Available at: http://www.telegraph.co.uk/news/worldnews/centralamericaandthecaribbean/haiti/7005646/Haiti-earthquake-rescuers-still-struggling-without-working-airport-port-or-roads.html. Accessed 29 April 2012.
15. FEMA, op. cit.
16. Multihazard Mitigation Council. 2005. *New Study: Disaster Mitigation Is Cost Effective and Reduces Future Losses*. Available at http://www.nibs.org/index.php/mmc/news/Entry/newstudydisastermitigationiscosteffectiveandreducesfuturelosses Accessed 29 April 2012.
17. Intergovernmental Panel on Climate Change. 2001. Cost-effective Mitigation. Available at: http://www.ipcc.ch/ipccreports/tar/wg3/index.php?idp=51. Accessed 29 April 2012.
18. Stern N. 2006. *Stern Review on the Economics of Climate Change*. London: Her Majesty's Treasury. Available at: http://webarchive.nationalarchives.gov.uk/+/http:/www.hm-treasury.gov.uk/sternreview_index.htm. Accessed 29 April 2012.
19. American Society of Civil Engineers (ASCE). 2009. *Guiding Principles for the Nation's Critical Infrastructure*. ASCE. ISBN: 978-0-7844-1063-9.
20. Hinshaw RE. 2006. *Living with Nature's Extremes: The Life of Gilbert Fowler White*. Boulder, CO: Johnson Books. ISBN: 1-55566-388-5.
21. FEMA: National Response Framework. Available at http://www.fema.gov/emergency/nrf/. Accessed 30 April 2012.
22. Lagadec E. 2007. *Unconventional Crises, Unconventional Responses: Reforming Leadership in the Age of Catastrophic Crises and Hypercomplexity*. Washington, DC: Center for Transatlantic Relations. ISBN: 10:0-9788821-8-0.

CHAPTER 8

Public Health Role in Catastrophes

Rick Bissell and Thomas Kirsch

CONTENTS

Basic Vocabulary 172
Infectious Disease Vocabulary 172
Disease Control Mechanisms 175
Catastrophes and PH 177
    PH Priorities 180
    Infrastructure and Support Needed for PH 181
Role of Surge Capacity Planning in Catastrophes 181
References 182

In all catastrophes, whether or not the event is caused by a health phenomenon like a pandemic, the event will cause significant threat or actual damage to the affected population at the very time that people need their very best physical, mental, and emotional performance capability to deal with losses and move productively toward stabilization and some kind of recovery. The role of public health (PH) in this context must not be underestimated: it plays a direct role in helping people survive and recover from physical insults, and a crucial role in helping both individuals and communities marshal their resources for the daunting tasks ahead in reconstruction and recovery.[1] PH also plays an important role in protecting the health of disaster response personnel.[2] We will see some of these issues discussed more in the pandemic and New Madrid Seismic Zone (NMSZ) scenarios, but you would do well to think about PH considerations throughout the chapters that follow, so that you can start integrating the PH viewpoint into your emergency management (EM) thinking. Note: This chapter and the explanations of PH principles and techniques as they relate to catastrophes are not meant to make you "public health savvy," but rather to give you sufficient understanding that you can contribute to bridging some of the gaps that tend to exist between PH practitioners and emergency managers in the context of catastrophes.

BASIC VOCABULARY

PH is a broad inter-disciplinary field of applied science, using some of its own methods and tools, as well as borrowing concepts and methods from medicine, biology, sociology, psychology, anthropology, statistics, and ethics. *It is important to keep in mind that public health is broader than medicine, it focuses on populations, while medicine typically focuses on individuals.* People sometimes have difficulty comprehending how PH and medicine articulate with each other. There are some similarities with the articulation between EM and front-line emergency response practitioners. Both PH and EM are oriented toward the well being of the entire catchment population, while medicine and "rescue" personnel typically channel their efforts toward one person at a time. People who worked at the individual level such as medicine or first response often staff the ranks of both PH and EM organizations. In both cases, there are staffers who practice both at the public and individual levels.

It is also helpful to note that medicine and first response tend to be more technology oriented, while PH and EM are more organizational and use knowledge of science and management methods to make sure resources are applied where they might do the most good. Finally, both PH and EM have a strong history of trying to prevent and mitigate situations before they evolve into emergencies. While medical and first response personnel do participate in prevention activities, they are most often engaged in trying to ameliorate problems that have already exerted themselves.

One of the core tools in PH is called *epidemiology*. While the field of epidemiology can deal with epidemics, it is much broader and is intrinsic to virtually all aspects of PH. It is the discipline that combines the use of biomedical, human behavior, and statistical tools to investigate, describe, and analyze population-based health phenomena. Epidemiologists are intimately involved in discovering the pathways and extent of infectious disease outbreaks, but are equally important in investigating all kinds of other disorders, including chronic diseases, injuries, auto-immune diseases, mental health problems, and even such behavioral problems as homicide and suicide. Epidemiologists also play an important role in helping scientists test new medical and pharmacological treatments for effectiveness in a trial population.

Surveillance is one of the tools used by epidemiologists to analyze how health phenomena come about (e.g., injuries, STDs) and are propagated (Figure 8.1). For PH officials in a disaster situation, surveillance is also one of the key tools used to determine what the health response needs are, and whether the disaster response is having its intended effect of decreasing symptoms or needs. For an excellent description of this, see Sundnes et al.[3]

INFECTIOUS DISEASE VOCABULARY

The word "etiology" is one that emergency managers will hear PH workers use frequently, and is a very useful word that should be incorporated into EM. It means the entire causal chain and pathway of a disease or health condition. For example,

PUBLIC HEALTH ROLE IN CATASTROPHES 173

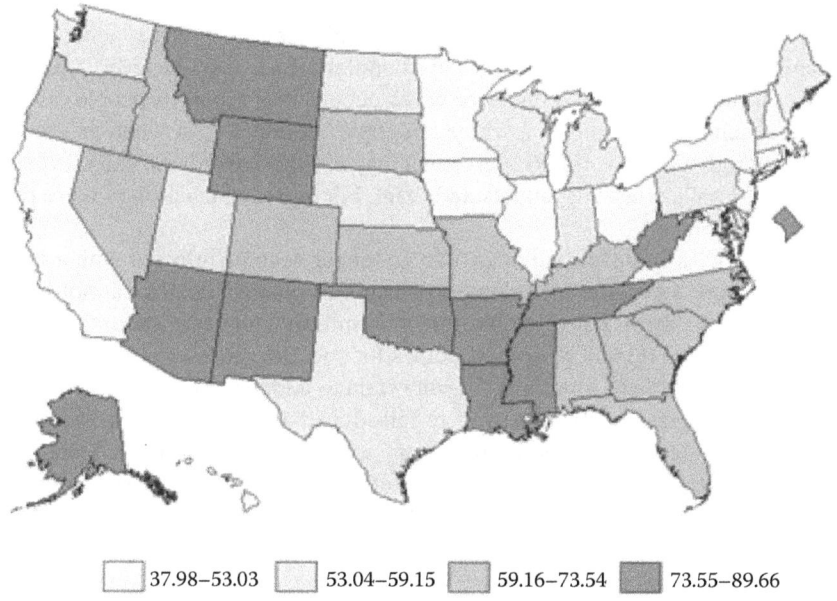

Figure 8.1 Surveillance data mapping example.

the etiology of malaria includes a microbial blood parasite that is transmitted from human to human (or animal to human in some cases) via a particular kind of mosquito. When a mosquito bites a human or other primate that carries the parasite that causes malaria, the blood that the mosquito ingests carries the parasite into the mosquito's digestive tract. The parasite has to mature in the gut of the mosquito before it is capable of infecting another human. The mosquito, in turn, lives only in certain temperature and humidity conditions. Once the infected female mosquito bites a human, it transmits the parasites and that human becomes a new "host" for the parasite. The mosquito is termed a "*vector*" because it transmits the disease. Armed with knowledge of the etiology of malaria, PH personnel can strategize points in the process where an intervention can take place to stop disease transmission. For example, swamp drainage or the use of insecticides can minimize the vector (mosquito) population, and the use of window screens or bed netting can decrease the probability that mosquitoes can bite new victims. In a similar way, an emergency manager who knows the etiology of floods in a particular community or geography can strategize methods of mitigation (Figure 8.2).

It is important that emergency managers understand the three "emic" words. "Endemic" is when a disease just exists in a population at a baseline level, "epidemic" is when an unusually large number of cases occurs in a group of people (as small as a single school, or as big as a whole country), *"pandemic"* is when an epidemic spreads throughout the world. PH personnel may use these words casually, expecting that their EM colleagues will understand them. For more explanation of these terms, see Friis and Sellers.[4]

"Immunity" is when an individual can no longer become infected with a specific organism. There are some infectious organisms to which humans cannot become immune (e.g., malaria). For other microbes, immunity can occur naturally because of surviving a prior infection, or by vaccines for specific illnesses (e.g., measles).

The concept of "herd immunity" is important to understand, as it plays an important role in strategies to control new or re-introduced diseases, and helps emergency managers understand why it is not necessary to inoculate everyone in a population when supplies are limited. To access more information on this, please see the Friis book, previously mentioned (Ref. 4). The CDC website (www.cdc.gov) also provides a

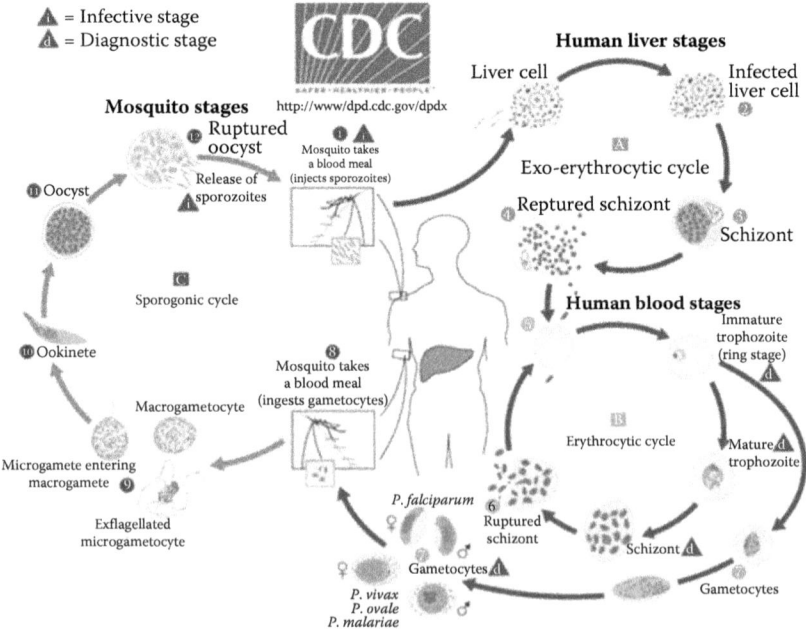

Figure 8.2 Vector-borne disease life cycle of malaria. (www.cdc.gov.)

good description of herd immunity and how it is used to control the spread of diseases in a population in which 100% vaccination cannot be achieved. In short, the concept is taken from veterinary medicine, in which it was found that one can decrease the probability of disease spread in a herd of domestic animals by vaccinating a significant percentage of the herd, without having to vaccinate all of the animals. In order for disease causing microbes to spread in a population, they need to pass from an infected individual to others that are vulnerable to the microbe. If one vaccinates a majority of the animals in the herd, the probability increases that the microbes will not find sufficient vulnerable individuals to spread widely, and the infection stops.

Social distancing, *quarantine*, and *isolation* are all strategies for decreasing exposure to microbes (viruses, bacteria, etc.) that are passed from one person to the next. Emergency managers may become involved in preparation for and enforcement of quarantine and isolation orders, because they require facilities, food delivery, and, potentially, law enforcement. Note that social distancing has taken on new meanings recently, to include increasing the distance between individuals when talking (at least 3–6 ft), the use of N95 disposable particulate respirators or surgical masks on people who are ill or suspected of being contagious, and the use of numerous strategies to maintain hand sanitation. Older forms of social distancing may include such strategies as canceling or prohibiting the congregation of people (e.g., church services, athletic events, school, etc.), or prohibition of travel.

Note that quarantine and isolation are similar in some ways, but significantly different in practice. Quarantine is applied both to ill individuals as well as people who have been exposed to a disease but have not yet come down with it. Quarantine usually consists of limiting people to their own homes or some other controlled living situation, so that they will not come into contact with unexposed individuals. Isolation, on the other hand, is usually done within hospitals or other medical institutions, and is targeted at people who are clinically sick with the dangerous disease. These patients are maintained in a room that has significant means of limiting the escape of microbes, including the use of negative air pressure to keep contaminated air from the isolation room from escaping. Isolation is expensive, difficult, and is severely limited by the small number of medical isolation rooms found in any given community (Figure 8.3).

DISEASE CONTROL MECHANISMS

Understanding the very basics of disease spread is an important first step to comprehending why PH officials will suggest specific interventions. Influenza is generally transmitted (spread) by waterborne or aerosolized droplets. These are small droplets that are expelled during breathing, coughing or sneezing, or some other mechanical means. These may also be called aerosolized or airborne droplets. Microbes can catch a ride with such droplets and these can be directly breathed in, or passed by touching a contaminated surface (that someone coughed on), and then touching a mucous membrane like the mouth or nose.

Vectors are things that transmit microbes, but they are not usually microbes themselves. We are familiar with animate vectors, for example, insects and animals, but

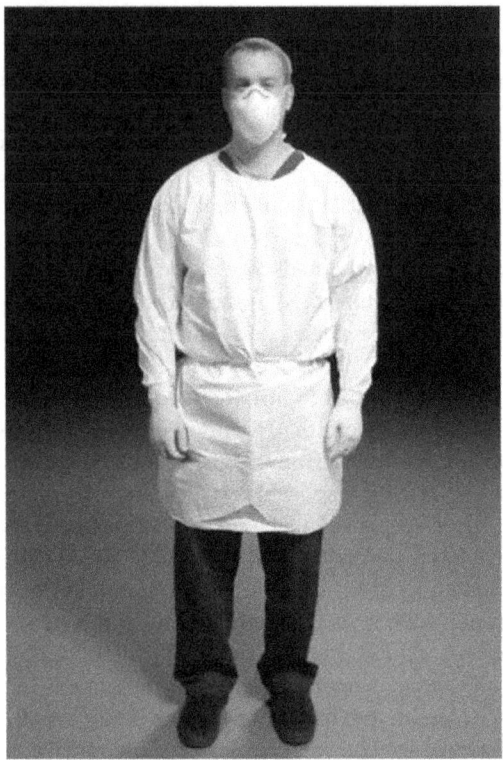

Figure 8.3 Some common personal protective equipment. (www.cdc.gov.)

inanimate transportation devices may also serve as vectors. For example, it is believed that the arrival of West Nile Virus in the United States was made possible by mosquitoes brought to New York onboard a jet from Egypt.[5] A few years ago the severe acute respiratory syndrome (SARS) epidemic was extended from China to the Toronto area of Canada by means of air transportation.[6] And, in an example many parents will quickly recognize, when young girls share hair brushes they are sometimes unwittingly converting their brushes into inanimate vectors that are carrying head lice from girl to girl. Vectors can be an intermediate cause of a PH disaster, as in the case of SARS, or they can suddenly become a threat source in communities suffering from a disaster such as an earthquake or flood, in which the normal vector-control mechanisms are interrupted or destroyed.

Disease control virtually always starts with an epidemiologic investigation, so that health personnel will know what they are working with. Once the organism and its etiology are known, PH specialists will invoke a control campaign, using one or more of the following tools: vaccination, social distancing (including quarantine and isolation), sanitation, vector reduction, treatment of infected individuals, and education of the public as to risks and means of preventing transmission. These are the most common mechanisms employed to control disease spread in a human population. The concepts are simple; implementation is often not. Epidemiologic investigation can be a sizeable undertaking, requiring significant logistical assistance. Quarantine and isolation are legally supported in some jurisdictions, not in others. Even when supported legally, it is difficult to enforce quarantine. Best is to get the population to cooperate voluntarily.

One of the reasons that it is not sufficient to simply treat everyone who comes down with an epidemic disease is that most all such diseases have what is called an "incubation period," a time during which infected individuals do not yet show symptoms but are fully capable of passing the microbe on to others. If we wait until people show symptoms of the disease, it will be too late to keep them from infecting others and the disease will continue to expand its population base. Second, if it is possible to prevent disease transmission by way of a vaccine or other methods, it is considerably less expensive than to wait and treat those who become ill. This is particularly true in a pandemic scenario. For more explanation, see Haddix.[7]

CATASTROPHES AND PH

It does not matter what kind of event provokes the catastrophe, all catastrophes lead to significant health impacts.[8] Because the healthcare system in the United States is consistently working at close to 100% of capacity during normal conditions, it does not take much to overwhelm it. Catastrophes provoke a significant increase in demand for healthcare services at the same time that many of those services are, themselves, affected directly by the event and unable to provide even the normal level of preventive and curative care services. This imbalance can constitute a major problem for the public and thus also for emergency managers, one which will be made infinitely more complicated if EMs and PH personnel do not understand each other's skills and needs.[9]

The health effects from a disaster or catastrophe can be termed *primary or secondary*. Primary health effects are those that are caused directly by the event's causal agent (e.g., winds or flooding in a hurricane), or as a result of the direct effects of the event (e.g., the shaking of the earth in an earthquake causes buildings to fall. The falling debris causes injury). Note that some event types cause multiple kinds of health effects. For example, hurricanes can lead to injury from flying debris, injury from falling structures or trees, and drowning. See the Noji book, Reference 1 (Figure 8.4). They also expose victims to unseen biological and chemical hazards as they wade through floodwaters.

Secondary effects are those that are indirectly caused by the catastrophic event. For example, hurricanes may not directly carry microbial infection, but they can promote disease transmission if humans densely crowd together to seek shelter, or if fresh water supplies are contaminated and ingested without filtration or boiling. In some catastrophes the human response to the event may provoke more damage to health than the event itself. For example, we now know that placing survivors in

Figure 8.4 People seeking high ground after a hurricane. (Photo courtesy of www.fema.gov.)

tightly packed "refugee" camps, while convenient for care providers and response teams, can be a recipe for significant increases in infectious disease and can also lead to conflict among survivors (Noji).

Mass relocation can be another secondary cause of PH deterioration following disasters, and this is one that is particularly likely to be the case in catastrophes. We are currently seeing that sea level rise is causing slow-onset catastrophes in several low-lying countries, which are now contemplating having to evacuate the entire populations of the island countries to someplace else. See some news coverage of the cases of the Maldives and Tuvalu in current news sources. To start, see:

- Sinking Island's National Seek New Home. www.cnn.com/2008/WORLD/asiapcf/11/11/maldives.president.html?iref=newssearch
- Tuvalu. www.hinduonet.com/fline/fl1825/18250630.htm
- Disappearing Islands. http://itotd.com/articles/499/disappearing-island-nations

As will be mentioned in the chapter on Mass Relocation, when large numbers of people relocate from one environment to another, they encounter microbes to which their immune-response systems are not accustomed, often resulting in high infection rates. Likewise, the migrants can bring with them diseases that can prove dangerous or fatal to the people already occupying the land into which the migrants are relocating. For a good historical account of this process, see books by Mc Neill[10] and Diamond.[11] The importance of the relationship between mass relocation, PH, and catastrophes is that many kinds of catastrophes are likely to result in mass relocations, a problem not normally seen with disasters.

There is a long list of secondary causes of health status decreases following large disasters and catastrophes. The factors in Table 8.1 are only a few of the more prominent causes, and we need to remember that they often combine. For example, loss of employment can lead to loss of housing and sanitation, and decrease in nutritional status. All of these can have important effects on the survivors' emotional status, which, in turn, can affect physical health status, and the energy available to work on finding solutions to disaster losses. Because of our lack of national experience with catastrophes, we do not have direct experience with the group psychology/depression of a community of survivors who, because of the size of the event, know that little help will be forthcoming any time soon. It could be that catastrophes will provoke more severe emotional response than disasters, because of the extended period of time needed before much outside help is available. This reality may contribute to group depression, or, alternatively, it could contribute to group self-help dynamics. Regardless of which way it goes, each way has a secondary effect on health status.

If you look at it from a basic health maintenance perspective, all the things shown in Table 8.1 are the basic components of health in a population. Catastrophes have the capability of taking away, or making scarce all of these basic components. Once this is realized, we should come to see that all catastrophes are also potential or real PH catastrophes, hence the importance of involving PH in every stage of catastrophe readiness and response.

Knowledge of the determinants of health outcome is very useful in helping predict what kinds of assistance will be needed and for how long. This is not a calculation that EMs will want to take on, but it is useful for them to recognize that the health outcome of a population can be affected by more than just the ferocity of the event, and that some of the determinants can be manipulated to create better outcomes. Likewise, emergency managers should recognize that pre-event deficits in nutritional status, education, or vaccine history can lead to considerably worse outcome and the need for more intervention.

Table 8.2 points out once again the multi-disciplinary character of the relationship between a population's catastrophe experience and its health outcome, emphasizing the

Table 8.1 Some Causes of Secondary Health Effect from Catastrophes

Crowding in shelters enhances disease transmission
Water contamination transmits microbes
Injuries from debris clearing
Mass relocation can lead to violence, starvation, disease transmission
Loss of housing and sanitation
Loss of food and potable water
Loss of healthcare facilities and personnel
Loss of employment
Loss of organized government support services

Table 8.2 Some Determinants of Health Outcome in a Catastrophe

Magnitude and extent of the event
Pre-event health status:
- Nutritional status
- Immunological experience/vaccines

Educational level
Preparedness level of individuals and families
Weather conditions
Preparedness and training of healthcare workers (Bissell et al. 2004)

need for a multi-agency collaborative, coordinated approach to catastrophe response, as described by McEntire, Ruback, Wachtendorf, Bissell, and others in this book. See also works by Lagadec[12] and Kirch[13] et al., describing the European planning efforts to minimize the health impact of catastrophes, based on a strong emphasis on a broad collaborative approach rather than a singular command and control organizational methodology. See also Bissell et al. (2004), for a description of evidence that PH preparedness contributes to a better health outcome in major disasters.[14]

PH Priorities

The PH priorities in a major disaster are

- Clean water and sanitation (Figure 8.5)
- Safe and adequate food
- Shelter
- Epidemiologic surveillance/info
- Access to labs
- Access to pharmaceuticals
- Clinical personnel and facilities

These PH priorities can change a bit in terms of which has top priority, depending on the conditions and the response stage currently underway, but all seven entries here are things emergency managers should assume that PH personnel will be asking for. Obviously, some will be considerably more difficult to obtain than others in any given set of circumstances. Note that PH personnel have direct control over very few of these functions, and no control at all over some of the basics (food, housing, and the provision of water). The National Response Framework foresees different organizations being responsible for the provision of these basics at the local level,

Methods	Kills Microbes	Removes Other Contaminants (Heavy Metals, Salts, and Most Other Chemicals)
Boiling	Yes	No
Chlorination	Yes	No
Distillation	Yes	Yes

Figure 8.5 Effectiveness of water treatment. (http://www.ready.gov/managing-water.)

requiring multiagency coordination in order to make available basic necessities that are among the top priorities for PH. Emergency managers will need to play a core role in coordinating between the agencies that carry discrete responsibilities and, where necessary, finding replacements when agencies expected to be available in disasters are not in a catastrophe.

Infrastructure and Support Needed for PH

Keep in mind that catastrophes are likely to require much more time for recovery than is the case for most disasters. Therefore, catastrophes will likely require water supply solutions that are more sustainable than that which might be jerry-rigged in a disaster, because of the fact that, in a catastrophe, the "temporary" solution is likely to have to last a lot longer before permanent reconstruction can take place. The same concept holds true for shelter ... it may take considerable time before permanent shelter again becomes available, therefore requiring that, where possible, temporary shelter should be as sustainable as possible. Experience in catastrophe response in developing countries indicates that people will work on repairing their own shelters, if possible, if tools and materials are made available.

Note that the PH priorities require considerable expertise at logistics, and some are quite resource-hungry. PH departments may be capable of coordinating the influx of qualified personnel into the catastrophe zone, but will likely need help with all of the logistics, transport, and communications functions listed here. The Department of Health and Human Services maintains medical and PH response teams, some of which consist of volunteers within the National Disaster Medical System (NDMS), and some of whom are full-time uniformed personnel of HHS who are trained and maintain readiness status. The Centers for Disease Control and Prevention (CDC) also has trained PH responders and investigators based around the country. These federal personnel constitute a significant potential PH workforce in a catastrophe, but they are limited by two factors: (1) they often lack local knowledge and contacts and (2) they have only short-term self-sufficiency in terms of transportation and supplies, after which they may depend on local coordinators to make it possible for them to continue functioning. Given the complexity and magnitude of catastrophes, such teams will only be effective if they benefit from multi-agency, multi-disciplinary coordination with strong support from EM. Put plainly, to be effective in a catastrophe, PH will depend on EM to coordinate and potentiate the many services needed to assist PH workers, and those that are needed directly by the public but which are not under the control of the health sector (housing, food, etc.).

ROLE OF SURGE CAPACITY PLANNING IN CATASTROPHES

Surge capacity is a measure of the ability of a hospital or clinical care system to rapidly adjust to caring for a sudden increase in the number of patients. This has become a primary concept in PH agencies as they conduct pandemic flu planning.

Other kinds of disaster may also cause surges in patient numbers, and, if they coincide with a decrease in the numbers of facilities available (due to destruction or loss of personnel), the concept of rapidly increasing clinical care capability in surviving facilities might be viable ... at least in disasters with limited geographic spread. In catastrophes, the surge capacity would have to be seen as applying to the national level. In a pandemic, everyone would be overwhelmed and the amount of surge capacity available is miniscule compared to the need which would exist. The NDMS, HHS, and CDC teams mentioned previously all have plans for bringing health personnel into affected areas, and, in the case of NDMS, transporting patients out of the affected areas to receive care in other parts of the country. Whether these resources and plans would be sufficient to meet the need depends on the circumstances of the catastrophe, but none of them will be effective in a catastrophe without substantial assistance from, and coordination with non-PH agencies and organizations. So, while we talk about "surge capacity" at the national level for catastrophes, it all still depends on coordination at the local level to make the most effective possible use of scarce resources. For more information on NDMS go to http://www.hhs.gov/aspr/opeo/ndms/index.html.

Note that there are two basic strategies or mechanisms for creating a surge of capacity. The first is to enhance the number of clinicians and other workers taking care of patients or victims by using staff who are already internal to the organization (e.g., hospital, EMS agency), by bringing in all available staffing shifts at once. This strategy might be called an "internal surge." A second strategy is to bring in outsiders and incorporate them into the organization's tasks. This might be termed an external surge strategy and a good example of it might be the disaster operations of the American Red Cross, in which the organization plans for and trains for the utilization of outside volunteers in disaster responses. Most surge capacity planning in the healthcare sector assumes an internal surge strategy, or, at best very limited use of outsiders. The severe conditions of catastrophes may well benefit more from a pre-planned external surge capacity strategy, given the extreme need levels at the same moment that internal resources are highly limited. Emergency managers can help move jurisdictional health authorities toward more concentration on external strategies during the preparedness phase by providing planning assistance.

REFERENCES

1. Noji E. 1997. The nature of disaster: General characteristics and public health effects. Chapter 1 in *The Public Health Consequences of Disaster*, Noji E. (ed.). Oxford University Press, USA. ISBN: 0-19-509570-7.
2. Landesman LY. 2001. *Public Health Management of Disasters*. American Public Health Association, Washington, DC. ISBN: 0-87553-025-7.
3. Sundnes KO and Birnbaum ML. 2003. Health disaster management: Guidelines for evaluation and research in the Utstein style. *Prehospital and Disaster Medicine*, 17(Suppl. 3). ISBN: 1049-023X.

4. Friis RH and Sellers TA. 2004. *Epidemiology for Public Health Practice*. Jones and Bartlett Publishers, Sudbury, MA. ISBN: 0-7637-3170-6.
5. Lanciotti RS, Roehrig JT, Deubel V, Smith J, Parker M, Steele K, Crise B et al. 1999. Origin of the West Nile virus responsible for an outbreak of encephalitis in the northeastern United States. *Science*, 17; 286(5448): 2333–7.
6. Mangili A and Gendreau, MA. 2005. Transmission of infectious diseases during commercial air travel. *Lancet*, 365(9463), 989–996.
7. Haddix A. 2002. *Prevention Effectiveness: A Guide to Decision Analysis and Economic Evaluation.* Oxford University Press, New York.
8. Baxter PJ. 2002. Catastrophes—Natural and man-made disasters. Chapter 3 in *Conflict and Catastrophe Medicine*, Ryan J, Mahoney PF, Greaves I and Bowyer G. (eds.). Springer-Verlag, UK. ISBN: 1-85233-348-0.
9. Bissell RA. 2007. Public health and medicine in emergency Management. Chapter 16 in *Disciplines, Disasters and Emergency Management*, David A. and McEntire. (eds.). Charles C. Thomas Publisher, Springfield, IL. ISBN: 978-0-398-07743-3
10. McNeill WH. 1976. *Plagues and Peoples*. Bantam Doubleday Dell Publishing Group, Inc., New York, NY. ISBN 0-385-12122-9.
11. Diamond J. 1999. *Guns, Germs and Steel: The Fates of Human Societies*. Norton Books, New York, NY. ISBN 0-393-31755-2.
12. Lagadec E. 2007. *Unconventional Crises, Unconventional Responses: Reforming Leadership in the Age of Catastrophic Crises and Hypercomplexity*. Center for Transatlantic Relations. Johns Hopkins University, Washington, DC. ISBN 10: 0-9788821-8-0.
13. Kirch W, Menne B, and Bertolini R. 2005. *Extreme Weather Events and Public Health Responses*. Springer-Verlag, Heidelberg. ISBN: 3-540-24417-4.
14. Bissell RA, Pinet L, Nelson M, and Levy M. 2004. Evidence of the effectiveness of health sector preparedness in disaster response: The example of four earthquakes. *Family and Community Health (special issue: Disaster Management in Public Health)*, 27(3), 193–203.

CHAPTER 9

Catastrophes, Mass Displacement, and Population Resettlement

Anthony Oliver-Smith

CONTENTS

Introduction 186
Mass Displacement 186
Defining Mass Displacement 187
Complexity and Causation 189
Catastrophes and Mass Relocations 191
Global Climate Changes and Mass Relocation 193
Defining Environmentally Forced Migrants 194
Estimating Environmentally Induced Displacement and Migration 195
Mass Relocation and the Legal Status of Forced Migrants 196
Global Climate Change and Local Vulnerability 198
Demographic Movement 200
Continua of Relocation 201
The Consequences of Mass Relocation 202
And after Displacement and Forced Migration? 204
Involuntary Migration, Displacement, and Recovery 206
Understanding Mass Displacement and Resettlement 207
Impoverishment Risks and Reconstruction Model 208
The Complexity of the Displacement and Resettlement Process 210
Psychological, Social, and Cultural Impoverishment 210
Factors in Success/Failure of Post-Disaster Resettlement 211
Resettlement, Reconstruction, and Development 213
Resettlement Action Plans 214
The Arenal Dam Resettlement Project 215
The Near Future 217
References 218

INTRODUCTION

The purpose of this chapter is to present an overview of the field of displacement and resettlement research, focusing on the development of conceptual approaches, policy positions, and practice problems in the various forms of displacement and resettlement associated with catastrophic events. The range of forms that catastrophic forced displacement and resettlement are projected to take will be considered. Emphasis will be placed on developing an understanding of the factors that generate both the short- and long-term risks and consequences in major dislocations, deriving understanding from data and perspectives from other forms of displacement and resettlement, including conflict and development-caused relocations. The chapter will also identify and analyze the key components of resettlement planning as developed for infrastructural projects, assessing their utility for crafting appropriate standards and strategies for potential future mass relocation.

MASS DISPLACEMENT

Mass displacement after catastrophe, involving the physical relocation of people, is an extremely complex process, which if not properly planned and managed (with the full participation of affected people), may result in long-term hardship for the displaced as well as potential conflict with resident populations and environmental damage in locations in which they are resettled. The complexity of the process is a challenge that is being and has been confronted by researchers and practitioners alike for the last 50 years. Indeed, the literature on displacement and resettlement from a variety of causes has grown significantly over that time.

In the last half century, researchers on development-induced displacement, refugee studies, and disaster research[1-4] have learned that involuntarily displaced peoples face many similar challenges. Although the places and peoples are geographically and culturally distant and the sociopolitical environments and causes of dislocation dissimilar, there emerge a number of common concerns and processes. Displaced people of all descriptions must cope with the consequent stresses and the need to adapt to new or radically changed environments. All may experience privation, loss of homes, jobs, and the breakup of families and communities. All may suffer the endangerment of structures of meaning and identity. All must mobilize social and cultural resources in their efforts to re-establish viable social groups and communities and to restore adequate levels of material and cultural life.

Analyzing the risks and developing adequate responses to population displacement have been the focus of a number of fields toward crafting appropriate standards and strategies for future catastrophe-driven mass relocation. Central to these tasks are the issues of rights, poverty, vulnerability, and other forms of social marginality that are intrinsically linked to displacement. While the field of displacement and resettlement studies has achieved significant advances over the last half century, it must be recognized that deficiencies in planning, preparation, and implementation of involuntary resettlement projects have produced far more failures than successes. Therefore, the applicability of displacement and resettlement research to potential mass relocations will require refinement and development to deal effectively with these challenges. A key element in any development of the field will, however, continue to be the recognition that the displaced must be seen as active social agents with their own views on rights and entitlements, which have to be considered in any displacement and in the planning and implementation of resettlement projects.

DEFINING MASS DISPLACEMENT

Mass displacement is composed of two processes: forced migration and resettlement. Forced migration takes place because of the occurrence of a disaster, including climate-induced environmental change, a conflict or a development project that renders the abode of a population uninhabitable, either temporarily or permanently. Resettlement may be undertaken individually or in small groups, but in larger contexts of communities, resettlement involves the planned re-establishment of displaced peoples in a new location with appropriate settlement design, housing, services, and an economic base to enable the community to reconstitute itself and achieve adequate levels of resilience to normal social, economic, political, and environmental variation. That such satisfactory outcomes have not been common constitutes a major humanitarian crisis.

Mass relocation, also frequently called forced migration or involuntary displacement and resettlement, refers to the uprooting of large numbers of people from their home locations. Although the term "mass" refers to large numbers, it is vague and not well defined in its application. Nonetheless, we should not fail to recognize that potential displacements of enormous size are projected for the near future. Even currently, more than a million people dispersed by the combination of Hurricane Katrina and an ad hoc and poorly conceived government response constitutes a mass displacement. Similar disaster-associated mass displacements have occurred after the 2006 South Asian tsunami and the even more recent Fukushima catastrophe. Certainly, the displacement of close to 1.5 million people by the construction of the Three Gorges dam in China qualifies as a mass displacement (see Figure 9.1).

However different the driving forces and policies may have been, for forcibly uprooted people recovery and reconstruction take place in a new setting, generally far from familiar environments and people. In other words, getting to where they are going does not solve the problem. They may have stopped moving, but that is just the beginning of another process, resettlement. In all too many cases, resettlement, particularly when done at the community level, ends up becoming a secondary disaster. Therefore, when disasters, conflicts or development damage or destroy communities, uprooting people, displacing them far from homes and jobs, the process of recovery is made doubly complex. Some mass relocations will involve sudden rapid onset events that evoke at initial stages elements of emergency management strategies such as evacuation and temporary shelters. Other approaches to deal with

Figure 9.1 Hurricane Katrina survivors arrived at the Houston Astrodome Red Cross Shelter after being evacuated from New Orleans. Thousands of survivors were at the Astrodome after the Superdome became unsafe following the levee breaks in New Orleans. Many thousands never returned. (http://www.fema.gov/photolibrary/photo_details.do?id=14461.)

mass relocations may resemble the resettlement of political refugees in strategies to integrate the displaced into existing communities. Still other forms will be the result of planned mitigation projects and will draw on models from development-forced resettlement, community development, and urban planning. Recently, greater attention has been paid to resettlement to reduce exposure to natural hazards.[5] Some mass relocations may involve several of these forms of displacement and resettlement. Finally, some mass relocations will constitute simply mass migrations, evoking very little formal institutional response. The challenge of mass displacement thus requires inputs from all of the phases of emergency management, and many social, scientific, and management disciplines.

In some circumstances, because catastrophes involve different time/space scales (lasting longer, encompassing wider areas), crossing ecological, jurisdictional, and national boundaries, impacting heterogeneous populations, they will require multiple strategies and inter- and multi-national efforts and cooperation. At the same time, mass relocation may involve masses of people, but responses will need to address culturally and socially defined constituent population groups. Regardless, uprooted people generally face the daunting task of rebuilding not only personal lives, but also those relationships, networks, and structures that support people as individuals that we understand as communities. The social destruction wrought by these phenomena takes place both at the individual level and at the community level. In most cases, solutions must be durable. There is often little hope of return.

Given the paucity of research on catastrophes and mass relocations, particularly in contemporary times, much of what follows is drawn from research and practice in the fields of refugee studies, disaster research, migration, planning, and development-forced displacement and resettlement (DFDR).

COMPLEXITY AND CAUSATION

The question of causation of mass displacement at first glance would appear to be fairly straightforward. That is, wars have uprooted people since time immemorial, although governments have been known to use conflict as a pretext to displace populations considered disloyal or merely in the way. Development projects have displaced close to half a billion people since 1950, although there are many examples in history of a development that was defensive or ceremonial in nature that displaced thousands as well.[6] Although both conflict and development present their own complications, the question of environmental catastrophe as a driver of mass displacement is more complex.

Since the 1980s, researchers have linked the issue of catastrophic environmental change with human migration, explicitly designating as "environmental refugees" people who are forced to leave their homes, temporarily or permanently, due to the threat, impact or effects of a hazard or environmental change.[7] Other scholars attribute the displacement of people to a more complex pattern of factors including political, social, economic as well as environmental forces.[8-10] Natural disasters are seen to cause temporary displacement, but not some idea of authentic, that is, permanent migration. Indeed, if permanent migration does occur as the result of a disaster, it is seen as more the result of deficient responses of weak or corrupt states rather than an altered environment as expressed in the form of a natural hazard impact. Certainly, Hurricane Katrina exemplifies this perspective. Black's critique that focusing on environmental factors as causes of migration often obscures the role of political and economic factors is well taken, and echoes the position held by most disaster researchers today that focusing solely on agents reveals little about the political or economic forces that together with agents produce disasters or, for that matter, any forced migration that might ensue. It is worth noting that some environmental disasters, for example, permanent inundation due to sea level rise, will result in permanent dislocation of those whose normal habitat is now under water or unusable due to water table infiltration.

Seeking single-agent causality is always highly problematic. There are two fundamental questions regarding causality. The first asks what empirical evidence is required for legitimate inference of cause–effect relationships. The second suggests that if we are willing to accept causal information about a phenomenon, what kinds of inferences can be drawn from that information?[11] The key word here is "inferences." Clear and direct relationships of causality are hard to come by. In the strictest sense of the word, if A causes B, then A must always be followed by B. In common parlance, when we say A causes B, as in smoking (A) causes cancer (B), what we should really say is that smoking causes an increase in the probability of cancer.[12] In other words, in the case of catastrophes, A increases the risk of B, forced migration (see Figure 9.2).

Figure 9.2 Haitian refugees await relocation to camps in Guantanamo Bay, Cuba. (http://cgvi.uscg.mil/media/main.php?g2_itemId=113072.)

Therefore, it is difficult to point to the environment, even in catastrophes, as the single cause of anything. By the same token, eliminating the environment as the single cause of forced migration hardly warrants discounting it as one of a multiplicity of forces at work in generating mass relocation. It is important to remember here that a catastrophe is also not defined in terms of its event aspect only, but in terms of both the processes that set it in motion and the post-event processes of adaptation and adjustment in recovery and reconstruction. Forced migration can be part of the process prior to the event or after, but it is not inevitable. We know that disasters are not caused by a single agent but by the complex interaction of both environmental and social features and forces. By the same token, disaster outcomes are rarely the result of a single agent (i.e., a hurricane), but are brought about by multiple complex and intersecting forces acting together in a specific social context that is complex in its own right. Seeking single causes for a complex outcome is usually difficult in any context, and particularly so with forced migration, whether the obvious "cause" is international or civil conflict, development projects, or natural or technological disasters.

The issue of causality raises a number of important issues. Establishing causality in mass relocation may become key in determining mitigation efforts. In some circumstances, causality will determine jurisdiction and responsibility for assistance. Thus, establishing causality in mass relocation may lead either to meaningful efforts to mitigate drivers or no action at all. By the same token, causality becomes a crucial issue in assigning responsibility for people dislocated by a catastrophe which may not be legally defined as war or persecution, thus leaving the displaced bereft of any meaningful assistance under international agreements on refugees. At present there are no internationally established conventions or covenants for legal protections or responsibilities for environmentally displaced peoples, although a number of initiatives have been formulated for that purpose.[13]

CATASTROPHES AND MASS RELOCATIONS

There is a wide array of catastrophic events that can generate mass displacements. A number of fundamental questions will prove important for developing mitigation and response policies and practices. Emergent trends or patterns of potential mass-scale events that will produce forced displacement and resettlement must be identified. Equally important, if not more so, will be the identification of the specific forms of social vulnerability that increase the likelihood of mass displacement. How the policy discourse and practice of institutional players (states, international development, and aid agencies) will frame, define, and categorize catastrophe-forced displacement and resettlement will be crucial in formal institutional responses. In addition, the link between vulnerability with rights and entitlements and the capacity to reconstruct livelihoods must be clearly established.[14]

By vulnerability we mean the characteristics of a person or group in terms of their capacity to anticipate, cope with, resist, and recover from the impact of a natural hazard. It involves a combination of factors that determine the degree to which someone's life and livelihood is put at risk by a discrete and identifiable event in nature or society.[15] Clearly, one of the fundamental tasks that societies must address is some kind of adjustment to the hazardous features of the environment to which they are exposed. These adaptations will almost always be approximate in that all impacts from a hazard will not be completely absorbable. Were that not the case, that is, if the society could absorb all impacts of a hazard without effect, it would not be a hazard. Therefore, both exposure to a hazard and the capacity to adapt to it are fundamental aspects of vulnerability.[16]

Vulnerability and risk refer to the relationships between people and the environment including the physical setting and the sociopolitical structures that frame the conditions in which people live. Risk, vulnerability, and resilience address the degree to which at a given point in time a society is adapted to the hazards of its environment. Vulnerability is fundamentally a socially derived condition that refers to the degree to which a socioecological system is either susceptible or resilient to the impact of natural hazards. More aptly labeled "social vulnerability," it is the outcome of various factors, including awareness of hazards, settlement and infrastructural patterns, social, economic and political marginality, public policy and administration, the level of societal development, and institutional capacities in disaster and risk management.

The concept of vulnerability is fundamentally a political ecological concept, integrating not only political economic, but environmental forces in terms of both biophysical and socially constructed risk. Vulnerability links the relationship that people have with their environment with social forces and institutions and the cultural values that sustain or contest them. In so far as vulnerability is socially produced, risk is therefore not evenly distributed across the social spectrum. Vulnerability thus explicitly links environmental issues, such as hazards, with the structure and organization of society, and the rights associated with membership.

Vulnerability to the dynamic interactions of society and environment is particularly accentuated in the developing world, where people have fewer resources either to manage threats or to recover from impacts. It is clear that the differential endangerment is a violation of human rights, and is deeply embedded in the patterns of inequality that characterize the distribution of both risk and vulnerability. Therefore, overwhelming as catastrophes threaten to become, their impacts, like any disaster, will be socially, politically, and economically mediated, distributed, and interpreted. The measures taken to mitigate and respond will be similarly structured.

There are relatively few contemporary studies of disaster-caused community uprooting and resettlement that have been the result of planned policy and action in the United States and elsewhere, but these have been relatively small events involving smaller populations.[17-19] Their utility in understanding and responding to mass relocations remains to be assessed. A frequent response to catastrophe throughout history has been mass forced migration, but most cases have not evoked significant or effective policy or practice responses. In general we must look to history for detailed discussions of these processes.

In the Irish potato famine, for example, formal institutional responses actually exacerbated conditions, forcing huge numbers of starving peasants to leave the country by whatever means were available, often to North America or Australia as indentured servants, with a significant percentage of them dying while underway. There were few formal institutional measures undertaken to assist them in either the displacement or the resettlement processes and the hardships and discrimination they endured in their new locations are well documented.

The Great Flood of 1927 in the lower Mississippi Valley displaced nearly 700,000 people, approximately 330,000 of whom were African Americans. The displaced individuals were subsequently interned in 154 relief "concentration camps" where they were forced to work. Although there were many reasons for African Americans to leave the South, the flood and its consequences, especially the forced labor in the camps, were the final motivation for migrating for thousands.[20]

The great economic depression of the 1930s, combined with several years of inadequate rainfall and elevated temperatures in the Great Plains resulted in the widespread failure of small farms, producing a migration of hundreds of thousands of people from the region to the west coast of the United States.[21]

In the contemporary context, Hurricane Katrina in 2005 uprooted about 1.5 million people from New Orleans and the Gulf Coast, 300,000 of whom are expected to remain permanently displaced. Their displacement, however, was not due to environmental reasons alone, but to inappropriate and inadequate policy, incompetent practice, and the political economy of reconstruction as well. New Orleans depended on an inadequate levee system to protect it from storm surges. The response system of the city, the state of Louisiana and the Federal Emergency Management Agency (FEMA) proved woefully inadequate. In addition, local interests saw the displacement of African Americans as an opportunity to reconfigure the social environment[22,23] (see Figure 9.3).

Figure 9.3 Five of the 1,355 buses used to evacuate New Orleans following Hurricane Katrina. (http://www.fema.gov/photolibrary/photo_details.do?id=15512.)

GLOBAL CLIMATE CHANGES AND MASS RELOCATION

Although contested by some selected interests for economic or political reasons, global climate change has been projected to become one of the major forces producing mass relocations in the near future. The Millennium Ecosystem Assessment (MEA)[24] concluded that 15 of 24 assessed ecosystem services were being degraded or used unsustainably, with serious effects for poor, resource-dependent communities. Among the issues the MEA calls attention to is the fact that 10–20% of drylands are already degraded affecting as many as 2 billion people. Increasing pressure on dry land ecosystems will affect the provision of ecosystem services such as food and water for humans, livestock, irrigation, and sanitation. There will as well be likely increases in water scarcity due to climate change in highly populated regions that are already under water stress. Droughts are also increasing in frequency and their continuous reoccurrence can overwhelm community-coping capacities. When coping capacities and adaptation strategies of communities are overcome by the loss of ecosystem services, droughts and loss of land productivity can act as triggers for the movement of people from dry lands to other areas.[25–27]

The recent reports from the Intergovernmental Panel on Climate Change[28] affirm that human-induced factors are responsible for generating significant increases in temperatures around the world. Among the local consequences of this rise in temperature are: increases in the rate of sea level rise; increases in glacial, permafrost, Arctic and Antarctic ice melt; and more rainfall in specific regions of the world. Worldwide changes include: more severe droughts in tropical and subtropical zones;

increases in heat waves; changing ranges and incidences of diseases; and more intense hurricane and cyclone activity.

All of these changes are projected to affect natural systems globally, inducing alterations in hydrological, terrestrial, biological, and aquatic subsystems. And all of these changes also have great potential for generating processes that may lead to the uprooting of large numbers of people, forcing them to migrate as individuals and families or permanently displacing them and/or relocating them as communities. Global climate changes, in addition, will also combine with other factors, such as environmental contamination, to drive people from their homes.

While all of the changes mentioned have the potential to uproot people, there are basically three major expressions of global climate change that will be the principal contributing forces that uproot people. These forces are: loss of ecosystem services, loss of land, and increased intensity and frequency of climate-based natural disasters.[29] Nevertheless, any forced migrations that take place will be the outcome of the intersection of these physical events with the socially constructed patterns of vulnerability that characterize the locality affected.

However, despite the fact that the reality of environmental change, and specifically climate change, is generally accepted, there is considerable uncertainty about local manifestations of global environmental change and what necessary adjustments will be induced in natural and human systems.[30] The uncertainty, in fact, characterizes the problem both at the level of physical impacts and at the level of responses and adaptations in human communities. Indeed, the projected effects of environmental change, particularly as they pertain to specific human communities, have entered as much into political controversy as they have into academic and scientific debate. The actual processes through which major population dislocations might occur are still only partially understood.[31] The UNHCR sees five displacement scenarios emerging in the near future: hydrometeorological disasters, population removal from high risk areas, environmental degradation, the submergence of small island states, and violent conflict.[32]

DEFINING ENVIRONMENTALLY FORCED MIGRANTS

Since the 1980s, researchers have linked the issue of environmental change with human migration, designating as "environmental migrants," "environmental refugees," "climate migrants," or "environmentally displaced peoples," people who are forced to leave their homes, temporarily or permanently, due to the threat, impact or effects of a hazard or environmental change, but other researchers dispute the accuracy of the term, finding it misleading. They attribute the displacement of people to a complex pattern of factors, including political, social, economic, as well as environmental forces. The failure to reach a consensus definition of environmental migration has impaired efforts to diminish the uncertainty that surrounds the issue. Without the parameters of an established definition, it is difficult to state whether people have been displaced by climate change or some other driver such as economic motives.

Most of the definitions offered in the literature address the issue of an environmental disruption, whether a sudden disaster from the occurrence of a natural hazard or a slower onset process of resource degradation of either natural or anthropogenic origin. Clearly, environmental events and processes may drive mass displacement and migration. The impact of natural hazard occurrence, such as Hurricane Mitch in Honduras, uprooted thousands, many of whom migrated to the United States in 1998. In some cases, emergency evacuation either before or after a hazard event can result in permanent migration such as occurred with hundreds of thousands in Hurricane Katrina. Slower onset processes such as droughts have also stimulated various levels of migration in Africa. However, many environmental impacts that uproot people are often shown to be far from naturally generated, but rather have their origins in human policies and practices, as the environmental destruction in New Orleans tragically demonstrated in Hurricane Katrina.

Black's critique that focusing on environmental factors as causes of migration may obscure the role of political and economic factors is well taken, and echoes the position held by most disaster researchers today. Focusing solely on agents reveals little about the political or economic forces that together with agents produce disasters or, for that matter, any forced migration that might ensue. But these objections in turn elide the fact that the environment, and its resources as well as its hazards, is itself socially constructed and is always channeled for people through social, economic, and political factors, even in the best of times.[33] Nevertheless, the projections for climate change, however conjectural at this point, indicate the increasing role that major environmental changes, such as sea level rise that may submerge entire small nations, may play in driving mass displacement and migration.

ESTIMATING ENVIRONMENTALLY INDUCED DISPLACEMENT AND MIGRATION

One of the complications of the lack of a consensus definition is the enormous disparity in estimates of people who have been or will be displaced by the effects of environmental change. Estimates are at least in part contingent on how environmental migration is defined and who will fall under a given definition. The range of estimates is considerable, ranging from 24 to 250 million, which suggests that estimating the displaced is far more complex than imagined, as the following table illustrates[34]:

El-Hinnawi (1985)	50 million
The Almeria Statement (1994)	135 million
UNHCR (2002)	24 million
Myers (2005)	200 million
The Stern Review (2006)	200 million by 2050
Nicholls (2006)	50–200 million by 2080
Friends of the Earth (2007)	200 million by 2050
Christian Aid (2007)	250 million
Global Humanitarian Forum (2009)	20 million in 2009

Moreover, the failure of most of those who have offered estimates to specify the methods by which they arrived at their numbers has generated significant scientific debate and presented policy makers with confusing data. There is also no commonly agreed upon methodology.[35] Some estimates are based on field reports from relief agencies. Some are based on population figures in areas that are experiencing environmental change. Few have solid bases for the numbers that are estimated. Probably the most reliable figures at present are produced by the International Displacement Monitoring Center (IDMC) and the Norwegian Refugee Council (NRC) that place the number of people displaced by natural disasters at over 42 million people, using a baseline of events from the EM-DAT database to produce a core data set for events where over 50,000 people were affected. Data on the displaced from each event is then sought from organizations involved in relief for those events.[34]

The debate over this issue, with claims of millions of environmental refugees being produced versus counterclaims that the evidence is uneven, unconvincing, and counterproductive, has been active since the 1980s. However, it is clear that to develop adequate responses to these issues and uncertainties regarding the social impacts of climate and other environmental changes, we must begin by addressing them at the multiple levels at which they exist, and particularly in the complex interrelationships between nature and society both conceptually and specifically as expressed in local contexts.

In the final analysis, environmental change does not necessarily undermine human security in the absence of poverty, lack of economic opportunity, lack of state support, good governance, and social cohesion with surrounding groups, but at present we know very little about the interplay between environmental change, ecological systems, socioeconomic vulnerability, and patterns of forced migration.[36] Finally, in addition to conflict, disasters, and development projects, mass relocation has also been generated by a variety of political and economic factors. Governments may displace large populations as a form of political reorganization for greater social control, ethnic separation, border security, or resource acquisition.

MASS RELOCATION AND THE LEGAL STATUS OF FORCED MIGRANTS

Since society structures and distributes both environmental risks and impacts, human rights are a central issue in both catastrophes and any mass relocation that may result. In cases of conflict and development, the intentionality and coercion exercised in the displacement constitutes a gross human rights violation. In disasters and catastrophes, the social vulnerability of those most affected is often the result of a compendium of denials of fundamental human rights. Although in catastrophes damage and death may be so widespread as to affect all social classes, the capacity to recover will be based on social and economic assets held unequally prior to the event.

In climate change, equity is a core principle of the Framework Convention on Climate Change. Regarding the impacts of climate change effects, two concepts of human rights and justice pertain. Procedural justice refers to who makes the crucial decisions on climate change. Who decides what strategies to adopt? And indeed, who is responsible for the decisions that produced actions that resulted in climate change? Indeed, the people least responsible for climate change, people in the developing world, are those who will likely suffer the greatest impacts. Distributive justice refers to inequities in the distribution of risk, vulnerability, and impact that have resulted in selective victimization.[37] Most of the people most vulnerable to climate change are in the developing world. Climate change and our adaptations to it, such as relocation as a mitigation strategy, threaten to exacerbate exactly those forces that cause present insecurities and will likely increase that insecurity in the future.

Moreover, both our adaptations and the distribution of impacts are distributed unequally in terms of their effects on attempts by nations in the global south to develop, to reduce poverty and vulnerability. Adaptations to climate change may exacerbate past injustices (underdevelopment, colonialism) that are in effect the conditions that produced the patterns of underdevelopment and vulnerability to climate change and other disasters.[38]

Although the issue of environmentally displaced peoples has generated significant debate over the last 20 years, appropriate policies pertaining to environmentally displaced peoples or other internally displaced populations have yet to attain legal status. Moreover, according to the International Federation of Red Cross and Red Crescent Societies,[39] "there are no well recognized and comprehensive legal instruments which identify internationally agreed rules, principles and standards for the protection and assistance of people affected by natural and technological disasters. As a result, many international disaster response operations are subject to ad hoc rules and systems, which vary dramatically from country to country and impede the provision of fast and effective assistance—putting lives and dignity at risk."[40]

The category "refugee" with all its attendant rights also still applies only to a very specifically defined group of people who, in fleeing for their lives, have crossed an international border. However, over the last decade there has been increasing concern regarding internally displaced persons (IDPs) and their rights, and there is increasing recognition that the causes of displacement and resettlement are far wider than wars and civil conflicts. Despite this there are still no nationally or internationally binding agreements or treaties that guarantee the rights of people who have been uprooted by other causes, such as environmental disruption, disasters, or development projects (such as the Three Gorges Dam project in China). The United Nations Guiding Principles on Internal Displacement defines IDPs as "... persons or groups of persons who have been forced or obliged to flee or leave their homes or places of habitual residence, in particular as a result of or in order to avoid the effects of armed conflict, situations of generalized violence, violations of human rights or natural or human made disasters, and who have not crossed an internally recognized state border."[41] However, although widely recognized as an international standard, and certainly helpful in guiding non-governmental organizations (NGOs) and other aid organizations in assisting IDPs, the guiding principles have not been agreed upon in a binding covenant or treaty and have no legal standing. We must also recognize the very real potential for Global Climate Change to generate displacements and migrations across international borders.

Despite the attention that the issue of environmental displacement has garnered in recent years, there are no legally binding internationally recognized instruments that pertain to the needs of people displaced by environmental causes. Recognition of this lack has prompted a number of proposals for appropriate forms of governance pertaining to environmentally displaced peoples.[42,43] Recognizing the problem of complicating the status of legally defined refugees, these proposals argue against including environmentally displaced peoples under the 1951 Geneva Convention Relating to the Status of Refugees. Instead, they propose new legal instruments designed specifically to address the needs of environmentally displaced peoples. Given the dearth of appropriate policies for IDPs, the need for developing adequate legal protections and assistance programs for populations facing potential displacement by forces generated by global climate change becomes urgent.

GLOBAL CLIMATE CHANGE AND LOCAL VULNERABILITY

Certainly, vulnerability science has made clear that exposure alone does not determine outcome. The challenge lies in determining not just exposure (such as absolute exposed land and absolute exposed population) but specific lands and populations in different socially configured conditions of resilience or vulnerability. For example, the problem with assessing the exposure of both land and population to sea level rise is that we are dealing with more than projected increases in sea level. We must also consider various future projections about different societal and environmental trajectories including greenhouse gas emissions, demographic change, migration trends, infrastructural development, mitigation strategies, adaptive capacities, vulnerabilities, and patterns of economic change, all of which will play out in different ways, according to the political, economic, and sociocultural dispositions of national governments, international organizations, and general populations.

As mentioned earlier, the concept of social vulnerability will be key in identifying beforehand those groups that may suffer substantial displacement, but vulnerability assessment is still at an early stage of development. However, the poor and underdeveloped regions of the world are likely to have fewer resources to deal with climate change. That notwithstanding, the poor, particularly the rural poor, because they observe environmental factors more acutely to ensure their livelihoods may be more aware of creeping environmental changes than urban people.

Global climate models currently lack sufficient resolution to profile types and magnitudes of changes to be expected in specific local sites. There are also real limitations in our abilities to assess human vulnerabilities to these projected, yet ill-defined threats. The interaction of multiple, sometimes rapidly changing stresses, such as economic shocks, natural hazards, and so on, with systemic chronic stresses such as malnutrition and poor health, in shaping vulnerability and the dynamic interaction of these forces across social and geographic scales means that levels of vulnerability are hard to predict.⁴⁴ Moreover, slow onset disaster processes are not seen in many cases as immediately threatening, thereby forestalling preparedness and mitigation.

However, as United Nations Framework Convention on Climate Change (UNFCCC) Article 4.8 makes clear, there is some basis for establishing some broad scale levels of exposure and vulnerability. UNFCCC Article 4.8 provides that The Parties shall give full consideration to what actions are necessary ... to meet the specific needs and concerns of developing country Parties arising from the adverse effects of climate change and/or the impact of the implementation of response measures, especially on:

1. Small island countries
2. Countries with low-lying coastal areas
3. Countries with arid and semiarid areas, forested areas, and areas liable to forest decay
4. Countries prone to natural disasters
5. Countries with areas liable to drought and desertification
6. Countries with areas of high urban atmospheric pollution
7. Countries with areas of fragile ecosystems, including mountainous ecosystems
8. Countries whose economies are dependent on income generated from the production, processing, and export and/or on consumption of fossil fuels and associated energy-intensive products
9. Land-locked and transit countries

Potential forces leading to mass displacement in these UNFCCC identified regions as well as other exposed and vulnerable locations will be

1. *Rapid Onset Drivers and Evacuation*: Displacement (dismantling of infrastructural and socioeconomic patterns by a disaster agent) and evacuation (physical transfer to a different location). Mega-earthquakes and large hurricanes are examples of some rapid onset events that could lead to evacuation and mass displacement.
2. *Slow Onset Drivers and Forced Migration*: Many catastrophes, impacting large numbers of people and wide areas, will be slow onset processes, including drought, desertification, sea level rise, salinization, deglaciation, and the more recent volcanic eruption in Iceland and the British Petroleum (BP) oil spill in the Gulf of Mexico.
3. *Climate Change Mitigation Projects and Displacement*: Climate change and disaster mitigation projects potentially will displace large numbers of people. Large-scale projects such as dams, coastal defenses, water transfer schemes, and renewable energy complexes developed in the name of mitigation and adaptation are also likely to induce major population displacements.⁴⁵
4. *Relocation as Mitigation*: Historically, relocation of communities at risk has been undertaken by many societies, usually without a great deal of success.⁴⁶ At present, there are few examples of mass relocation as mitigation. There are, however, a number of examples of small-scale voluntary resettlement as mitigation that have enhanced the resilience and reduced the vulnerability of communities, including many examples from FEMA's now-defunct Project Impact program. Moreover, recent efforts in Latin America have produced guidelines

for relocation for disaster risk reduction[47] and several cases of at least partially successful relocation of communities, although none of them would qualify as "mass relocation."[48]

Mitigation aims to increase the self-reliance of people in hazard-prone environments to demonstrate that they have the resources and organization to withstand the worst effects of the hazards to which they are vulnerable. In other words, disaster mitigation, in contrast to dependency creating relief, is empowering.[49] Mitigation thus brings in issues of development in that anything that increases the resilience and security of society can be defined as a form of development.

Although the problem seems to be an enduring one, until relatively recently, most of the literature has characterized disaster-induced displacement as temporary, suggesting that people eventually return.[50] However, a great deal of this research has been excessively event-focused both temporally and spatially and has given far less attention to the longer term, more geographically dispersed aspects of post-event recovery or reconstruction. Today, with broadened and deepened spatial and temporal scales of analysis, natural disasters, rather than unanticipated and unique events caused by a natural agent, are seen to be much more explainable in terms of the "normal" order of things. That is, the conditions of inequality and subordination in the society, rather than the accidental geophysical features of a place, are the primary sources of vulnerability. This perspective has shifted the focus away from the disaster event and toward the vulnerability of peoples embedded in the "on-going societal and man–environment relations that prefigure [disaster]."[51] While expanded intensities of hydrometerological phenomena might suggest that catastrophic impact might transcend local vulnerability differentials, it is worth noting that the ability to recover will still be socially constructed.

DEMOGRAPHIC MOVEMENT

When people are subject to internal or external forces that force them to alter their location in space, the resulting movement takes a number of different forms that vary along the spectrum of a number of different characteristics. If the threat is immediate, flight or escape to the closest safe location is a frequent response. Such safe havens may prove to be permanent.[52] An impending threat may result in an evacuation that may resemble flight or may be more organized or administrated by internal or external agents (Hurricane Katrina, for example). Displacement similarly can occur as the result of flight or be more planned in the sense that people are organized and obliged to move from one residence site to another either temporarily or permanently. If the movement is thought to be permanent, resettlement in the form of the creation of a new residence site may actually be the outcome.[53] Finally, as mentioned earlier, forced migration can involve permanent, longer distance moves generally into very different environments. Some of the forms of demographic movement may lead to others as in flight or evacuation, which may lead to displacement and resettlement or eventually to forced migration (see Figure 9.4).

Figure 9.4 Pakistani flood victims sit on the floor of a U.S. Army helicopter as part of U.S. and Pakistani efforts to evacuate them from the town of Khyber in Pakistan. (http://www.army.mil/media/142583.)

CONTINUA OF RELOCATION

Each form of demographic movement may vary along a number of scales or continua between opposites associated with certain characteristics that refer largely to the social and environmental relations expressed in the particular context. The following set of paired responses is useful in understanding the types of demographic movement that occur in mass displacement:

- Proactive or reactive
- Voluntary–involuntary
- Temporary–permanent
- Physical danger–economic danger
- Administrated–non-administrated

These five pairs are far more points on a series of continua rather than closed or opposing categories. In addition, these concepts have to be treated with a certain flexibility, and should not be taken as hard and fast categories because the reality of particular occurrences of forced migration tends to be too complex to nail down within rigid categories. Looking at each kind of demographic movement along the various continua presented reveals the wide variability that each can display. Flight, for example, generally tends to be proactive and forced, but not administered, can be temporary or permanent, tends to be associated with physical danger and may result in permanent displacement, resettlement, or forced migration. Evacuation, usually a response to physical danger, can have similar outcomes, can be proactive or reactive but tends to be administered to a greater or lesser degree.

In disasters, I make a distinction, one that holds for development-induced movement as well, between forced displacement and forced migration. Displacement can be an administered involuntary process of moving a population. Displacement can be temporary or permanent, and may be a response to both physical and economic harm. Migration involves moving further away, to different environments and for longer periods of time, if not permanently, and will vary in the degree of voluntariness or involuntariness. Except in extreme cases, the coercive power or push factors in disaster-induced forced migration will vary and may be balanced to some degree by pull factors or positive inducements to move.

THE CONSEQUENCES OF MASS RELOCATION

Most large-scale displacement very frequently involves whole communities and in many cases whole regions. This becomes significant particularly with regard to consequences and losses, because what often becomes lost is the community network that enabled people to access resources; not just material resources, but social and emotional support that in stressful times in the displacement of communities becomes all the more a significant issue. The community is more than the sum of the total number of individuals and the loss of community for displaced people, particularly when the loss is the outcome of aid policies that do not take community into account, can be devastating.

When an entire community is displaced and resettled, it is not simply lifted up and set down whole in a new site. In most cases the community is reconfigured in specific ways. Most resettlement projects, particularly in the developing world, directly or indirectly further two fundamental processes, the expansion of the state and integration into regional and national market systems. Neither of these processes of inclusion is particularly simple or straightforward, but in most cases, they produce a restructuring of social, economic, and political relationships toward the priorities of the larger society. In many respects, resettlement will not necessarily destroy "local cultures" as much as it appropriates them and restructures them in terms of values and goals often originating from far beyond the local context. Such a process involves the reduction of local culture, society, and economy from all their varied expressions to a narrow set of institutions and activities that make them compatible with the purposes of the larger society.[54]

If we are to both understand and respond effectively to potential mass displacements from catastrophes, we need to identify those pertinent sources of theory and information that can inform appropriate policy formation and practice. The process of resettlement in cases of involuntary uprooting has proven to be a particularly challenging one. In point of fact, the record of successful resettlement projects is dismal. The vast majority of these projects, whether from disasters, development or conflict-driven displacement, leave local people permanently displaced, disempowered, and destitute. For the vast majority of the displaced, the causes of dislocation and the uprooting process itself are nothing less than catastrophic both at the personal level and at the level of community. These forces, natural and technological disasters, political conflict and large-scale development projects, are what I have called "totalizing phenomena" in their capacity to affect virtually every domain of human life.[55]

For people affected by disasters and other environmental changes, forced migration or displacement and resettlement often constitute a second disaster in their lives. The complexity of disasters reverberates in the losses that people experience and in the process of recovery. Serious disasters inflict terrible losses on people and communities, often shredding families and uprooting communities to radically changed or new environments. Displacement both compounds and makes permanent many of the losses incurred in disaster. Those who can reconstruct *in situ*, even in much diminished circumstances, generally stand a better chance at recovery.

The destruction or loss through uprooting of livelihood and community require affected people to engage in a process of reinvention. As human beings are social creatures, the reinvention of the self will be intimately linked to the reinvention of social bonds and community as the principal form of social living of humankind. The process of reinvention or recovery will have both material and social aspects. Material and social losses compound each other. Those who are uprooted, having suffered almost complete loss, like political refugees, must migrate with fewer resources with which to reconstruct their lives.

Material elements such as housing, the possessions of a lifetime, infrastructure, services like electricity and potable water, healthcare, transportation and communication, and nutrition can all be endangered, damaged, or destroyed in catastrophes or lost in displacement. In addition to physical damage, material losses resonate profoundly as well in the social world, compounding the serious losses also inflicted in the economic, social, and cultural life of survivors. For example, material damages frequently mean the loss of livelihoods, whether through destruction or loss of worksite, tools and equipment, land or common property resources, or physical injury. Loss of livelihood and the capacity to sustain oneself endanger individual and social identity producing a loss of status and resulting in marginalization and social disarticulation. The loss of a house is also the loss of a place in the social world. And the community, the social world, is endangered by such individual losses.

The dispersal, displacement, or death of family members fragments not only a household, but erodes the social cohesion of a community as well. Disaster-caused deaths shred those networks of relationships that form the basis of personal and social identity, setting people adrift, without those ties that anchor the self in the social world. Survivors of serious disasters, in which there is great loss of life and prolonged devastation and displacement, may also suffer a loss of personal identity, the partial loss of the self. The loss of significant others in high mortality disasters is also a loss of the self in that the part of the self that was invested in the lost relationship is also lost. Thus, the loss of a child means that one has lost that part of the self that was a parent. The loss of status, the social leveling, the reduction to a common level of misery can constitute an assault on the sense of the self.

Cultural identity is often placed at risk in uprooted communities. The loss and destruction of important cultural sites, shrines, religious objects, the interruption of important sacred and secular events and rituals undermines the community's sense of itself. Disasters and displacement may endanger the identification with an environment that may once have been seen as nurturing and central to cultural identity but is feared and distrusted in the aftermath.[56] Displacement for any group can be a crushing blow, but for indigenous peoples it can prove mortal. Land tenure is considered to be an essential element in the survival of indigenous societies and distinctive cultural identities.

These losses of community, family, and self compound each other to create another form of loss, the loss of meaning. These events and the prolonged conditions of deprivation and displacement can shake the foundations of personal worldview and identity. They challenge the culturally constructed vision in which the world is a logical place, where life makes sense. Major disasters and displacement rob people of the social context in which they lived meaningful lives, judged to be significant by others around them. This loss of personal relationships and the social context in which they were expressed and in which the individual was affirmed may leave people bereft of a sense of meaning, a sense of purpose in life. Religious belief can also become a casualty in the aftermath of disasters.

When people are forced from their known environments, they become separated from the material and cultural resource base upon which they have depended for life as individuals and as communities. Moreover, a sense of place has been shown to play an important role in individual and collective identity formation, in the way time and history are encoded and contextualized, and in interpersonal, community and intercultural relations.[57-60] A sense of place is crucial in the creation of what Giddens calls an "environment of trust" in which space, kin relations, local communities, cosmology, and tradition are linked.[61]

In summary, removal from one of the most basic physical dimensions of life can be a form of removal from life. The disruption in individual or community identity and stability in place, resulting in resettlement in a strange landscape can baffle and silence people in the same way a strange language can.[62] Culture loses its ontological grounding and people must struggle to construct a life world that can clearly articulate their continuity and identity as a community again. The human need for "environments of trust" is fundamental to the sense of order and predictability implied by culture.

AND AFTER DISPLACEMENT AND FORCED MIGRATION?

There has been much speculation regarding the number of people who may be forced to migrate by catastrophic environmental change or disruption but surprisingly little about where they go and what they are going to do when they get there. From other forms of forced migration and displacement, we can project that there will be at least four options.

Assimilation with co-ethnics sometimes reduces the traumatic effects of displacement, but not always. Angolan refugees in Zambia never felt displaced because they moved in with co-ethnics even though they had crossed a political border.[63] On the other hand, Inuits in Alaska cannot conceive of living in someone else's community, even though they may also be Inuit. They say it would be like living in someone else's house.[64,65]

Camps: Camps are often seen as a temporary solution for political refugees, but they have a tendency to become permanent as in the case of the Palestinians whose "camps" have evolved into neighborhoods, villages, or towns, although still seen by many as temporary. In some cases, once a camp is established it may become a permanent fixture, even though different refugee populations may pass through it *en route* to repatriation or resettlement in a foreign country as in the Tongorara camp in Zambia that has housed successive waves of different refugees from regional conflicts over a generation. Camps are originally never meant to be a durable solution and are established as temporary emergency facilities, often with minimum infrastructure that over time becomes more permanent, but still less than satisfactory. The temporary status of camps, despite long-term residence, often forestalls major efforts at development at both the household and local levels (see Figure 9.5).

Urbanization: The vast majority of people displaced over the last 40 years by Indian dam construction have migrated to urban slums disappearing into those vast populations of poor and vulnerable people that strain the capacities of environments, administrations, and infrastructures to meet urban needs.[66]

Resettlement: The outcomes of the vast majority of planned resettlement projects have been very poor, resulting in the impoverishment of the affected populations.[67] Projects are frequently poorly planned, underfunded, and badly implemented leaving affected populations destitute and disempowered. Such projects compound the losses experienced in displacement and can constitute severe violations of human rights.[68,69]

Figure 9.5 Rwandan refugee camp in East Zaire. (Public domain photo from http://article.wn.com/view/2010/09/02/UN_to_release_Congo_genocide_report_in_October_g/.)

INVOLUNTARY MIGRATION, DISPLACEMENT, AND RECOVERY

If, in fact, the uprooted are resettled in some systematic way, the quality of the resettlement project itself may play a major role in the capacity of the community to recover from the trauma of displacement. Such projects are really about reconstructing communities after they have been materially destroyed and socially traumatized to varying degrees. Reconstructing and reconstituting community is an idea that needs to be approached with a certain humility and realism about the limits of our capacities. Such humility and realism have not always characterized the planners and administrators of projects dealing with uprooted peoples to any major extent to date. Indeed, the goals of such undertakings frequently stress efficiency and cost containment over restoration of community. Such top-down initiatives have a poor record of success because of a lack of regard for local community resources. Planners often perceive the culture of uprooted people as an obstacle to success, rather than as a resource.

Reconstructing/reconstituting a community means attempting to replace through administrative routine an evolutionary process in which social, cultural, economic, and environmental interactions arrived at through trial and error and deep experiential knowledge develop, enabling a population to achieve a mutually sustaining social coherence and material sustenance over time. The systems that develop are not perfect, are often far from egalitarian, and do not conform to some imagined standard of efficiency. The idea that such a process could be the outcome of planning is ambitious to say the least. One of the best outcomes that might be imagined for resettlement projects is to work out a system in which people can materially sustain themselves while they themselves begin the process of social reconstruction. The least that could be hoped for might be that resettlement projects not impede the process of community reconstitution. However, if the level of impoverishment experienced by most resettled peoples is any indicator, even adequate systems of material reproduction are beyond either the will or the capabilities of most contemporary policy makers and planners. This does not bode well for the victims of potential mass displacements. We must be aware of the potential for events of catastrophic scale to overwhelm the organizational, logistic, and material capabilities of even the most informed and prepared of disaster managers and teams.

There is an inextricable tie between material and social reconstruction. However, reconstruction must be much more than being simply materially sustained while reconstituting the community. To be sure, prolonged severe material deprivation in certain circumstances has been shown to erode the basic identities and interactions upon which community is based.[70] To what extent is some basic level of materiality a necessary pre-condition for social reconstruction? And conversely, to what extent does social reconstruction in some form of cooperative action undergird and enable material reconstruction? No community can survive without a material base, but once these basic elements are re-established, they must be continually reproduced through cooperation, which is not always based on material interest, if the community is not to sink into prolonged dependency. In effect, the material and social rebuilding processes must be mutually reinforcing. Indeed, they must in some sense be mutually constitutive. The built environment in which we live is a material expression of our social relations.[71] It is both expressive of and shapes our social relations. Nowhere does this relationship become more crucial than in the process of community reconstruction. Material reconstruction can both support and express social reconstitution. Material reconstruction can be a confirmation of social reconstitution. It can also undermine the process severely and very frequently has. The form and delivery of housing after disasters are frequently the cause of considerable conflict and resentment that impede the process of social reconstitution. In the aftermath of a devastating avalanche, the population of Yungay, Peru was riven with hostilities over the distribution of emergency shelters. Moreover, when permanent housing became available, the various forms it took soon began to express class and ethnic divisions.[72]

UNDERSTANDING MASS DISPLACEMENT AND RESETTLEMENT

As is evident from this discussion, the social scientific literature on displacement and resettlement is clustered around three themes: civil and military conflicts, disasters, and development projects. The relatively scant literature from disaster-driven displacement focuses largely on temporary shelters, with a few cases dealing with permanent resettlement of small communities.[73–75] The research from conflict-driven uprooting focuses largely on temporary camps, repatriation and individual, and family refugee resettlement to foreign countries.[76,77] The literature on DFDR generally deals with resettlement of communities of varying size and sometimes entire regions affected by large-scale infrastructural projects.[78–83] It is clear that catastrophe-driven mass relocation must draw on these other fields for insights into how best to understand and respond to the potentially large-scale displacements projected for the not too distant future. This research is also being complemented by a growing concern regarding IDPs.[84,85]

Over the last half century, various researchers have developed a variety of conceptual approaches to the problem of mass relocation. First, Scudder alone and subsequently with Elizabeth Colson developed an approach based on the concept of stress to describe and analyze the process of involuntary dislocation and resettlement.[86,87] The Four Stage Framework, as Scudder now calls it, emphasizes how most resettlers can be expected to behave during each of the four stages, passage through which must be completed if the resettlement project is to be successful.[88]

They posited that three forms of stress resulted from involuntary relocation and resettlement: physiological stress, psychological stress, and sociocultural stress. These three forms of stress, referred to as multidimensional stress, are experienced as affected people pass through the displacement and resettlement process. Physiological stress is seen in increased morbidity and mortality rates. The impoverishment that generally results from forced migration or displacement may lower both social resilience and individual resistance to disease, particularly among the young and the elderly. Psychological stress, seen as directly proportional to the abruptness of the relocation, has four manifestations: trauma from the uprooting process, guilt about having survived, grief for a lost home and anxiety about an uncertain future. Serious implications from psychological stress include the "Dying of a broken heart" syndrome with prevalence among the elderly.

Sociocultural stress is manifested as a result of the economic, political, and cultural effects of relocation. The lack of economic support, evidenced in deficient livelihood possibilities, has been shown to be a major source of stress. A lack of leadership often emerges as former leaders who failed to protect the interests of the community or to mount credible resistance to resettlement also produces anxiety. Other forms of stress result from the reduction in cultural inventory: loss of traditional patterns, institutions and symbols, and conflict with the host community.

The resettlement process itself is represented as occurring in four stages, which Scudder labels:

1. Planning for resettlement before physical removal
2. Coping with the initial drop in living standards that tends to follow removal
3. Initiating economic development and community-formation activities
4. Handing over a sustainable resettlement process to the second generation of resettlers and to non-project authority institutions[89]

The planning stage involves the decisions taken by authorities regarding the population to be relocated, particularly those that influence the length and severity of the stressful coping stage. The coping stage begins when the population to be relocated is first affected. Generally speaking the coping stage is the longest and the stage in which the most severe multidimensional stress is experienced. The general attitude of people during the coping stage is conservative in order to avoid the possibility of further risk and stress.

The handing over stage begins when people begin to abandon their conservative risk avoidance strategies and express greater initiative and risk-taking behavior. Scudder and Colson, and subsequently Scudder, emphasize that this stage is often never realized since many projects remain trapped in the coping stage by inept and inappropriate policy and implementation. Equally difficult to attain is the final stage of handing over. Achieving the handing over stage signifies that the resettlement project has been successful. They define success by the act of local management of taking over economic and political affairs and the phasing out of external agencies and personnel from day-to-day management of the community. The community has become able to assume its place within the larger regional context that includes host communities and other regional systems.[90,91]

IMPOVERISHMENT RISKS AND RECONSTRUCTION MODEL

At roughly the same time that Scudder and Colson were developing their model, an approach began in an emerging political ecology that focused on the linked ideas of vulnerability and risk. Vulnerability was initially employed in disaster research to understand the vast differences among societies in disaster losses from similar agents. An alternative perspective on human–environment relations, emphasizing the role of human interventions in generating disaster risk and impact, found that these sets of relations coalesced in the concept of vulnerability.[92]

As these concepts gained currency, Cernea began to write about the risks of poverty resulting from displacement from water projects.[93] He subsequently developed his now well-known Impoverishment Risks and Reconstruction (IRR) approach to understanding (and mitigating) the major adverse effects of displacement; the IRR identifies eight basic risks associated with displacement.[94,95] The model is based on the three basic concepts of risk, impoverishment, and reconstruction. Deriving his understanding of risk from Giddens's (1990) notion of the possibility that a certain course of action may produce negative effects, Cernea models displacement risks by deconstructing the "syncretic, multifaceted process of displacement into its identifiable, principle and most widespread components. These are: (a) landlessness, (b) joblessness, (c) homelessness, (d) marginalization, and (e) food insecurity, increased morbidity, loss of access to common property resources, and social disarticulation."[96] He further asserts that the probability of these risks producing serious consequences is extremely high in badly or unplanned resettlement. All these risks follow the displacement process with the threat of a second calamity that entails such risks that can translate directly into losses. Cernea's IRR model is designed to predict, diagnose, and resolve the problems associated with DFDR.[97]

One of the principal risks in displacement and resettlement is social disarticulation, including the scattering of kinship groups and informal networks of mutual help.[98] The disarticulation of spatially and culturally based patterns of self-organization, social interaction, and reciprocity constitutes a loss of essential social ties that affect access to resources, compounding the loss of natural and man-made capital. Thus, in displacement and resettlement, people's adaptations to the social disarticulation produce new dynamics that influence their access and control over resources, often leading to a process of further impoverishment. Therefore, understanding institutional processes in resettlers' adaptive strategies will be crucial for identifying the socioculturally specific nature of the risks Cernea identified as inherent in forced displacement, thus helping to explain why displacement and resettlement so often result in greater impoverishment of affected households.

Moreover, Cernea's model points to strategies to counter the risks of resettlement. Each risk can be confronted with the means to reduce it. For example, recognizing the loss of land should produce plans for land-based resettlement. The loss of jobs or livelihoods points to the need for re-employment in the new community. The loss of a home underscores the need for appropriate housing. The disarticulation of community, marginalization, and expropriation must be responded to by efforts at community reconstitution, greater social inclusion, and the restoration of community assets. Food insecurity and diminished health can be prevented by appropriate safety net programs.[99] Indeed, the similarities in challenges faced by displaced and resettled people, regardless of cause or driver, have been noted by several scholars as requiring greater attention from researchers.[100] The commonalities between development and disasters increase the further in time from the initial event. Over time, there is a greater degree of commonality in the challenges people face whether they are victims of development or disaster. Thus, the survivors of Hurricane Katrina were faced with the same persisting issues as those of development survivors: homelessness, unemployment, marginalization, the loss of neighborhood and community, mental and physical health challenges, and powerlessness.[101,102]

THE COMPLEXITY OF THE DISPLACEMENT AND RESETTLEMENT PROCESS

Chris de Wet has sought to incorporate Cernea's important insights into a more comprehensive approach.[103] Asking why resettlement so often goes wrong, de Wet sees two broad approaches to responding to the question. The first approach is what he calls the "Inadequate Inputs" approach, which argues that resettlement projects fail because of a lack of appropriate inputs: national legal frameworks and policies, political will, funding, pre-displacement research, careful implementation, and monitoring. Optimistic in tenor, the inadequate inputs approach posits that the risks and injuries of resettlement can be controlled and mitigated by appropriate policies and practices. De Wet, on the other hand, finds himself moving toward what he calls the "Inherent Complexity" approach. He argues that there is a complexity in resettlement that is inherent in "the interrelatedness of a range of factors of different orders: cultural, social, environmental, economic, institutional, and political—all of which are taking place in the context of imposed space change and of local level responses and initiatives."[104] Moreover, these changes are taking place simultaneously in an interlinked and mutually influencing process of transformation. And further, these internal changes from the displacement process are also influenced by and respond to the imposition from external sources of power as well as the initiatives of local actors. Therefore, the resettlement process emerges out of the complex interaction of all these factors *in ways that are not predictable and that do not seem amenable to a linear-based, rational planning approach.*

De Wet suggests that a more comprehensive and open-ended approach rather than the predominately economic and operational perspective of the inadequate inputs approach is necessary to understand, adapt to, and take advantage of the opportunities presented by the inherent complexity of the displacement and resettlement process. While some might see this perspective as unduly pessimistic, *the fact that authorities are limited in the degree of control they can exercise over a project creates a space for resettlers to take greater control over the process.* The challenge thus becomes the development of policy that supports a genuine participatory and open-ended approach to resettlement planning and decision making.[105]

PSYCHOLOGICAL, SOCIAL, AND CULTURAL IMPOVERISHMENT

Ted Downing and Carmen Garcia-Downing contend that insufficient attention has been paid to the psycho-socio-cultural (PSC) impoverishment inflicted by involuntary displacement. Mitigation of PSC damages has proven much more problematic, seldom considered by projects as constituting a risk that requires mitigation. The authors argue that five fallacies block discussions and actions, providing those who should bear responsibility with an untenable rationale for not addressing the issue. The first fallacy, the "compensation is enough" fallacy, asserts that compensation payments meet all the moral and economic obligations due to displaced peoples. The second fallacy impeding action is the "strict compliance" fallacy, which holds that adherence to project plans, policies, and laws adequately addresses resettlement risks. If the policies, politics, and economics have been addressed but PSC impoverishment still occurs, a third fallacy is to "blame the victims" themselves because they are seen as incapable of understanding or taking advantage of economic opportunities offered to them. A fourth fallacy, "the clock stops with construction," asserts that responsibilities to displaced people end at the completion of the resettlement action plan (RAP) or with the completion of the construction phase. And finally, the fifth fallacy, the fallacy that "someone else should pay," holds that the project designers, governments, and financiers are not legally or economically liable for PSC changes.

The Downings argue that in the PSC realm, it is highly unlikely that a predisplacement routine culture may be recovered, let alone be restored. However, this does not mean that nothing can be done. PSC recovery must be measured by criteria different than those for economic recovery or legal liability. Relative success is determined by how well the transformed routine culture answers the primary questions of the displaced compared to the predisplacement culture. The primary questions include: Who are we? Where are we? How do we relate to one another? The policy/practice-relevant question thus becomes, "What can be done to facilitate the new routine culture so that it adequately addresses the primary cultural questions faced by the displaced peoples?"[106]

FACTORS IN SUCCESS/FAILURE OF POST-DISASTER RESETTLEMENT

Complexity notwithstanding, there are fundamental questions that have proven to be key in the success or failure of resettlement projects. In material terms, the needs of individuals, households, communities, and the extra-local systems of which they are parts and the organized responses to these needs are numerous, diverse, and interconnected. While there are urgent needs in any uprooting crisis, relatively adequate procedures have actually been developed to respond to these, although a uniform standard has yet to be reached, despite the much-debated Sphere project guidelines for reaching such standards.[107] Unfortunately, the procedures put in place to cope with emergency needs are rarely linked to key features of community organization, although they can have a determining role in the development of the longer-term rehabilitative system, often with very negative impacts on the long-term viability of the community.

Although seemingly obvious, the issue of employment for the uprooted over the long term has often been neglected and resettlement projects often end up as impoverished, dependent communities requiring continued inputs of aid over long periods of time. From both a material and a psychological standpoint, economics drives the process of reconstruction and/or resettlement. Employment provides needed income to replace or improve upon those personal and household needs not provided by aid, but it is also a form of action that enables people to return to being actors, rather than being acted upon as disaster victims, refugees or development displacees all of which are essentially passive rather than active roles. Uprooting causes many people to lose the means of production, such as land, tools, or access to other resources and they will be unable to resume normal activities until such resources are obtained.

In addition, four issues of organization and design can be identified as significant in the success or failure of resettlement projects. *Poor choice of site for resettlement is one of the most frequently mentioned causes of resettlement failure.* Sites for resettlement are often chosen using factors other than the welfare and development of the population, such as availability or price rather than proximity to resources or employment. The design or layout of the settlement has been cited as a source of sufficient dissatisfaction to result in abandoning the resettlement site. Ease of construction, misconstrued concepts of efficiency, and the imposition of urban middle class values on rural populations seem to lie at the root of such problems as monotonous, uniform designs for resettlement sites. Housing design and reconstruction are often blamed for the rejection or failure of resettlement projects. Faulty construction and inferior materials in houses become quickly evident with use and create difficult living conditions, particularly regarding thermal protection in different seasons. Projects that suffer failure, or at best partial success, are often characterized by policies that depend very little on consultation with the affected population. The three previously mentioned problems (poor site selection, inappropriate design, and unsatisfactory housing) derive from a lack of consultation with, and participation by, the affected people. This lack is generally due to a disparagement of local knowledge and culture on the part of policy makers and planners.[106,108]

Thus, life-sustaining activities and homes and life are the most deeply felt needs in establishing a long-term system for dealing with material necessity in the stress of uprooting and resettlement, whatever the cause. Whether it is due to sudden disaster onset, the explosion of civil violence, or the bad or absent planning of development projects, resettled people are frequently housed in "temporary" quarters, which in all too many cases become permanent; however, inadequate and inappropriate they may be.

House form and settlement design that are donor-driven endanger the connection that people establish with their built environment; the forms and design violate cultural norms of space and place, private and public life, inhibit the reweaving of social networks and, inhibit the re-emergence of community identity.[109] Additionally, the design of settlements that place living quarters in dense proximity, which is convenient for relief agencies, significantly increases the probability of infectious disease transmission with the community.[110]

There may be a difficult trade-off between reconstituting economic resources (especially land and property) versus the social and cultural benefits gained by staying together. This is especially true in development-induced displacement when a project has opted for land for land replacement and the host population density is high. It may be difficult or even impossible to settle a community together on sufficient land. Or people may need to move far from extra-community networks in order to have both sufficient land and avoid dispersal of the community itself. This creates hard questions. However, until people resume employment, they remain dependent on external resources and recovery remains incomplete.

RESETTLEMENT, RECONSTRUCTION, AND DEVELOPMENT

In effect, resettlement must be approached as development. If mass relocation results only in the dispersal of affected populations to poverty-stricken slums, or warehousing them in "temporary" or otherwise permanent camps (rural slums), the process of resettlement will compound the trauma and human rights violations of uprooting and consign them forever to misery. Moreover, after 40 years of application in development-forced displacement, the compensation principle has been amply demonstrated to be utterly inadequate in restoring livelihoods to displaced people.[111,112] Therefore, resettlement projects must be configured as development projects. The projects must include the appropriate investments to enable people to become active and self-sufficient members of resilient communities.

However, to date, relatively few nations have either the necessary legislation or the administrative structure and capacity to competently undertake the task of resettling displaced populations. China has established comprehensive legislation regarding resettlement and several other nations are considering various legislative initiatives.[113] However, generally speaking, a mix of public agencies, with a wide array environmental, social, and economic responsibilities, is assembled and charged with planning and implementing resettlement, frequently creating projects with serious internal contradictions and conflicting agendas.[114] For example, in the context of development-forced displacement, there is a significant debate between the national governments and multilateral agencies that wish to require "free, prior and informed consultation" before resettlement and local peoples and their allies who demand "free, prior and informed consent." To a large extent, except in mitigation projects, the impact of a catastrophic event or process may preclude the opportunity for consultation, consent, or even preparation. In resettlement for disaster risk reduction projects (mitigation), the basic requirement is a credible risk analysis that establishes that risks cannot be mitigated and that the only viable option for public safety is resettlement.

Nonetheless resettlement projects are frequently underfunded and compensation packages are unequal to the task of restoring livelihoods and well-being. For example, in the United States, 33 federal, state and county agencies were involved in the relocation of the community of Allenville, Arizona away from a flood plain. Although this comparatively small relocation was successful, the project was characterized by an at times bewildering complexity in which the various rules and operating procedures of the agencies involved became a major impediment to the successful resettlement of the population.[115]

Such has been the case for the Inuit villagers of Shishmaref and Newtok in Alaska, who are threatened by serious coastal erosion and sea level rise due to climate change. Although they have opted for resettlement, the villagers' plans have been frustrated by the lack of clear responsible agencies and a systematic strategy for resettlement on the part of state and federal authorities.[116] There is, in fact, no lead agency, responsible for relocation planning and the coordination of all the various agencies working on housing, transportation, community infrastructure, education, health, and other related needs.[117] This confusion and lack of expertise and coordination produced resettlement budgets that ranged between $100 and 200 million dollars for a village of roughly 600 people. *Given potential large-scale relocations in the future, there is an unquestionable and urgent need for development of a coherent administrative infrastructure, including a responsible lead agency empowered by appropriate legislation to deal with these challenges.*

A study by the World Bank's Operations Evaluation Department of five major bank-funded dam projects concludes that while better planning has occurred, it has not led generally to better involuntary resettlement. Furthermore, the public agencies charged with resettlement have not responded adequately to the challenge of resettlement. They also find that income restoration strategies, whether based on land for land or other options, have not in general been successful. The key to success in their opinion is genuine commitment to the resettlement process as a development opportunity by the borrower country.[118]

One of the key elements in such a commitment to a resettlement process is the adequate preparation of design and implementation staff. Resettlement projects, based on their dismal performance, were known until a relatively short time ago as "career killers" in the development banks. Now, due to the greater recognition of the importance of improving resettlement project performance, there has been an expansion of specialists in the field. Nonetheless, at the level of design and implementation, the need for training resettlement professionals appears as an imperative both for the present and for the future. The definition of the format and content of such training should be a research priority.[119]

RESETTLEMENT ACTION PLANS

Resettlement Action Plans (RAPs) are now a requirement of multilateral lending institutions such as the World Bank, the Interamerican Development Bank and the Asian Development Bank prior to undertaking the resettlement of any population for the construction of an infrastructural project.[120TM]

RAPs are generally prepared according to specific planning principles that include a policy and budget framework that emphasize income enhancement and entitlements derived from consultation with affected people, and emphasize the strengthening of local institutional capacity. A RAP generally includes an introductory description of the projects, detailing efforts to minimize resettlement. Censuses and socioeconomic surveys are essential for identifying the characteristics of the affected peoples and their needs and cultural requirements. Since resettlement requires access to land for new communities, as well as crucial human rights issues, the national legal framework, and the institutional arrangements for responsible agencies must also be detailed in the RAP. After resettlement sites have been selected, based on available land and adequate access to natural (arable land, water, etc.) and social resources (roads, markets, etc.), income restoration plans must be established. The RAP must also include a detailed schedule for implementation that includes participation and consultation, the redress of grievances, monitoring and evaluation as well as a budget sufficient to carry out all these tasks. Additional quantitative and documentary data should also be included in annexes.

THE ARENAL DAM RESETTLEMENT PROJECT

Despite the general failure to develop resettlement projects that do not impoverish affected populations, there have been some cases whose relative success points the way to improved practice. Assessing success, however, is challenging. Scudder (2009) maintains that resettlement cannot be adequately evaluated for success for at least two generations, thus complicating the analysis because success (or failure) may be due as much to exogenous factors (other development projects or climatic variation, for example) as to appropriate planning.

The Arenal Hydroelectric Project in Costa Rica is considered by many to have succeeded in improving the standards of living and returning control over their own lives to the resettled people 5 years after the implementation of the project.[121] The Arenal Hydroelectric Project involved the construction of a dam 70 m high that would produce a reservoir of 1.75 million cubic meters (or 88 square kilometers) that necessitated the displacement and resettlement of about 2500 people (roughly 500 families). The area in which the project was located was characterized by the "humid tropics cattle-ranching complex," with little or no commercial agriculture. Subsistence agriculture was declining as well. When the dam project was approved, resettlement planning by the Instituto Costarricense de Electricidad (ICE), the national electricity company/dam builder/resettlement agency, began 2 years before any actual construction. The preparatory period consisted of 11 steps or phases. These 11 phases were

Phase I: Ethnographic Sample Survey of Communities
Phase II: Information Campaign and Meetings with Families
Phase III: Census of People and Property to Be Affected
Phase IV: Making Public the Planning Data
Phase V: New Settlement Site Selection
Phase VI: Action Plan for Resettlement Prepared
Phase VII: Land Acquisition
Phase VIII: Participation of the Affected Population
Phase IX: Financial Mechanism for Restitution of Property
Phase X: Construction of New Settlements
Phase XI: Community and Agricultural Development

The first 2–3 years (1976–1979) of the new communities were difficult. After the resettled people cleared the new lands, they planted traditional crops such as maize, manioc, plantains, and bananas. Seeds and cuttings were made available to the farmers as soon as their new plots had been allocated. The agricultural system in the new settlements was initially the traditional slash and burn technology. Subsequently, new vegetable, tree, and pasture crops, that had been field tested during the construction phase, began to be cultivated, particularly a new variety of coffee. Individual farmers obtained loans from the National Bank of Costa Rica to intensify production, and the farmers as a group organized a marketing cooperative. In the first years of the project, income from coffee increased by roughly 100% over pre-resettlement levels. New grasses for cattle fodder also enabled farmers to increase cattle pastured from one animal per hectare to three.

Income from these initiatives stimulated the purchase of additional farmlands, the construction of outbuildings on farms, purchase of vehicles, and the construction of a rural school building with no assistance from the government. The success of the families in the farming sector nourished success in the commercial sector. Shopkeepers and their families benefited by the increased levels of cash income in the communities. Levels of fixed capital and inventory values in the new communities range between 50% and 200% greater than in the old settlements. Furthermore, social organizational features developed in the new communities in the form of a school committee, a sports committee, and the continuation of the Catholic Church committee. A new road constructed by the project linked the new communities to market centers and fostered the development of several small dairy farms. However, this road was not paved until years after resettlement, and became virtually impassible during the rainy season, causing Arenal to lose its status as a market center and become a peripheral community in the basin.

Materially, the resettlement project was a resounding success—all promised infrastructure was well built and in place at the time of resettlement. However, recent assessments of the project indicate that economic activities were not as successful as initial evaluations indicated.[122] ICE actually paid very little attention to economic reconstruction other than putting the necessary infrastructure in place. The loss of the major employer in the basin (a foreign-owned cattle operation), increased geographic isolation, a rugged topography, increased rainfall, lower soil fertility, and a lot size too small for cattle or other commercially viable agricultural products (maximum of 6 hectares) were to blame for declines in economic activity, Families that had money to invest in buying more land or purchasing inputs to increase soil fertility could succeed in their agricultural endeavors, but most did not have access to these extra funds. A number of other agricultural experiments, including macadamia and cardamom, were attempted but none were successful at a large scale. As discussed above, coffee was the best attempt at generating a new agricultural economy, but most people today complain that the terrain was not well suited for coffee and that the trees took too long to produce good beans. While many families planted coffee initially, most went into debt from this effort rather than profiting from it. The cooperative closed down in the early 2000s. With regard to commercial businesses, many that were directly transferred from the original town closed or transferred ownership within the first few years post-resettlement due to a lack of clients once the community was no longer the commercial center of the valley.

In sum, despite the many successes of the resettlement project, life in Arenal was difficult for years post-resettlement. As in many rural areas, people moved from activity to activity just trying to survive, which was a major shift from the bustling market center of old Arenal. Many families simply abandoned ship in the first few years, leaving their homes vacant. Today, the general opinion is that residential tourism, spurred by the attractive mountainous terrain and views of the lake (i.e., the reservoir created by the dam), which began in the 1990s, can be credited for the economic success seen currently.[120] Nonetheless, it can be reasonably claimed that the general level of well-being of the community and the community's adaptive capacity is at least partially due to the planning process undertaken prior to the resettlement project. Partridge attributes the successes achieved in the project to three basic steps in the preparation process. Good data collection and community studies carried out by social scientists resulted in a resettlement plan than was both realistic and practical. He also emphasized the importance of consultation with the people to be relocated and their meaningful participation in the preparation process.[123]

THE NEAR FUTURE

Although estimates of the numbers of people who may be uprooted by catastrophes and climate change are problematic, the potential for mass displacement is real. It is also worth noting that among the statistics being cited, those pertaining to displacement by natural disaster are considered the most credible. Produced by the IDMC and the NRC, the number of people displaced by natural disasters is placed at over 42 million people, using a baseline of events from the EM-DAT database to produce a core data set for events where over 50,000 people were affected. Data on the displaced from each event is then sought from organizations involved in relief for those events.[124] However, at this point in time, in regard to climate change, it is more probable in most cases that climate change effects are only making matters somewhat worse for the majority of the world's most vulnerable people. Where displacement is occurring, it is generally the outcome of multiple factors, including environmental, political, and economic causes. In fact, at present, the problems afflicting, for example, the slum dwellers of Mumbai are not primarily climate change, but rather the conditions of poverty and exclusion that they are consigned to by the larger political economy encompassing their region, nation, and the world.

However, if predictions from the Intergovernmental Panel on Climate Change (IPCC) and other research organizations are even half right, and confidence in estimates for sea level rise, coastal erosion, desertification, and other forces that may displace people is considerably higher than that, then we must be prepared for significant increases in the role environmental factors will play in displacement in the relatively near future. In addition, although the number of refugees, asylum seekers and internally displaced people diminished slightly in the middle years of the current decade, it has begun increasing again.[125] We must also add the intentional displacement of many millions by vast infrastructural and other development projects, currently estimated to reach 15 million people a year. Thus, on the one hand, we are facing unusual changes that will generate very particular and potentially devastating threats, including large-scale displacements of people. On the other hand, we have the scientific tools at present to make predictions with sufficiently high probabilities that allow us to prepare to meet those threats.

Given the likelihood of increasing numbers of people being affected by displacement, there is a certain urgency to improve policies and practices for adaptation, mitigation, and assistance for uprooted peoples. It is imperative that legal frameworks be established both nationally and internationally to protect the welfare and human rights of people displaced by radical environmental change, development projects, and complex humanitarian emergencies. Further, such legal frameworks must lay the groundwork for stronger, more effective policies and practices to mitigate the impacts of displacement and resettlement. Displaced people should be actively involved in the planning and implementation of resettlement projects, which should be understood and organized as development projects with the aim of not just restoring pre-project levels, but improving conditions and the fair and equitable distribution of benefits. Given the lamentable record of failure of resettlement projects, the need for training of resettlement professionals is acute both currently and for the future.[126]

While predicting the precise number of people who will likely be displaced by direct impacts of disasters or the effects of climate change, or for that matter, those resettlement projects designed to mitigate their effects are not possible, it is likely to be large. *Where exposure and vulnerability assessments indicate risk that cannot be mitigated, assistance should be provided for gradual spontaneous migration before larger-scale resettlement becomes the only remaining option.*[127] Given its complexity, organized resettlement should be avoided if at all possible, but current projections indicate that national governments as well as local authorities should recognize that planned resettlement must be prepared for as an option for people threatened by mass displacement by environmental catastrophes.

REFERENCES

1. Hansen, A. and Oliver-Smith, A. 1982. *Involuntary Migration and Resettlement: The Problems and Responses of Dislocated People*, CO: Westview, p. 344.
2. Cernea, M. M. 1996. Understanding and preventing impoverishment from displacement: Reflections on the state of understanding, In *Understanding Improverishment from Development-Induced Displacement*, edited by C. McDowell, Providence, RI: Berghahn Books, pp. 13–32.
3. Turton, D. 2003. Refugees and "Other Forced Migrants": Towards a Unitary Study of Forced Migration, Paper presented at the Workshop on Settlement and Resettlement in Ethiopia, January 28–30. Addis Ababa.
4. Oliver-Smith, A. 2009. *Development and Dispossession: The Crisis of Development Forced Displacement and Resettlement*, Santa Fe: SAR Press.
5. Correa, E. 2011b. *Preventive Resettlement of Populations at Risk of Disaster: Experiences from Latin America*, Washington DC: World Bank and the Global Facility for Disaster Risk Reduction.

6. Correa, op. cit.
7. El-Hinnawi, E. 1985. *Environmental Refugees*, Nairobi, Kenya: United Nations Environment Programme.
8. Wood, W. B. 2001. Ecomigration: Linkages between environmental change and migration, In *Global Refugees and Global Migrants*, edited by A. R. Zolber and P. M. Benda, pp. 42–61, New York: Berghahn.
9. Black, R. 2001. Environmental refugees: Myth or reality?, *UNHCR Working Papers*, (34): 1–19.
10. Castles, S. 2002. Environmental change and forced migration: Making sense of the debate, *UNHCR Working Papers*, (70): 1–14.
11. Pearl, J. 2000. *Causality: Models, Reasoning and Inference*, Cambridge: Cambridge University Press.
12. Spirtes, P., C. Glymour, and R. Scheines. 2000. *Causation, Prediction and Search*, Cambridge, MA: MIT Press.
13. Biermann, F. and I. Boas. 2010. Preparing for a warmer world: Towards a global governance system to protect climate refugees, *Global Environmental Politics*, 10(1): 60–68.
14. Morvaridi, B. and G. Chatelard. 2004. Displacement and resettlement in the Middle East : Access to rights as a regional policy issue, Fifth Mediterranean social and political research meeting, IUE, Florence.
15. Wisner, B., P. Blaikie, T. Cannon, and I. Davis. 2004. In *At Risk: Natural Hazards, People's Vulnerability and Disasters*, 2nd ed., London: Routledge.
16. Adger, W. N., J. Paavola, and S. Huq. 2006. Toward justice in adaptation to climate change, In *Fairness in Adaptation to Climate Change*, edited by W. N. Adger, J. Paavola, S. Huq and M. J. Mace, pp.1–20, Cambridge, MA: MIT Press.
17. Correa, 2011, op. cit.
18. Oliver-Smith, A. 1991. Success and failures in post-disaster resettlement, *Disasters*, 15(1): 12–24.
19. Perry, R. W. and A. H. Mushkatel. 1984. *Disaster Management: Warning, Response and Community Relocation*, Westport, CT and London, UK: Quorum Books.
20. Barry, J. M. 1997. *Rising Tide: The Great Mississippi Flood of 1927 and How It Changed America*, New York: Simon and Schuster.
21. Egan, T. 2006. *The Worst Hard Time*, Houghton Mifflin: Boston.
22. Freudenberg, et al., 2007, op. cit.
23. Rodriguez, H. and D. Marks. 2006. Disasters, vulnerability, and governmental response: Where (How) have we gone so wrong?, *Corporate Finance Review*, (May/June) 5–14.
24. Millenium Ecosystem Assessment. 2005a. *Ecosystems and Human Well-Being: Synthesis*, Washington, DC: Island Press.
25. Millenium Ecosystem Assessment. 2005b. *Ecosystems and Human Well-Being: Desertification Synthesis*, Washington, DC: World Resources Institute.
26. Renaud, F. and J. Bogardi. 2007. Forced Migrations due to degradation of arid lands: Concepts, debate and policy requirements. In King C, Bigas H, Adeel Z (eds) Desertification and International Policy Imperative. *Proceedings of a Joint International Conference*. Algiers, Algeira 17–19, December 2006 UNU Desertification Series No. 7 United Nations University. Tokyo, Japan, pp. 24–34.
27. Warner, K., M. Hamza, A. Oliver-Smith, F. Renaud, and A. Julca. 2010. Climate change, environmental degradation and migration, *Natural Hazards*, 55: 689–713.
28. IPCC. 2007. Summary for Policymakers. In Climate Change 2007: The Physical Science Basis. Contribution of Working Group I to the Fourth Assessment Report of the

Intergovernmental Panel on Climate Change. Soomon, S., C. Qin, M. Manning, Z.Cher, M. Marquis, K.B. Avery, M. Tignor and H.L. Miller (eds). Cambridge University Press, Cambridge, United Kingdom and New York, NY, USA.
29. Renaud, et al., 2007, op. cit.
30. Dessai, S., K. O'Brien, and M. Hulme. 2007. Editorial: On uncertainty and climate change. *Global Environmental Change*, 17: 1–3.
31. Adamo, S. B. 2008. "Addressing Environmentally Induced Population Displacements: A Delicate Task," A Background Paper for the Population-Environment Research Network Cyberseminar on "Environmentally Induced Population Displacements", August 18–29 2008. (www.populationenvironmentresearch.org).
32. United Nations High Commissioner for Refugees. 2009.
33. Oliver-Smith, A. 2002. Theorizing disasters: Nature, culture, power, In *Culture and Catastrophe: The Anthropology of Disaster*, edited by S. M. Hoffman and A. Oliver-Smith. Santa Fe, NM: The School of American Research Press.
34. Yenotani, M. 2011. Displacement due to Natural Hazard-Induced Disasters. Global Estimates for 2009 and 2010. IDMC & NRC, Oslo.
35. Gemenne, F. 2011. Why the numbers don't add up: A review of estimates and predictions of people displaced by environmental changes. *Global Environmental Change*, 21s: s41–s49.
36. Hamza, M. 2007. "Challenges in Measuring Vulnerability in Complex Environments: Environmental Transformations and Tipping Points of Population Displacement and Humanitarian Crises," Expert Working Group "measuring Vulnerability" United Nations University Institute for Environment and Human Security, Bonn, November 19–22, 2007.
37. Hamza, op. cit.
38. Adger, et al., Ibid.
39. International Federation of Red Cross and Red Crescent Societies. 2004. World Disasters Report IFRC: Geneva.
40. IFRC, Ibid.
41. http://www.amnestyusa.org/pdf/UN_guidingprinciples_intdispl.pdf.
42. Biermann and Boas, op. cit.
43. Koivurova, T. 2007. International legal avenues to address the plight of victims of climate change: Problems and prospects, *Journal of Environmental Law and Litigation*, 22(2): 267–300.
44. Dow, K., R. Kasperson, and M. Bohn. 2006. Exploring the social justice implications of adaptation and vulnerability, In *Fairness in Adaptation to Climate Change*, edited by W. N. Adger, J. Paavola, S. Huq, and M. J. Mace, pp. 79–97, Cambridge, MA: MIT Press.
45. De Sherbinin, A., M. Castro, F. Gemenne, M. M. Cernea, S. Adamo, P. M. Fearnside, G. Krieger et al. 2011. Preparing for resettlement associated with climate change, *Science*, 28(2011): 456–457.
46. Oliver-Smith, 1991, op. cit.
47. Correa, E. 2011a. *Populations at Risk of Disaster: A Resettlement Guide*, Washington DC: World Bank and the Global Facility for Disaster Risk Reduction.
48. Correa, 2011b, op. cit.
49. Boyden, J. and Davis, I. 1984. *Editorial: Getting Mitigation on the Agenda*. Bulletin 18, University of Reading Agricultural Extension and Rural Development Centre.
50. Oliver-Smith, 1991, op. cit.
51. Hewitt, K. 1983. *Interpretations of Calamity*, Winchester, MA: Allen & Unwin, Inc.
52. Oliver-Smith, 1992, op. cit.

53. Correa, 2011, op. cit.
54. Garcia Canclini, N. 1993. *Transforming Modernity*, Austin: University of Texas Press.
55. Oliver-Smith, 2006, op. cit.
56. Oliver-Smith, 1992, op. cit.
57. Altman, I. and S. Low. 1992. *Place Attachment. Volume 8 Human Behavior and Environment: Advances in Theory and Research*, New York: Plenum.
58. Malkki, L. H. 1992. National geographic: Rooting of peoples and the territorialization of national identity among scholars and refugees, *Cultural Anthropology*, 7(1): 24–44.
59. Rodman, M. C. 1992. Empowering place: Multilocality and multivocality, *American Anthropologist*, 94(3): 640–656.
60. Escobar, A. 2001. Culture sits in places: Reflections on globalism and subaltern strategies of localization, *Political Geography*, 20: 139–174.
61. Giddens, A. 1990. *The Consequences of Modernity*, Cambridge: Polity Press.
62. Basso, K. 1988. Speaking with names: Language and landscape among the western apache, *Cultural Anthropology*, 3(2): 99–130.
63. Hansen, A. 2005. Black and white and the other: International immigration and change in metropolitan Atlanta, In *Beyond the Gateway: Immigrants in a Changing America*, edited by E. M. Gozdziak and S. F. Martin, pp. 87–109, Lanham, Maryland: Lexington Books.
64. Bronen, R. 2009. Forced migration of alaskan indigenous communities due to climate change: Creating a human rights response, In *Linking Environmental Change, Migration and Social Vulnerability*, edited by A. Oliver-Smith and X. Shen, SOURCE No. 11, United Nations University Institute for Environment and Human Security.
65. Marino, E. 2009. Immanent threats, impossible moves and unlikely prestige: Understanding the struggle for local control as a means toward sustainability, In *Linking Environmental Change, Migration and Social Vulnerability*, edited by A. Oliver-Smith and X. Shen, SOURCE No. 11, United Nations University Institute for Environment and Human Security.
66. Koenig, D. 2009. *Urban Relocation and Resettlement: Distinctive Problems, Distinctive Opportunities*, pp. 119–140 in Oliver-Smith (2009) *Development and Dispossession: The Crisis of Forced Displacement and Resettlement*, Santa Fe: School of Advanced Research Press.
67. Cernea, M. 1997. The risks and reconstruction model for resettling displaced populations, *World Development*, 25(10): 1569–1588.
68. Scudder, T. 2009. Resettlement theory and the Kariba case: An anthropology of resettlement, In *Development and Dispossession: The Crisis of Development Forced Displacement and Resettlement*, edited by A. Oliver-Smith, Santa Fe and London: SAR Press and James Currey.
69. De Wet, C. 2006. Risk, complexity and local initiative in involuntary resettlement outcomes, In *Towards Improving Outcomes in Development Induced Involuntary Resettlement Projects*, edited by De Wet, Chris, pp. 180–202, Oxford and New York: Berghahn Books.
70. Dirks, R. 1980. Social responses during severe food shortages and famine, *Current Anthropology*, 21(1): 21–44.
71. Harvey, D. 1996. *Justice, Nature and the Geography of Difference*, Oxford: Blackwell Publishers.
72. Oliver-Smith, 1992, op. cit.
73. Correa, 2011, op. cit.
74. Oliver-Smith, 1990, op. cit.

75. Perry and Mushkatel, 1989, op. cit.
76. Haines, 1996, place holder.
77. Martin, S. F., P. W. Fagen, K. Jorgensen, L. Mann-Bondat, and A. Schoenholz. 2005. *The Uprooted: Improving Humanitarian Responses to Forced Migration*, Lanham, MD: Lexington Books.
78. Cernea, 1990, 1996, op. cit.
79. Oliver-Smith, 2009, op. cit.
80. McDowell, C. 2001. Involuntary resettlement, impoverishment risks, and sustainable livelihoods, In *The Australasian Journal of Disaster and Trauma Studies* (http://www.massey.ac.nz/~trauma/issues/2002/mcdowell.htm).
81. Scudder, T. 1981. What it means to be dammed: The anthropology of large-scale development projects in the tropics and subtropics, *Engineering & Science*, XLIV(4): 9–15.
82. Scudder and Colson, 1982, op. cit.
83. De Wet, 2006, op. cit.
84. Deng, F. and R. Cohen. 1999. Masses in flight: The global crisis of internal displacement. The forsaken people: Case studies of the internally displaced, *Human Rights Quarterly*, 21(2): 541–544.
85. Koser, K. 2007. The Global IDP Situation in a Changing Humanitarian Context. UNICEF Global Workshop on IDPs. Brookings Institute (September 4, 2007).
86. Scudder, 1981, op. cit.
87. Scudder and Colson, 1982, op. cit.
88. Scudder, 2009, op. cit.
89. Scudder, 2009, op. cit.
90. Scudder and Colson, op. cit.
91. Scudder, 2009, op. cit.
92. Hewitt, op. cit.
93. Cernea, 1990, op. cit.
94. Cernea, 1996, op. cit.
95. Cernea, M. M. and McDowell, C. 2000. *Risks and Reconstruction: Experiences of Resettlers and Refugees*, Washington, DC: World Bank.
96. Cernea, 2000, op. cit.
97. Oliver-Smith, 2009, op. cit.
98. Cernea, 2000, op. cit.
99. Cernea, 1997, op. cit.
100. Button, G. 2009. Family resemblances between disasters and development forced displacement: Hurricane Katrina as a comparative case study, In *Development and Dispossession: The Crisis of Forced Displacement and Resettlement*, edited by Oliver-Smith, A, pp. 255–274, Santa Fe: School for Advanced Research Press.
101. Button, Ibid.
102. Cernea, 1997, op. cit.
103. De Wet, 2006, op. cit.
104. De Wet, Ibid.
105. De Wet, Ibid.
106. Oliver-Smith, 1991, op. cit.
107. Sphere Project. Humanitarian Charter and Minimum Standards in Disaster Response. 2004.
108. Downing, T. and C. Garcia-Downing. 2009. Routine and dissonant cultures: A theory about the psycho-socio-cultural disruptions of involuntary resettlement and ways to mitigate them without inflicting even more damage. In Oliver-Smith A (ed). *Development

and Dispossession: The Crisis of Forced Displacement and Resettlement. Santa Fe: School of Advanced Research Press, pp. 225–253.
109. Oliver-Smith, 1991, op. cit.
110. Toole, M. J. 1997. Communicable disease and disease control. Chapter 5, In *The Public Health Consequences of Disasters*, edited by E. K. Noji, New York: Oxford University Press.
111. Cernea, 2009, op. cit.
112. Scudder, 2009, op. cit.
113. Cernea, 2009, op. cit.
114. Cernea, 2005, op. cit.
115. Perry and Mushkatel, 1984, op. cit.
116. Marino, 2009, op. cit.
117. Bronen, op. cit, p. 7.
118. Picciotto, R., W. van Wicklin, and E. Rice. 2001. Involuntary resettlement: Comparative perspectives, In *World Bank Series on Evaluation and Development*, Vol. 2, Washington, DC: World Bank.
119. De Sherbinin, et al., op. cit.
120. Stocks, G. 2011. Evaluating the Long-Term Effects of Dam-Caused Displacement and Resettlement in Nuevo Arenal, Costa Rica. Presented at the Annual Meeting of the Society for Applied Anthropology, Seattle, WA.
121. Partridge, W. 1993. Successful involuntary resettlement: Lessons from the costa rican arenal hydroelectric project. I, In *Anthropology and Involuntary Resettlement: Policy, Practice and Theory*, edited by S. Guggenheim and M. Cernea, Boulder, CO: Westview Press.
122. World Bank 2004 Involuntary Resettlement Sourcebook. Washington, DC: The World Bank.
123. Partridge, op. cit, p. 367.
124. Yenotani, op. cit.
125. United Nations High Commission for Refugees. 2010. *Ten Years of Statistics: UNHCR Statistical Yearbook*, Geneva: UNHCR.
126. De Sherbinin, op. cit.
127. De Sherbinin, Ibid.

CHAPTER 10

Emergent Organizations and Networks in Catastrophic Environments

Tricia Wachtendorf

CONTENTS

Overview 225
Common (mis)Conceptions..226
Strengths and Short-Comings of Incident Management Systems 232
Emergent Groups and Networks 234
The Phenomenon of Convergence 239
Facilitating the Integration and Visibility of Emergent Organizations and
Networks 245
Acknowledgments..253
References..253

OVERVIEW

This chapter focuses on the emergent nature of organizations and organizational networks, their tasks, and their structures in catastrophic environments. Of particular note is that many of the features as traditionally described by researchers of disaster environments reveal themselves in catastrophic cases. Indeed, the consideration of the term "catastrophe" as something distinct from disasters is a relatively recent research phenomenon. The two terms have often been used interchangeably—sometimes in the same sentence—to describe the same event, to the extent that the usage appeared to represent a preference for word variation rather than signify a qualitative difference between the two terms. As noted elsewhere in this volume, recent scholarship has attempted to undertake the differentiation of the concepts, most notably Quarantelli (2005) in his post-Hurricane Katrina essay, as well as others in their expansion of the topic, catastrophe characteristics, and argument that degree versus dichotomous considerations of the terms is a more useful approach

(Wachtendorf et al., under review). In this chapter, we will highlight several findings that are relevant to both an understanding of disasters and catastrophes, but we will also point to differences and circumstance where catastrophic environments offer unique circumstances for emergent organizations and networks. Through the course of the chapter, we will discuss and refute several common but inaccurate assumptions about disasters and catastrophic events. Importantly, we will describe the strengths and short-comings of incident management systems in contending with emergent networks in catastrophic events. Emergent groups and networks are defined, and we will highlight the conditions in which they develop. Later in the chapter, we describe the role that people-convergence plays in the development and functioning of emergent networks. We close with an examination of the factors that facilitate the effective integration and visibility of emergent organizations and networks.

COMMON (MIS)CONCEPTIONS

Common misconceptions about disasters not only affect our popular understandings of such events, but they also can affect the ways in which we consider and plan for them. Although often discussed within the disaster context, these myths and realities (see Fischer, 2008 for an overview) hold particular implications for catastrophic events.

First, a common misconception is that we will see widespread role abandonment by emergency responders. In fact, research indicates that emergency responders generally do not abandon their responsibilities, particularly after assurances that their family is safe (see Trainor and Barsky, 2011 for an overview of the literature). In catastrophes, however, we can expect that local officials may be unable to fulfill their response roles (Quarantelli, 2005). This is not to imply a wholesale abandonment of responsibilities as suggested by the long-held myth, but rather an acknowledgement of how the catastrophic environment may present very different considerations and contexts. For example, some officials who are not immediately deemed essential may adhere to mandatory evacuation orders and leave the area as instructed by other authorities. Even if their intention is to return to the area once the threat has passed, damage to transportation infrastructure into the area may limit their ability to do so. In other cases, the officials themselves may become victims of the event. Alternatively, it may prove extremely difficult for emergency responders to determine or respond to emerging needs. Communication lines may be down and there may be general uncertainty about where citizenry are, let alone what type of assistance they require. Different from role abandonment, catastrophic situations may see a greater need for additional support to work alongside designate responders.

Second, responses are often portrayed as the work of isolated heroes. In fact, responses are multi-organizational. Even the smallest role can result in lives saved; and the larger the event, the more likely a range of organizations will play critical response roles. Unlike movies such as *Dante's Peak* and *Volcano*, where the foresight and heroic efforts of the very few guide effective components of the response, successful responses rely on a range of activities performed by many people. To extend the discussion even further, not only are isolated individual actions often the focus of disaster responses, but these efforts are often portrayed as governmental. That is, disaster responses—at least in the American context—are frequently portrayed as falling under the sole responsibility of government organizations. We know, however, that responses include participation by a range of individuals, groups, agencies, and businesses. Some of these roles are legislatively mandated or formally contracted (such as the role of the American Red Cross in shelter provision or the roles of some trucking companies in transporting supplies should an event occur). Others simply, or not so simply, emerge as the event unfolds. Some organizations exist prior to the event, some are quite formal in their organizational structure, some only develop in the aftermath of the event, and some are quite informal in their organizational structure.

MYTHS AND REALITIES OF DISASTERS (AND CATASTROPHES)

Myth: Widespread role abandonment by emergency responders

- Research indicates that emergency responders generally do not abandon responsibilities, particularly after assurances that their family is safe.

Myth: Responses are solely actions of isolated heroes

- Research indicates that responses are multi-organizational.

Myth: Responses are solely the responsibility of government organizations

- Research indicates that responses includes full range of individuals, groups, agencies, and businesses.

Myth: Centralized decision-making and response are always appropriate

- Research shows that while authority, leadership, and accountability are necessary, communication and coordination as well as resource management are better than command and control approaches (Drabek and McEntire, 2002).
- Complex disasters necessitate *decentralized* decision-making structures and networks. That is, a decentralized network will emerge in post-event environment of a large-scale disaster or catastrophe. The challenge is to maximize coordination and communication across that network.

The Disaster Research Center (DRC) developed a typology of organizations that play roles in disaster events (Dynes, 1970). Established organizations use routine organizational structures and engage in routine tasks. A fire department responding to fire-suppression activities is a good example of an established organization. Expanding organizations engage in the same tasks pre- and post-event, but utilize new organizational structures. The American Red Cross—mandated to perform specific disaster-related tasks but expanding during events to include new volunteers—exemplifies this organizational type. Extending organizations use pre-event organizational structures, but engage in novel tasks. Consider a middle school that unexpectedly is used to provide shelter for its students. It may rely on the organizational structure previously in place (i.e., the roles of the principal, vice principal, teachers, secretaries, custodial staff, and students themselves), but the tasks these participants engage in during the sheltering operation are quite novel compared to their routine activities. Finally, emergent organizations utilize new organizational structures and engage in new tasks. Bucket brigades of community residents and workers engaged in spontaneous search and rescue efforts after a structural collapse is an often-used example of an emergent organization. Such emergent groups in the aftermath of disasters are common. For example, on May 12, 2008, the town of Yingxiu was one of many communities in Sichuan Province that suffered devastating effects of the catastrophic earthquake. Three quarters of the population of this small town were killed in the event. Earthquake and rain-induced landslides made roads to the town impassable, and local citizens initially had to perform search and rescue operations before government help arrived, including in this middle school where many students died (see Figure 10.1).

ORGANIZATIONS IN DISASTERS

Structures

	Old	New
Old Tasks	Established (e.g., fire dept)	Expanding (e.g., American Red Cross volunteers)
New	Extending (e.g., school providing shelter)	Emergent (e.g., search and rescue bucket brigades)

See: Dynes, R.R. 1970. *Organized Behavior in Disaster.* Lexington, MA: D.C. Heath.

It is important to note that even in established, expanding, and extending organizations, some level of emergence is likely. When the event takes on catastrophic characteristics, a greater level of emergent activity is likely. Emergency events are more likely to be dealt with by established organizations. Consider a large multi-vehicle traffic accident on an interstate highway, involving some hazardous material spillage. Certainly, we would expect some emergent activity on the part of by-standers and people who stop their own vehicles to help. Perhaps some would initially help with rescuing victims and providing first aid. Others may try to safely divert oncoming traffic, provide rides to non-injured victims, or offer their cell phones. For the most part, however, on-site response activities would quickly be assumed by firefighters, police officers, emergency medical technicians, Department of Transportation personnel, tow-truck drivers, and hazardous materials cleanup crews: Organizations operating with similar organizational structures doing what they are used to doing.

Disasters—with a greater level of complexity, ambiguity, and unexpected circumstances that exceed a community's ability to cope—are more likely to include

Figure 10.1 School destroyed by the May 12, 2008 earthquake in the town of Yingxiu. (Photo courtesy of the Disaster Research Center, University of Delaware, copyright 2008. All rights reserved.)

the other three types of organizational actors. There certainly is some debate in the disaster research field regarding the extent to which the September 11, 2001 terrorist attacks constitute a disaster or a catastrophe. Although high in consequence, the event does not meet many of the thresholds offered in Quarantelli (2005) or Wachtendorf et al.'s (2008) taxonomy. Still, bicycle couriers delivered food, GIS personnel from around the city came together to form a mapping station at the emergency operations center, and volunteers from across the country came to help staff supply warehouses and guard checkpoints (Wachtendorf, 2004). Expanding organizations such as the American Red Cross and the Salvation Army played a very active role; and emergent groups formed to help with the evacuation, attempted search and rescue operations, and provided support services for family members looking for loved ones.

In catastrophes, however, the involvement of expanding, extending, and particularly emergent organizations rises to new levels as established capacities and response capabilities are exceeded. These other types of organizations must step in, at least temporarily, to fill response gaps. If they do not, it will take much longer for needs to be met by established groups. Consider the 2010 Haiti earthquake. Government buildings collapsed and many government staff were killed when the earthquake struck on January 12. Although the United Nations had a strong presence in the country for many decades, many of their warehouses were destroyed and key operational staff members were also killed. The capacity to contend with routine needs was arguably inadequate, let alone the new needs that became critically apparent after a devastating earthquake. Ports were damaged, access to the airstrip was limited, and road access was extremely difficult. In the early days, local residents, churches, and community groups needed to perform many of the immediate response activities. Unable to simply rely on mutual aid from neighboring jurisdictions, supplies and expertise (particularly medical expertise to contend with severe crush injuries) were required from outside the impact and immediately surrounding areas. Organizations working within the country needed to integrate a diverse set of paid and volunteer personnel coming from many different nations as well as residents who were directly integrated into the recovery operation (see Figure 10.2).

Another common misconception about disasters is that centralized decision-making and response are always appropriate. Indeed, as Drabek and McEntire (2002) note, the command and control model that is often recommended in disaster response *incorrectly* assumes that the government is the only responder; information from outside official channels is inaccurate; role abandonment will occur; standard operating procedures will always function; citizens are inept, passive, and irrational; society will breakdown; and ad hoc emergence of the kind so common in disasters is counter-productive. This is not to say that if one asks a proponent of the command and control structure, one would hear these ideas as clearly articulated as Drabek and McEntire present. That said, the assumptions are evident in the policies, practices, and orientation of the overarching approach, and not without practical consequence. Drabek and McEntire argue that while authority, leadership, and accountability are necessary, communication and coordination as well as resource management are better than command and control approaches. Indeed, complex disasters necessitate *decentralized* decision-making structures and networks. That is, a decentralized network will emerge in the post-event environment of a large-scale disaster or catastrophe, even if the intention is to follow a centralized model. Following the 2011 Tohoku earthquake in Japan, many of the most devastated areas were initially cut off from Prefecture officials. In some cases,

Figure 10.2   Local residents hired by USAID to help with the debris removal effort after the January 12, 2010 Haiti Earthquake. (Photo courtesy of the Disaster Research Center, University of Delaware, copyright 2011. All rights reserved.)

communities lost key local officials to the tsunami waves as they stayed behind to help in threatened areas. Pre-tsunami planning and consideration regarding responsibilities for particular tasks was important, but to lose sight of survivors' needs to self-organize in shelters, share resources, and engage in response and early recovery operations in improvised manners ignores the decentralized reality on the ground in those early days (see Figure 10.3). That ability to self-organize and operate in a decentralized manner is a positive attribute of community response. The challenge is to maximize coordination and communication across that decentralized network.

Disasters, and certainly catastrophes, disrupt the patterns of what can be absorbed by routine procedures. As Tierney (2002) states, these types of events are largely defined by their need for improvised responses. Even when formal planning has occurred, conditions will merit an improvised response, which will involve unanticipated participants and activities. In high consequence events such as catastrophes, organizations with more formal and pre-established roles will need to work with or along-side organizations that are less formal in their disaster role and whose very presence is emergent in nature.

Figure 10.3 Picture of shelter along Japan's tsunami impacted coast three months after the 2011 catastrophe. Residents grouped themselves by neighborhood into different classrooms, and took votes on whether to partition areas or have open space and whether or not to allow food in the sleeping quarters. (Photo courtesy of the Disaster Research Center, University of Delaware, copyright 2011. All rights reserved.)

STRENGTHS AND SHORT-COMINGS OF INCIDENT MANAGEMENT SYSTEMS

Management systems, such as the incident command system, can offer some structure in contending with emergence during large-scale events. Yet these systems fall short in appreciating or contending with the phenomenon of emergence. Given our assertion that considerable emergence is highly likely in catastrophic events, such management systems prove problematic in their actual implementation in these types of events.

Incident Management System (IMS) is a "generic term for the design of ad hoc emergency management teams that coordinate the efforts of more than one agency under a unified command" (Christen et al., 2001; 1). IMS has both proponents and critics in the disaster research community. Christen et al. (2001) provide a detailed overview of IMS. According to them, proponents of IMS highlight the organizing system as a means to effectively delegate and coordinate authority, joint problem solve, and identify a clear chain of authority. The system developed as a result of the lack of coordination among organizations responding to California wildfires in the 1970, where identified challenges included

- Lack of clear leadership (either due to role ambiguity or turf battles between jurisdictions)
- Lack of collaborative organizational structures that outlined command chains
- Lack of common terminology
- Lack of joint communications systems
- Lack of logistics and resource priority-setting systems

Previously known as the Incident Command System, IMS expanded in California and was adopted by law enforcement agencies in such 1980s incidents as a plane crash in San Luis Obispo County and planning for the Los Angeles Olympic Games, and by hospitals in response to the 1989 Loma Prieta earthquake. As Christen et al. (2001) explain, proponents of IMS highlight advantages of the unified management system. First, it offers a functional management system that integrates personnel from different home organizations. Second, IMS enables the identification of an incident manager or a unified management team when jurisdictional areas or responsibilities overlap. Third, the system offers standard terminology that facilitates cooperation (although some minor regional variance remains). Fourth, IMS offers rules for chain of command, unity of command, and span of control. Fifth, IMS establishes protocols for communications and flow of information. Sixth, there is an emphasis on logistics planning and centralized resources allocation. Finally, IMS puts planning functions on an equal level with operations and logistics functions.

Still, the effectiveness and appropriateness of IMS is widely disputed in the disaster research community. Other scholars point to the command and control approach often inherent to the implementation of IMS. For example, because of the shortcomings of the command and control structure highlighted earlier by Drabek and McEntire (2002), incident management systems such as the incident command system (ICS) fall short in appreciating or contending with emergence in organizations and social networks. Waugh (2006b) notes that while the hierarchical structure of ICS had demonstrated positive outcomes in large fire responses, the "unity of command may not be practical in many complex emergencies, such as pandemics or even large-scale terrorist incidents" (p. 402). Waugh contends that ICS is highly centralized in its decision processes (2006a), which may not fit within the system of shared governance prevalent in the United States, and in fact may generate problems for the local response efforts (2006b). Waugh (2006a) elaborates, pointing to the hierarchical organizational structure of this model, the very formal roles involved, and the extent to which ICS becomes difficult to operationally implement in large disperse disasters. Said another way, ICS may be better suited to organizations such as police departments, fire departments, and other organizations with a culture of hierarchy and division of roles that are reflected by the models of operation within this system. In contrast, other organizations—particularly non-governmental and emergent groups—may rely on consensus-building, informal, or anti-bureaucratic models. When they become part of a disaster or catastrophic response, the ICS system might fall short in taking into account their potential contribution and organizational culture (Waugh, 2006a). Given that private citizens are often the first to respond to a disaster (Tierney, 2006), and that formal organizations may experience unique limitations during a catastrophe in working to activate an expedited response, any multi-organizational structure would need to account for the presence of both new and not-previously-connected groups, many of whom would be unfamiliar with the planned-for multi-organizational structure. Rigidly adhering to the original plans can thus result in significantly decreased effectiveness.

While Waugh (2006b) argues IMS, and ICS in particular, have serious flaws when it comes to contending with complex events, he does concede a more "consensus-based decision process" (p. 402) within a unified command system may prove suitable. Still, most approaches to a unified command system focus on unifying uniformed personnel and organizations more traditionally involved in emergency management (Waugh, 2006a), thus excluding emerging resources or organizations.

Some contend that the problems associated with IMS have more to do with improper implementation of a potentially valuable coordination system (DeCapua, 2007). Yet others such as Buck et al. (2006) assert that ICS works best when its users are part of a specific community, when response needs are routine to those users, and when social and cultural emergence is at a minimum. In fact, Buck et al. (2006) claim, based on their research of urban search and rescue teams, that ICS is a way through which coordination can begin to emerge in disaster environments rather than an organizing system that can easily serve as a comprehensive organizing principle of disaster management. Official organizations which have established mutual trust and have experience working together may greatly benefit from these organizing principles. The mistake, however, is when the principles come to form set action scripts that do not fully account for or engage emergent behavior.

EMERGENT GROUPS AND NETWORKS

Recent catastrophic events such as the 2008 Miramar cyclone, the 2008 China earthquake, Hurricane Katrina in 2005, the Pakistani earthquake in 2005, and the Indian Ocean tsunami in 2004 have shown repeatedly how existing government emergency plans often fail to adequately meet victims' needs during the initial aftermath (Majchrazak et al., 2007). Even in areas where formal planning has occurred at some level, the event's scale, magnitude, and scope can contribute to communication breakdowns, unexpected conditions, the inability to garner or verify timely information, and an overall difficulty in mobilizing sufficient personnel and material resources in the days leading up to and immediately following the event. That is, the need to improvise response activities is not always a failure of vision on the part of the emergency management organizations (although sometimes that may, indeed, be the case), *but demonstrate clearly that an effective disaster response involves both planned and improvised actions* (Wachtendorf, 2004). Emergent groups and networks often form in response to these conditions. Although particular challenges accompany their presence in the response and early recovery environment, they also frequently fill gaps and address pressing needs.

Emergent groups are newly formed, engage in new tasks, operate with a sense of great urgency and levels of interdependence, and function in response to constantly changing environments and conditions (Dynes, 1970; Drabek and McEntire, 2003; Majchrazak et al., 2007). Sometimes groups disband after their tasks are accomplished. Other times, groups "develop an ideology, formal cadre, and organizational structure much like a grouping social movement ... [and transform their] goals to address more general community needs ..." (Tierney et al., 2001, p. 116). Emergent community groups develop both before (community-oriented groups) and after (task-oriented groups) events. Many of these groups have few monetary sources; however, volunteer time and commitment are important factors for mobilizing efforts. Such groups usually are comprised of a consistent and active core, a larger number of participants who support efforts, and a still larger group of supporters who play a nominal role (see Tierney et al., 2001 for this summary of a study conducted by the Disaster Research Center).

Indeed, be they disasters or events that occur at a catastrophic level, trans-system social ruptures—or events that Quarantelli et al. (2006) identify as jumping across different societal boundaries disrupting the social fabric of different social systems—may be particularly well suited to see an exceptional amount of emergent behavior and the involvement of informal emergent groups. Events such as the quick transnational spread of computer viruses or widespread epidemics may not have a clear point of origin and local community solutions may not be sufficient to address the threat. Given the high levels of ambiguity and potential for planning gaps, emergent groups and networks may be particularly likely in these environments.

Majchrazak et al. (2007) provide a strong summary of the characteristics of emergent groups: their membership composition frequently changes; they consist of geographically distributed and diverse unfamiliar group members; they need to adapt to unstable task definition, flexible task assignments, and fleeting membership; and they often pursue multiple simultaneous and possibly conflicting purposes. Some members may be acting with altruism while others out of self-interest. Some may know each other, others may not, and indeed they may never see each other again after the response ends. Indeed, while the formal system operating under the command and control model may assume that organizations involved in the response network are known ahead of time, and have trained or planned together, many emergent groups do not follow this model (Bigley and Roberts, 2001; Trainor, 2004).

Emergent response groups often operate outside of official lines of authority; however, they are also influenced by these authority mechanisms that in turn influence the response environment. Either emergent groups must find a way to make inroads into these official mechanisms, navigate in concert with them, or—on occasion—find ways to circumvent them. According to Majchrazak et al. (2007, p. 151), these groups often adopt "a learn-by-doing (versus decision-making) action-based model of coordinated problem solving, in which sense making and improvisation are the norm rather than the exception ... The urgency of the situations means that the objective of coordination is to achieve minimally acceptable and timely action, even when more effective responses may be feasible—but would take longer and use more resources."

Emergence is likely when members perceive a present threat, when the social climate is supportive of emergence, when social ties are in place—at least to some degree—before the mobilization, when the social setting legitimizes the groups, and when resources are available (Quarantelli et al., 1983). Let us remember what makes catastrophic events potentially distinct from the disasters. Catastrophes can involve situations with widespread damage to the built environment (including those relied on by emergency organizations) and the sharp and concurrent loss of most community functions. Local officials likely cannot undertake their usual roles and help from nearby communities cannot be provided. The mass media and the political arena can become even more critical areas for claims-making than in disasters, particularly as debates ensue regarding who is to blame and who is responsible for ensuing events and tragic circumstances. And in catastrophes, we might see mass out-migration from impacted areas, a phenomenon less likely in what we might categorize as a disaster. For all of these characteristics (Quarantelli, 2005; Wachtendorf et al., 2008), the situation can extend well into the recovery period. Consequently, the level of emergence necessary to contend with these severe and unanticipated conditions is likely to be greater than for more typical disaster situations.

Emergent activity in response to crisis has a strong cultural component. In some societies where formal emergency management organizations are non-existent, emergent activity may be the only or primary response to high-consequence events (particularly before outside help arrives). In other cases, there may be less of a history of emergent activity. For example, the convergence of individuals and groups after the 1995 Kobe earthquake in Japan, as well as their informal participation in the response, was considered unusual, whereas the occurrence would have been considered a typical social behavior were the same event to have happened in the United States (Tierney et al., 2001). This is in contrast to the convergence of helpers after the 2011 Tohoku earthquake and tsunami that struck Japan, where the phenomenon was more prevalent, particularly among organizations that originally formed in response to the Kobe disaster.

According to Drabek (1996: 21-11), the term emergent multi-organizational networks (EMONs) describes the "structure of relationships that form among organizations, or segments of organizations, that are focused on [specific activities or response functions]." EMONS form during the emergency period for a limited time in order to address emerging needs. In catastrophic events, EMONS are often simultaneously comprised of a range of established, expanding, extending, and emergent organizations.

Emergent organizational networks are defined as such not necessarily because they are comprised of emergent groups, but because of the newly-formed relations between organizations. Consider EMONS in search and rescue operations. Most search and rescue operations are carried out by local community organizations and individual participants. For example, during the Guadalajara Mexico gas explosion, search and rescue teams arrived too late to rescue survivors. These activities were undertaken by neighbors, friends, and family members in the community, while search and rescue teams were more active in body recovery (Aguirre et al., 1995). At the same time, these search and rescue operations often see a time period where various emergent groups of actors must begin to work with formal responders (i.e., police, fire, military, official search, and rescue teams). Eventually, the emergent groups may cease their participation (voluntarily or involuntarily) or become a part of more officially sanctioned efforts. The EMON will, in other words, be in flux and dynamic in nature. Following the Indian Ocean tsunami, many formal and informal groups came together to form multi-organizational networks around debris removal. Even when formal organizations, such as USAID, provided resources it was often an emergent group of local citizens and organizations that undertook much of the work (see Figures 10.4 through 10.6).

Research on emergent networks has shown that challenges for their successful operation can include lack of standardization, fragmentation, lack of interorganizational communication, ambiguity of authority, and poor utilization of special resources. Coordination problems can be overcome when there are high levels of consensus (particularly when participating organizations understand their roles, the roles of others, and the overall purpose of the network), when there is an identified lead with legitimate authority and personal influence, when there is a central coordinating mechanism, and when units have had frequent interaction with each other prior to the actual event, even if the interaction was not related to emergency, disaster, or catastrophic planning. (Much of the key work on EMONS as described above has been undertaken by Drabek. For a brief review of the above points, see Tierney et al., 2001.)

Figure 10.4 Fishing village in Tamil Nadu, India, where village women play a key role in collecting and burning debris 3 weeks after the 2004 Indian Ocean tsunami. (Photo courtesy of the Disaster Research Center, University of Delaware, copyright 2005. All rights reserved.)

Figure 10.5 Town of Kinniya, Sri Lanka, where community residents—including many school teachers—engage in debris removal one month after the 2004 Indian Ocean tsunami. (Photo courtesy of the Disaster Research Center, University of Delaware, copyright 2005. All rights reserved.)

Figure 10.6 Those clearing debris left by the 2004 Indian Ocean tsunami at Relief Camp Peraliya, Sri Lanka wear USAID shirts, but groups are comprised primarily of community residents with no formal association to the relief organization. (Photo courtesy of the Disaster Research Center, University of Delaware, copyright 2005. All rights reserved.)

A key point should immediately become evident. On the one hand, catastrophes are characterized in ways that lead us to expect considerable emergence. Centralized approaches and incident management systems are often criticized for an inability to adequately account for this emergence and its contribution. That said, other research points to coordination problems that accompany emergent networks. How does one reconcile such seeming contradictions? What is a well-intentioned emergency manager to do?

Well perhaps it returns to the nature of what an incident management system is. Remember that a few paragraphs earlier, we cited Buck et al.'s (2006) assertion that ICS as a comprehensive organizing system is different from a system for coordination that emerges in disaster environments. Arguably, then, what might be needed is not an absence of a system or a rigid pre-designated system imposed upon transpiring events, but rather an emergent system that reflects the emergent characteristics the EMON. What is at stake, then, is the organizing principles (with special emphasis on the fluid and plural nature for the word "principles") of the system rather than whether or not a system exists. As Drabek and McEntire (2003, p. 108) explain, one of the goals should be to move away from a "more rigid and autocratic command and control model through greater emphasis on more participative efforts."

The lack of clear leadership, for example, may prove less important for the operation of the group's task, but may prove problematic for a network's ability to communicate regularly in the challenging environment of a catastrophe. Those attempting to organize the EMON may suggest that a leader should be assigned to represent the emergent group or the cluster of groups. Unfortunately this strategy of leadership assignment within a specific reporting structure may only solve the coordination challenge on paper. In reality, however, emergent groups have "fleeting" and "volitional member participation" and are "geographically distributed with diverse and unfamiliar group members" (Majchrazak et al., 2007, p. 157 drawing on Drabek and McEntire, 2003). The individual designated as the key contact person may: leave; change in their operational role; have reduced involvement; or simply not prove to be the individual who fulfills a leadership role as response tasks unfold. Moreover, emergent groups "pursue multiple, simultaneous, changing and possibly conflicting purposes" and they need to adapt to "unstable task definitions" (Majchrazak et al., 2007, p. 157 drawing on Drabek and McEntire, 2003). As the role of a particular emergent group changes over time, where they find themselves in a network may very quickly bear little resemblance to where they were initially assigned or observed.

STUDENT ACTIVITY 1

Students should form small working groups of 5 or 6 people. Using the figure on expanding Transactive Memory Systems (TMS) theory to emergent response groups, each group should develop a different catastrophic event scenario (perhaps based on hazard type to ensure there is no duplication in the class) and apply features of the chart to specific examples regarding how they may play out in that particular event. Students should briefly present their application to the class at the end of the exercise. Students should articulate how the features presented by Majchrazak et al. (2007) impact the established way of considering TMS theory. The goal of the exercise is to reinforce the application of TMS to emergent response groups (Figure 10.7).

THE PHENOMENON OF CONVERGENCE

This section provides an overview of the phenomenon of personal or people convergence and its impact on emergent networks. While a review of the overall phenomenon of convergence is not provided in this session, the reader may reference the chapter on logistics for additional information.

Personal or people convergence involves the influx of people to areas associated with the disaster milieu (Kendra and Wachtendorf, 2003; Fritz and Mathewson, 1957) (see Figure 10.8). Sometimes they converge from within areas impacted by the disaster or relevant to the response, sometimes from areas immediately surrounding the response milieu, and sometimes they come from great distances. People convergers may help to form emergent groups, become part of emergent networks, or comprise the population to which emergent groups and networks respond. Convergence can be extremely helpful and often needed, but can also bring with it complex challenges.

STUDENT ACTIVITY 1

Majchrzak, Jarvenpaa, and Hollingshead: *Perspective*
Organization Science 18(1), pp. 147–161, © 2007 INFORMS

Exhibit 5 Expanding TMS Theory to Emergent Response Group

Characteristics of Emergent Response Groups*	Implications for Knowledge Coordination	Current TMS Theory	Suggested Extensions to TMS Theory for Emergent Response Groups	Implications for Research Topics in Organization Science
• Unstable task definitions and assignments • Pursuit of multiple, conflicting, and changing purposes and perspectives • Fleeting and sometimes unclear membership • Geographically distributed, diverse, unfamiliar group members • Volitional member participation, based on urgent personal needs	• Action-based coordination • Learning-by-doing model • Minimally acceptable timely action suffices • Opportunistic coordination with emergent leaders, emergent coordination principles, emergent coordination channels	Task-relevant expertise serves as basis for task assignment and specialization	**TMS Indicator 1: Expertise Specialization** • Task-relevant expertise often not present, so any knowledge of relationships, tools, or tasks and ability and willingness to act on that knowledge may serve as basis of task assignment and specialization • Knowledge flexibility, sufficiency, and motivation as additional bases for task assignment and specialization	• Evolving nature of expertise in a group • Convening focus on domain knowledge to actionable knowledge • Keeping volunteers engaged when their initial needs are met
		Validation of expertise needed for effective group functioning	**TMS Indicator 2: Credibility in Member Expertise** • Replace credibility with trust in action • Moderate levels of trust more conducive to building a TMS than high levels • Trust encouraged without observing member behavior • Development of swift trust	• Examining nature of trust as it evolves • How group dynamics affect trust • When trust and expertise credibility differ • Conflicts of swift vs. generalized trust
		Shared mental model of who knows what necessary for efficient coordination	**TMS Indicator 3: Knowledge Coordination** • Knowledge coordination occurs by observing and recognizing action scenarios, identifying ways to contribute to scenarios, and quickly devising simple coordination mechanisms • Community-developed narratives describing events & scenarios may help coordination	• Finding ways to overcome communication difficulties • Using IT to facilitate narrative evolution and communication • Coordinating with multiple conflicting action scenarios

* Drabek and McEntire (2003).

Figure 10.7 Expanding TMS theory to emergent response groups.

1. Returnees
2. Anxious
3. Helpers
4. Curious
5. Exploiters
6. Supporters*
7. Mourners/Memorializers*

* These two additional types were noted in the 2001 World Trade Center disaster. Their presence was partially accounted for by the protracted nature of the response.

Figure 10.8 Types of personal convergence.

The extent to which of each convergence type is seen by others as having legitimate claims to an area often contributes to the access that is awarded to participants. There are several different types of people convergers, each operating with different motivations (Figure 10.8).

Returnees include residents, business owners, and employees of the area. They may converge as they permanently return home or to work, or to temporarily gather and check on property. The *anxious* includes family members and friends looking for loved ones. The *helpers* category constitutes local personnel, personnel from neighboring jurisdictions serving under mutual agreements, uniformed or skilled personnel from outside area, and other volunteers with limited skills and without affiliation (both from within and outside the impacted area). Unaffiliated helpers successful at gaining entrée often are have particular skills; are able to identify, or create, niche markets for themselves; and are able to work largely unsupervised. The *curious* includes political officials, celebrities, and the general public, all interested or curious to see areas associated with the event. *Exploiters* include merchants coming to sites and overcharging victims for goods and services, people falsely claiming that proceeds of various goods and collection efforts will go to charity, and other individuals looking for ways to commit fraud. Based on their research following the 2001 terrorist attacks in New York City, the categories *supporters* and *mourners/memorializers* were added by Kendra and Wachtendorf (2003) to the original list developed by Fritz and Mathewson (1957). Supporters include convergers who come to show their support for and solidarity with either victims or responders; while mourners or memorializers come to commemorate or remember those who have died. The connection to the converger and the victim may be a family or friendship tie, but not necessarily. In protracted responses, and particularly those that have a strong galvanizing political context (such as the 2001 attacks on the World Trade Center), the presence of these two types of convergers during the response phase is more likely.

The scale (scope and magnitude) of the event, accessibility of location, and the level of media attention given to it can amplify the level of convergence.

Consequently, catastrophic events are more likely to attract a higher level of convergence than disasters; although, for example, a catastrophic event that occurs in a remote area with little media attention may indeed receive a smaller degree of convergence than a smaller event more easily accessible and with greater attention placed on its occurrence.

Understanding the types of convergers who may be present after a catastrophic event sheds light on how, when, and where emergent groups and networks may manifest themselves. For example, as returnees come back to an impacted area, new groups may form to contend with food, shelter, and information needs. As anxious family members converge to various sites, emergent networks of counselors—both those part of government organizations as well as individual volunteers—may likewise converge to relevant sites to provide assistance. Advocacy groups of survivors may develop in response to new and unmet needs, and networks may form as different groups begin to address different interests. The range of helpers who converge to a site—some part of newly emergent groups, others from established, expanding, and extending organizations—may all play roles in addressing key response and recovery needs, thereby forming emergent multi-organizational networks.

There are, of course, challenges in contending with these convergers. For example:

- Who has legitimate claim to access particular areas?
- Who has legitimate claim to restrict access for different convergers?
- Whose presence hinders response or recovery efforts?
- Who has much needed skills and how are those identified?
- When is the presence of particular convergers most appropriate?
- How does one determine who has indeed converged?
- How does one convey and receive information from these groups?

Yet we must not lose sight of the fact that emergent groups of convergers often have valuable roles to play and may be present precisely because the formal anticipated response is unable (or unwilling) to meet these needs.

For example, during the response to the 2001 World Trade Center attacks, a range of vessels converged toward Lower Manhattan to help evacuate residents and commuters from the island. The U.S. Coast guard played a major role in these activities (see Figure 10.9) but so did harbor pilots as well as so many other vessel operators who found themselves in close proximity to the collapsing buildings, including tugs, ferries, dinner cruise boats, and private vessels. This activity was not previously planned for, and the participants became part of an emergent network of organizations (including some emergent groups) to help with this unmet need. While some individual boat operators who converged were less well suited than others to provide assistance, this was an emergent—and successful—network that very quickly met an emergent, unanticipated need. (For more information, see Kendra et al., 2003 of Wachtendorf et al., 2010.) People convergence can occur in a range of, shall we say, events with a tragic and immediate nature. Earlier, we considered that the September 11 attacks may be better described as a disaster than

EMERGENT ORGANIZATIONS AND NETWORKS 243

Figure 10.9 NEW YORK, New York (Sept. 11)—Coast Guard crewmembers patrol the harbor after the collapse of the World Trade Center. Terrorists hijacked four commercial jets and then crashed them into the World Trade Center in New York, the Pentagon and the Pennsylvania countryside. (USCG photo by PA3 Tom Sperduto. The U.S. Coast Guard Imagery Server is provided as a public service by the Office of Assistant Commandant for Governmental and Public Affairs.)

a catastrophe. Yet we saw tremendous participation by private citizens and extending organizations after Hurricane Katrina as boat operators of all sorts converged to help rescue Gulf Coast survivors from their roof tops and second floor windows. The July 22, 2011 terrorist attacks at a youth camp on the Norwegian Island of Utoya (following a deadly car bomb detonation in central Oslo) by a political extremist certainly brought the grief of disaster to Norwegians. Yet by more conceptual definitions of the response capacity, the event could better be described as an emergency despite the death and injury to over 100 people. Here, too, however, private boat operators converged to the island to help rescue and evacuate those still fleeing the bullets of the attacker. What makes the challenges of convergence different in catastrophes again ties in to the characteristics of the phenomenon.

There is no one answer to the questions of how to best deal with convergence and emergence, as the nature of the event and community will affect the best approach. What is clear, however, is that emergence is inevitable in a community-wide disaster, and indeed, most disaster planning implicitly depends on emergence (Kendra and Wachtendorf, 2007). Given the characteristics of catastrophe (Quarantelli, 2005), some non-planned form of response will be necessary to contend with the impacts. If local officials are unable to undertake their usual roles, for example, integrating people (convergers) into the response effort transforms it from a recommended action into a very necessary one. As mass out-migration is another characteristic of catastrophe, the requests and needs of returnees might be very different following a catastrophic event compared to a disaster where mass out-migration does not occur, or occurs for a shorter length of time. For example, residents returning after a disastrous hurricane may come back within a relatively short time period and may be able to stay in close proximity to their communities until temporary housing or rebuilding can occur, and may be relatively easy to communicate information to. After a catastrophe such as the 2011 Tohoku earthquake and tsunami, evacuees may be uprooted and stay at great distance from their original homes, may be scattered across a vast geographic area, and may be difficult to communicate with given the extent to which they may be dispersed. Convergence, too, is inevitable, although how it manifests will be closely tied to cultural context. Planning efforts should consider how to best make use of emergent groups and how to best incorporate them into the response networks even while acknowledging that the particular players may not be identified before the event. Moreover, some emergent activity may run counter to the overall goals of the larger response. For example, a group may decide to breach security checkpoints to provide assistance in an affected area despite efforts to reduce the presence of helpers in a location where hazards remain present. Issuing an edict of no participation will likely not meet the goals of either those trying to respond to an emergent need or those trying to control the area. Coordination and discussion, although sometimes difficult to achieve, is more likely to help stakeholders recognize the viewpoints of the other and work out an acceptable solution (see Figure 10.10).

Figure 10.10 A supply distribution area, staffed by converging helpers, in Mississippi a few weeks after Hurricane Katrina made landfall. (Photo courtesy of the Disaster Research Center, University of Delaware, copyright 2005. All rights reserved.)

STUDENT ACTIVITY 2

In the aftermath of Hurricane Katrina, emergent groups, previously existing groups undertaking new tasks or with new organizational arrangements, and established organizations all formed new organizational networks as they contended with the many response needs. Different types of groups played more predominate roles than others in different stages of the response and early recovery, both with respect to the tasks they worked on and the segments of the community they worked with. One of the challenges was coordinating and communicating across these networks. Imagine that you become part of an emergent group that has come together to address a particular response need in this catastrophic event. What steps might you and those in your group take to become a connected part of the emergent multi-organizational response network? Remember the severe impact to communication systems, infrastructure, facilities, and community function that would contribute to the setting in which you would need to work.

FACILITATING THE INTEGRATION AND VISIBILITY OF EMERGENT ORGANIZATIONS AND NETWORKS

When conducting research on relief provision after Hurricane Katrina, Wachtendorf et al. (2005) found that as new groups become part of the response milieu and as emergent networks form, one of the key challenges in coordinating responses is ensuring network visibility. The authors found that principal actors were often unaware of not only what assets various organizations had or did not have available, but also which organizations were a part of relief supply networks and what role they may have played. For example, one responder noted the need for a broker—in addition to Voluntary Organizations Active in Disasters (VOAD)—to handle donations, without any knowledge that additional brokers were active in the response. Indeed, there were groups doing just that. One of these groups, Compassion Alliance, worked with both government and VOAD groups as well as with extensive network of the faith-based community, seeking to match need with supplies and keeping inventories. Many established and emergent key actors were unaware of the formal roles outlined in response plans. As existing groups took on new roles or other groups emerged, information about key organizations was often unknown across the social network. In catastrophic events like Hurricane Katrina, where convergence and emergence may play an even larger role than in typical disasters, network visibility—allowing for both open and coordinated systems—becomes paramount.

Clearly, an emergency management agency will not be aware of every potential participant in a potential catastrophic response. At the same time, there are steps that can be taken to facilitate network visibility. Greater effort can be made to identify organizations that can serve as information bridges between networks.

During routine periods, certain organizations can play pivotal roles in bridging smaller clusters of organizations. These organizations can play equally important roles during a catastrophic event. For example, key emergency response organizations may not be well connected to all the private truck transport companies in a community or across a region; however, by building ties with the associations with which those companies belong, an information mechanism can be built to communicate activities to and from the larger, more formalized, response network. Emergent groups quickly connect with each other or with somewhat established organizations. The more bridge organizations a response network can foster, the more likely it will generate a tie to the emergent groups. However, simply building ties is not enough to coordinate an emergent network. There needs to be a concentrated effort to use these ties to obtain visibility for both existing and new members, particularly as the network changes throughout the response and early recovery.

Emphasizing pre-event community partnership building can produce substantial dividends after a catastrophe strikes, even if the partnership building had little or nothing to do with disaster-related issues. Community-partnership building can play an important role in enhancing network visibility, although engaging in these partnership-building strategies must take place before an event occurs. Wachtendorf (2005) suggests that incorporating groups not traditionally involved in disaster response or mitigation decision-making can provide a perspective that may otherwise have been overlooked. It can also generate new information on knowledge, skills, and resources that may augment a catastrophic response. Furthermore, the inter-organizational networks developed from comprehensive mitigation planning and implementation can have positive effects on a community's disaster response.

Substantial research and development is needed in the area of open system technology platforms that better visually represent complex, emergent, and dynamic networks—not just those that were pre-planning before the event. Rather than simply generating long lists that may prove not to be user-friendly during an unfolding crisis, these platforms would need to show the newly developing network in real time and in a way that enables better processing of information (much in the same way that Geographic Information Systems have helped to process location-based information). At the same time, any development or implementation of technological solutions would need to account for the ability to: input information into the system in a timely manner; the successful communication of information to all organizations that should be represented in the networks; the continuity of infrastructure that supports these technologies; access (and maintenance) of the technology—particularly in poorer communities, for organizations with limited resources, and to emergent organizations who may not have anticipated involvement; as well as user-friendly approaches. Enhanced technology is *not the solution* to the challenges of visualizing emergent networks. Seeing does not necessarily help us interpret and act on information in effective ways. Still, technology could play important roles in helping us gather, account for, and mine emerging data, so long as it does not become interpreted as a solution to the social problem of catastrophic response and recovery.

One might suggest that establishing a volunteer coordinator position would serve several purposes, specifically recruiting emergent groups, coordinating emergent groups, and advising both the groups and established actors in a response effort. I would contend, however, that although likely helpful, such a position within an existing management system would not suffice and indeed may deflect attention away from the more comprehensive interaction necessary between anticipated and unanticipated organizational involvement. In the end, a catastrophic response will require interaction between a range of established and emergent organizations, let alone those expanding and extending organizations that alter their organizational structure or tasks during the crisis period (Dynes, 1970).

The solutions to contending with these challenges, unfortunately, are complex. One can empathize with the policymaker or practitioner looking for a straightforward solution to grapple with these issues. Technologically-driven platforms may help. Pre-existing relationships that operate and are reinforced during routine periods may facilitate post-catastrophe awareness and interaction. Designated coordination roles and pre-identified organizations that can bridge clusters within the network may prove beneficial. Yet, perhaps, more important than all of these strategies is awareness that multiple approaches are necessary to ensure network visibility, communication, and coordination. It is in catastrophic situations—when resources are stretched, information is lacking, and capacity is most compromised—that appreciation of the potential of emergent organizations and networks is most critical. In such

RECOMMENDED READINGS

Buck, D.A., J.E. Trainor, and B.E. Aguirre. 2006. A critical study of the incident command system and NIMS. *Journal of Homeland Security and Emergency Management*, 3(3), 1.

Drabek, T.E. and D.A. McEntire. 2002. Emergent phenomena and multi-organizational coordination in disasters: Lessons from the research literature. *International Journal of Mass Emergencies and Disasters.*, August, 22(2), 197–224.

Kendra, J.M. and T. Wachtendorf. 2003. Reconsidering convergence and converger legitimacy in response to the world trade center disaster. *Terrorism and Disaster: New Threats, New Ideas* (ed. Lee Clarke). *Research in Social Problems and Public Policy*, (11), 97–122.

Majchrazak, A., S.L. Jarvenpaa, and A.B. Hollingshead. 2007. Coordinating expertise among emergent groups responding to disasters. *Organization Science* 18(1), 147–161.

Quarantelli, E.L., with K.E. Green, E. Ireland, S. McCbe, and D.M. Neal. 1983. Emergent citizen groups in disaster preparedness and recovery activities: An interim report. Newark, DE. University of Delaware, Disaster Research Center.

Tierney, K.J., M.K. Lindell, and R.W. Perry. 2001. *Facing the Unexpected: Disaster Preparedness and Response in the United States*. Washington, DC: Joseph Henry Press.

Figure 10.11 Recommended additional readings.

stressful circumstances, it could be all too easy to focus on jurisdiction and protocol and to see emergent participation as inept, counter-productive, and damaging. Yet dismissing their participation outright undermines the very resiliency of our communities: the ability to draw upon latent capacities in concert with our contingency planning and then improvise in various ways to contend with the unexpected. It is unlikely that a community that has not engaged in any pre-planning will fare well during a catastrophe. But it is also unlikely that a community that solely relies on anticipated organization and tasks during a catastrophic response will fare well either. These complex events demand complex approaches, which—in the end—will demand our best and brightest formal responders working alongside, in a coordinated but creative fashion, our most dedicated and knowledgeable emergent organizations (Figure 10.11).

CASE STUDY*

EXISTING AND EMERGENT RESPONDERS IN HIGH CONSEQUENCE EVENTS

After the attacks on the World Trade Center, thousands of people converged to New York City to offer their assistance. Uniformed officers from within the city, as well as those from across the country, came to assist in security, fire suppression, and rescue and recovery operations. Iron and construction workers came to work on the site, as did architects and planners who were familiar with the layout and design of the Twin Towers. Personnel from city, state, and federal agencies were involved in tasks as varied as coordination, debris removal, environmental monitoring, remains recovery, and warehouse inventory. Non-profit personnel were providing food and counseling. Media from around the world were seeking to report on events. Private sector personnel were restoring utilities and providing needed equipment. Everyday citizens were volunteering en mass in any way they could, be it delivering coffee, providing massages, and sorting donations to more specialized tasks such as assisting in mapping projects. In short, the city had to contend with an outpouring of much-needed assistance while at the same time ensure that: (1) security was maintained in a post-terrorist environment; (2) only essential personnel with adequate protection were allowed into hazardous areas; and (3) the number of people in response-related areas and facilities was kept to a manageable number. Consequently, credentialing of personnel (determining qualifications and issuing of credentials or badges) quickly emerged as an important task during the response period.

Initially, the credentialing procedure was relatively rudimentary. The only protocol in place was to allow access to city, state, or federal agency personnel with valid agency badges. Several non-profit organizations would also be allowed

---

* Case study prepared by Tricia Wachtendorf and supported by grants from the Multidisciplinary Center for Earthquake and Engineering Research (MCEER), New Technologies in Emergency Management, No. 00-10-81 and Measure of Resilience, No. 99-32-01; by special supplemental funding provided by the National Science Foundation, and by the Public Entity Risk Institute No. 2001-70 (Kathleen J. Tierney, principal investigator). Revised for reprint and with permission for use in this chapter.

access with their badges, including the American Red Cross and the Salvation Army. Those in charge of site security quickly realized this would prove inadequate in the aftermath of such a catastrophic disaster. Citizens who provided critical assistance in the hours after the attack found themselves within the secured zone. Some opted not to leave, and therefore it became difficult to restrict their access. Others familiar with the city and blessed with a talent for negotiation were able to talk their way into the restricted areas. Furthermore, those coordinating the response did not want every agency worker with a badge to have access to all areas associated with the operations. At the same time, some people whose expertise was indeed much needed were unable to quickly gain access due to their outsider status. For example, some private sector individuals who were contacted by telephone to transport necessary equipment were initially unable to cross into Manhattan as they were without city credentials or official written authorization. After waiting for hours, checkpoint security finally let them through stating that they must be legitimate if they chose to wait that long. Critical supplies were delayed, yet in the end the system did not actually serve any additional security function to limit access if waiting a long time was the ultimate criterion for entry. Architects with detailed knowledge of the Twin Towers—important information as rescue workers were hoping to identify voids where survivors might be trapped—were delayed in gaining access because they did not have a city agency badge. Although we now know that there was little hope in finding any more survivors than were rescued, this delay could have had important and tragic ramifications. Coordinators of the response needed to devise a system to restrict access to the many response-related sites (e.g., the impact zone, the emergency operations center (EOC), the disaster field office (DFO), the mortuary, the family assistance center (FAC), the warehouses, and the recovery operation on Staten Island) in such as way that allowed in those who were needed at a given time period and limited or prevented access for those whose assistance was not needed at that area or at that phase of the response. However, with operations underway at various sites (particularly when the EOC was in the process of re-establishing itself), credentialing proved extremely challenging.

Why was it so important to limit access to Ground Zero? We must remember that this was an extremely dangerous environment, with overhead hazards from damaged buildings, unstable debris piles, and fires raging beneath the surface for months. Heavy equipment was in operation. Personal protection equipment was sometimes in limited supply and it was essential to attend safety meetings or have access to updates on site safety. It was important, particularly after the effort transitioned from rescue to recovery, to limit the number of personnel operating in the confined area and to ensure that those working at the site were properly protected, informed of safety procedures and changes in operations, and best equipped to provide needed services. Moreover, whether the site was the impacted zone or one of the many other sites and facilities, emergency coordinators needed to consider the turnover of assistance providers. As new helpers came in and others transitioned out, there needed to be some way to account for how many people would have access and to where.

A number of steps were taken in New York City, each bringing with it unintended consequences that also needed to be contended with. The evolving credentialing system included a series of badges introduced at the EOC and the impacted zone. At the EOC, we saw a fairly simple badge issued with the Office of Emergency Management (OEM) Insignia—something that could have been easily reproduced on any home computer—that needed to be shown with any form of photo identification. Changes were made, including the addition of a "P" for podium access, numbers of the piers where the EOC, DFO, and FAC were located, to a more sophisticated laminated and photo badge system where a variety of site access points were outlined. A significant amount of time was spent waiting in line for these badges as they evolved—particularly if one was away from the EOC when the change occurred. Yet when the laminated photo badges were initially issued, individuals themselves could indicate where they wanted access to without a screening process.

An entirely different badges system evolved for contractors at the impact site, with new badges being issued in different colors over time and with no individual identifiers in the first few months. The color system was an effort both to account for workers who had since been replaced by others and the changing restrictions on the number of personnel allowed at the site. Sometimes contractors did not have enough badges and had to improvise entry strategies including the sharing of badges, with individuals transferring them back and forth through the checkpoints. Eventually a photo identification badge was issued. An entirely separate volunteer credentialing and assignment operation was set up at the Jacob Javits Convention Center. All the while, some agency badges were enough to allow entry, even without the new credentials. Agencies such as the American Red Cross were in charge of their own volunteer screening.

Each time a change was made, information needed to be disseminated to checkpoint personnel. Sometimes checkpoint security included uniformed personnel who were themselves convergers from outside the jurisdiction and not within a network to learn about the changes in a timely manner. When the white contractor badge was no longer valid, this generated some delays for those with the white laminated EOC badge. In another case, newly-introduced contractor badges were handed out without regard to new access protocol, essentially defeating the purpose of the new badge.

New York City was dealing with an unprecedented disaster within its jurisdiction, and an unprecedented number of people who were generously offering assistance. With the destruction of its EOC, emergency coordinators and site security recognized that existing protocol was no longer appropriate given emerging needs and adapted to their changing emergency environment. Although the size of the disaster and the city impacted generated a tremendous convergence of helpers, smaller communities could be quickly overwhelmed with less convergence.

INSTRUCTIONS

Students should be divided into groups of four and imagine that each group represents a different set of stakeholders in a medium-sized city impacted by a catastrophic event.

Groups may include the following: local emergency managers; local fire and police departments; local government agencies such as public works, transportation, health and human services, sanitation, and so on; federal agencies including but not limited to FEMA; large non-profit groups such as the American Red Cross, Second Harvest, and the Salvation Army; an emergent group of small community-based non-profit groups and local businesses; a group of local citizens who are also impacted by the event who form an emergent organization; and an emergent group of people who have converged from outside the area to provide assistance.

Each group should consider the following sets of questions from the perspective of the stakeholder group they are assigned to represent and develop a credentialing plan to contend with both existing and emergent groups. Student groups adopting the perspective of an emergent group should identify a purpose around which the group has formed (e.g., search and rescue; delivery of certain supplies; communication of information; debris clean-up; shelter provision; victim advocacy; among others).

After spending 30 min working through the questions in their respective groups, the class should reconvene and compare how different stakeholders may respond differently to the questions. The answers to the questions may vary depending on the type of disaster or catastrophe. For example, the credentialing process may be somewhat different in the aftermath of a hurricane or a flood than in the aftermath of a pandemic or chemical release. Depending on the time available, students may wish to repeat the exercise, considering the questions from the perspective of a different stakeholder group in response to a different catastrophic event. The instructor could also adapt the exercise to constitute as a take-home paper assignment or an essay question on a final exam.

1. Briefly describe the system you would recommend implementing.
2. How should *local, state, and federal government employees* be dealt with under this system?
3. How should the system distinguish government employees who should have access from those who should not?
4. How should national or large non-profit organization employees be dealt with under this system?
5. Should there be a way to distinguish non-profit organization employees who should have access from those who should not? If so, how?
6. How should *community and faith-based organization employees* be dealt with under this system? Consider a broad range of community and faith-based organizations, not just those with a history of working with the emergency management community.
7. Should there be a way to distinguish community and faith-based organization employees who should have access from those who should not? If so, how?
8. How should *private sector employees* be dealt with under this system?
9. Should there be a way to distinguish private sector employees who should have access from those who should not? If so, how?
10. What should the credentialing strategies be for *helpers from outside the impacted area compared to those from within the area*? Consider a number

of different types of helpers, including but not limited to police officers, fire fighters, various medical personnel, construction workers, translators, formal and informal rescue crews, counselors, childcare workers, food providers, researchers, skilled equipment operators, environmental monitors, media and those with expert knowledge (such as the architects mentioned in the case study).

11. Who should determine who will have site access and how will they make that determination?
12. At what sites or facilities will that determination take place? What if those sites or facilities are not accessible during the catastrophe?
13. Will more than one credentialing system be in place? If so, will that pose any conflicts or inconsistencies in the way in which the systems are implemented?
14. Will additional documentation be necessary to acquire or use a badge (e.g., one or two pieces of other identification, photo identification, or professional documents)? Is it reasonable to expect that an individual will have quick access to these documents in the aftermath of a disaster? Even if it is, how will exceptions be handled?
15. How will lost badges be dealt with?
16. Is any specialized equipment needed to manage your credentialing system? How will your community acquire this equipment and how will it be maintained or updated?
17. To what extent will your community credentialing strategies rely upon the functioning operation of other systems (e.g., access to facilities with pre-produced badges, access to scanner equipment, operation of communication systems, and operation of electrical systems)?
18. What are the resources in your community that could be valuable to this process, either in planning for a disaster/catastrophe credentialing program or in the midst of a response should improvisation become necessary?
19. What protocols will be in place for access to specific facilities? Are these protocols readily transferable to a new facility? How adaptable are those policies to emergent needs?
20. If you find yourself presented with unanticipated needs, how can you best limit access to only key personnel while at the same time not instituting barriers to people who may legitimately fulfill emergent needs?
21. What should the process be to transition personnel out of an area, or decreasing access over time?
22. How should credentialing protocol and changes to that protocol be communicated to those seeking credentials and those checking credentials? What are the potential gaps in that communication that may impact your stakeholder group?
23. Should there be a process for making exceptions to protocol? If so, what? There will be many cases where those with essential skills or resources must be granted access without waiting for standard protocol to be implemented.
24. How will you determine if changes need to be made to your credential system in the midst of the disaster?
25. Finally, what are the major barriers to participation in response that most impact your group and how can they best be dealt with (you should feel free to speculate beyond the area of credentialing).

ACKNOWLEDGMENTS

This chapter is based upon work supported by the following grant numbers. Multidisciplinary Center for Earthquake and Engineering Research (MCEER), New Technologies in Emergency Management, No. 00-10-81 and Measure of Resilience, No. 99-32-01; by special supplemental funding provided by the National Science Foundation, Public Entity Risk Institute No. 2001-70; University of Delaware Research Foundation; National Science Foundation 1123924, 1034627, 0624083, 0554949, 0510188, 1138643, and funding provided by the Disaster Research Center and the Earthquake Engineering Research Institute for quick response fieldwork. Any opinions, findings, and conclusions or recommendations expressed in this material are those of the author(s) and do not necessarily reflect the views of the funding agencies.

REFERENCES

Aguirre, B.E., D. Wenger, T.A. Glass, M. Diaz-Murillo, and G. Vigo. 1995. The social organization of search and rescue: Evidence from the Guadalajara gasoline explosion. *International Journal of Mass Emergencies and Disasters*, 13, 93–106.

Bigley, G.A. and K. Roberts. 2001. The incident command system: High reliability organizing for complex and volatile task environments. *Acad. Management Journal*, 44, 1281–1300.

Buck, D.A., J.E. Trainor, and B.E. Aguirre. 2006. A critical study of the incident command system and NIMS. *Journal of Homeland Security and Emergency Management*, 3(3), 1.

Christen, H., P. Maniscalco, A. Vickery, and F. Winslow. 2001. An overview of incident management systems. *Perspectives on Preparedness*, September 4. Accessed on June 30, 2012. http://www.hcanj.org/docs/An_Overview_of_Incident_Management_Systems.pdf.

DeCapua, M. 2007. Letter to the editor regarding incident command system. *Journal of Homeland Security and Emergency Management*, 4(1), 4.

Drabek, T.E. 1996. *The Social Dimensions of Disaster.* Federal Emergency Management Agency: Washington, DC.

Drabek, T.E. and D.A. McEntire. 2002. Emergent phenomena and multi-organizational coordination in disasters: Lessons from the research literature. *International Journal of Mass Emergencies and Disasters,* August, 22(2), 197–224.

Drabek, T.E. and D.A. McEntire. 2003. Emergent phenomena and the sociology of disaster: Lessons, trends and opportunities from the research literature. *Disaster Prevention and Management*, 12(2), 97–112.

Dynes, R.R. 1970. *Organized Behavior in Disaster.* DC. Heath: Lexington, MA.

Fischer, H.W. III 2008. *Response to Disaster.* University Press of America, Inc.: Lanham, MD.

Fritz, C. and J.H. Mathewson. 1957. Convergent Behavior: A Disaster Control Problem. *Special Report for the Committee on Disaster Studies*. National Academy of Sciences, Washington, DC.

Kendra, J.M. and T. Wachtendorf. 2003. Reconsidering Convergence and Converger Legitimacy in Response to the World Trade Center Disaster. *Terrorism and Disaster: New Threats, New Ideas* (ed. L. Clarke). *Research in Social Problems and Public Policy,* (11), 97–122.

Kendra, J. and T. Wachtendorf. 2007. *Emergence and Convergence in the Post-Disaster Environment: Recent Research Perspectives*, Training program created for the Public Entity Risk Institute.

Kendra, J.M., T. Wachtendorf, and E.L. Quarantelli. 2003. The evacuation of lower Manhattan by water transport on September 11: An unplanned success. *Joint Commission Journal on Quality and Safety*, 29(6), 316–318.

Majchrazak, A., S.L. Jarvenpaa, and A.B. Hollingshead. 2007. Coordinating expertise among emergent groups responding to disasters. *Organization Science,* 18(1), 147–161.

Moreland, R.L. and L. Argote. 2003. Transactive memory in dynamic organizations. In R.S. Peterson, E.A. Mannix, eds. *Leading and Managing People in the Dynamic Organization*. Lawrence Erlbaum: Mahwah, NJ.

Quarantelli, E.L. 2005. *Catastrophes Are Different from Disasters: Implications for Crisis Planning and Managing Drawn from Katrina. Understanding Katrina: Perspectives from the Social Sciences.* Social Science Research Council. http://understandingkatrina.ssrc.org.

Quarantelli, E.L., P. Lagadec, and A. Boin. 2006. A heuristic approach to future disasters and crises: New, old, and in-between disasters. (eds. H. Rodriguez, E.L. Qurantelli, and R.R. Dynes) *Handbook of Disaster Research*. Springer: New York, NY, pp. 16–41.

Quarantelli, E.L., with K.E. Green, E. Ireland, S. McCabe, and D.M. Neal. 1983. *Emergent Citizen Groups in Disaster Preparedness and Recovery Activities: An Interim Report*. University of Delaware, Disaster Research Center: Newark, DE.

Tierney, K.J. 2002. *Lessons Learned from Research on Group and Organizational Responses to Disasters.* Paper presented at Countering Terrorism: Lessons Learned from Natural and Technological Disasters. Academy of Sciences, February 28–March 1.

Tierney, K.J. 2006. Recent Developments in U.S. Homeland Security Policies. (eds. H. Rodriguez, E.L. Quarantelli, and R.R. Dynes) *Handbook of Disaster Research*. Springer: New York, NY, pp. 405–412.

Tierney, K.J., M.K. Lindell, and R.W. Perry. 2001. *Facing the Unexpected: Disaster Preparedness and Response in the United States*. Joseph Henry Press: Washington, DC.

Trainor, J.E. 2004. *Searching for a System: Multi-Organizational Coordination in the September 11th World Trade Center Search and Rescue Response.* Masters Thesis. Department of Sociology and Criminal Justice and Disaster Research Center. University of Delaware, Disaster Research Center: Newark, DE.

Trainor, J.E. and L. Barsky. 2011. *Reporting for Duty? A Synthesis of Research on Role Conflict, Strain, and Abandonment Among Emergency Responders during Disasters and Catastrophes*. Miscellaneous Report 71. University of Delaware, Disaster Research Center: Newark, DE.

Wachtendorf, T. 2004. *Improvising 9/11: Organizational Improvisation in the World Trade Center Disaster,* Dissertation #35. University of Delaware Disaster Research Center: Newark, DE.

Wachtendorf, T. 2005. *Partnering to Foster Disaster Resistant Communities*. Invited Presentation to the Disaster Resistant California Conference, Sacramento, CA, May 17.

Wachtendorf, T., B. Brown, J. Holguin-Veras, and S. Ukkusuri. 2008. Network visibility in emergency supply chain management. Paper presented at the workshop on improving disaster supply chain management: Key supply chain factors for humanitarian relief sponsored by the Stephenson Disaster Management Institute, Baton Rouge, Louisiana. November 18.

Wachtendorf, T., B. Brown, J. Holguin-Veras, (Under review). Catastrophe Characteristics and their Impact on Critical Supply Chains: Problematizing Materiel Convergence and Management Following Hurricane Katrina.

Wachtendorf, T., J.M. Kendra, and B. Lea. 2010. Community behavior and response to disaster (eds. E. Daily and R. Powers). *International Disaster Nursing*. World Association of Disaster and Emergency Medicine and Cambridge Press.

Waugh, W.L. 2006a. Mechanisms for collaboration in emergency management: ICS, NIMS, and the problem of command and control. *Power Point Presentation to the Collaborative Public Management Conference*, The Maxwell School of Syracuse University, Washington, DC, September 28–30. Accessed August 30, 2008 at http://www.maxwell.syr.edu/parc/AAA%20-%20Powerpoints/William%20Waugh.ppt/.

Waugh, W.L. 2006b. Terrorism and Disaster. (eds. H. Rodriguez, E.L. Quarantelli, and R.R. Dynes) *Handbook of Disaster Research*. Springer: New York, NY, pp. 388–404.

CHAPTER 11

Methods of Planning and Response Coordination

Jasmin R. Ruback, A. Scott Wells, and Brian J. Maguire

CONTENTS

Overall Complexity of Catastrophe 258
Strategic Thinking with Regard to Catastrophe Response 259
Policies for Catastrophe Planning and Response...260
Current Legislation for Catastrophe Response Planning......................................264
Presidential Preparedness Directive-8 (PPD-8)..265
New Methods in Catastrophe Response Planning Innovations: Research,
Theory, and Tools 266
    New Research..266
    New Theory and Decision-Making Tools...268
    Change of Focus of Planning 268
    Predictive Modeling Techniques...269
Catastrophe Planning Practices 270
The Integrated Planning System (IPS) 270
The Catastrophic Planning Program 271
The North Atlantic Hypercomplexity Approach 273
Future of Catastrophe Planning and Response Coordination: Conclusion............277
References..278

Working collaboratively creates strength, and thus it is the planning process, not the final plan, that is most important. We have had to learn this lesson the hard way, first after the attacks of September 11, 2001, when responding agencies could not effectively communicate, and then again after Hurricane Katrina, when the enormity of the event overwhelmed the largely uncoordinated response. Planning is about anticipating and adapting to changed and changing circumstances. The threats facing us change (e.g., the magnitude, scope, and increased overall complexity of the events), the resources we want to protect change (e.g., populations move and grow), and the agencies charged with protecting us change (e.g., politicians increase, or more often, decrease resources, and they shift policy focus areas and departments). Typically, national and state response systems have been slow to change, but criticisms of recent responses to catastrophes have meant that these agencies have had to adapt at a quicker pace.

As described earlier in this book, catastrophes are different from disasters in numerous ways. When it comes to planning for catastrophe response, we need to remember that catastrophes are complex, and of four primary types, all of which have to be planned for:

1. Natural catastrophes include pandemics, hurricanes, and earthquakes
2. Scientific accidents include calamities at nuclear reactors and mishaps at biological laboratories
3. Other unintended human-caused disasters such as global warming
4. Intentional catastrophes such as terrorism and nuclear attacks

OVERALL COMPLEXITY OF CATASTROPHE

Some kinds of resources may not ever be sufficient in some catastrophes, even with the use of national assets such as healthcare facilities and personnel. Especially since Hurricane Katrina, medical professionals have been concerned about the issues related to scarce resource allocation (such as removing patients from ventilators to make the machines available for disaster victims). The fallout from catastrophic events is interdependent, and the effects are magnified. Thus, if electrical power is down, being unable to travel because there is no gasoline and the roads are out makes the situation even more unbearable. Providers of energy (electricity, gasoline, natural gas, heating oil) are highly networked, even across national boundaries, and a disruption from a disaster in one place will likely affect distribution in other places. Information services are also highly linked and tied into the availability of electrical power; both systems are vulnerable to disruption that can take many weeks or months to reset. Financial losses are so high that no single source will be able to cover them. Communities need funding right away. The operational tempo for responding to a catastrophic event must speed up as the response needs on the ground become greater, the need to help injured people grows, the distances spanned become longer, and the political pressures increase.

The mainstream disaster planning techniques currently used in the United States cannot be directly applied to catastrophe planning because they are fundamentally inadequate for complex, multi-jurisdictional events. Therefore, new strategies, policies, methods, and practices to catastrophic planning are needed and are being developed.

STRATEGIC THINKING WITH REGARD TO CATASTROPHE RESPONSE

Successful strategic thinking occurs in an environment where individual leaders and managers have had education, training, and practice using strategic thinking skills. Managers without that education, training, and practice will do what they do best—focus on accomplishing their short-term and focused tactical and organizational objectives.

Planning never stops. There is no one way to accomplish a mission once an event occurs. The process of planning allows for the sharing of knowledge and the flexibility needed for catastrophe response. While many organizational cultures require strict adherence to established protocol, a successful response to catastrophes require flexible leadership. The responders have to be creative to adapt to the real-world situation and any constraints. This means taking initiative and doing things differently, despite leadership. Current policy initiatives focus on the need to assess changing conditions and integrate responses that are scalable, flexible, and adaptable.[1]

In the past, the need for flexibility was evidenced during the invasion of Grenada in 1983. According to General Schwartzkopf, the initial wave of Army helicopters was met with a fierce barrage of gunfire. Some were able to make it to a nearby Navy helicopter carrier. As the battle was raging, an urgent message was sent from the Navy's comptroller in Washington telling the admiral not to refuel Army helicopters because the "funds-transfer arrangement was not worked out." The Admiral read the message, turned to his chief of staff and said: "This is bullsh**. Give them the fuel."[2] During the same invasion, the helicopter carrier that Schwartzkopf was on began sailing directly past the students' dormitories. The general looked down and saw a deck full of Marine helicopters. He summoned the Marine colonel and told him he wanted the helicopters to be used to protect the students. The colonel said it would take 24 hours to staff the helicopters with Marines. Schwartzkopf said the helicopters could be staffed with Army Rangers and the job could be done in an hour. The colonel said: "We don't put Army soldiers on Marine helicopters." After trying to reason with him, Schwartzkopf had to finally resort to giving the colonel a direct order to put the Army soldiers on the Marine helicopters.[3]

Although prior experience is generally helpful for dealing with a disaster, it is not always the case that experience in less serious events leads to better outcomes in more serious events. Using risk management techniques that worked in previous emergencies, or even in previous disasters, may prove futile or even detrimental in the environment of a catastrophe. For example, researchers have found that managers "do not accept the idea that the risks they face are inherent in their situation." Rather, they believe that risks can be reduced by using skills to control the dangers.[4] In particular, "the methods that had been employed successfully for the 243 previous major disaster declarations since January 2001 proved inadequate for Hurricane Katrina's magnitude."[5] Perhaps the single most important lesson for experienced managers is that the event may be beyond their control.

Successful planning also considers variables associated with the workforce. During the SARS outbreak in Toronto, 436 of the city's 850 paramedics had to be quarantined.[6] Dan Hafling, an emergency department physician, researcher, and director of emergency management and disaster medicine for the Inova Health System in Virginia, estimates that between a quarter and a third of hospital workers will not come to work during a pandemic or chemical/biological/radiological attack.[7] How can agencies prepare for large-scale events with the possibility that a large proportion of their workforce will be unavailable? What can be done during the planning phase to increase the number of workers who may respond?

Table 11.1 is a tool to help with the planning process. It identifies three types of groups and the objectives they need to focus on during three periods of time. The three groups are

1. "Community," which refers to the whole community, including citizens;
2. "Agency," which primarily means response and infrastructure agencies such as police, fire, EMS, public health, water and energy departments, and;
3. "Government," which includes local, state, and federal officials.

The three time periods are pre-event, event, and post-event. Therefore, in the pre-event period, the community should focus on: Sufficient public education (e.g., planning, alternate evacuation routes, ways to be a disaster volunteer, etc.); Community level drills (for both volunteers and for non-volunteers); and insure that there are sufficient food and water resources for the community for one week.

POLICIES FOR CATASTROPHE PLANNING AND RESPONSE

The focus in the United States is on integration of the Whole Community which is, "an approach to emergency management that reinforces the fact that FEMA is only one part of our nation's emergency management team; that we must leverage all of the resources of our collective team in preparing for, protecting against, responding to, recovering from and mitigating against all hazards; and that collectively we must meet the needs of the entire community in each of these areas."[8]

Such a comprehensive level of integration is not easy. Management officials must recognize that other agencies may have drastically different cultures—as well as different policies and procedures. Integration of leaders should take place prior to events happening, in joint policy development, training, and exercising. This will require changes in funding practice for planning and training.

Beyond the integration of agencies, planning also needs to include the management of voluntary responders. "Volunteers have an important role to play in strengthening the capacity of local communities to manage the effects of disaster. Information exists to facilitate increased citizen involvement in disaster mitigation but has not been effectively communicated to help individuals and organizations identify and embrace appropriate volunteer opportunities."[9] Major

Table 11.1 Critical Success Factors Related to Strategic Thinking

	Community	Agency	Government
Pre-event	Sufficient public education Community level drills Sufficient food and water for one week	Mobilization and response plans are based on realistic scenarios Mobilization capacity and capability is adequate to meet expected needs Adequate resources are available for initial response in high threat areas Interorganizational coordination is preplanned	Domain awareness and detection capability are created and maintained Mobilization and response plans are based on realistic scenarios Mobilization capacity and capability is adequate to meet expected needs Adequate resources are available for initial response in high threat areas Interorganizational coordination is preplanned; stakeholders are identified
Event	Local resources are rapidly and efficiently integrated into predetermined response organization Evacuations proceed in orderly fashion	Mobilized response resources are rapidly and efficiently integrated into predetermined response organization Coordinated multiorganization, networked response system is established Ability to manage the collection, synthesis, analysis, and internal and external distribution of information is established Organizational and operational adaptability and agility is maintained	Situational awareness is obtained and shared across distributed organizational networks Resources in place are capable of initial life and safety response Resource mobilization is based on accurate estimates of needs for people, funds, and equipment Resource mobilization is governed by preplanned organizational structure and process
Post-event	Repopulation occurs as resources and infrastructure become available	Continuing needs are identified Organizational learning is accomplished	Continuing needs are identified Plan for transition to local support of continuing needs is developed and followed External resources are demobilized according to established plans and procedures Resources are provided to support economic and social recovery Organizational learning is accomplished

Source: Adapted from Bullen CV, Rockart JF. *A Primer on Critical Success Factors.* MIT. 1981. Available at: http://dspace.mit.edu/bitstream/handle/1721.1/1988/SWP-1220-08368993-CISR-069.pdf?sequence=1. Accessed December 13, 2008.

planning problems are possible. For example, there is a possibility that thousands of volunteers may show up at the scene(s) of a catastrophe, and, managed correctly, might add crucial assistance when the deficits are greatest. Without appropriate management, volunteers may impede rescues, disrupt crime scenes, and may themselves become victims. However, experienced volunteer managers and coordinators may provide needed leadership if there is planning beforehand. The availability (and value) of volunteers may be influenced by pre-event planning and training. Citizen involvement initiatives may help educate and prepare people to assist during critical events. Pre-event training programs and meetings may also serve as ways to help establish and document the volunteer's credentials. Drills should also be used as opportunities to test plans for providing food, water, and shelter to volunteers. After the catastrophe, citizens who are not volunteering may place more burdens upon strained resources (if they're not part of the solution, they're part of the problem). Historical anecdotes describe people in catastrophic circumstances who feel helpless and then abandon any sense of responsibility. For example, during the Bubonic Plague in Medieval Europe, some people "decided that since life was short, indulging in pleasures while you could was the order of the day."[10] Thus, it is important to consider ways for communities to recruit and prepare volunteers before an event and to do real-time training for volunteers during an event.

Another integration issue involves methods of integrating international responders into the response effort to a major catastrophe in the United States. There have been calls for such plans: "The Department of State, in coordination with the Department of Homeland Security, should review and revise policies, plans, and procedures for the management of foreign disaster assistance. In addition, this review should clarify responsibilities and procedures for handling inquiries regarding affected foreign nationals."[11] Many smaller countries have well-established plans and protocols for integrating assistance coming in from other countries. Catastrophes can be so large and overwhelming that even the wealthiest countries should be prepared to effectively integrate outside assistance.

The overall planning procedure often brings unlikely neighbors together for a common cause. The plans can go from simple to complex, yet all of the parts work together as a whole. For example, the U.S. military is not often thought of as a humanitarian organization and yet, just in recent years alone, it has engaged in disaster relief efforts in Japan, Haiti, and Pakistan. Masters and Cropsey[12] also note the U.S. military's increasing role in working on an international level to make the seas safer; an endeavor that has some humanitarian roots but one that also supports global commerce.

In the midst of a future crisis that may devastate an entire region, plans often require a strong basis of credibility and trust in order to be implemented in a timely fashion. Every one needs to know what to do and to have some knowledge of the other key players in the effort (see Figure 11.1).

One way of improving the potential and practice of integration is to adopt these three planning activities that facilitate the process of working together.

METHODS OF PLANNING AND RESPONSE COORDINATION

Figure 11.1 FEMA organized planning meeting to discuss removal of the April tornado debris in AL. (http://www.fema.gov/photolibrary/photo_details.do?id=47074.)

1. *Standardization.* Planners need standard terminology, doctrine, and procedures so that we can better understand and integrate our efforts.
2. *Integration.* Planning needs to be integrated both horizontally across the major areas of emergency management—prevention, protection, response, recovery, and mitigation as well as across neighboring jurisdictions. Integration of planning efforts should also occur vertically among our local, state, and federal governments.
3. *Collaboration.* This is a term of art for planning purposes that means working together for a common outcome. Implied in this is that each party must relinquish part of its self-interest, its autonomy, for the greater good. True collaboration means sacrifice, which is only achieved when trust and credibility are established.

But what happens when that credibility and trust are not there?

In the midst of a future crisis that may devastate an entire region, plans often require collaboration. A strong basis of credibility and trust must be established in order for plans to be implemented in a timely and synchronized fashion. Everyone needs to know what to do and to have some knowledge of the other key players' efforts.

Even so, there are many sources of potential conflict. Conflicts with planning occur when some individuals who are not at the table should be, when people are included for the wrong reasons, when there are conflicting motivations, when there is confusion about authority and responsibility, when communication breaks down, when people feel as though a plan is being forced upon them, and also when blame gets assigned to a wrong party. This can lead to fear. Specifically fear of failure. Very little gets accomplished in this environment, as the focus moves to avoiding blame versus accomplishing the mission.

Conflict can also occur among agencies. Some degree of conflict or friction is inherent among the three levels of the U.S. government, and this friction can work its way into planning. For example, the federal government is concerned about the most destructive scenarios while state and local governments are generally more concerned about the most likely scenarios. Consequently, the federal government stresses planning activities for low-probability but high impact catastrophic events. State and local governments, while cognizant of the potential events, have limited time and resources for planning, so they generally gravitate to the more likely events. Additionally, the federal government is interested in capability gaps at the state and local levels. Knowledge of the gaps in medical, search and rescue, sheltering, and commodities will help the federal government plan better. State and local governments may be somewhat reluctant to reveal their gaps, as they could be interpreted as evidence that the states are not taking all the measures necessary to protect their constituents.

The planning process is made more complex because partners have different levels of knowledge of, and experience with, disaster planning. For example, some individuals do not know that the federal government generally will not respond to a disaster unless asked by the state. Additionally, some kinds or planning are not mandated, and so they are not done. Another complexity involves the resources available for planning. Coalitions can be difficult to build if coalition partners have differing resource levels. In such cases, there can be insensitivity to issues like available time and funds. Some communities within the region may be growing at different rates putting more pressure and urgency on some to plan faster than others. While planning, it pays to consider everyone a potential partner and to start the dialog. Learn to respect differences. Conflict resolution in the planning process can take time but the investment will build stronger trust and commitments for the future.

For disasters involving presidential declarations, when the federal government gets involved, the center of gravity for response operations shifts more toward the federal end of the continuum. This shift results in a planning process centered on the local level and a response process authority centered on the federal level. Inevitably, then, there is some disconnect between the plans for an incident and the actual response to it.

CURRENT LEGISLATION FOR CATASTROPHE RESPONSE PLANNING

Two pieces of legislation in the aftermath of Hurricane Katrina, the Post-Katrina Emergency Reform Act and amendments to the Homeland Security Act of 2002, have greatly changed and expanded the responsibilities of FEMA. Among the many changes that expand FEMA's roles and responsibilities are requirements to address catastrophe preparedness. For example, in Sections 503 and 504 of the Federal Emergency Management Act (6 U.S.C 313) of the Homeland Security Act of 2002 as amended by the Department of Homeland Security Appropriations Act, 2007—there are specific catastrophe requirements to:

"... partner with State, local, and tribal governments and emergency response providers, with other Federal agencies, with the private sector, and with nongovernmental organizations to build a national system of emergency management that can effectively and efficiently utilize the full measure of the nation's resources to respond to natural disasters, acts of terrorism, and other man-made disasters, including catastrophic incidents."

"The Administrator shall provide Federal leadership necessary to prepare for, protect against, respond to, recover from, or mitigate against a natural disaster ... including ... developing a national emergency management system that is capable of preparing for, protecting against, responding to, recovering from, and mitigating against catastrophic incidents."

The Stafford Act is the Nation's primary authority for all-hazards emergency management; the FEMA Administrator exercises a variety of powers under the Stafford Act on behalf of the President and the Secretary of Homeland Security. Homeland Security Presidential Directives make the Secretary of Homeland Security responsible for domestic incident management and national continuity operations and activities, respectively. For the most part, these functions are carried out by FEMA.

PRESIDENTIAL PREPAREDNESS DIRECTIVE-8 (PPD-8)

PPD-8 is an explicit policy statement that the security and resilience of the United States must be strengthened through systematic preparation for the threats that pose the greatest risk to the security of the nation, including acts of terrorism, cyber attacks, pandemics, and catastrophic natural disasters. The PPD-8 effort is being delivered through the National Preparedness System and the National Preparedness Goal, which provides the capabilities required to prevent, protect against, mitigate, respond to, and recover from the threats and hazards that pose the greatest risk to the nation. A national preparedness system is being assembled, and new tools and guidance are being developed. Currently being developed are new national planning frameworks and interagency operations plans that utilize the National Preparedness System to identify the roles and responsibilities of the departments and agencies with roles in the five mission areas of preparedness (e.g., prevention, protection, mitigation, response, and recovery).

According to PPD-8, planning for catastrophic disasters must be better coordinated and predicated on nationally agreed-upon, risk-based preparedness standards. National efforts to ensure resilience after catastrophic events must focus on improving existing preparedness. This preparedness requires close collaboration with all partners in the establishment of shared objectives and capability standards at the federal, state, local, regional, tribal, territorial, nongovernmental, and private sector levels. Moreover, the public is engaged and integrated as part of the solution to achieving greater overall catastrophic preparedness. Planning assumptions address risk-based worst-case scenarios (maximums of maximums) with resource thresholds that are intended to challenge preparedness at all levels of government. These scenarios will enable planners to seek innovative, non-traditional solutions to catastrophic events. Partnerships in planning for these events will also extend beyond traditional coalitions. Plans will be supported by training, technical assistance, and grants. Ultimately, these plans will be validated through robust exercises designed to overload the system so that additional capability shortfalls can be identified and addressed (Bottom-Up Report, DHS 2010). Some of these scenarios are also being discussed at the regional rollouts of the National Disaster Recovery Framework discussed in Chapter 12.

It must be noted that there may be a problem using exercises that utilize catastrophic disaster scenarios for which neither the public nor leadership have links or prior experience.

NEW METHODS IN CATASTROPHE RESPONSE PLANNING INNOVATIONS: RESEARCH, THEORY, AND TOOLS

There are four ways in which catastrophic response planning has been improved. These four innovations are

- New research
- New theory and decision-making tools
- Change in focus on planning approaches
- Predictive modeling techniques and analysis

New Research

At the end of 2011, FEMA released the Catastrophic Event Study Final 11-28-11, which examined eight specific catastrophic events/disasters (Loma Prieta Earthquake 1989, Hiroshima—Atomic Bomb 1945, Southeast Asian Tsunami 2004, Three Mile Island (TMI) Nuclear Power Plant Accident 1979, Hurricane Katrina 2005, Chernobyl Nuclear Power Plant Accident 1986, Haiti Earthquake 2010, Terrorist Attacks—September 11, 2001, and preliminary data from the Pakistan Floods 2010). The purpose of the project was to research and validate previously identified national response requirements in the first 72 hours of a catastrophic event. FEMA identified and prioritized 13 essential emergency response operations (Critical Communications, Public Messaging, Search and Rescue, Health and Medical Treatment, Safe and Secure Environment, Emergency Shelter, Command, Control, and Coordination, Life-Saving Access and Egress, Stabilize Infrastructure, Essential Services and Commodities, Recovery/Temporary Storage of Deceased, Situational Assessment and Critical Transportation).

"There were multiple lessons learned in the response to each of the eight events, which spanned 65 years of emergency response. Some were overarching and critical to current planning for a catastrophic improvised nuclear device event or a natural disaster. Some of these lessons are especially important.

1. *Problem Conditions.* Pre-existing social, economic, infrastructure, and political problems can be magnified and exacerbated by catastrophic events and affect the speed and effectiveness of response, rescue, and recovery efforts.
2. *Devastation Is Overwhelming.* Manmade and natural disasters can devastate entire communities, resulting in the need for total rebuilding, relocation of the population, and/or abandonment of the area, not just stabilization and repair. In the past, disaster plans at local, state, and federal levels did not take into account the possibility of large-scale devastation of entire communities that would require years for recovery (see Figure 11.2).
3. *Services and Agencies Were Overwhelmed.* During the first 72 hours access into the devastated areas may not be possible, and mutual aid partners may be occupied with their own local response. Even in notice events where many state and federal assets are pre-deployed, effective response coordination was lacking. In addition, agencies and departments responsible for emergency response and management can suffer losses themselves, may be incapacitated, and may be overwhelmed by a catastrophic event. Thus, planning for additional staffing and resources after a catastrophic event needs to broaden the radius of mutual aid agreements and take into account the additional time it will take for deployment and staging.
4. *Inadequacy of Conventional Emergency Response Plans and Procedures.* Each of the events in this study exemplified one or more ways in which the conventional emergency management response protocols at the time of the event were not adequate for the event. Importantly, lives and property were lost in some cases because responders lacked important knowledge.
5. *Lack of Understanding of Incident Command System (ICS).* The scope and duration of all eight events highlight the need to be able to expand control to coordinate multiple agencies and then consolidate multiple commands among mutual aid partners, military personnel, and rapid response teams. Response efforts were slowed

Figure 11.2 As an example of overwhelming devastation: Haitian women sit on rubble from a collapsed building in Port-au-Prince after 7.0 magnitude earthquake. (http://www.army.mil/media/115195.)

by lack of understanding of ICS and by individual agency/department plans at all levels that were not standardized or based on ICS.
6. *Need for Interoperability and Compatibility.* All of the events studied involved multiple agencies and departments working together during the response and recovery. Incompatibility of plans and procedures and lack of interoperability of radio frequencies hampered local and mutual aid responder-coordination.
7. *Emergency Public Information Issues.* Media reports, regardless of their degree of accuracy, were primary sources of information on event severity and location. In the absence of information management by emergency management officials, local reports presented isolated coverage of those events that the media could access, and thus an incomplete picture of the overall situation."[13]

New Theory and Decision-Making Tools

Catastrophe theory provides a way of classifying catastrophes so that we can visualize them pictorially, understand their different characteristics, and gain an intuitive feel for how they arise and what we might be able to do about them.[14] Models are metaphors for reality. There are both physical and mathematical models to predict the economy, the weather, building designs, and so on. When it comes to predictions that involve human behavior, the rules are much less clear, and computer models are correspondingly less able to provide accurate forecasts.[15] Still there are rules that can be used, such as those from game theory, which uses rigorous mathematics to predict outcomes when the proponents in a situation choose strategies that are guided solely by the logic of self-interest.[16]

There are two relatively new and untried decision-making tools to help emergency managers plan for catastrophe: (1) the Catastrophic Incident Annex to the National Response Framework and (2) the Catastrophic Incident Supplement (CIS) to the Catastrophic Incident Annex to the National Response Framework. Together, these tools establish "the context and overarching strategy for implementing and coordinating an accelerated, proactive national response to a catastrophic incident."[17]

These tools serve to cut bureaucracy and speed up the pace for providing lifesaving and life-sustaining resources in catastrophic events.

Change of Focus of Planning

All-hazards planning is the conventional planning methodology being used in most U.S. jurisdictions, and it is the FEMA-supported methodology for jurisdictional disaster response planning. The basic concept is that the responses to disasters are essentially the same, irrespective of the causes. Thus, the focus of these plans is to develop general procedures that can be applied across the full spectrum of types and magnitudes of disasters.

However, the complexity and broad reach of catastrophes are too immense to be adequately addressed by a one-design-fits-all approach, such as is found in all-hazards planning and preparedness. Moreover, neighboring jurisdictions may use the same all-hazards-based approach to planning and preparedness, but come up with significantly different actual response plans to a given disaster type. This was the case in many of the neighboring jurisdictions affected by Hurricane Katrina. When the targeted disaster becomes a catastrophe covering many jurisdictions, the uncoordinated and dissimilar response plans of individual jurisdictions make it difficult to conduct a coordinated response to the catastrophe. In sum, multi-jurisdictional scenario-specific catastrophe response planning can significantly decrease the conflicts and inefficiencies that would otherwise exist.

On the other hand, scenario-based planning uses a specific scenario to establish a framework for modeling disaster effects and resources needed and for evaluating regional emergency management capabilities. This process uses decision matrices that can be manipulated to provide a means for quickly determining baseline estimates for resource needs and identifying possible shortfalls for various events. In the planning stages, the information provided by the matrices allows the entire emergency management system to be analyzed for gaps.

The nation is moving to a composite approach that combines both all-hazards and scenario-based planning. Organizations and jurisdictions generally start with all-hazard planning to address the vast majority of their plans. This is supplemented by scenario-based planning for those specific incidents requiring unique approaches, resources, and authorities.

Predictive Modeling Techniques

For catastrophe response planning, the nation uses a variety of predictive modeling techniques that are scientifically based. Here, we discuss one of them in detail, HAZUS.

HAZUS-MH is a standardized methodology for analyzing potential losses from floods, hurricane winds, and earthquakes. In HAZUS-MH, current scientific and engineering knowledge is coupled with the latest geographic information systems (GIS) technology to produce estimates of hazard-related damage before, or after, a disaster occurs. These estimates provide a relatively realistic and comprehensive set of consequences upon which to base planning assumptions. Potential loss estimates analyzed in HAZUS-MH focus on three types of losses:

- *Physical damage*, to residential and commercial buildings, schools, critical facilities, and infrastructure;
- *Economic loss*, including lost jobs, business interruptions, repair and reconstruction costs; and
- *Social impacts*, including estimates of shelter requirements, displaced households, and the size of the population exposed to scenario floods, earthquakes, and hurricanes. (http://www.fema.gov/plan/prevent/hazus/index.shtm). HAZUS has been used by FEMA for many years. It continues to be refined and is updated often (see Figure 11.3).

In addition to HAZUS-MH, a second modeling technique that could be used is the gap analysis. Gap analysis allows emergency managers to determine their local capacity and the resources on hand, the resources required in a catastrophic event, and the

Figure 11.3 Current HAZUS logo from FEMA. (http://www.fema.gov/plan/prevent/hazus/index.shtm.)

gaps (what is missing) in between current and needed capacity. Gap analysis provides critical information as to what resources will be needed on the local, state, and national levels, providing critical lead time to gather resources and provide assistance to citizens in need. Determining the gap between the resources available and the resources required during a catastrophic event gives state and federal agencies a heads up on the types of resources that will be required during a catastrophic event. In summary, both HAZUS and gap analysis play an important role in catastrophic preparedness. In the sciences in general, the strongest results come from using multiple methodologies and multiple measures. These techniques are not in competition with each other but used together can provide a stronger tool for policy decision makers to rely on.

Some of the other modeling tools are

- HurrEvac (Hurricane Evacuation) to help in the tracking of hurricanes and assist in evacuation decision making;
- SLOSH (Sea, Lake, and Overland Surges from Hurricanes) to enable estimates of storm surge heights and winds resulting from historical, hypothetical, or predicted hurricanes by taking into account pressure, size, forward speed, track, and winds;
- The US Army Corps of Engineers' modeling tools which rely on geo-spatial capabilities to provide hurricane disaster estimates of debris volumes; water, ice, as well as commodity needs and estimates of effected households. NISAC (National Infrastructure Simulation and Analysis Center) utilizes advanced modeling and simulation capabilities to analyze critical infrastructure interdependencies and vulnerabilities.

CATASTROPHE PLANNING PRACTICES

This section describes three main planning practices for catastrophes: the Integrated Planning System (IPS), the Catastrophic Planning Program (CPP), and the North Atlantic Hypercomplexity approach. Our focus in describing them is on (1) planning approaches they take, (2) their strengths and weaknesses, and (3) available case studies.

THE INTEGRATED PLANNING SYSTEM (IPS)

One method that has been used by the U.S. government, but which has now been discontinued, is the so-called Integrated Planning system. This system used 15 National Planning Scenarios to develop generic federal plans (Strategic Plans, CONPLANS,

OPLANS, and Tactical Plans).[18] It involved all of the federal departments and agencies that have roles in federal response and recovery activities. This scenario-based regional planning and exercise program used a traditional "top-down" approach to authority. DHS developed the Strategic Statement and Strategic Plans, FEMA developed the CONPLANs, and supporting federal agencies developed operational plans (OPLANS) and Tactical Plans. The integrated planning approach uses a wide range of scenarios but, in the prior U.S. version, focused on terrorism scenarios. These IPS scenarios are generic; in other words, they can occur in practically every jurisdiction.

Such integrated planning has various strengths:

- It has access to classified information.
- It was created by professionals with a great deal of expertise.
- It involves many different agencies and departments in the federal government.
- It plans for the most destructive event, not the event that is the most common or the one that local individuals have the most experience with (e.g., hurricanes, drought).
- Its ability to easily fit into a traditional incident command structure makes it simpler for participants to grasp what their roles and responsibilities will be.
- The approach is scenario-based, forcing jurisdictions at all levels to figure out how they would actually respond to a highly challenging set of circumstances, one of which is that immediately surrounding jurisdictions are struggling with the same issues and will not be able to provide aid.
- The scenario exercise component encourages high-level politicians and decision makers to participate.
- This approach is already in practical implementation, although still on a trial basis.

THE CATASTROPHIC PLANNING PROGRAM

The Catastrophic Planning Program (CPP) has a national orientation that involves integrating local, state, federal, regional, and national organizations. This program uses an intensive regional "bottom-up" approach based on a single scenario. For example, in the New Madrid Seismic Zone (NMSZ) Catastrophic Earthquake Planning Project, eight states (Alabama, Arkansas, Illinois, Indiana, Kentucky, Mississippi, Missouri, and Tennessee) and four Federal Emergency Management Agency (FEMA) regions (IV, V, VI, and VII) were asked, "What do we do if an earthquake hits the central United States tomorrow?" Forty-one local jurisdictions conducted planning, workshops, and exercises to develop their plans. This was followed by states using the products and insights from the local level to develop state plans. In turn, the FEMA regions use the state products as the foundation for developing their regional earthquake plans. Lastly, the national-level plan was developed after all these local, state, and regional planning activities were completed. The Catastrophic Planning Program addresses incidents that are of the greatest threat to our nation. This program focuses on catastrophe response planning for a specific location large enough to encompass many jurisdictions. This type of planning approach is scientifically sound and scenario-driven, is focused on capability and required resources, based on collaboration and partnerships, and is holistic in nature. Credible, worst-case earthquake scenarios using HAZUS earthquake modeling were developed for each of the eight NMSZ states. FEMA embedded support planners in each of the four participating FEMA Regions and in each of the eight NMSZ states, to facilitate scenario-driven planning and identification of required resources based on a bottom-up, local approach.

The CPP has strengths:[19]

- It is national in its orientation involving local, state, regional, and federal organizations working together to develop plans that are integrated. It is the only program that integrates all levels of government in the planning process. All three levels of government are working together as plans are built and exercises and workshops are conducted. For example, state and federal organizations participate in the local workshops throughout the New Madrid Seismic Zone.
- The result was a national plan that was integrated and synchronized at all levels of government because all levels of government worked together to create the plan.
- The planning activities are generally concurrent rather than sequential in nature. While this is a bottom-up planning program driven from the local level, in reality, all levels of government are planning together. States and federal partners are not waiting for the locals to finish their plans before starting. All levels are talking and sharing information in the process through workshops and exercises. This is very important for the unique and catastrophic events such as earthquakes where there is a lot of discovery work.
- The bottom-up procedure encourages ownership of the plan by the individuals who develop it at the local level. By participating in this exercise, individuals are able to apply regional planning activities to other events and other types of regional planning activities like mitigation.
- The CPP is more realistic and detailed than other approaches, thereby fostering more interdependencies.
- The individuals involved in the CPP process are the actual operators, decision makers, and supervisors of the staff who will respond to the disaster. They know their community.
- The CPP requires local-level assessment, solution finding, and relationship building across a large multi-jurisdictional geographic area, thus decreasing reliance on state and federal resources in an actual catastrophe. This approach is consistent with the observation that local areas are likely to be isolated for a considerable period of time in catastrophes.
- The local character of much of the planning is more likely to include non-governmental and private for-profit organizations, as well as the general citizenry, thus enhancing the potential for local solutions during times of isolation.
- The process is designed to be on-going, not built around specified set-time, high-visibility exercises.
- Local-level politicians and decision-makers are more likely to participate than is the case with the top-down process, which focuses more on high-level decision makers.

There are, however, some weaknesses of the Catastrophic Planning Program:

- The NMSZ plans' focus on response operations is a disadvantage, in that recovery from a catastrophic earthquake is monumental. Lead designers intentionally limited this plan to response as they thought it would take a more focused approach

METHODS OF PLANNING AND RESPONSE COORDINATION

Figure 11.4 Collapsed home, Talca, Chile as a result of the 2010 earthquake. (Photo courtesy of Rick Bissell.)

to write plans at all levels of government for a disaster that impacts eight states and four regions. CPP planners have always believed that the CPP would be a two-phased approach, with a New Madrid recovery plan following the response plan.
- It is expensive.
- It is scenario and site-specific.
- It is more complicated than the planning that relies on the all-hazard approach. It requires modeling, gap analysis, and damage estimates.
- The CPP is a very time-consuming process, competing for time and planning resources against many other more pressing immediate needs.
- The lack of a single response plan can be seen as confusing by some.
- Some federal officials may feel uncomfortable with the lack of control that is inherent in a planning process that is more focused on local and regional resources and decision makers (see Figure 11.4).

THE NORTH ATLANTIC HYPERCOMPLEXITY APPROACH

A group of emergency management personnel in France, England, and some other European countries have argued that three related variables differentiate catastrophes from other types of crises:[20]

1. They are "hypercomplex" because of the extremely high degree of interdependent linkages in modern societies regarding the production and delivery of basic life-supporting services, such as food, water, electricity, natural gas, oil, and communications.

From an American perspective, hypercomplexity also describes large and even medium size incidents. In our system of democracy there are so many different jurisdictions—both vertically and horizontally—that decision making is never found in one control center, except for the smallest of small incidents.
2. Because of these hypercomplex linkages, the focus of decision making cannot be limited to a single control center.
3. Because of these linkages, the event affects other jurisdictions, countries and continents, as well as to other aspects of human life, such as health, economics, and security.

For example, a major earthquake in the New Madrid Seismic Zone may have the same causes as any other earthquake, but, because of the strategically interlinked character of that area of the United States, responses to the zone would have to come from many areas of the United States, Canada, Mexico, and perhaps even Europe. The delivery of much natural gas, oil, and gasoline to the U.S. East Coast may be stopped or severely restricted, and it would take months to get the delivery of these resources restored across the New Madrid-area routes. Other countries may be called upon to provide tanker deliveries to the East Coast. Major failures would occur in the electrical grid, again affecting parts of the East Coast and Midwest and maybe even causing outages in the linked-in power supply system from Canada. Canada may be asked to help re-route and re-supply power to East Coast and upper Midwest population centers. Communications failures may severely interrupt commerce affecting many countries. The loss of barge traffic on the Mississippi River could lead to famine and social–political unrest in parts of the world that depend on grain shipments coming down the Mississippi from the U.S. and Canadian grain belts. This cascade would require New Madrid-induced responses to countries like Bangladesh and Zimbabwe by organizations and countries far outside of the NMSZ.

This hypercomplexity thinking has now crossed the Atlantic and has become one of the activities of the Center for Transatlantic Relations, coordinated through the Johns Hopkins University School for Advanced International Studies (SAIS), and has resulted in several multinational meetings in Washington, involving researchers and emergency management practitioners from several European countries, as well as the United States and Canada. One of the practical outcomes of the hypercomplexity approach to visualizing preparedness and response to catastrophes has been the formation in several European countries of:

1. A system of "alignments" between governments, industries, and non-governmental organizations in the pre-event phase, which will facilitate easier collaboration and coordination when response is required, and
2. The development of a new functional group within the response coordination structure, called a "rapid reflection force." These groups are composed of representatives of responding agencies, industries, NGOs, politicians, and scientists with the responsibility to think through the potential consequences and potential networks affected by the crisis event, and to suggest on a real-time basis points where

interventions may be effective. The RRFs are not operational groups, but rather a sort of rapid response think tank with broader representation and roles than are found in typical American planning sections of the incident management system.

At its core, the hypercomplexity approach, as discussed within the Center for Transatlantic Relations, is based on the assumption that catastrophes cannot be managed, and that the best we can do is to recognize the complexity and use that recognition to help drive the most effective possible utilization of available resources. Because of this assumption, the hypercomplexity approach does not envision a single locus of control or coordination, but rather a more decentralized collaboration that is better able to assign resources and to trace causes and remedies through complex networks of multi-functional, multi-jurisdictional relationships. Some might say that the approach allows for a more "organic" response to complex events than can be achieved through a hierarchical control system. This entire approach to planning for and responding to catastrophes is still in the development process, but is evidenced by concrete actions being taken in several European countries.

The North Atlantic approach has several strengths:

- The approach forces planners to recognize distant causes and effects of catastrophes, thus making response planners think more broadly, including thinking about the probability that there will be out-of-area consequences. Likewise, it encourages pre-event recognition that very distant actors may provide some of the most important resources during the response period.
- The very term "hypercomplexity" is consonant with the sociological research that indicates that complexity is one of the key variables that differentiates catastrophes from disasters.
- The hypercomplexity conceptual model mandates planning and coordination with a very broad array of non-governmental actors and organizations, thus significantly broadening the resources that can be brought to bear on the needs provoked by catastrophes.
- The development of multi-institutional, multi-disciplinary "rapid reflection forces" adds to the ability of response operations planners to anticipate needs, required actions, and, importantly, reactions to specific response activities. This consideration of down-stream effects of disaster-response actions is otherwise difficult in time-stressed operations planning, and it has been oft noted that certain decisions made during the disaster response period can significantly increase the level of complication and difficulty in the following recovery period.

The North Atlantic approach also has some weaknesses:

- To date, this approach is not as much an operational model, as it is a conceptual model aimed at helping the users of virtually any planning method to improve their outcomes.
- The conceptual model is young and is still in the stages of development and refinement. As such, there are no guidebooks like those offered by the CPG series from FEMA.
- This model lacks, to date, specific benchmarks planners could use to document their progress in the planning process.

In summary, each of these approaches being offered at this point in time is still under development, with outcomes that remain unclear. It might be that none of them will survive intact, but each has some strengths and weaknesses, as well as characteristics that might make one of them more appropriate for a particular application (country, culture, political structure, hazard type, etc.). Yet, they all serve a clear purpose in trying to work within a complex catastrophe response planning environment.

The integrated planning system has a definite measure of reality to it. For planning purposes it has access to classified information essential to our current environment. This system, with its orientation toward national level government, includes the assumption that when a serious catastrophe occurs, local and regional governments may not be able to respond. The national government must be prepared to step in quickly to assist communities and states overwhelmed by low-probability and high-consequence events.

On the other hand, the CPP approach says, "Don't count out the resilience, resources and ability of the local and state government and its partners." The authors of this chapter who have significant combined experience in both practice and disaster research, know that when people are aware of risks and know what to do, strength is built. The CPP approach is more of a departure from the traditional federal way of preparing for disasters. It too focuses on specific scenarios, but relies on a more ground-level effort of analyzing needs and finding solutions and less on building a structured single common plan. The "hypercomplexity" approach, currently in discussion in several North Atlantic countries, is more of a conceptual model of what needs to be considered in the planning and response process than an actual planning model. Some countries, such as France, have begun to implement some aspects of the hypercomplexity model in their planning, scenario testing, and actual response modalities, including such functions as the "rapid reflection forces." This approach is interesting in that it focuses on systems and on intervening at key points during a response. However, it is in a theoretical stage and future work needs to connect it more to the decision makers on the ground.

These catastrophe-focused planning models recognize the need to go beyond the traditional all-hazards planning that is based on single jurisdictions. The "integrated planning" model may be more appropriate in political and response systems that are highly structured around authority relationships, such as is often found in civil defense agencies. However, it is likely to miss valuable resources that lie outside of traditional authority relationships. The CPP approach is likely to be more comfortable in societies and political systems that operate on the basis of distributed power and decision making, where the highest level authorities can trust that lower level jurisdictions can make appropriate decisions without central government input. The hypercomplexity model is, for the most part, not a response model, and can be integrated into other actual planning and response approaches with some modifications to those approaches.

All three of these approaches present considerable challenge to current and future emergency managers. We look forward to seeing the development of more holistic and operational catastrophe-focused planning and response models.

Table 11.2 summarizes the three approaches we have discussed.

Table 11.2 Comparison of Planning Approaches

	Top-Down Integrated (IPS)	Bottom-Up Regional (CPP)	Hypercomplexity
Response time	Unknown	72 hours stabilization	Unknown
Type of responders	Federal	National	All
Broad range issues	No	Yes	Yes
Type of approach	Top down	Bottom up	Both
Incident control	Centralized	Both	Decentralized
Event focus	Terrorism	Natural	Natural
Regional focus	No	Yes	Yes

FUTURE OF CATASTROPHE PLANNING AND RESPONSE COORDINATION: CONCLUSION

In this chapter we discussed how the magnitude, scope, and complexity of a catastrophic event affect its impact. We also discussed how legislation and executive policies determine the direction, scope, and detail of emergency management planning. Innovations in research, theory, tools and techniques have greatly improved planning for catastrophes, as have increased individual experience, more strategic thinking, and greater use of multi-disciplinary collaboration. Our review of bottom up, top down, and hypercomplex planning approaches suggests what has and has not worked and what needs to be considered to prepare for future threats, particularly global threats.

> "… globalization has also intensified the dangers we face— from international terrorism and the spread of deadly technologies, to economic upheaval and a changing climate"
>
> **President Obama**
> *National Security Strategy of 2010*

We live in a risk environment where threats and hazards to the United States are growing. Presidential Policy Directive/PPD-8 National Preparedness, released on March 30, 2011, provides a path forward for addressing these threats. It calls for a new approach to preparedness, one that moves the nation from a government-centric approach to one where preparedness for risk is the shared responsibility of all levels of government, of the private and nonprofit sectors, and of individual citizens.

PPD-8 also calls for the nation to focus planning and resources on our greatest risks. Our first responsibility is to focus on hazards and threats of catastrophic proportions. Replacing the Target Capabilities List, which drove federal preparedness initiatives in the last administration, PPD-8 calls for establishing the essential operations (also known as core capabilities) needed to keep our nation secure and resilient as promulgated in the National Preparedness Goal. Consequently, catastrophic disaster planning is evolving to a capabilities-based approach. Because the core capabilities are based on the greatest risks, conceptually, this approach institutionalizes catastrophic disaster planning as the conventional way of planning, rather than the exception.

> "Since the terrorist attacks of September 11, 2001 this nation has recognized how remote threats and distant trouble can pose near and present dangers to our shores ... As we develop new capabilities and technologies, our adversaries will seek to evade them ... We must constantly work to stay ahead of our adversaries"
> *Quadrennial Homeland Security Review (Feb 2010)*[21]

In the United States, over the next few years, a new national preparedness system will be initiated to institutionalize the concepts in PPP-8. Preparedness will have five mission areas: prevention, protection, response, recovery, and mitigation. Core capabilities will be the main driver for planning. Each mission area will identify the essential operations or core capabilities necessary to achieve a secure and resilient nation. Capability targets will be established for each of the core capabilities. Importantly, they will provide performance measures for planning and assessment.

Integration of all components into a preparedness system will be a hallmark of this new approach. Moreover planning will be an integral part of this preparedness system, such that plans will be integrated both vertically among all levels of government, and horizontally across jurisdictions and functional areas.

Collaborative work will create professional strength among agencies and disaster specialists. But we also need to remember the families, friends, and neighbors for whom these plans are made. Information regarding catastrophic threats that could potentially affect them needs to be communicated so that they understand what those threats are and encourage them to prepare for them, which will help us all to respond and recover if those threats become reality.

REFERENCES

1. DHS/FEMA. National Response Framework.
2. Schwarzkopf HN. 1993. *The Autobiography: It Doesn't Take a Hero*. Bantam Books, USA. pp. 289–290.
3. Schwarzkopf HN. 1993. *The Autobiography: It Doesn't Take a Hero*. Bantam Books, USA. p. 294.
4. Shapira Z. 1995. *Risk Taking: A Managerial Perspective*. Russell Sage Foundation Publications, New York. p. 73.
5. Ibid, p. 127.
6. Silverman A, Loutfy MR, Simor A. 2004. Toronto emergency medical services and SARS [letter]. *Emerg Infect Dis*. Available from: http://www.cdc.gov/ncidod/EID/vol10 no9/04-0170.htm. Accessed July 11, 2010.
7. Levine S. 2005. Leaders share flu pandemic concerns: Federal plan prompts a deeper look into worst-case health, business scenarios. *Washington Post*. November 7, 2005. Available at: http://www.washingtonpost.com/wp-dyn/content/article/2005/11/06/AR2005110601232.html. Accessed July 11, 2010.
8. FEMA. *Whole Community*. Last modified: 12 Dec 2011. Available at: http://fema.gov/about/wholecommunity.shtm. Accessed 2 March 2012.

9. *Preventing A Disaster Within The Disaster: The Effective Use and Management of Unaffiliated Volunteers.* Points of Light Foundation & Volunteer Center National Network Pub. Available at: http://www.community.ups.com/downloads/pdfs/disasterbook.pdf. Accessed December 12, 2008.
10. Johnson TJ. *A History of Biological Warfare from 300BCE to the Present.* Available at: http://www.aarc.org/resources/biological/history.asp. Accessed 2 March 2012.
11. White House Report. 2006. *The Federal Response to Hurricane Katrina: Lessons Learned.* 2006; Feb. p. 63. Available at: http://www.whitehouse.gov/reports/katrina-lessons-learned.pdf. Accessed December 14, 2008.
12. Masters J. *Disaster Relief in a Dangerous World.* Interview of Seth Cropsey; 22 March, 2011. Available at: http://www.cfr.org/united-states/disaster-relief-dangerous-world/p24463. Accessed 2 March 2012.
13. FEMA 2011 Catastrophic Event Study.
14. Fisher L. 2011. *Crashes, Crisis, and Calamities. How We Can Use Science to Read the Early-Warning Signs.* Basic books Group, New York. p. 37.
15. Ibid.
16. Ibid, p. 131.
17. The Catastrophic Incident Annex. http://www.fema.gov/pdf/emergency/nrf/nrf_CatastrophicIncidentAnnex.pdf.
18. National Planning Scenarios http://www.fema.gov/txt/media/factsheets/2009/npd_natl_plan_scenario.txt.
19. Wells S. 2009. Value of Catastrophic New Madrid Planning Background Paper. Prepared for the Federal Emergency Management Agency.
20. Lagadec E. 2007. *Unconventional Crisis, Unconventional Responses: Reforming Leadership in the Age of Catastrophic Crisis and Hypercomplexity.* Center for Transatlantic Relations, Washington, DC.
21. Department of Homeland Security. 2010. Quadrennial Homeland Security Review. Available at: http://www.dhs.gov/xabout/gc_1208534155450.shtm.

CHAPTER 12

Catastrophic Disaster Recovery
An Institutional Network Perspective

Gavin Smith

CONTENTS

Overview 281
What Is a Catastrophe and Its Relationship to Disaster Recovery? 282
The Emergence of a National Recovery Policy 284
The Disaster Recovery Assistance Framework 286
Dimensions of the United States Disaster Recovery Assistance Framework 287
    Resource Rules and Understanding of Local Needs 288
    Timing of Assistance 288
    Horizontal and Vertical Integration 290
The Role of Planning: Transforming the Dimensions of the Disaster
Recovery Assistance Framework 291
Catastrophic Disaster Recovery in the United States: Future Recommendations 294
Conclusions and Final Thoughts 298
References 299

OVERVIEW

This chapter draws on a conceptual approach developed as part of the text "Planning for Post-Disaster Recovery: A Review of the United States Disaster Assistance Framework" (Smith 2011). The framework provides insights into the challenges inherent in large-scale disasters, particularly the difficulties associated with the coordination of those who are involved in disaster recovery operations. The framework also provides a useful way of differentiating recovery operations following disasters and catastrophes. Disasters, including catastrophes, have been defined by the level of physical damages, disruption to infrastructure, dislocation of social systems, and their effects on national economies.[1-3] Both types of events also expose issues that presage a disaster, including degraded natural systems, social inequities, conflict, fragile and/or uni-dimensional economies, and high rates of exposure to natural hazards.

An important characteristic of catastrophic disasters, and one that has not been effectively studied nor recognized in practice, is the severe strain placed on larger organizational networks that address the stressors to physical, social, economic, and environmental systems, including the process needed to systematically address their breakdown, reconstitution, or even their formation after a disaster. More recently, Federal Emergency Management Agency (FEMA) and a growing number of states are beginning to develop national programs and policies in support of pre-event planning for post-disaster recovery. Understood in this changing policy context, disaster recovery can be understood as "the differential process of restoring, rebuilding, and reshaping the physical, social, economic, and natural environment through pre-event planning and post-event actions."[4] The definition highlights the varied elements of recovery (i.e., physical, social, economic, and natural environment). It also describes the recovery process in the context of both pre-event planning and post-event actions. Thus, the process of recovery from a disaster is viewed through an inter-institutional lens and is described in the context of those organizations that comprise disaster recovery assistance networks.

WHAT IS A CATASTROPHE AND ITS RELATIONSHIP TO DISASTER RECOVERY?

The close association between the definition of catastrophe and the nature of the recovery that follows merits a brief discussion. As noted in Chapter 1, catastrophe and its connectivity to disaster are tied to the scale and nature of the event in question. Among the descriptive characteristics that have been used to differentiate these phenomena include the magnitude, duration, speed of onset, and breadth of the event. Additional factors include the severity of disaster-related impacts, the timing of the event, and the pre-event characteristics of the geographic area affected.[5] Pre-event characteristics of a community, region, or nation may include the level of preparedness, including planning, the prevalence of social capital, economic wealth, and hazard vulnerability. It is the intersection of the physical nature of the hazard event in question and the pre-event conditions that exist in the area affected that helps to define disaster.[6,7] In the United States, disasters are typically defined as events that exceed the capacity of a local or state government to effectively respond to and recover from them using the existing resources they possess. According to FEMA, when a state's capacity to deliver resources needed by communities is exceeded (as defined on a county-level per capita threshold), states can request a federal disaster declaration which, if accepted, results in the release of federal assistance as promulgated under the Robert T. Stafford Disaster Relief Act. This approach reflects a history of disaster policy in the United States that remains focused on the roles of the government and less on inter-organizational governance. This government-centric metric does not account for the capacity of larger assistance networks, their significant geographic and temporal variability, and the ability of such networks to expand or contract over time based on the type and scale of the disaster experienced.

In fact, it conflicts with the more recent efforts of FEMA to address these limitations through the National Disaster Recovery Framework (NDRF), the "whole of community concept," and Presidential Policy Directive 8: National Preparedness (PPD-8) which all seek to expand the involvement and accountability of stakeholders beyond members of the public sector (Figure 12.1).[8–10]

Bissell notes in his definition of catastrophe that events of this nature can strain or even exceed the capacity of a national government to effectively respond to a disaster (Chapter 1). Conceptually, this is the idea behind the whole community, which is defined as: "a means by which residents, emergency management practitioners, organizational and community leaders, and government officials can collectively understand and assess the needs of their respective communities and determine the best ways to organize and strengthen their assets, capacities, and interests."[11] Bissell similarly calls for a new kind of response planning, one that will be discussed in this chapter as it relates to the challenges associated with disaster recovery. In this chapter, I propose another way of differentiating disasters and catastrophes, which is the degree to which larger disaster assistance networks, building on more traditional government-focused networks, are created and used to recover from disasters when they occur. Thus, a central premise of this chapter is to describe the collective abilities of these larger networks to guide formal and informal disaster recovery operations. The power and efficacy of these networks are compromised by weak links across participants whereby potential collaboration may be unrealized and in some cases remain latent as disaster recovery is typically dominated by the management of poorly designed and coordinated, largely reactive federal programs and policies rather than the pre-event fostering, nurturing, and sustaining of a much broader network of resource providers. Thus, catastrophe is described here as an event that results in physical, social, economic, and environmental impacts of a sufficient magnitude and duration that exceed the collective institutional capacity of disaster recovery assistance networks. Focusing on catastrophe in this manner represents an extension of the long-standing recognition in the United States that disasters exceed the capacity of governments to sufficiently manage their impacts[12] and are socially constructed non-routine events.[13–16] This definition also recognizes that catastrophes

- Shared understanding of community needs and capabilities;
- Greater empowerment and integration of resources from across the community;
- Stronger social infrastructure;
- Establishment of relationships that facilitate more effective prevention, protection, mitigation, response, and recovery activities;
- Increased individual and collective preparedness; and
- Greater resiliency at both the community and national levels.

Figure 12.1 FEMA's whole community concept. (Federal Emergency Management Agency. 2011. *A Whole Community Approach to Emergency Management: Principles, Themes and Pathways for Action*. FDOC 104-008-1, December, p. 3.)

can occur when existing networks, some of which possess the latent, but unrealized potential needed to address major disasters, fail to harness this capacity. This builds on the idea furthered by Bates and Peacock,[17] who have described disasters as an event that exceeds existing institutionalized actions and behavior (1989) as well as those of Lagadec[18] who describes the hypercomplexity of varied organizations involved in a crisis (2007). This chapter also posits that the absorptive capacity of larger networks to address what amount to a shock to institutional systems is much greater than the more narrowly defined clusters of public sector and non-profit organizations traditionally assigned disaster-related duties and it is up to the public sector to help create the conditions in which collaboration can thrive across disaster recovery assistance networks.[19]

THE EMERGENCE OF A NATIONAL RECOVERY POLICY

A key shortfall in the United States Disaster Recovery Assistance Framework is the limited emphasis placed on pre-event capacity-building initiatives across larger assistance networks. In its current form, the Disaster Recovery Assistance Framework is dominated by the post-disaster management of federal assistance, although efforts are being made to address these limitations through the post-Katrina adoption of the NDRF and FEMA's "whole of community" concept. While these efforts offer promise, it is still unclear who should assume specific duties, who should take on leadership roles, and how differing organizations plan for recovery and collaborate in the aftermath of a disaster. We had a powerful indicator of just how unprepared the United States government was for a large-scale disaster recovery operation, and how our government continues to be dominated by a response orientation, as described in the National Response Framework (NRF). It was not until 2011 that the Federal Government developed the National Disaster Recovery Strategy after being required to do so by the Congress following Hurricane Katrina. When the storm struck in 2005, it took six years to recognize the fundamental weaknesses in the system, mandate change, and begin developing an implementation strategy. At this point, the operationalization of these federal initiatives is still a work in progress. This chapter posits that the current federal system and approach to post-disaster recovery assistance remains fundamentally flawed and the United States is still ill-equipped to address major disasters and catastrophes, as key partnerships with members of a larger assistance network are still lacking. The most recent passage of the Post Katrina Emergency Management Reform Act (PKEMRA) and the new NDRF are certainly steps in the right direction. However, the NDRF still places a disproportionate focus on the role of the government and much less on the myriad organizations that play an important, albeit unrecognized role in disaster recovery. Federal disaster recovery assistance remains driven by narrowly defined, highly prescriptive programs, which in turn strongly influence the actions of states and local governments who tend to react to and focus their efforts on the administration of these programs after a disaster rather than invest the time needed to develop inclusive pre-event plans for post-disaster recovery. The other members of the assistance network often remain marginalized and struggle to find their place in recovery operations, reacting to the identified gaps in assistance rather than developing enduring partnerships identified well before an event.

The whole of community program (which is still under development), like the NDRF, offers promise if it can be effectively operationalized to address the shortfalls identified in this chapter. The recommendations at the end of this chapter will focus on the ability of the emerging policies associated with the NDRF and the whole of community program to address the defining characteristics of the Disaster Recovery Assistance Framework. Efforts to recover from catastrophic disasters further expose the weaknesses in the Disaster Recovery Assistance Framework as a number of unique demands are placed on those responsible for recovery operations and a number of organizations that may or may not be part of the established assistance networks, but rather are drawn into recovery operations with little advance notice or involvement in pre-event planning activities (see Figure 12.2).

PHYSICAL

- Large-scale damages to public infrastructure, housing, and businesses that lead to the resettlement of major population centers, including housing and supporting physical infrastructure;
- Catastrophes may require the construction of major emergency and transitional housing communities and the re-establishment/relocation of regional infrastructure (e.g., energy source, water, sewer, and transportation), including the creation of temporary transportation systems to convey food, water, medical supplies, and reconstruction materials.

SOCIAL

- The slow or nonexistent delivery of critical, life-supporting assistance (e.g., food, water, and housing), the provision of public safety, and the slow reconstruction of communities may result in large-scale social unrest and the potential involvement of the military (challenging the Posse Comitatus Act of the United States which sets strict limitations on military operations in domestic affairs);
- The magnitude of mass casualties may exceed state, regional, and national mortuary, forensic, and medical capabilities;
- The needs of disaster refugees may exceed state, regional, and national capacities and require the involvement of international relief organizations;
- Catastrophes may result in the collapse of federal, state, and local governments, requiring assistance from other governments in nonaffected areas (this may be due to the death of key elected officials, destruction of government facilities and records, and financial collapse—see economic system).

Figure 12.2 Catastrophic disaster impacts to physical, social, economic, and environmental systems and potential actions by members of assistance networks.

ECONOMIC

- Catastrophes may result in the collapse of state, regional, and national economies, requiring the sustained infusion of capital and financial management capabilities needed to reconstitute the flow of goods and services and assume the costs associated with reconstruction;
- The level of damages and the associated recovery needs may exceed state or national production and the distribution capacity of the private sector associated with the delivery of an adequate supply of building materials;
- Loss of employment opportunities may result in the large-scale exodus of the predisaster workforce (including professionals);
- Catastrophes and the associated reconstruction demands will require the development of large-scale housing for construction, debris management, and other disaster management employees.

ENVIRONMENTAL

- Catastrophes can cause long-term impacts to ecosystems, including the environmental contamination (nuclear, chemical, and biological) of cities, regions, and agricultural areas that render them uninhabitable or unable to produce food;
- Public health issues tied to catastrophes may exceed the capacity of the national healthcare system to treat the sick and injured and track the long-term implications of the event;
- Catastrophes can cause large-scale changes to ecological systems (e.g., collapse of barrier islands, widespread loss of forests in areas prone to landslides, mudflows, and floods, regional degradation of wetlands and floodplains) that serve to protect and/or are adjacent to human settlements.

Figure 12.2 (Continued).

THE DISASTER RECOVERY ASSISTANCE FRAMEWORK

Disaster recovery as practiced in the United States is best characterized as reactive in nature and focused on the post-disaster delivery of assistance with little emphasis placed on the building of strong local capacity designed to confront three principle challenges. These include: (1) obtaining resources that meet the local needs, (2) effectively timing the distribution of resources, in both the pre- and post-disaster environment, and (3) building organizational networks that are horizontally and vertically integrated. Three types of resources, including funding, policy-based, and technical assistance (training, education, and outreach) are delivered by a diffuse network of organizational actors. Members of the network include public sector organizations (federal, state, and local governments); quasi-governmental, and non-governmental organizations (community development corporations, homeowner's associations, special service districts, regional planning organizations, professional associations, and colleges and universities); non-profit relief organizations (non-profits, community-based organizations, and foundations); private sector organizations (businesses and corporations, financial and lending institutions, insurance, and media); international aid organizations and nations; and emergent groups and individuals. The makeup and location of organizations within these networks are highly varied due to a number of pre- and post-disaster-related factors, including the degree of pre-event planning for post-disaster recovery, previous experience in disaster recovery, the creation of recovery committees, the scope of the disaster, and the needs of communities that emerge after disasters.

Disaster recovery assistance networks are comprised of differing members and subject to change over time. Those participating in the assistance network are shown as broad organizational types. For instance, members of the private sector may include small businesses, corporations, and varied types of private sector organizations including disaster recovery contractors, members of the insurance industry, developers, financial investors, and the media. The makeup of a given disaster recovery assistance network may differ due to the scope of the disaster, with differing organizations assuming roles in catastrophes that may not be needed following smaller disasters that adhere to the traditional disaster relief programs established under the Robert T. Stafford Disaster Relief Act of 1988. Commonly referred to as the Stafford Act, this federal legislation tends to dominate the organizational "shape" of the United States disaster recovery assistance network as states and local governments as well as many other organizations tend to react to the narrowly defined federal programs. For instance, state and local governments tend to focus their efforts on the administration of these programs rather than investing the resources needed in the pre-disaster environment to develop programs that address local needs. The unmet local needs are often exacerbated following catastrophic events and yet, states and local governments have done little to prepare for such conditions. The federal government has not invested time in the pre-disaster timeframe to assist states and local governments build the capacity to deal with this eventuality.

DIMENSIONS OF THE UNITED STATES DISASTER RECOVERY ASSISTANCE FRAMEWORK

The United States Disaster Recovery Assistance Framework is characterized by three dimensions: (1) the varied understanding of the local needs among the members of the disaster recovery assistance network, as exemplified by the rules associated with the resources they provide, (2) the timing of the delivery of those resources, and (3) the degree of horizontal and vertical integration among the members of the network. The dimensions help explain the complexities of disaster recovery, including what amounts to a significant increase in complexity during an event that is characterized as a catastrophe. The study of these dimensions also provides insights into strategic points of intervention, including planning techniques that can be used to improve the functionality of the framework.

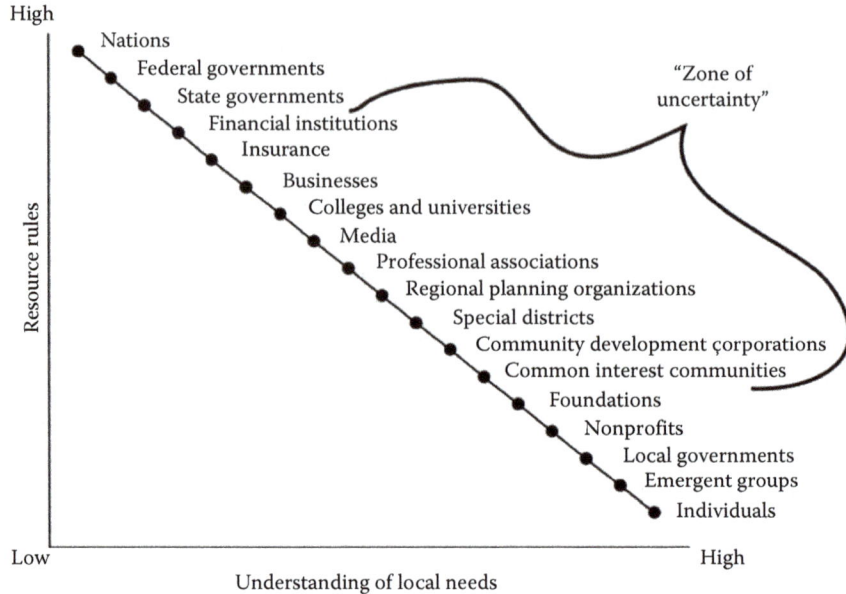

Figure 12.3 Stakeholder rules and understanding of local needs across the disaster recovery assistance network. (*Planning for Post-Disaster Recovery: A Review of the United States Disaster Assistance Framework* (Smith 2011, p. 14).)

Resource Rules and Understanding of Local Needs

The organizations in the disaster recovery assistance network possess great variation in the degree to which the rules governing the distribution of the resources they possess or manage are prescriptive and the degree to which these strategies address local needs. The divergence between resource rules and understanding of the local needs is clearer at the margins of the network. For instance, the federal government typically administers highly prescriptive rules with limited input from those they directly affect at the local level, whereas individuals tend to have the best understanding of local conditions and few rules governing the types of resources (e.g., information) they provide. Many of the other organizations in Figure 12.3 are cast in a "zone of uncertainty" as less research has been done to fully understand their roles in recovery and how these roles can be coordinated with others. Public sector practitioners tasked with recovery operations often discount the importance of other members of the network and fail to involve them in pre-event planning and post-disaster decision making. This has important policy implications for disaster recovery operations, including catastrophes.

Timing of Assistance

The timing of resource (funding, policy, and technical assistance) delivery among members of the network is critical to recovery due to three interrelated issues: (1)

the timing of differing types of resources delivered by individual organizations, (2) the coordinated timing of resource delivery across organizations, and (3) the effect of pre- and post-disaster resource delivery among and between organizations. One powerful example highlighted in *Planning for Post-Disaster Recovery: A Review of the United States Disaster Recovery Assistance Framework* is between non-profits and local governments (see Figure 12.4). In this instance, non-profits following Hurricane Katrina quickly rebuilt low-income housing destroyed after the storm before local governments adopted more stringent building codes requiring higher elevation standards. If these two organizational types had better coordinated the delivery of resources, namely funding and technical assistance, in the case of non-profits and policy and funding in the case of local governments, the homes rebuilt by non-profits could have been elevated using federal hazard mitigation funding, thereby protecting them from future storm-related flooding. Instead, high levels of pre-event social vulnerability, endemic to low-income residents on the coast, were perpetuated.

When one recognizes that all members of the assistance network deliver or influence the three types of resources over time, the coordination of the timing of these resources can become highly complex and again dramatizes the importance of developing pre-event coordinative strategies across these groups. It also shows that the temporal distribution of disaster recovery assistance is often dominated by a post-event mindset. Little emphasis has been placed on the pre-event capacity building initiatives that are so important to disaster recovery, including the value of gaining a better understanding of the resources available across the network and how they can be better coordinated in both the pre- and post-disaster environment. Disaster

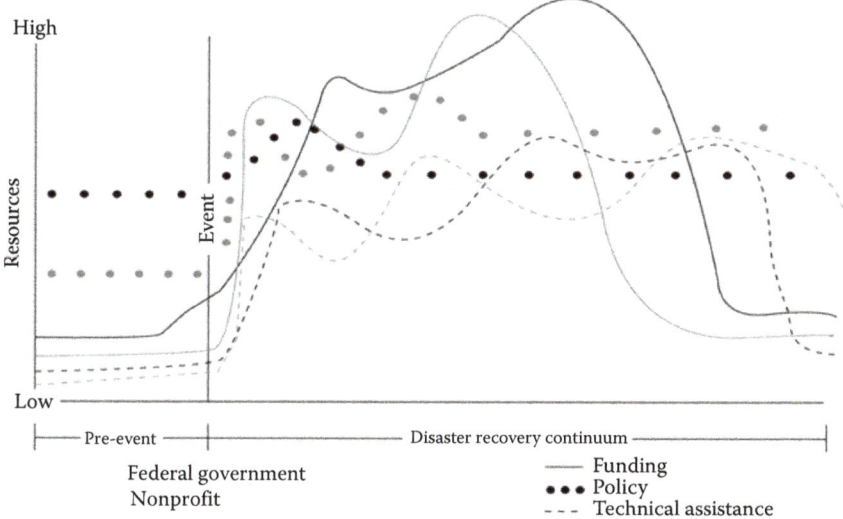

Figure 12.4 Hypothetical timing of assistance: An example of federal government and nonprofit stakeholders. (*Planning for Post-Disaster Recovery: A Review of the United States Disaster Assistance Framework* (Smith 2011, p. 17).)

recovery exercises, training, educational workshops, and other time-intensive investments focused on the building of pre-disaster collaborative relationships are infrequently undertaken. Instead, most members of the assistance network either focus on the administration of post-disaster federal grant programs or react to these programs by developing ways to address the identified shortfalls after disasters strike. Another issue associated with the timing of assistance and one that is directly related to planning is the notion of speed versus deliberation.[20] Following disasters, there is a strong desire to return to a sense of normalcy as quickly as possible. Intense pressure is put on elected officials at all levels of government to act quickly, and the speed at which communities recover is often an overriding metric of success. Yet to achieve a recovery that addresses important issues tied to the equitable distribution of resources, the incorporation of risk-reduction measures into reconstruction efforts and the effective inclusion of members of the assistance network require time to deliberate how this should be done. Ideally, these conversations have been held prior to a disaster and incorporated as a policy into a pre-disaster recovery plan. The failure to plan and coordinate the timely distribution of resources is greatly exacerbated after catastrophic disasters as the number of organizations involved and the types of resources delivered can increase significantly. Further complicating matters is the involvement of outside organizations that may be unfamiliar with more traditional pre-event assistance networks that have formed to deal with more routine events.

Horizontal and Vertical Integration

The concept of horizontal and vertical integration has been used to explain a number of inter-organizational policy issues, including disaster recovery.[21] The application of this concept helps explain how the combined effect of strong horizontal and vertical integration across networks can help improve the collective understanding of local needs and the timing of assistance. Figure 12.5 provides a simple, yet powerful way to characterize the concept. Strong horizontal integration is characterized by robust local relationships. Vertical integration is reflected in relationships with those that provide external assistance. Type 1 communities possess strong horizontal and vertical integration, and as such, they tend to possess a good understanding of local

Vertical / Horizontal	Strong	Weak
Strong	Type 1	Type 2
Weak	Type 3	Type 4

Figure 12.5 Community types by degree of horizontal and vertical integration. (From Berke, P. R., J. Kartez, and D. Wenger. 1993. *Disasters* 17(2): 93–109.)

needs and available indigenous resources and have established close relationships with other community-based organizations. They also possess a good understanding of the external resources provided by those located outside of the community, including the rules that drive how these resources are distributed. Thus, Type I communities are among the best positioned to address the problems cited in this chapter. Type II communities are characterized by strong-horizontal, but weak-vertical integration. In many cases, this is reflective of smaller, rural communities that may have a close knit network of local organizations and yet lack a clear understanding of external resources and the recovery organizations that provide them. Type III communities maintain strong vertical ties, but possess a weak horizontal integration. In this case, communities may have a good understanding of external resource providers but have not invested the time needed to develop strong local relationships. This can result in a strong reliance on external aid (that often fails to meet certain local needs) while discounting the varied types of assistance that can be provided by local groups. Type IV communities typically face the greatest challenges in recovery, all things being equal, as they are defined by weak local relationships and weak vertical ties. The limited understanding of external programs and poor connectivity among local groups can lead to overwhelmed communities as external assistance may not be understood, nor have effective local networks been established to share the burden of program administration, or identified unmet local needs.

Applying the horizontal and vertical integration concept of disaster assistance networks to catastrophic disaster recovery involves an expansion of the interorganizational dimension. For instance, in the case of catastrophes, the involvement of other nations and international aid organizations reflect an expansion of the vertical dimension. The failure to recognize this important aspect of recovery was evident following Hurricane Katrina as the federal government did not have in place international agreements with other nations to accept the delivery of assistance. The horizontal integration of "non-traditional" community-level organizations into the disaster recovery assistance network often takes time to develop, whereas in other cases, new organizations may emerge to address the unmet needs that are not accounted for by traditional local emergency management-related organizations. In other cases, horizontal networks may be expanded during disasters to include community and regional organizations from outside an affected community. In the case of catastrophic disasters, these expanded horizontal linkages may be more difficult to form as nearby communities may also be affected.

THE ROLE OF PLANNING: TRANSFORMING THE DIMENSIONS OF THE DISASTER RECOVERY ASSISTANCE FRAMEWORK

Each dimension of the disaster recovery, including the rules governing the distribution of available resources and understanding of local needs, the timing of assistance, and the level of horizontal and vertical integration found in assistance networks can be improved through the application of recognized planning techniques and processes (Figure 12.6). Transforming the dimensions of the United

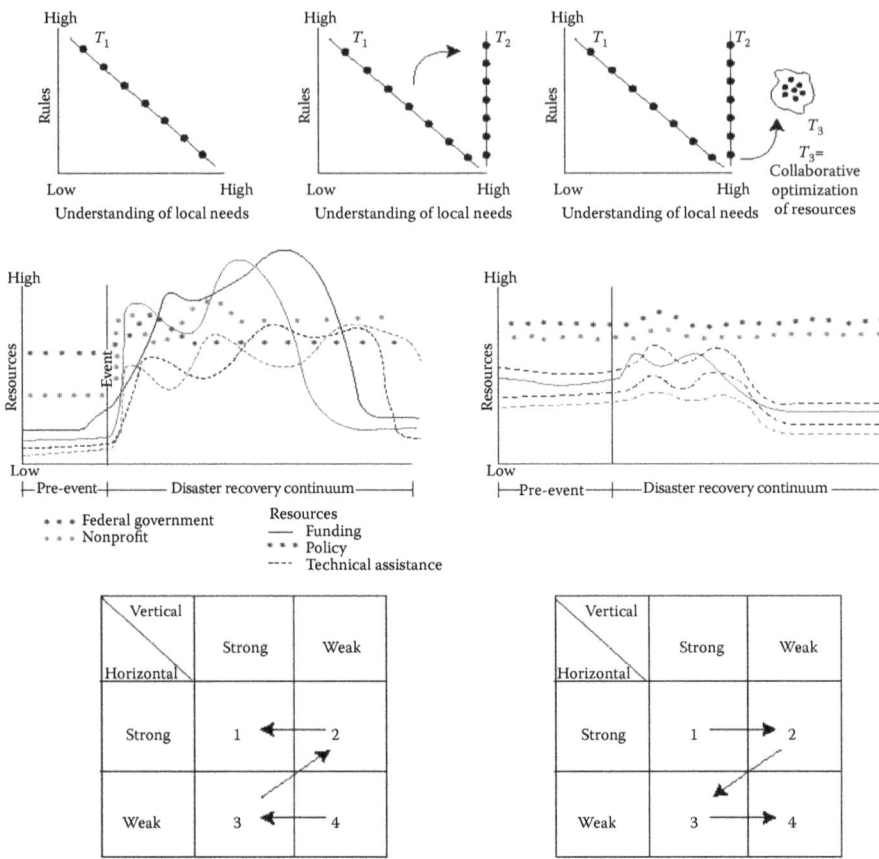

Figure 12.6 Transforming the United States disaster recovery assistance framework. (*Planning for Post-Disaster Recovery: A Review of the United States Disaster Assistance Framework* (Smith 2011, p. 27).)

States Disaster Recovery Assistance Framework from a largely reactive enterprise to one that embraces pre-event planning for post-disaster recovery requires gaining a greater understanding of local needs, and altering the existing funding strategies, policies, and capacity-building regimes across the network; improving the coordinated delivery of resources over time; and improving the level of horizontal and vertical integration of assistance networks through regular and sustained interactions. The act of planning provides a procedural forum to meaningfully engage members of the assistance network over time. Planning is also grounded in the efforts designed to transform knowledge to action[22] and protect public health and safety.[23] All of these elements are directly relevant to disaster recovery. For instance, planning has a rich history of advancing participatory practices, including the application of alternative dispute resolution (ADR) techniques to address multi-party conflicts.[24,25] While the response literature is replete with examples of acts of altruism,[26] the process of disaster recovery is often contentious due to the conflicts associated with the competition for scarce resources (including their equitable distribution), debates surrounding the rules governing assistance, and the timing and/or length of time it takes to deliver assistance and the closely associated pace of recovery.[27]

A central finding of the book, *Planning for Post-Disaster Recovery: A Review of the United States Disaster Assistance Framework*, was the realization that in those cases where effective recovery was taking place, organizations did, in fact act collaboratively. Furthermore, differing organizational types in assistance networks facilitated this process, albeit after the disaster had already occurred. The difficulty in identifying good pre-disaster cases for the book highlights the ongoing problems associated with encouraging pre-disaster recovery planning. Thus, while most of the disaster recovery planning literature emphasizes the importance of pre-event planning for post-disaster recovery,[28,29] states and local governments have largely failed to effectively plan for disaster recovery, nor have land-use planners actively embraced this responsibility.[30-32] This tends to result in a reactionary process of adaptive planning, which can result in good outcomes,[33] although in many cases, states and local governments struggle to administer the resources provided by others and fail to implement a broader recovery vision tied to reducing future hazard vulnerability, addressing socially vulnerable populations, or incorporating pre-existing planning goals into post-disaster reconstruction strategies.[34]

The process orientation of good plans allows for multiple, often competing, values and ideas. The utilization of ADR procedures, including mediation, facilitation, and policy dialog, provide tested means to address what appear to be competing interests among members of the assistance network. One of the primary benefits of the planning process is to gain a greater understanding of those striving to address a common problem or issue. In the case of disaster recovery, the lack of understanding of local needs, the reluctance to involve those directly impacted by resource delivery policies, and the formulation of these ill-informed rules are symptomatic of the often dysfunctional nature of the United States Disaster Recovery Assistance Framework. This is reflected in the graphic shown as T_1, a typical disaster recovery assistance network. Planning can help all members gain a greater understanding of local needs regardless of the prescriptiveness of their programs and policies as seen in the time series denoted as T_2. Through continued dialog and organizational learning, members of the assistance network can, in fact, change the way they distribute resources, including through the use of a more collaborative approach that recognizes local needs and changes in the level of prescriptiveness, ideally resulting in an optimal distribution of resources (T_3).

The timing of resource delivery, including before and after disasters and across members of the assistance network also suffers from a lack of planning. The application of planning principles to temporal aspects of disaster recovery includes placing a greater emphasis on pre-event planning and capacity building while recognizing the realities of post-disaster adaptive planning. It also means developing a disaster recovery plan that describes an overall vision for recovery, the types of resources delivered by differing members of the network, and how these resources should be temporally coordinated to avoid unnecessary duplication, avert engaging in counterproductive actions, and enable the achievement of complimentary goals as specified in the plan. The second set of graphics in Figure 12.5 shows a temporal change in the distributional shape of how resources can be provided if inter-organizational planning takes place. For instance, more time is spent in the pre-disaster period engaging in planning and other capacity-building initiatives and a greater investment in the resources needed to accomplish this aim is achieved. As a result, fewer resources are needed in the aftermath of an event, all else being equal.

Good plans also foster strong horizontal and vertical integration across organizations. Studies have shown that planning can lead to changes in community type, moving from a Type 4 community to a Type 1 community.[35-38] Conversely, a breakdown in planning can lead to regressing from one with high horizontal and vertical integration to one with lower levels of integration. The ability to build strong horizontal and vertical integration across disaster recovery assistance networks requires an ongoing commitment to foster trusted relationships as well as investing the time required to develop both informal and formal agreements among members to coordinate the delivery of assistance.

It is important to recognize that while the planning process provides the means to transform the dimensions of the disaster recovery assistance framework, this potential remains largely unrealized. There are several reasons for this including the limited, but improving commitment to a national disaster recovery strategy (the NDRF), the limited number of state and local disaster recovery plans, the limited involvement of land-use planners in this process, and an overall lack of awareness among members of disaster assistance networks that planning offers a means to address the identified shortfalls in the current system. The importance of engaging in an inclusive, sustained, and collaborative recovery planning process is magnified when discussed in the context of catastrophic disasters. Next, the recommendations discussed provide a roadmap for the emerging national commitment to disaster recovery, which requires addressing a number of fundamental problems if it is to succeed.

CATASTROPHIC DISASTER RECOVERY IN THE UNITED STATES: FUTURE RECOMMENDATIONS

The recommendations presented here are intended to guide what still amounts to a nascent national disaster recovery strategy in the United States. These limitations may, in fact, be found in other countries and they may seek to compare their assistance framework with that found in the United States to see if the recommendations offered here are of value. Among the most important factors to consider is the importance of sound pre-event recovery planning. For this to occur in a meaningful and sustained manner, a number of national, state, and local policy issues must be recognized and addressed.

Shift the balance of resource delivery from large-scale post-disaster financial assistance to include a greater focus on pre-event resources, including those tied to capacity building, communication, and planning. The current emphasis on post-disaster assistance and a virtually nonexistent commitment to pre-event capacity building, including planning, is a basic and long-standing problem that must be altered to emphasize the role of pre-event planning; building partnerships; and engaging in training, education, and outreach initiatives. In the current model, which can result in the provision of massive amounts of post-disaster aid in communities that are unprepared to deal with these large sums of money and other resources, it should not be surprising that the disaster recovery process overwhelms the assistance network as they have failed to coordinate post-event responsibilities that account for this eventuality. To better address this problem, the federal government should work with local networks to assess their collective recovery capacities and based on this assessment, develop a capacity building strategy that is undertaken prior to a disaster. Viewed nationally, this capacity building effort should involve a substantial commitment of the resources that would normally go to communities in the aftermath of disasters.

Pre-event investments should be coupled with a long-term strategy to hold those recipients of assistance more accountable, both in terms of the quality of their recovery plans as well as a greater commitment to a more comprehensive risk-reduction strategy. A recent national study of state and local hazard mitigation plans, for instance, found that local governments are not effectively incorporating land-use measures into these plans.[39] The continued expenditure of millions and in some cases billions of dollars following major disasters without a concomitant requirement that more needs to be done to avoid or lessen the likelihood of future disasters in these same areas is not sustainable and should be redirected into a more effective national disaster recovery policy.

Enhance the involvement of non-traditional stakeholders in policy formulation, planning, and post-event actions, including those that may assume some of the duties unique to a catastrophic disaster. The strength of disaster recovery assistance networks is their diversity and their ability to change over time to include new members, some of which emerge in the aftermath of an event to provide very specific assistance, only to go away once their work has been completed. Other non-traditional partners may include nations and international aid organizations, which tend to focus on the delivery of assistance to developing countries, which disproportionately represent areas in which catastrophic disasters occur. Described in the United States context, international disaster recovery assistance is in fact unique, and as such, attempts to provide a wide range of aid to the United States following Katrina were often ill-coordinated or simply refused as our country did not have adequate mechanisms in place to effectively accept and distribute the resources offered.[40] To improve the extension of vertically integrated communities to include other nations, and to better share with potential donors information about local needs, the development of improved international agreements regarding disaster assistance delivery are required.[41]

Businesses, including corporations, consultants, financial institutions, the insurance industry, and the media are all representative of private sector stakeholders in recovery and ones that will play an increasingly important role in catastrophic disaster recovery. For instance, most of the United States' infrastructure is privately owned and decisions made regarding its repair and potential relocation following a catastrophic disaster will require a close working relationship with power and other utility companies, ports, and airports. Furthermore, the hazards management profession is becoming increasingly privatized as contractors assist communities write plans, implement pre- and post-disaster grants, draft federal policy and implement guidance materials, pick up debris, and design and reconstruct communities after disasters. Private financial investors provide much needed capital to fund the repair and reconstruction of privately owned buildings and infrastructure while insurance companies distribute payouts to policyholders, including re-insurance following major disasters. Yet the clear integration of their critically important actions is not always well-coordinated with the activities of the public sector and other members of the assistance network. Policy change, including that which is focused on catastrophic disaster recovery planning, should embrace the involvement of "non-traditional" stakeholders as much of what disaster recovery entails is beyond the purview of emergency managers. Examples include economic development, serving as advocates for socially vulnerable populations, grants management, infrastructure repair, and housing assistance among other activities (for a more comprehensive list of potential activities tied to catastrophic disaster recovery, see Figure 12.1).

Enhance federal, state, and local capacity and commitment to plan for post-disaster recovery. Building the capacity of federal, state, and local governments is an important yet still unrecognized role for most members of the public sector. While the recent development of the NDRF appears to mark a change in thinking at the federal level, it remains uncertain the degree to which FEMA, housing and urban development (HUD), and other federal agencies will be given the resources needed to engage in what amounts to a national education, training, and outreach effort to build the collective capacity of disaster recovery assistance networks across the United States, including state and local government officials. The failure to invest in the necessary delivery of pre-event training, education, and outreach efforts will likely result in weak plans and low levels of participation among members of the assistance network. While capacity building necessarily entails enhancing the collective capacity of larger assistance networks (as discussed in the next recommendation), the ability to provide federal, state, and local government officials with the technical skills needed to coordinate the development and implementation of strong plans represents part of a more complex challenge. In addition to training, members of the public sector need to be informed or educated about the merits of actively engaging in an ongoing commitment to pre-disaster planning and post-disaster updates to these plans as conditions change, new members join the network, and unique conditions arise following disasters. Similarly, a much larger outreach campaign is required to encourage the participation of members of the larger assistance network, many of whom may not initially recognize their role in this process, including those roles triggered by a catastrophe.

Maximize the collective strength of the larger disaster recovery assistance network. Factors used to describe the collective strength of inter-organizational networks often include diversity, regular communication and information sharing, and the role of boundary spanning organizations that link those groups that may not normally interact. In each case, pre-event planning can help to actualize collective strength, which is often initiated by an organization within a network that assumes a leadership role. For instance, research has shown that while differing members of the disaster recovery assistance network can play this role, non-profits are often at the center of these types of activities. In other cases, states, quasi governmental organizations, or the private sector may play a pivotal role in helping to coordinate actions across the network.[42] Regardless of who helps to pull together members of the network, the power to positively affect recovery outcomes is closely associated with the harnessing of this collective strength. Until recently, the current array of federal, state, and local government collaborative operations in emergency management have tended to focus on response and not disaster recovery operations, while other relevant planning activities have not recognized their important role in disaster recovery.

Modify the existing collaborative operations and the scope of plans in emergency management. The emergency management profession is dominated by a response orientation. This is reflected in a number of federal, state, and local policies, programs, and plans, many of which espouse collaboration. Improvements to national policy should include the expansion of these largely response-oriented operations to address disaster recovery-related issues. In many ways these operational policies reflect a more mature and distinct response assistance network that offer lessons for those involved in the emerging NDRF. Specific examples and suggested changes that merit attention include:

- Improving the linkage between the NRF and the NDRF;
- Better integrating state and local plans, including comprehensive land-use plans, comprehensive emergency management plans, and hazard mitigation plans;
- Expanding the pre- and post-disaster role of the emergency management assistance compact to support recovery outreach and raining;
- Incorporating disaster recovery courses into college and university programs;
- More effectively utilizing the recognized strengths of non-profits that are part of National Organizations Active in Disasters (NVOAD) and coordinating their activities with others in disaster recovery assistance networks;
- Including clear recovery metrics in national emergency management accreditation program evaluation criteria and;
- Broadening the training of Community Emergency Response Teams (CERT) to include recovery-related activities (for a more detailed discussion of collaborative operations see Smith 2011, pp. 345–366).

Improve the integration of disaster recovery issues identified in this chapter with ongoing FEMA Catastrophic Planning initiatives. In 2007, the House Committee on Oversight and Government Reform conducted a hearing to assess where FEMA stood relative to its preparedness for a future event in the light of how Hurricane Katrina dramatically illustrated the limitations of the federal agency and its partners. As part of the hearing, the committee asked the Department of Homeland Security Office of Inspector General to assess FEMA's readiness for a future catastrophic disaster.[43] The evaluation provides insights into two important issues: (1) the study found that the "new FEMA" (i.e., a term used to describe the federal agency after taking a number of steps to strengthen its capabilities post-Katrina) was improved but still unprepared for a catastrophic disaster and (2) the scorecard developed by the Department of Homeland Security does not adequately address disaster recovery.

In 2008, FEMA created the Task Force for Emergency Readiness Pilot Program (TFER) that sought to improve FEMA's capacity to integrate federal and state catastrophic planning efforts. The pilot program selected five states to participate. Interestingly, according to the United States Government Accountability Office, the program sought to "emphasize horizontal integration of planning efforts across sectors, jurisdictions, and functional disciplines, as well as vertical integration among state, regional, and federal agencies."[44] Yet the TFER evaluation criteria, like that found in the United States Office of the Inspector General (USOIG) report, do not adequately address catastrophic disaster recovery-related elements (Smith 2011, pp. 47–50). Both reports highlight what is still a major concern; that is, the disaster recovery assistance framework remains immature and the development of a new national recovery strategy has yet to be institutionalized within the agency responsible for its implementation. Until this occurs and the collective power of a well-coordinated recovery assistance network can be achieved and replicated across the United States, it remains uncertain how effective this new approach will fare when tested in a major disaster or catastrophe.

CONCLUSIONS AND FINAL THOUGHTS

The United States is in the midst of a potential transformation in the way the federal government and members of the larger disaster recovery assistance network address disaster recovery. The development of the NDRF, whole of community concept, and PPD-8 offer significant potential, if the resources are provided to the federal government in the pre-disaster timeframe to develop the collective capacity of disaster recovery assistance networks. The development of an enduring commitment to build the collective pre- and post-event capacity of this network to address the multitude of issues that arise following disasters and catastrophes remains to be seen. Understood relative to catastrophes, the importance of a broad network of participants, including those that are not typically invited to the table, cannot be understated as the physical, social, economic, and environmental impacts are likely to be massive and to date are largely unplanned for.

In the United States and around the world, disaster losses are growing exponentially. In the United States, Hurricane Katrina has been cited as the closest we have come as a nation to what could be called a catastrophe. Many of the catastrophic planning scenarios developed by FEMA may be much worse in terms of the level of damages and loss of life. In *Planning for Post-Disaster Recovery: A Review of the United States Disaster Recovery Framework*, I proposed the creation of the Disaster Recovery Act, which was intended to address many of the problems discussed in this chapter through the operationalization of new and existing policies, programs, and initiatives, with the ultimate aim of strengthening disaster recovery assistance networks and the policy framework itself. This idea has gained traction and legislation has been drafted that incorporates many of the ideas expressed here. Given the continued increase in disaster losses in the United States, and the real and significant threats associated with our changing climate and weather patterns in areas built to reflect past meteorological conditions, the relevance of planning for post-disaster recovery, including those disasters defined as catastrophes, is more important than ever.

REFERENCES

1. Quarantelli, E. L. 1998. *What Is a Disaster? Perspectives on the Question*. Routledge: London.
2. Lagadec, E. 2007. *Unconventional Crises, Unconventional Responses: Reforming Leadership in the Age of Catastrophic Crises and Hypercomplexity*. Center for Transatlantic Relations.
3. Quarantelli, E. L. 2005. *What Is a Disaster? New Answers to Old Questions*. Routledge: London.
4. Smith, G. and D. Wenger. 2006. Sustainable disaster recovery: Operationalizing an existing framework. pp. 234–257. In *Handbook of Disaster Research*. Editors H. Rodriguez, E. Quarantelli, and R. Dynes. New York: Springer.
5. Quarentelli, 1998, op. cit.
6. Peacock, W. G., B. H. Morrow, and H. Gladwin. 1997. *Hurricane Andrew and the Reshaping of Miami: Ethnicity, Gender, and the Socio-Political Ecology of Disasters*. Gainsville: University Press of Florida.
7. Quarantelli, 2005, op. cit.
8. Federal Emergency Management Agency. 2011. *A Whole Community Approach to Emergency Management: Principles, Themes and Pathways for Action*. FDOC 104-008-1, December.
9. Federal Emergency Management Agency. 2012. *National Disaster Recovery Framework*.
10. President Barack Obama. 2011. *Presidential Policy Directive 8 (PPD-8): National Preparedness*, March 30, 2011.
11. FEMA, 2011, op. cit., p. 3.
12. Federal Emergency Management Agency. 2007. *National Response Framework*. Washington, D.C.: Federal Emergency Management Agency. Available at http://www.fema.gov/pdf/emergency/nrf/nrf-base.pdf.
13. White, G. 1945. *Human Adjustment to Floods*. Research Paper no. 29. Chicago: Department of Geography, University of Chicago.
14. Kreps, G. A. and T. E. Drabek. 1996. Disasters are nonroutine social problems. *International Journal of Mass Emergencies and Disasters* 14: 129–153.
15. Mileti, D. 1999. *Disasters by Design: A Reassessment of Natural Hazards in the United States*. Washington, DC: Joseph Henry Press.
16. Freudenberg, W. R., R. Gramling, S. Laska, and K. T. Erickson 2009. *Catastrophe in the Making: The Engineering of Katrina and the Disasters of Tomorrow*. Washington, DC: Island Press.
17. Bates, F. L. and W. G. Peacock 1989. Long term recovery. *International Journal of Mass Emergencies and Disasters* 7(30): 349–365.
18. Lagadec, op. cit.
19. Smith, G. 2011. *Planning for Post-Disaster Recovery: A Review of the United States Disaster Assistance Framework*. USA: Public Entity Risk Institute. ISBN 978-0-9793722-5-4.
20. Olshansky, R. B. 2006. Planning after Hurricane Katrina. *Journal of the American Planning Association* 72(2): 147–153.

21. Berke, P. R., J. Kartez, and D. Wenger 1993. Recovery after disasters: Achieving sustainable development, mitigation and equity. *Disasters* 17(2): 93–109.
22. Friedmann, J. 1987. *Planning in the Public Domain: From Knowledge to Action.* Princeton, NJ: Princeton University Press.
23. Kent, T. J. 1991. *The Urban General Plan.* 2nd Edition. San Francisco: Chandler.
24. Forester, J. 1987. Planning in the face of conflict: Negotiation and mediation strategies in local land use regulation. *Journal of the American Planning Association* 53(3): 303–314.
25. Godschalk, D. 1992. Negotiating intergovernmental development policy conflicts: Practice based guidelines. *Journal of the American Planning Association* 58(3): 368–378.
26. Dynes, R. R. 1970. *Organized Behavior in Disaster.* Lexington, MA: Heath Lexington Books.
27. Smith, 2011, op. cit.
28. Schwab, J., K. C. Topping, C. C. Eadie, R. E. Deyle, and R. Smith. 1998. *Planning for Post-Disaster Recovery and Reconstruction.* Chicago: American Planning Association.
29. Smith and Wenger, op. cit.
30. Spangle, W., R. Meehan, H. Degenkolb, and M. Blair 1987. *Pre-Event Planning for Post-earthquake Rebuilding.* Los Angeles, CA: Southern California Earthquake Preparedness Project.
31. Smith and Wenger, op. cit.
32. Smith, G. and V. Flatt. 2011. *Assessing the Disaster Recovery Planning Capacity of the State of North Carolina.* Research Brief. Durham, NC: Institute for Homeland Security Solutions.
33. Ganapati, N. E. and S. Ganapati. 2009. Enabling participatory planning after disasters. *Journal of the American Planning Association* 75(1): 41–59.
34. Spangle and Associates. 1990. *Rebuilding After Earthquakes: Lessons from Planners.* Portola Valley, CA: William Spangle and Associates.
35. May, P. 1989. Disaster recovery and reconstruction. In *Managing Disaster: Strategies and Perspectives.* Editors L. L. Comfort. Durham, NC: Duke University Press.
36. Berke, Kartez, and Wenger, op. cit.
37. Bolin, R. and L. Stanford. 1998. The Northridge earthquake: Community-based approaches to unmet recovery needs. *Disasters* 22(1): 21–38.
38. Smith and Wenger, 2006, op. cit.
39. Berke, P., W. Lyles, and G. Smith. Impacts of federal and state mitigation policies on local land use policy. *Journal of the American Planning Association*, currently under review.
40. Smith, 2011, op. cit. pp. 198–204.
41. Smith, Ibid, pp. 225–228.
42. Smith, Ibid.
43. United States Department of Homeland Security. Office of Inspector General. 2008 March. FEMA's preparedness for the next catastrophic disaster. OIG-08-34. Washington, D.C.: Department of Homeland Security.
44. United States Government Accountability Office. Report to Congressional Requesters. 2011 April. Catastrophic Planning: States Participating in FEMA's Pilot Program Made Progress, but Better Guidance Could Enhance Future Pilot Programs. GAO-11-383. Washington, D.C.: Government Accountability Office.

CHAPTER 13

Pandemic Scenario

Rick Bissell and Thomas Kirsch

CONTENTS

Overview 301
    Why Do We Care? 302
Influenza 303
Pandemic Flu Scenario 304
Coordinating a Response 305
    Principles of Pandemic Response 305
    Priority Setting 306
Scene Safety/Worker Protection 307
Control of the Pandemic 308
    And Other Healthcare Needs 309
What About Other Basic Societal Needs? 310
Short Overview of Federal Plans 311
    The DHHS Pandemic Flu Plan 312
    Department of Homeland Security Pandemic Plan 314
Barriers to Effective Preparedness for a Pandemic Catastrophe 315
Potential Long-Range Problems 316
References 317

OVERVIEW

This chapter is intended to present the complicated problems and dynamics that would likely accompany a very probable but relatively slow-onset catastrophe, a pandemic of a new or "novel" version of an influenza virus. We say that this is probable because it is in the natural order of viruses that they mutate into new versions of an old virus. This new version is particularly potent because our immune system does not recognize it, and so cannot accurately protect the body against it. Because of the high probability of such an event happening during the professional lifetime of many readers, and because the vocabulary and methods of public health (PH) are foreign to many emergency managers, we have chosen to use the pandemic scenario to: (1) expose emergency managers to the methods and terminology of PH practitioners, with whom emergency managers will have to work closely; (2) help readers grasp the social/economic/political/security complications that could result from a pandemic, and; (3) present a compelling scenario in which the typical tools of emergency management (EM) and emergency response are not the primary resources in combating the event and its direct effects. The importance of the pandemic scenario is demonstrated by the fact that both the U.S. Department of Homeland Security (DHS) and the Department of Health and Human Services (DHHS) have chosen pandemics as a primary planning and preparedness focus.

Note that this chapter is not intended to provide any reasonable level of expertise in planning for and response to a pandemic. Rather, it is intended to familiarize readers with the vocabulary, concepts, strategies, and complications that surround the pandemic scenario. This familiarization level is intended to help you to productively work with PH experts on tasks related to pandemic preparedness and response. The content presented here is not intended to represent the expert-level discussions of PH strategies or analyses one might find on an expert panel or in a PH graduate program. If you have interest in learning more about this field, there is excellent material available on the web, primarily from the World Health Organization (who.org) or the U.S. Centers for Disease Control and Prevention (cdc.gov). Many schools of PH also offer courses in epidemic or pandemic response within their infectious disease control programs.

The vocabulary and concepts used in this chapter were explained in Chapter 8 on Public Health. If you are not familiar with the field of PH and have not yet read Chapter 8, do so prior to reading this chapter on the pandemic scenario as an example of a catastrophe.

Why Do We Care?

A severe pandemic could kill hundreds of millions of people worldwide and disrupt the entire fabric of society. It could severely deplete the number of personnel available to carry out all primary functions, ranging from medical care to law enforcement, food delivery, utilities management, banking, and EM. If banks, industries, and businesses shut down, a general financial crisis may result. This is a real challenge for emergency managers, because the lead specialists will be PH and medical personnel who have disease control knowledge, but who also have very limited access to the resources and logistics needed to carry out an effective emergency response that would cover the entire population of the country. Emergency managers will play a key role in coordinating the myriad agencies and resources needed to confront a pandemic. Depending on the characteristics of the microbes involved, a pandemic could prove to be one of the most humanly destructive and difficult catastrophes to confront.

INFLUENZA

Influenza is currently expected to be the most likely cause of a new pandemic. "The Flu" is not a common cold with runny noses and a cough. It is an infection that causes high fever and severe muscle pains, with fatigue, cough, and headaches. It starts rapidly over just a couple of hours and people who get an influenza infection often say it feels like they "got hit by a truck." Currently, the most likely influenza virus that could become a deadly pandemic is called the H5N1 virus. It has led to deaths in Asia, mostly in people who handle birds (in many parts of Asia, families typically keep a small flock of chickens and ducks), but has been spread throughout most of Asia and some parts of Europe and Asia Minor by bird flocks. Most humans who contract H5N1 are people who are bird handlers or consumers. However, a small number of people have been infected by close contact with infected humans. At the time this is being written in 2012, the virus has not shown the ability to transmit easily from one person to another (see Figure 13.1).

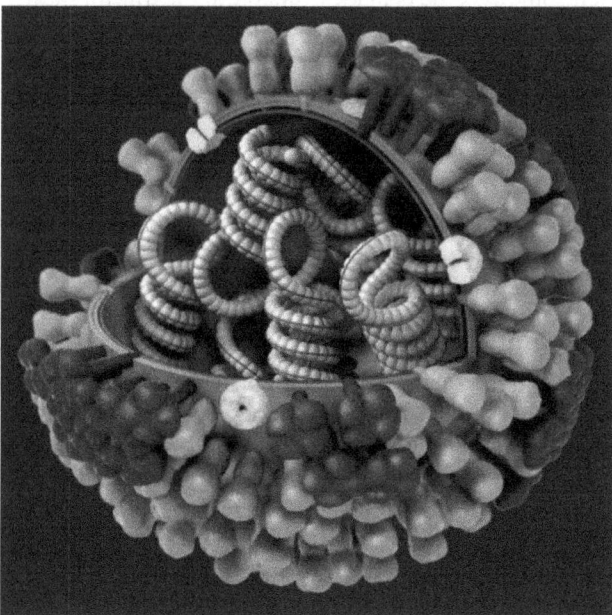

Figure 13.1 The three-dimensional (3D) depiction of the influenza virus: The spikes on the outside represent the surface proteins which the virus uses for entering the host cell. The H and N numbers in the virus name actually tell us the type of surface proteins found on the virus. The coils shown inside represent the genetic material, which in the case of the influenza virus is RNA. (http://phil.cdc.gov/phil/details.asp (Image # 11878).)

PANDEMIC FLU SCENARIO

This scenario is based on an abbreviated version of that which is used by the CDC and WHO in some of their planning. A "novel" microbe is one to which the human population has no experience or immunity.

The current (at the time of this writing) case fatality rate (percentage of those who contract the disease and end up dying from it) for the H5N1 avian flu virus is over 50%. It is not easy to predict what the case fatality rate would be if the virus were to mutate such that it would pass easily from human to human. There is some evidence that, in the process of becoming more easily transmittable, viruses tend to become less lethal. Current planning assumes a case-fatality rate of somewhere around 2–5%, equaling 600,000–1,500,000 fatalities in the United States over a 6–12-month period. An estimated 500,000 died in the United States in the 1918–1919 flu pandemic, with a much lower population base than we have now. If the case fatality rate is in the double digits and 50% of the population is attacked by the virus, many millions could perish in the U.S., and perhaps hundreds of millions (or more) in the world at large.

Since influenza pandemics typically come in waves, it is possible that a vaccine might become available for, or during the second wave. Vaccines for a novel virus typically take 4–6 months to prepare and manufacture once the virus is isolated and validated. Even if some vaccine is made available at the time of the second wave, the current manufacturing methods are limited and the amount available would be insufficient to meet the demand for many months after the first dose becomes available. Research is currently underway to speed up the process of new vaccine development.

Given the millions that would become ill, the U.S. medical care system would be totally overwhelmed early on, and only able to address the needs for a tiny percentage of those who are extremely ill. Most "care" would have to take place at home. Reverberations throughout the economy and government services would be enormous, in some cases leading to a secondary disaster due to a lack of basic services and food deliveries. As is the case in many other kinds of disasters, the threats that come to humans can be primary and secondary. In the case of an influenza pandemic, the virus itself would be the primary cause of suffering. However, on a society-wide basis, it might be that a significant portion of the catastrophe would come from human responses to the virus. Not wanting to be exposed to the virus, many are likely to follow "social distancing" strategies to the extreme, and not show up for work. DA Jones and others have found evidence of significant probable absenteeism in critical goods transport systems,[1] and other critical functions such as healthcare.[2,3] Delivery of food may be problematic. Residents of cities may be particularly vulnerable to food shortages, in that almost all food is transported in from the outside, and few Americans keep substantial food stored for emergencies (or even winter). Rural residents may be closer to food sources. One of the things that enabled Americans to withstand the 1918–1919 pandemic was the fact that so many kept canned stores of food, and raised at least some of their own food.

Law enforcement availability is a special concern, due to the role that law enforcement would play in keeping the basic systems safe in times of desperation. Some countries have decided to give law enforcement personnel the top priority for anti-viral medications or vaccines, should a pandemic become a reality. The challenges to EM to help coordinate a response to this kind of scenario may be far greater than coordinating a response to many geophysical events. Absenteeism of emergency response workers of all kinds may at least temporarily take away from emergency managers many of their primary resources. It can be expected that the pandemic will not constitute the only emergency during this period of time, thus taxing response resources beyond their capacity, requiring EM, PH, and political leadership to triage or establish priorities for access to resources.

Since past influenza pandemics have come in waves, it is critical for PH and EM personnel to recognize that the end of the first wave does not necessarily represent the end of the pandemic; they should use the lull period fruitfully to prepare for the next onslaught.

COORDINATING A RESPONSE

Pandemic flu demands a response paradigm very different from the standard jurisdictional disaster response. Virtually everyone will be out of their comfort zone, and many normal assumptions will simply not work. While PH experts may understand disease control measures, it is emergency managers who have the ability to coordinate the massive logistical undertakings necessary for implementing measures to confront both the primary and secondary effects of the pandemic.

Coordinating a pandemic response is made even more difficult because of some of the built-in contradictions of the situation, and the role that fear will play in driving population behavior. The contradictions are unavoidable. For example, at the very time that one would normally call for mutual aid, little will be available because everybody will be affected. At the moment that cross-jurisdictional and multi-jurisdictional sharing of resources are most needed, people will not want to be mixing with others and, when healthcare resources are most needed, few will be available.

Because fear will play such an important role in people's behavior, one of the most important functions of emergency managers will be to help educate the public so as to decrease their fear response.

Principles of Pandemic Response

Emergency managers are accustomed to having threat or impact predictions from scientists who work with the various hazards we prepare for and respond to. Such predictions allow us to better prioritize our activities and provide us with a crucial tool for informing the general public regarding their vulnerability and the steps they should be taking. The World Health Organization (http://www.who.int/csr/disease/avian_influenza/en/index.html) has developed a six-phase alert model for avian influenza, which is based upon the calculated likelihood that the disease can convert from one that is mostly carried and transmitted by birds, to one that can be easily transmitted from human-to-human. It is this capacity to transmit easily from human-to-human that enables a virus or any other microbe to grow from a localized "outbreak" to a full-fledged pandemic affecting much of the world. The six WHO alert phases are

1. Low risk of human cases
2. Higher risk of human cases
3. Not any, or very limited, human-to-human transmission
4. Evidence of increased human-to-human transmission
5. Evidence of significant human-to-human transmission
6. Efficient and sustained human-to-human transmission

Note that the phases are on an ordinal scale and that the determination of what alert phase is currently present, is made by a group of PH experts based on the available up-to-date information. Measurements of some other hazards, for example earthquakes and hurricanes, are based more on directly measurable physical phenomena, that is, intensity of shaking or wind speeds. The difference between measures for earthquakes and hurricanes, on the one hand, and a potential pandemic microbe, is that the geo-meteorological measures connote intensity; the WHO pandemic phases represent stages of development of the microbe, in which potential intensity is inferred but not directly measured. Note also that the WHO phases, used worldwide, do not include phases that might be equivalent to some of the post-impact phases of EM.

The WHO phases can be applied to the entire world, or to a particular jurisdiction. For example, during the 2008 H5N1 outbreak (not pandemic), the world was rated as being at phase level 3, with limited human-to-human transmission, mostly in East and South Asia. At the same time, the United States considered itself at phase 0 (not listed by WHO), because there had been no human cases anywhere in the Americas. In 2009 and early 2010, there was a true pandemic outbreak of another novel influenza virus, H1N1, which reached WHO pandemic alert level 6, and in doing so, demonstrated a problem with the WHO rating system: it is based on the transmissibility of the disease, but not the ability of the disease to cause disastrous levels of fatalities. In fact, although there were deaths in many countries, they were at a relatively low level (with a few exceptions), and, in the end, the H1N1 pandemic is now seen as having been a practice session for more dangerous disease outbreaks. For the most part, there was little need for EM to become involved in the 2009–2010 H1N1 pandemic. However, the pandemic alert system is being revised, and in their work to assist PH agencies with preparedness and response to a pandemic, emergency managers should learn the meaning of the current alert phases for the microbe causing an outbreak, and keep informed about the alert phase changes. Updated information can be obtained from the U.S. Centers for Disease Control and Prevention (www.cdc.gov) or the World Health Organization (http://www.who.int/csr/outbreaknetwork/en/), and through local health departments.

Priority Setting

PH emergency managers typically employ a needs assessment as a core tool in priority setting. Different from "damage assessments" done by emergency managers following a seismic or weather disaster, the PH needs assessment evaluates what functions need to be addressed, thereby assisting with the setting of priorities. In the pandemic scenario, the needs that will be assessed will fall into three categories:

- Those functions required to control the pandemic and its sequelae
- Those functions needed to meet the needs of all other healthcare operations
- Those functions needed to meet basic societal–survival requirements, such as water, shelter, food, sanitation, heat, and so on

PH managers will be torn between utilization of already limited health system resources for pandemic response and reserving some portion of those resources for other unrelated life-threatening acute and chronic diseases. While emergency managers cannot help PH agencies make those tough decisions, it will help emergency managers to understand why the PH agencies might want to disallow pandemic patients from being seen in certain hospitals or other facilities which are being held aside to meet more routine healthcare emergencies.

The third needs assessment listed here relates to the basic societal–survival requirements. This is a huge arena in which emergency managers have experience and can fulfill a strong leadership role. In the pandemic scenario, the delivery of food may become a particular concern if "social distancing" behavior extends to those who deliver food stocks to grocery stores, and those who staff grocery retailers. Emergency managers may do well to help develop alternate food delivery plans when working with PH agencies and private retailers on jurisdictional pandemic preparedness plans.

SCENE SAFETY/WORKER PROTECTION

The concept of scene safety is drilled into first responders, however, in the pandemic scenario there are several related problems. One is that many responders will not understand what they need to do to mitigate their own personal exposure risk. Second, many may simply decide to stay home. The "scene" is also harder to define than is normally the case. During a pandemic, the "scene" is everywhere, but risks increase with direct human contact. A major pre-pandemic EM role is to help all first response agencies develop plans and supplies for protecting their own personnel (and their families) in case a pandemic becomes a reality. The Centers for Disease Control (www.cdc.gov), the Occupational Safety and Health Administration (www.osha.gov), and the American Red Cross (www.redcross.org) all provide worker protection guidelines for epidemics and other infectious disease exposures. In the event of a pandemic, state and local health departments will also provide guidelines. Several worker protection decisions that can be made during the early pre-event planning stages are

- Whether emergency response and public safety workers will receive priority status for obtaining the available vaccines or anti-viral drugs.

- Whether to stock supplies of surgical gloves, N95 masks (or whatever is recommended), eye protection, and other "universal precaution" supplies that might be needed to protect the emergency response personnel during an extended pandemic.
- Whether the families of the emergency response personnel should also receive prophylactic vaccines or medications.

Germany has reached the policy decision that law enforcement personnel will have top priority for receiving any available vaccine or medications for the disease causing the pandemic, with the rationale being that keeping order will be necessary to be successful with almost all other response activities. Some U.S. agencies have suggested giving active healthcare workers top priority. The reality of the division of powers in the American political system means that different priority decisions may be made in different jurisdictions. The important thing is to have a broad EM/ public health (PH) discussion about this topic at the appropriate jurisdictional level prior to needing to respond to an imminent pandemic. Politicians and the public will need to understand the rationale behind any priority strategy, and agencies will need to know what the policy is and how it should be enforced. Obviously, this policy should not cover only vaccines, but should also address other protection items that might be in short supply, such as masks, gloves, eye protection, and so on (see Figure 13.2).

CONTROL OF THE PANDEMIC

An attempt to gain control of the pandemic, at a minimum, the following tasks will need to be performed:

- Epidemiologic surveillance and updating
- Institution of prevention: social distancing, quarantine, and isolation (Who takes care of these people?)
- Distribution of vaccines and medicines (How to distribute and to whom?)
- Surge/overflow: Where, and with which healthcare workers?
- Family-centered self-care information

The basic tasks and tactics in the attempt to gain "control" of a pandemic are fraught with problems and limitations. The reality is that a pandemic, by definition, is beyond control. The real focus is on mitigating or minimizing the consequences as much as possible. The point is to plan for all these anticipated functions, trying to prepare for as many difficulties as possible, but remaining flexible. Note that each function mentioned on the list, except epidemiologic surveillance, is subject to ethical dilemmas as well as logistical ones. For example, when providing the public information on family-centered care of the ill in the home, what guidance do you suggest in terms of the distribution of care resources when individuals of different age groups and vulnerability levels come down ill simultaneously? As a starter, see: *Pandemic Flu Preparedness: Ethical Issues and Recommendations to the Indiana State Department of Health*, found at www.bioethics.iu.edu/pandemic-FluPrep_2007.pdf.

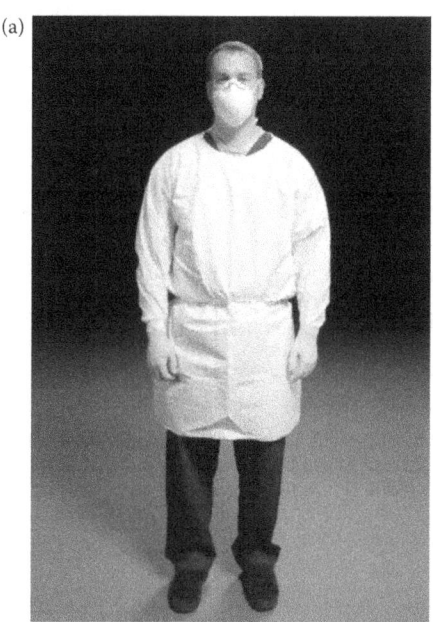 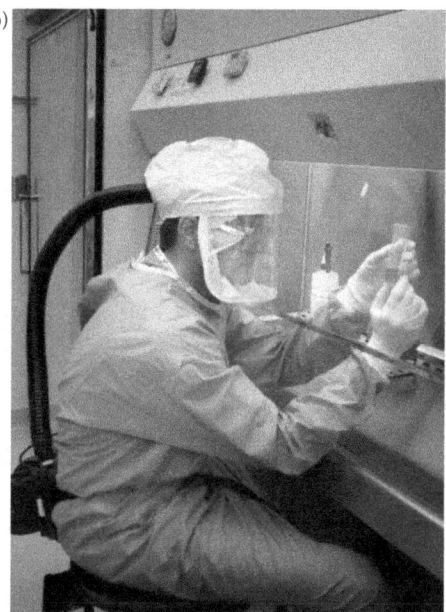

Figure 13.2 Personal protection equipment. (a) Shows personal protective equipment (PPE) which includes a surgical gown, surgical gloves, and an N95 respirator, all of which may be recommended for providers during a pandemic flu scenario. (b) Shows a scientist working with the influenza virus of 1918 in a laboratory. He is dressed for biosafety level 3 and is working under a constantly ventilating hood. (http://phil.cdc.gov/phil/details.asp (image # 7988 (b) and 10757 (a)).)

Another issue which will require collaboration between PH and EM personnel is the need to set up "surge facilities" at alternate care sites, perhaps schools, community centers, or nursing homes. PH authorities will be overly taxed in finding medical supplies and personnel to provide or oversee care of the sick in such facilities; they will not have the ability to manage the logistics of everything else that will be needed to make such surge facilities work (e.g., facilities management personnel, food services, water supply, etc.) (see Figure 13.3).

And Other Healthcare Needs ...

As mentioned previously, the existence of a pandemic does not mean that other healthcare needs suddenly stop. As a result, we are faced with the following questions:

- How to meet routine care and normal emergency care needs when hospitals are overflowing, and healthcare workers are absent?
- How to encourage healthcare workers to return to work?
- How to keep supplies available in a system that depends on just-in-time deliveries?

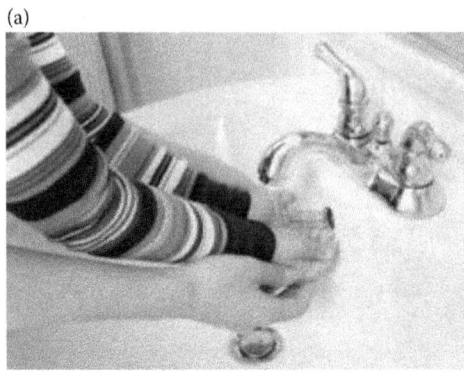 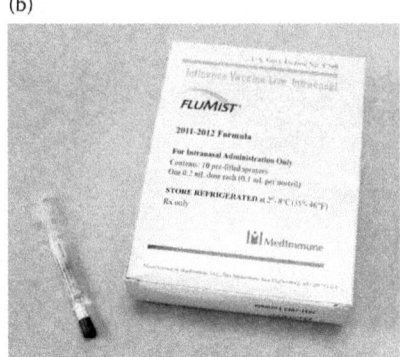

Figure 13.3 Containing and controlling the flu. In photo (a) we see an essential method by which the public can minimize the spread of the flu as well as many other infectious diseases with minimal effort. Washing hands. (http://www.cdc.gov/h1n1flu/faithbased/pdf/H1N1_FBO_toolkit.pdf?s_cid=cs_000.) Photo (b) shows a flu vaccine. (http://phil.cdc.gov/phil/details.asp (image # 14226).)

- How to prioritize care delivery to pandemic patients versus those whose lives or health are threatened by more routine injuries and illnesses?

There are no pat answers for these perplexing issues. Some hospitals have plans to house the families of healthcare workers in special protected facilities, but there is little agreement on whether this would even be attractive to workers. The supplies issue is just as vexing: In the United States, our society values efficiency and low cost over the safety margin that comes with having stocks of supplies in storage for emergency use. The federal government's strategic national stockpile (SNS) of pharmaceutical supplies is an attempt to mitigate the downside of just-in-time delivery systems, but it too has limits. The amount of supplies in the SNS is insufficient to meet broad long-term needs, and the delivery of supplies out of storage and into the hands of health agencies and health practitioners is likely to be difficult in times of high anxiety and low availability of transport. Second, the SNS covers only a limited range of healthcare supplies; it does not even begin to address other kinds of supplies necessary to social functioning, such as food and energy, which are also typically delivered by a just-in-time system. Obviously, when any kind of necessary supply is in short supply and the public is afraid that lack of access means potential poor outcome for themselves and their families, it is highly important that a pre-planned and coordinated system of security is implemented in such a fashion that ensures that supplies arrive at their destinations.

WHAT ABOUT OTHER BASIC SOCIETAL NEEDS?

Just to name a few, there are many basic societal needs that are outside of the purview of the healthcare sector:

- Law enforcement
- Food deliveries
- Fuel deliveries
- Utilities
- Monetary system
- Power plants
- Continuity of government

Each of these societal needs is a priority item and outside of the realm of the PH system. Therefore, EM will play a key role in coordinating the functions listed here. Prioritization may need to be based on the local situation and needs. Continuity of government is an issue that is important at all levels of government, and can best be addressed well ahead of any emergency period. Catastrophes are more likely to cause disruptions in governmental functions than are disasters. Completely aside from the catastrophe-caused disruptions to governments that have been discussed in other chapters of this book, pandemics carry the real risks that large numbers of key government personnel will become ill, and that another significant portion may decide not to report to work out of fear of becoming infected. The extent to which this may happen is open to speculation, and may depend ... on how well government agencies pre-plan to have onsite all the tools that are needed to protect the personnel. Another thing emergency managers may want to look into as part of their catastrophe planning process is the question of how they would operate under martial law.

The way that society and the government handle the issues outlined in this discussion will, to a large extent, determine whether the pandemic takes on truly catastrophic proportions. If society can keep order, provide for the distribution of food and other basic necessities, meet the needs of those who are quarantined, or orphaned, despite the catastrophic loss of life, the suffering due to the secondary effects of the event will not eclipse the direct effects of the disease. Emergency managers can and should exercise a major role in limiting those secondary effects.

SHORT OVERVIEW OF FEDERAL PLANS

There are obviously more than two federal agencies that have important roles in preparing for and responding to a pandemic, but we focus here on the two lead agencies, DHHS (Department of Health and Human Services) and DHS (Department of Homeland Security). The key PH agencies responsible for infection control are CDC, and the United States Public Health Service (USPHS), both of which are agencies within DHHS. Note that the federal plans that exist at the time of writing this chapter are a moving target and may have been revised by the time that you are reading this. It is likely that such changes will not be major. Nonetheless, refer to CDC, DHS, and DHHS websites for updated information on federal plans. For those outside of the United States, refer to WHO websites and those of your own country. We would also advise you to review your current state/provincial or territorial pandemic response plans, usually available through the jurisdictional health department, and often also available through the jurisdictional EM agency. Likewise, for readers outside of the United States, note that many governments have national pandemic preparedness and response plans which are coordinated with those of other countries via the World Health Organization. We will continue here with the focus on the United States, recognizing that most of the issues are similar virtually everywhere.

Dwight Eisenhower, at the time he was a general, is said to have stated that "Plans are nothing. Planning is everything." By this he meant that the planning process is more important than having a paper plan in contributing to actual readiness. In pandemic planning in the United States, numerous local and county jurisdictions have simply hired a consultant or appointed a single person to construct a plan, thereby losing out on the value of the planning process. Emergency managers have long recognized the value of the planning process, as compared to the paper plan, and could play an important role in helping health departments to design and organize a fruitful multi-agency and multi-government planning process in preparedness for pandemics.

The DHHS Pandemic Flu Plan

DHHS acknowledges up-front that response to a pandemic is beyond the scope of any one agency or even any one country. In the opening pages of the DHHS plan document, the agency states that it believes that pandemic flu planning is everyone's business, and confirms its commitment to work with other organizations ranging from the World Health Organization, scientific bodies, non-governmental organizations, and all levels of government. It also emphasizes the importance of preparedness at the community level. The DHHS plan focuses less on an organigram and more on tasks that need to be done to assure that resources, personnel, and coordination agreements will be on hand, should a pandemic response be required. While the plan is written by and for DHHS, it includes frequent references to local, state, and non-profit private agencies. This is a clear indication to planners that no one jurisdiction or level of government can plan in isolation for a pandemic response (see Figure 13.4).

The core of the DHHS plan is to enhance major components of critical preparedness and response actions, to include

- Intensifying surveillance and collaborating on containment measures—both international and domestic;
- Stockpiling of antiviral medications and vaccines and working with the industry to expand the capacity for production of these medical countermeasures;
- Creating a seamless network of federal, state, and local preparedness, including increasing healthcare surge capacity; and
- Developing the public education and communications efforts that will be very critical to keeping the public informed.

The DHHS plan includes some standardization, in the form of standardized evaluations and paperwork that must be completed by all jurisdictions, leading to

Figure 13.4 Up-to-date information on influenza. HHS has created a website dedicated specifically to the flu where information is available about seasonal flu as well as pandemic flu plans. (http://www.flu.gov/.)

some degree of uniformity of approach across jurisdictions and levels. The planning approach includes some funding for exercises, which is a valuable component of making plans "live." Note that the DHHS funding to jurisdictions is limited to health agencies even though the plan acknowledges the necessity of inter-agency cooperation.

The response portion of the DHHS Pandemic Flu Plan is based on the following:

- Federal roles:
  - Provide definitive reference laboratories and epidemiologic surveillance/information
  - Provide SNS of pharmaceuticals, vaccines, and other critical medical supplies and equipment
  - Coordinate the distribution of key medical supplies and personnel to states
  - Coordinate with the international agencies
- State roles:
  - Coordinate the flow of medical supplies and personnel
  - Coordinate the designation of alternate treatment sites
  - Coordinate placement of those needing treatment
  - Work with counties/cities in the designation of quarantine and isolation sites, and provide enforcement where necessary
  - Revise, amend, and suspend state laws addressing quarantine/isolation and medical practice codes
  - Report epidemiologic findings back to CDC and request a targeted assistance from DHHS
  - Provide state law enforcement manpower where local law enforcement may fall short on protecting vital sites and functions
- County/city roles:
  - Prioritize use of local healthcare resources among competing interests
  - Receive, store, and distribute SNS supplies
  - Provide law enforcement for key sites and services
  - Establish/enforce quarantine/isolation
  - Set up/maintain alternate treatment sites
  - Coordinate coroner and mortuary operations
  - Provide homecare information to the public
  - Provide/coordinate vaccine distribution
  - Coordinate distribution of food supplies where needed
  - Provide epidemiologic findings to the state's health department

PH works more on the basis of collaboration than the command and control approach sometimes invoked by EM. This is seen in the DHHS federal roles outlined. This may become problematical for emergency managers if they do not recognize the collaborative PH approach as being standard for the field, rather than thinking that the PH personnel are simply unwilling to take responsibility or "play" the game by EM rules. It is important for EM personnel to work with PH personnel in the preparedness stage to decide how emergency decision making will be accomplished, and not wait until a response to try to iron out the differences in the two disciplines.[4] Looking at the three lists of roles, federal, state, and local, it becomes apparent that many of the activities at state and local levels are essentially not possible without the assistance of EM, and the resources EM can coordinate. This is perhaps less the case at the federal level, but actually not so. In reality, the federal plan depends on the state and local resources for anything useful to be done, and the state and local agencies depend on close collaboration with EM. Given this reality, local and state populations cannot depend on, or assume that the "feds" will come to their rescue with all the needed resources in a pandemic catastrophe.

The DHHS plan affirms specific roles for the states. Note that, with the exception of law enforcement, the plan sticks to activities that are directly related to the health sector's response to the pandemic, and not the multi-sectoral responses needed for all the secondary impacts of the pandemic. Also note that there are no instructions for states that share borders with other countries regarding their collaboration with those countries.

In the DHHS plan, cities and counties are seen as the points of implementation for most tasks. At the local level, the DHHS plan mentions both food and law enforcement in addition to health-related tasks, but does not mention the myriad of other tasks that would be needed to protect the public or enhance probabilities of a good outcome. For example, mortuary and burial services come under the health department regulation in many jurisdictions. It is at the local level that emergency managers can make the most significant impact on the response to all of the connected emergencies or crises that would emerge in a pandemic. It is clear that a National Incident Management System (NIMS)-like joint operations center would be a good step in the right direction, but it will be even more important for emergency managers to have a basic understanding of what will be needed in a response. This can be greatly enhanced by multi-agency planning for pandemic response.

Department of Homeland Security Pandemic Plan

The DHS plan quickly establishes itself as a broader, more authority-oriented plan, although similar to the DHHS plan, it repeatedly mentions cooperation and coordination. Here is a brief overview.

- The pillars of pandemic preparedness are
  - Preparedness and communication
  - Surveillance and detection

- Response and command
- Goals
  - Limit spread and damage
  - Protect commerce and infrastructure
  - Assure governmental and economic continuity
- Preparedness
  - State and community level planning
  - Build SNS and distribution plan
  - Build national vaccine production capacity
  - Work with WHO and other international organizations
  - Build and exercise plans at all levels of government
  - Plan for medical and veterinary surge capacity
- Surveillance and response
  - Similar to the DHHS plan, with the exception of a section on sustaining infrastructure, critical services, and the economy
- Roles and responsibilities
  - Lead technical roles: DHHS and Department of Agriculture
  - Lead federal coordination: DHS

Note the DHS concentration on private sector services and continuity. DHS also clearly puts itself in the role of the lead federal coordinator in a pandemic, which may conflict with some other documents.

The DHS plan reaches out to non-health sectors that are not explicitly included in the DHHS plan, recognizing that DHHS does not have within its domain such things as commerce, physical infrastructure, data and communications infrastructure, food security and delivery, or protection of law and order. As noted in the chapter on political and legal issues, the legislation that created the DHS after the September 11, 2001 attacks gives broad powers to DHS to protect and support critical components of society in emergency circumstances.

BARRIERS TO EFFECTIVE PREPAREDNESS FOR A PANDEMIC CATASTROPHE

As has been the case with the rest of this chapter, the barriers mentioned here pertain to the United States. However, many countries have similar dynamics. The barriers to effective implementation of a robust response to a pandemic are enormous. Here is a short synopsis of the barriers:

Funding Limitations: While it almost always seems to be the case that there is insufficient funding at all levels of government and within the private sector to prepare for something that may not happen in the next 10 years, an even more frustrating limitation is based on the manner in which available funding is limited to specific agencies only. At the planning and preparedness stages, the agency-specific structure of the funding discourages the multi-disciplinary and multi-sectoral coordination that is promoted in the verbiage of the plans. That is to say that funding that is given to health departments with the intention of promoting multi-sectoral response planning and training cannot be shared with agencies that are not part of the health department structure.

Lack of Unity between Disciplines: At the state and local levels, numerous jurisdictions have been less than fully enthusiastic about pandemic planning. The relationship between EM and PH personnel is under-researched, making it hard to generalize similar problems or sensitivities. Recent research by Pinet and Bissell demonstrates a certain degree of reluctance on the part of some emergency managers to work closely with health professionals due to perceived attitudinal issues.[5] The personal feelings-level barrier is only a small (but potentially important) part of the dynamic. As mentioned earlier in the PH chapter of this book, PH and EM have at the core of their professional behavior some strong differences, which can drive each side to think the other is incompetent.[6] Many PH personnel have no concept of how the EM system operates, nor do they have first-hand experience with creating and testing viable emergency plans. This barrier can only be overcome when both sides are educated in the ways of the other, and are required to work together on common plans. It is our hope that this book also contributes to the process of increased understanding between emergency managers and PH specialists.

The lack of experienced emergency planners in health departments provides an opening for emergency managers to help health departments move in the direction of more complete and more inclusive planning. However, there is yet another barrier to this happening, in that many health departments require that candidates for their planning positions have a strong PH background, which few emergency managers do. As a result, many jurisdictional health departments have, in order to meet CDC preparedness requirements, hired consultants to write departmental pandemic response plans. This completely blocks the primary benefit that comes from planning: multi-group participation in the planning process, and joint decision making.

International Barriers: The issue of the United States being poorly prepared to accept and coordinate incoming international assistance is one that needs substantial high-level work, some of which is currently underway. When federal authorities work out the mechanisms for the incoming international assistance, emergency managers and PH personnel would need to be prepared to make the best use of such assistance. On the other hand, pandemics are less likely than other catastrophes to find international assistance offered, due to the probability that all countries will be struggling with the same problems.

POTENTIAL LONG-RANGE PROBLEMS

Some of the effects of a pandemic would have long-term impacts. If there is a large loss of life, many aspects of industry, education, and public safety services could find themselves lacking personnel with key skills. In some sectors of science, medicine, and technology, the loss of key people may set back otherwise promising-looking research and developments. These impacts could significantly delay any economic rebound from the catastrophe. Some markets may find themselves in a surplus situation. For example, if many have died there will be surplus housing for some time, greatly decreasing the value of homes, which for many is their primary investment.

Thus, we see the enormity of a serious pandemic, and that the stresses of the emergency period are followed by significant society-wide problems that will last for years. The actions that society takes during the pandemic can have a significant impact on what life is like for years afterwards.

REFERENCES

1. Jones DA, Nozick LK, Turnquist MA, and Sawaya WJ. Pandemic influenza, worker absenteeism and impacts on freight transportation. *Proceedings of the 41st Annual Hawaii International Conference on System Sciences*, January 7–10, 2008. ISBN: 978-0-7695-3075-8.
2. Wilson N, Baker M, Crampton P, and Monsoor O. The potential impact of the next influenza pandemic on a national primary care medical workforce. *Human Resources for Health*, August 11, 2005, 3:7.
3. Irvin C, Cindrich L, Patterson W, Ledbetter A, and Southall A. Hospital personnel response during a hypothetical influenza pandemic: Will they come to work? *Academy of Emergency Medicine Journal*, May 2007, 14(5, Suppl 1):13a.
4. For more information on this, please see: Bissell RA. Public health and medicine in emergency management. Chapter in *Disciplines and Disasters in Emergency Management: The Convergence and Divergence of Concepts, Issues and Trends from the Research Literature*. (2007) D. McEntire, ed. John Charles Thomas Publisher, pp. 213–223.
5. Pinet Peralta L and Bissell RA. *Barriers Between Emergency Management and Health Care: Results of a Multi-state Survey*. Unpublished manuscript, 2004.
6. Bissell. 2007, Op. Cit.

CHAPTER **14**

Training and Exercises for Catastrophes

Myra M. Socher

CONTENTS

Introduction 320
    Catastrophe versus Disaster: The Big Picture 320
    Catastrophe versus Disaster: Exercises 320
Training 321
    Dartmouth Interactive Media Laboratory: Virtual Terrorism Response Academy and Virtual-Medical Incident Management Institute (Managing Medical Surge) 322
    Use of Subject Matter Experts to Both Instruct in Response and Evaluate Exercises 322
        Webinars 322
Linking Training and Exercises 323
    Use of Exercises as a Primary Tool for Assessing Preparedness 323
    Why Have Exercises? 323
    Homeland Security Exercise Evaluation Program 323
    Exercise Planning Team 324
    Exercise Types 325
    Building Block Approach 327
    Exercise Documentation 327
    Exercise Design and Development: A Primer 327
    Exercise Design and Development: The Scenario 329
    Logistics 330
    Exercise Evaluation 330
    Combining Exercises Across the Country: The National Level Exercise Series 331
    Planning Timelines 332
    Preparedness Cycle 332
    Exercise Phases 332

Tabletop Exercise Design 333
The Situation Manual 333
Tabletop Formats and Facilitation Skills 335
Discussion Questions 335
Tabletop Exercise: Structure 336
Tabletop Attendee Roles 336
Agenda 336
Module One: Earthquake and Tsunami 336
Module Two: Response and Surge 336
Discussion Periods at the End of Module One and Module Two 337
Module Three: Recovery 337
Facilitator Questions 337
Hot Wash 338
References 339

A deadly contagion in the water supply cripples half of the capital, and Alex discovers that someone may be about to unleash the most devastating attack the United States has ever experienced.

Fact or fiction? Actually, an excerpt from James Patterson's latest book *Kill Alex Cross*. But, what if this was life imitating art?

INTRODUCTION

Catastrophe versus Disaster: The Big Picture

We have defined catastrophe in Chapter 1 of this book and provided some historical examples. The current history examples of the naturally occurring catastrophes include the Haitian earthquake as a geophysical event, and the famine in Somalia as a humanitarian catastrophe. But, what if the catastrophe were engineered by man—the detonation of a nuclear bomb in a heavily populated city or the release of a lethal agent such as smallpox in a confined space like the Kennedy Center in Washington, DC?

For responders to disasters on a small or large scale, it is essential that plans are understood; the methodology of response is known, and the overall response hierarchy is familiar. Note that this chapter's focus is on training for the response system in the United States, but much of it can be easily adopted for use in other countries.

Catastrophe versus Disaster: Exercises

In the characterization of catastrophes, we need to consider some of the criteria that define a catastrophe: normal day-to-day activities are not possible for private and public sector individuals; a large section of infrastructure is damaged and/or impacted; emergency services are operating with skeleton staff and often in makeshift facilities; the norm as we knew it is no more—we are unable to communicate and resources (food, medicines, shelter, etc.) are scarce. The 1918 Spanish Influenza was deemed a global public health emergency or catastrophe. Hurricane Katrina's devastation was a more contained catastrophe and will probably be viewed historically as a major disaster but not a catastrophe.

Many exercise design professionals opt not to stress their participants to the maximum to avoid the "sky is falling and there's nothing I can do about it" response. People throw up their hands in frustration and opt not to continue. However, since the advent of the Japanese tsunami—a truly catastrophic event—there is realization that "it" can in fact happen and therefore we need to prepare—to plan, to train, to exercise. Exercise criteria will differ widely—one smallpox patient could constitute the beginning of a public health catastrophe—but the overall goal for exercise designers is constant. The need exists to overwhelm the participants and force them to "inhabit" an environment where there is no structure and even the government is unable to function as expected.

TRAINING

This chapter provides an overview of the current and innovative means of training and testing response personnel and their organizations for disaster and/or catastrophe response. It contrasts the historical elements previously used with the more recent approaches developed in the last two decades.

Much of the didactic instruction is now provided in an interactive electronic medium versus the more traditional classroom model. This enables students to learn both during self-selected time slots and also at the pace best suited to their learning capability. As most students of disaster response and management are adult learners, this provides more flexibility and can reach a far wider audience than the older methods.[1]

Universities have found attrition in many classes that continue to offer the classic *one lecturer in a classroom full of students approach*. Eric Mazur, Professor of Physics and Applied Physics at Harvard, says, "I thought I was a good teacher until I discovered my students were just memorizing information rather than learning to understand the material." Today's lectures do not need to take place on a "bricks and mortar campus" as there is YouTube, iTunes, and lectures via iPods and so on.[2]

Training is now predominantly case/scenario-based and provides a "hands on" approach even when done in a virtual environment.

"Scenario-based training can provide effective decision-making training without the expense and risk of full-scale types of exercises, and can be self-paced to accommodate various levels of an individual's level of expertise and competence.

Scenario-based training helps practitioners connect theory with real-world applications/situations."[3]

Dartmouth Interactive Media Laboratory: Virtual Terrorism Response Academy and Virtual-Medical Incident Management Institute (Managing Medical Surge)

Two examples of interactive scenario-based training sponsored by grants from the Department of Homeland Security and developed by the interactive media laboratory at Dartmouth College's medical school are: the Virtual Terrorism Response Academy (VTRA)—http://iml.dartmouth.edu/education/pcpt/vtra/ and the Managing Medical Surge (MMS) module from the Virtual Medical Incident Management Institute (V-MIMI)—http://iml.dartmouth.edu/education/pcpt/vmimi/mms/, which includes an Anthrax Roundtable focusing on the management of the anthrax attacks in the National Capital Region.

"Do you know how to protect yourself and your citizens if terrorists attack using weapons of mass destruction? The Virtual Terrorism Response Academy's first course is Ops-Plus for WMD Hazmat. This interactive course offers fire, EMS and law-enforcement personnel more than 18 hours of practical, engaging training about CBRNE (chemical, biological, radiological, nuclear, and explosive) threats." The course can either be instructor-led or used individually.[4]

Use of Subject Matter Experts to Both Instruct in Response and Evaluate Exercises

Combining the emerging technology with innovative-instructional design is the hallmark of a superior distance learning or self-study program. Mentors and trainers drawn from the ranks of providers—fire, EMS, police, hospital, emergency management, and federal bureau of investigation (FBI)—offer a unique experience to learn from the masters without ever having to set foot in a lecture hall. Craig DeAtley in his 1988 course on disaster management at George Washington University coined the terms "Master of the Disaster" or "Commander of Chaos." When facing the management of a catastrophe, it is advisable to be the former and not the latter.

Webinars

A webinar is a combination of the words "web-based" and "seminar." A webinar can be a lecture, a presentation of some kind, a workshop, or an interactive meeting. Chris Garrett of Chrisg.com[5] defines the advantage of a webinar as a learning tool: "When you present your information live and interactive, the audience can question, clarify and drill down the parts that interest them [the] most. Rather than guess at what your audience most wants, allow them to ask you! This means teaching is deeper and accelerated in comparison to other forms of presenting content online."[6]

LINKING TRAINING AND EXERCISES

Use of Exercises as a Primary Tool for Assessing Preparedness

There is an intrinsic need to understand the use of exercises as the primary tool for assessing preparedness and identifying strengths and areas for improvement. Exercises enable an objective assessment of capability which, in turn, paves the way for an improved response during an actual event. They serve to test the adequacy of interagency and inter-jurisdictional agreements; refine procedures, roles, and responsibilities. They are also becoming popular as a tool to evaluate the efficacy of training programs.

Why Have Exercises?

The role of exercises in the overall preparedness model cannot be understated. Reading, listening, and learning from a didactic model constitute an excellent basis to prepare the student. However, the challenge of debating the issues with one's peers serves to solidify the thought processes. Furthermore, the ability to problem-solve in a low stress, fault-free environment provides an excellent forum for interacting with one's fellow-responders prior to an actual event. When a catastrophe occurs neither the time nor the place to be meeting your counterparts, testing your plans for the first time, or trying to determine what the command structure or lines of communication are, just to name a few benefits derived from a practice run, that is, an exercise. "Exercises provide an excellent tool to identify, analyze and quantify the strengths and gaps in our response system."[7]

Ensure that in the framework of a catastrophe exercise, the players are overwhelmed and under extreme pressure. This can be achieved by: an initial long period of little or no response; no rapidly available mutual aid; creating a sense of isolation; the loss of many colleagues—first responders and the coordinating personnel, resultant issues of concerns about one's own family, and the families of responders and emergency management personnel; and applying mental health stressors to both casualties and responders alike.

Homeland Security Exercise Evaluation Program

This is the how-to "book" on exercise design, execution, and evaluation. "Exercises allow personnel, from first responders to senior officials, to validate training and practice strategic and tactical prevention, protection, response, and recovery capabilities in a risk-reduced environment. Exercises are the primary tool for assessing preparedness and identifying areas for improvement, while demonstrating community resolve to prepare for major incidents. Exercises aim to help entities within the community gain objective assessments of their capabilities so that gaps, deficiencies, and vulnerabilities are addressed prior to a real incident."[8]

The Homeland Security Presidential Directive-8 (HSPD-8) mandated the establishment by the Department of Homeland Security of a standardized exercise policy and methodology to be used for the National Exercise Program. Common doctrine with common terminology (as seen in the National Incident Management System [NIMS]) provides the basis for interagency cooperation during an actual event. An integral component of the Homeland Security Exercise Evaluation Program (HSEEP) is the Multi-Year Training and Exercise Plan, which is established during a Training and Exercise Plan Workshop (T&EPW). Milestones are set for training and exercises and priorities are set for the evaluation of preparedness capabilities.

To develop exercises for local, state, and federal governments and to receive funding from any government agencies for this purpose, the student must ensure that they are in compliance with the HSEEP.

HSEEP Volumes I, II, III, and IV,[9] found at https://hseep.dhs.gov/pages/1001_HSEEP7.aspx, provide the foundation and guidance for developing exercises in compliance with HSEEP and therefore eligible for state and federal funding. The HSEEP website also provides access to many interesting readings and resources such as lessons learned, best practices, and templates—just to name a few.

Most areas of HSEEP are available without any special access capability although there are some sections such as certain documents in Volume IV (accessed through the secure HSEEP portal) and the National Planning Scenarios (accessed through the Lessons Learned Information Sharing. www.llis.gov) that do require a login process. Your organization will likely be able to sponsor your membership of these "secure sites." Graphics in this chapter are all accessible without a login.

Homeland Security Presidential Directive-5 (HSPD-5) which mandates the management of domestic incidents is key to both training and exercises. It provides for the following:

Purpose—"to enhance the ability of the United States to manage domestic incidents by establishing a single, comprehensive national incident management system."[10]

Policy—"to prevent, prepare for, respond to, and recover from terrorist attacks, major disasters, and other emergencies, the United States government shall establish a single and comprehensive approach to domestic incident management. The objective of the United States government is to ensure that all levels of government across the nation have the capability to work efficiently and effectively together, using a national approach to domestic incident management. In these efforts, with regard to domestic incidents, the United States government treats crisis management and consequence management as a single, integrated function, rather than as two separate functions."[11]

Exercise Planning Team

This should be structured along incident command system (ICS) principles as illustrated in Chapter 3 Exercise program management, HSEEP Volume I and shown later and is the pivotal organization for planning all exercise activities (Figure 14.1).

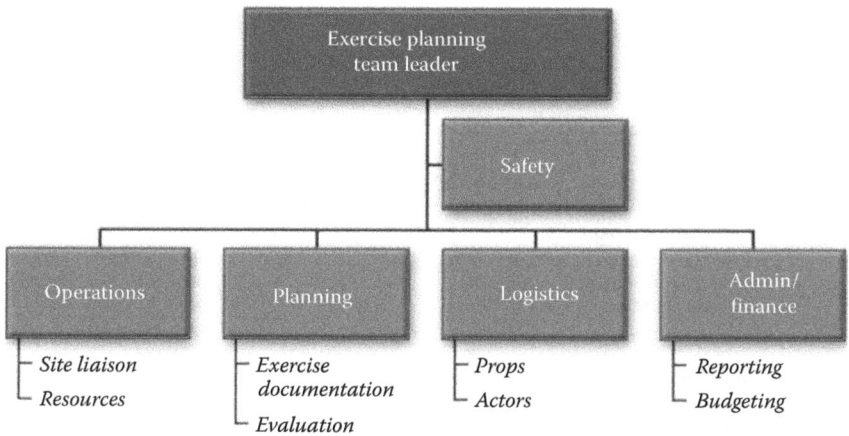

Figure 14.1 Exercise planning team. (HSEEP Volume I: *HSEEP Overview and Exercise Program Management.* Available at https://hseep.dhs.gov/support/VolumeI.pdf.)

Exercise Types

Figure 14.2, taken from Chapter 2, Exercise Program Management, HSEEP Volume I, focuses on the seven different types of exercises which comprise the two main categories: discussion- and operations-based. It provides a guide to the student on not only the primary exercise categories, but also the appropriate type to select for a specific purpose.

Utility/ Purpose		Type of Player Action	Duration	Real-Time Play?	Scope
Discussion-based exercises	Familiarize players with current plans, policies, agreements, and procedures; develop new plans, policies, agreements, and procedures	Notional; player actions are imaginary or hypothetical	Rarely exceeding 8 hours	No	Varies
Seminar	Provide overview of new or current plans, resources, strategies, concepts or ideas	N/A	2–5 hours	No	Multi- or single-agency
Workshop	Achieve specific goal or build product (e.g., exercise objectives, SOPs, policies, plans)	N/A	3–8 hours	No	Multi-agency/ single function

Figure 14.2 Exercise types. (HSEEP Volume I: *HSEEP Overview and Exercise Program Management.* Available at https://hseep.dhs.gov/support/VolumeI.pdf.)

Utility/ Purpose		Type of Player Action	Duration	Real-Time Play?	Scope
Tabletop exercise (TTX)	Validate plans and procedures by utilizing a hypothetical scenario to drive participant discussions	Notional	4–8 hours	No	Multi-agency/ multiple functions
Game	Explore decision-making process and examine consequences of those decisions	Notional	2–5 hours	No (though some simulations provide real- or near-real-time play)	Multi-agency/ multiple functions
Operations-based exercises	Validate plans, policies, agreements, and procedures; clarify roles and responsibilities; identify resource gaps	Actual; player action mimics reaction response, mobilization, and commitment of personnel and resources	May be hours, days, or weeks, depending on purpose, type, and scope of the excercise	Yes	Varies
Drill	Validate a single operation or function of an agency	Actual	2–4 hours	Yes	Single agency/ single function
Functional exercise (PE)	Evaluate capabilities, functions, plans, and staffs of Incident Command, Unified Command. Intelligence centers, or other multi-agency coordination centers (e.g., EOC's)	Command staff ctions are actual; movement of other personnel, equipment, or adversaries is simulated	4–8 hours or several days or weeks	Yes	Multiple functional areas/ multiple functions
Full-Scale exercise (FSE)	Validate plans, policies, procedures, and cooperative agreements developed in previous excercises through their actual implementation and execution during a simulated scenario; includes actual mobiliztion of resources, conduct of operations and integrated elements of functional excericse play (e.g., EOC's, command posts)	Actual	One full day or several days or weeks	Yes	Multi-angency/ multiple functions

Figure 14.2 (Continued).

Building Block Approach

The infancy-to-teen concept applies to exercise types—the more simplistic discussion-based exercise will precede the more sophisticated operations-based exercise. Not all classifications are always used. A common formula for an exercise series is tabletop, functional (command post), and full-scale. It is important to allow enough time between each for the lessons learned to be applied before the next exercise. Crawl–Walk–Run (Figure 14.3).

Exercise Documentation

Chapter 2, Exercise Planning and Conduct, HSEEP Volume II, provides a description of the documentation required for discussion- and operations-based exercises (Figure 14.4).

Exercise Design and Development: A Primer

For new exercise designers, as can be seen from the excerpt taken from HSEEP Volume II, there are numerous resources available to assist in the entire exercise process, "samples of exercise documents and formats can be found in *HSEEP Volume IV: Sample Exercise Documents and Formats*. These samples are presented as both examples and templates, intended for exercise planners to use and/or modify when designing and developing exercises." The materials presented in HSEEP Volume IV are pre-arranged in a manner consistent with the outline and contents of the HSEEP series of manuals, as described later. The content may also be searched or displayed based on user preferences and criteria input.

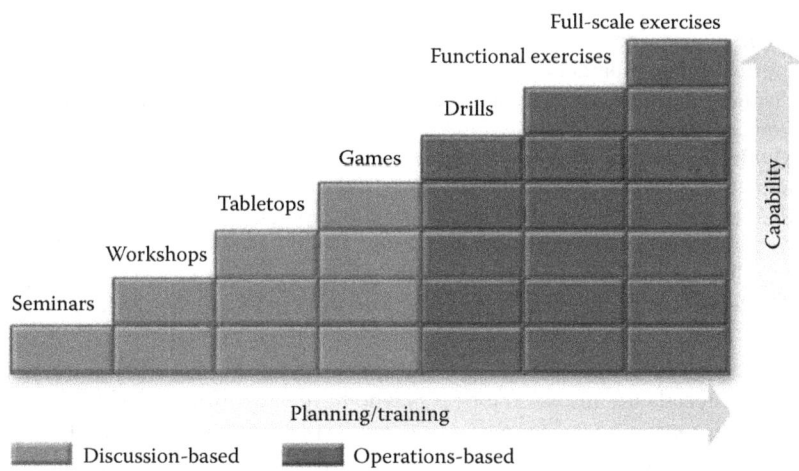

Figure 14.3 Building block approach. (HSEEP Volume I: *HSEEP Overview and Exercise Program Management*. Available at https://hseep.dhs.gov/support/VolumeI.pdf.)

Document Title	Exercise Usage	Distribution Audience	Key Document Features
Exercise evaluation guides (EEGs)	All evaluated exercises	Limited: Evaluators	Helps evaluators assess performance of capabilities, tasks, and objectives during an exercise
Situation manual (SitMan)	Discussion-based	Not limited: All exercise participants	Textual background for multimedia, facilitated exercise Includes administrative Information as well as scenario details
Multimedia presentation	Discussion-based	Not limited: All exercise participants	Supports SitMan, concisely summarizing written information Enhances exercise realism with audio/visual depiction of the scenario Focuses and drives exercise
Controller and evaluator (C/E) handbook	Operations-based	Limited: Controllers, evaluators	Supplements ExPlan with exercise administration Information and scenario details
Exercise plan (ExPlan)	Operations-based	Not limited: Players, observers	Includes general exercise information but does not contain scenario details Enables players to understand their roles and responsibilities in the exercise
Master scenario events List (MSEL)	Operations-based	Limited: Controllers, evaluators, simulators	A chronological listing of the events and injects that drive exercise play Produced in both short (i.e., quick reference) and long (i.e., all-encompassing) formats

Figure 14.4 Exercise documents. (HSEEP Volume II: *Exercise Planning and Conduct.* Available at https://hseep.dhs.gov/support/VolumeII.pdf.)

The topics provided in HSEEP Volume IV are as follows:

- Program management contains sample materials for use in developing and managing an exercise program.
- Planning contains sample materials for designing, developing, conducting, and evaluating exercises.
- Multimedia library contains video clips, sounds, and pictures that may be inserted into documentation or presentations to add a sense of realism.
- References contains homeland security community resources such as publications, websites, and acronyms/definitions.
- Volunteered materials contains examples of documentation posted voluntarily by the planners and program managers who used them in actual exercises and exercise programs.

These materials are intended for users who have varying levels of exercise experience. The information to support their use is included in the HSEEP volumes. The exercise timelines for discussion-based exercises and operations-based exercises further support the use of these materials by chronologically listing the step-by-step process and corrective actions that need to be accomplished during exercise planning and conduct. Many of the sample materials also contain brief descriptions and/or instructions for use.

Additionally, HSEEP has developed a toolkit designed to assist the exercise developer in design and development. (Access to the toolkit is restricted and is only available through the secure HSEEP portal.) The toolkit will simplify the planning process; will provide templates and guidance to aid exercise program managers; and assist in exercise conduct and evaluation in accordance with HSEEP guidance.

Once exercise planners have decided on the exercise goals and exercise type, they will need to tailor the final product to the exercising entity's needs as well as their proficiency in running exercises. It is recommended that you choose the format with which you feel most comfortable.

Exercises are like Lego for adults with the planning, dialog, and integration as the key components. Block by block, we have to build the essential components of the response initiative and ensure that all the pieces fit so as to make it work well. It is really a game that has serious implications.

Exercise Design and Development: The Scenario

The National Planning Scenarios are purely a guide and were designed to provide a base from which the target capabilities and universal task list were developed. When you design an exercise, you need to consider what it is you want to achieve—what piece of the response you want to test, what vulnerabilities you want to emphasize, and how the exercise should drive the group to try to find solutions. The scenario forces the evaluation of these criteria by using the objectives to develop the exercise evaluation plan or guides which, in turn, will highlight problem areas as well as strengths.

Chapter 4, Exercise Program Management, HSEEP Volume I, describes the four major components that comprise the exercise.

1. Capabilities—first assess what capabilities might be different for a catastrophe as compared to disasters ... for example, management and utilization of vast numbers of spontaneous volunteers. We tend to shun these folks in disasters, but we will have to avail ourselves of their assistance in a catastrophe. As a catastrophic event will overwhelm all our resources, the classic disaster-support structures will in most cases be non-functional.
2. Tasks—once we have defined the capabilities we intend to utilize in our catastrophe exercise we need to identify the critical tasks that we wish to exercise and evaluate.
3. Objectives—on the basis of the capabilities and tasks which are catastrophe-relevant, we can then use these to develop the exercise goals and objectives and then work these into the scenario.
4. Scenario—by definition, catastrophes are so large that it is not possible to take on the whole event in the scenario, so the design team will have to select a scenario that would represent a segment of the catastrophe response, perhaps a select three-county area or a metropolitan area such as the National Capital Region. It is important to build realistic catastrophe conditions into the scenario. Examples include lost communications, lack of mutual aid, delayed arrival of outside assistance, the

need to coordinate a massive post-event evacuation of the jurisdiction, arrival of federal "authorities" without prior notification, and so on.

The scenario is a chronological representation of activities leading up to an event followed by the situations that are caused by the event(s), the response that occurs, and the return of the community to pre-event status. In a catastrophe situation, the timeline will be prolonged and it is possible that there may never be a return to normalcy as previously known.

You are given the task of expanding your agency's emergency management plan to deal with catastrophic events. How do you best obtain stakeholder input for your project? Would you use a workshop or seminar or tabletop exercise?

Logistics

These are a key piece of a well-run and effective exercise and there should be considerable attention to detail in room selection, technological support, and built-in redundancy. (It is hard to use a projector if the bulb burns out and you do not have a spare one.) When a field exercise is being developed, logistics play an even more important role with numerous additional considerations such as actors and moulage; coordination between multiple locations; briefings for very important persons (VIPs); videotaping; and ensuring that all the pieces come together smoothly and in a timely manner.

To set the scene for a catastrophic exercise, we will need to ensure the availability of a large meeting space, invite large numbers of people representing numerous agencies—internal to the exercise location as well as external players to project the realism of the catastrophic event. We should write in frequent interruptions, conflicting information messages. Then add to this formula injects of personal tragedy information (i.e., it has just been learned that the entire staff directorate of the state Emergency Management Agency were killed in an explosion, and/or the local elementary, middle, and high schools were all decimated at mid-day). Make sure that the space and personnel logistics work the way the exercise team want them to, but not the way the participants might expect. Lights go out. Food disappears. Nearby toilets are overwhelmed when water pressure disappears. Create as realistic an environment as possible to prepare participants for a catastrophic event.

Exercise Evaluation

Without the evaluation there is no indicator of the level of preparedness. Strengths are identified as areas requiring improvement and ideally these "lessons learned" will be used to further refine plans and standard operating procedures (SOP) so that the response to a catastrophe that occurs further into the planning cycle will have better outcomes than if it had occurred earlier on in the cycle. To use a cliché, "we learn from our mistakes"— let's rather do that in an artificial environment than in a real one with lives at stake!

Exercise evaluation encompasses a four-pronged approach:

1. The exercise evaluation guides (EEG) which are linked to the goals and objectives and are used as a tool by evaluators (controller evaluators for operation exercises) to provide input to the After Action Report (AAR) and the improvement plan (IP).
2. The hot wash which is conducted directly after the exercise and provides participant feedback to the facilitator(s) and will also be incorporated into the AAR/IP.
3. The debrief which is a more formal forum for the exercise planning team members and does not include participants providing additional information for the AAR/IP.
4. The AAR/IP which is a formal set of documents following HSEEP format which is provided at a later date to the entity conducting the exercise. The findings may be presented during a formal AAR conference to which all participating agencies are invited. AARs can be posted on the lessons learned website mentioned earlier to be used as a planning resource by other agencies.

Combining Exercises Across the Country: The National Level Exercise Series

The purpose of these exercises is to prepare and coordinate a multiple-jurisdictional integrated response to a national catastrophic event. For example, national level exercise (NLE) 2011 was designated as a Tier I NLE. Tier I exercises (formerly known as the Top Officials exercise series or TOPOFF) are conducted annually in accordance with the national exercise program (NEP), which serves as the nation's overarching exercise program for planning, organizing, conducting, and evaluating NLEs. The NEP was established to provide the United States government, at all levels, exercise opportunities to prepare for catastrophic crises ranging from terrorism to natural disasters. NLE 2011 was a White House-directed Congressionally mandated exercise that included the participation of all appropriate federal department and agency senior officials, their deputies and staff, and key operational elements. The scenario revolved around a catastrophic earthquake occurring in the New Madrid Seismic Zone (NMSZ) and involved eight Central U.S. States: Alabama, Arkansas, Kentucky, Illinois, Indiana, Mississippi, Missouri, and Tennessee spread across four Federal Emergency Management Agency (FEMA) regions (IV, V, VI, and VII). While previous NLE's have focused on terrorism, this was the first to focus on a natural disaster.

Through a comprehensive evaluation process, the exercise assessed response and recovery capabilities both nationally and regionally. The exercise was designed to validate the following capabilities: communications; critical resource logistics and distribution; mass care (sheltering, feeding, and related services); medical surge; citizen evacuation and shelter-in-place; emergency public information and warning; emergency operations center (EOC) management; and long-term recovery.

Exercises such as NLE 2011 are an important component of national preparedness, helping to build an integrated federal, state, tribal, local, and private sector capability to manage a catastrophic event; and rapidly and effectively respond to and recover from any major disaster that occurs. Outcomes of the exercise may be found in the Quick Look Report (QLR) of June 14, 2011 at http://www.fema.gov/pdf/media/factsheets/2011/nle11_quick_look_report.pdf.

Planning Timelines

These will vary according to the complexity of the exercise. Exercise planners use shorter timelines for tabletop exercises (TTXs) than for full-scale exercises (FSEs). In addition, the TTX will only require two planning conferences (initial and final) while the functional exercise and the full-scale exercise will need three (initial, mid-term, and final). Examples of a timeline for discussion-based exercises can be found in HSEEP Volume I Appendix C, pages C1–C3.

Preparedness Cycle

Too often, the lessons learned from an exercise and recorded in an AAR (see later) are not considered when making changes to the existing emergency operations plans (EOPs) sometimes called emergency management plans (EMPs). The cycle can be termed the "cycle of life"—the exercise gives birth to a new series of issues to be answered in the next iteration of the plan. We plan, we train on the plan, we exercise the plan, we evaluate the efficacy of the plan, and then we start again.

Exercise Phases

Multi-year planning, stakeholder engagement, and resource management are essential ongoing processes that provide the basis for the planning, conduct, and evaluation of individual exercises. The success of individual exercises relies on the execution of five distinct phases, which are collectively known as the exercise cycle: foundation, design and development, conduct, evaluation, and improvement planning (Figure 14.5).

Figure 14.5 Exercise cycle. (HSEEP Volume I: *HSEEP Overview and Exercise Program Management*. Available at https://hseep.dhs.gov/support/VolumeI.pdf.)

Tabletop Exercise Design

In this chapter we focus on one aspect of exercises—the tabletop exercise. Well-defined objectives are the cornerstone of design and development. They should be simple, measurable, achievable, realistic, and task-oriented (SMART).

Key staff, decision makers, and elected and appointed officials are typical participants in a tabletop exercise. Sign-in sheets providing contact information for all participants are an essential component of the tabletop. This sets up contact lists that participants may use to share information and/or utilize during an actual event.

Timelines vary according to the complexity of the exercise. Exercise planners use shorter timelines for TTXs than for FSEs. In addition, the TTX will only require two planning conferences (initial and final) while the functional exercise and the FSE will need three (initial, mid-term, and final).

The schematic represents a timeline for a tabletop exercise (Figure 14.6).

The Situation Manual

The situation manual (SITMAN) is the "program" that the participants use during the exercise. It is a point of reference for them as they move through the exercise modules as well as providing historic and background information leading up the

Planning Conferences	Description	Prior to the Exercise
Concept and objective meeting (C&O)	Identifies the type, scope, objectives and purpose of the exercise Is typically attended by the sponsoring agency, lead exercise planner and senior officials	Prior to or concurrently with the initial planning Conference
Initial planning conference (IPC)	Lays the foundation for exercise development Gathers input from the exercise planning team on the scope, design, objectives, scenario, exercise location, schedule, duration and other details required to develop exercise documentation Assigns responsibility to planning team members	Three months
Final planning conference (FPC)	Uses a forum to review the process and procedures for exercise conduct, final drafts or exercise material and logistical requirements Ensures no major changes made to design or scope of the exercise or to any supporting documentation	Six weeks

Figure 14.6 Exercise planning conferences. Tabletop exercise planning timeline. (HSEEP Volume I: HSEEP Overview and Exercise Program Management. Available at https://hseep.dhs.gov/support/VolumeI.pdf.)

incident around which the exercise is focused. There is a section on rules of engagement and administrative and safety issues (i.e., how to evacuate the exercise facility in the case of a real-world event such as fire).

When designing a biological tabletop exercise, it is important for the planning team to discuss the elements represented in the graphic below, taken from HSEEP Volume IV (outside the secure portal):

- Is the agent chosen a communicable disease—are isolation and quarantine required?
- The lethality of the agent will determine the number of casualties. Using sufficient casualties to challenge them but not overwhelm them is usually the rule of thumb. *But, for the purposes of this book (Preparedness and Response for Catastrophic Disasters) it will be necessary to create a scenario with overwhelming numbers of both casualties and fatalities* (Figure 14.7).

The scenario provides the backdrop and storyline that drive the exercise—think of it as the "spine" around which the "body" is built. A good exercise is like a Broadway show: it is well-choreographed with something for everyone: you walk out of it feeling better than when you went in and it leaves you with food for thought. Humor is an essential component and it is important to remember that an exercise is a dry run. Most of us (fortunately) only get one shot at a catastrophic event and so we need to do it right the first time!

Ensure that in the framework of a catastrophe the players are overwhelmed and under extreme pressure. This can be achieved by: An initial long period of little or

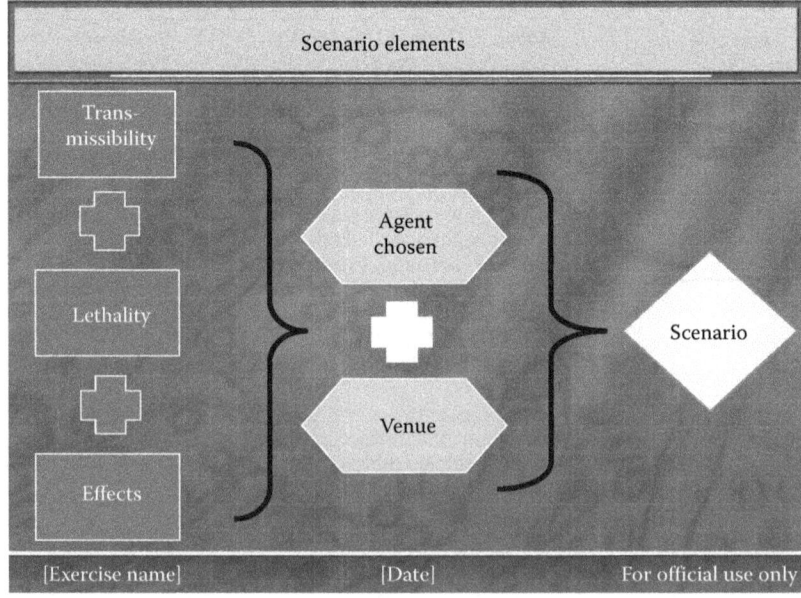

Figure 14.7 Scenario elements. (HSEEP Volume IV: *Library—Sample Exercise Materials*. Available at https://hseep.dhs.gov/hseep_vols/default1.aspx?url = home.aspx.)

no response; no rapidly available mutual aid; creating a sense of isolation; the loss of many colleagues—first responders and coordinating personnel; resultant issues of concerns about one's own family and the families of responders and emergency management personnel; applying mental health stressors to both casualties and responders alike.

For example let us use the Japanese tsunami scenario; put it in Southern California where it would hit a large coastal and low-lying population with at least two nuclear power plants in a densely populated area. Water to Southern California would be shut off; freeways would become impassable due to fallen bridges; and there would be very little escape. Naval facilities in San Diego would be on fire, as would petroleum plants near Long Beach. Mexico would spontaneously send aid. Disaster teams in California would be incapacitated and federal help would need to come from other areas of the United States. The stock market would plunge with Europe following suit and there would be outbreaks of rioting as well as subsequent disease outbreaks due to contaminated water.

Tabletop Formats and Facilitation Skills

Some facilitators are very comfortable conducting the entire exercise in a plenary (single large group) format while others prefer using functional or discipline-oriented breakout groups for discussion and the plenary group for the report-back sessions. The number of participants and location and size of rooms available may be determining factors as using a small room for a number of breakouts will result in sound issues. Another important factor to consider is the skill level of your primary facilitator. A strong facilitator is able to engage members of a large group and manage discussion while a less-experienced facilitator may be more comfortable in a smaller discipline-oriented structure—at least for the first few exercises until they have achieved a higher level of confidence in their ability. Facilitation is an acquired skill and is a role suited to a confident and outgoing individual who is also a subject matter expert. An important lesson to be learned is that so-called "war stories" or personal experiences should be kept to a minimum and only used where they provide a good illustration on how to deal with problems being confronted. Arrogance should not be mistaken for confidence and it is important to show respect to your audience and to involve all participants and not just the vocal ones.

Discussion Questions

The questions that the facilitator(s) use both to elicit information from the participants and to engender discussion constitute as important a component of the exercise as the scenario. Most experienced exercise designers will have a set of questions that they adapt to the scenario at hand, but for novices it is recommended that they consult with their exercise planning team and subject matter experts so as to arrive at a set of questions that produce the desired results. While the scenario is the spine, the questions used by the facilitators to drive the discussion constitute the cerebral cortex.

Tabletop Exercise: Structure

The moderator introduces oneself and gives a brief thumbnail sketch of credentials. One will briefly explain the rationale for conducting the exercise (what it is that we want to achieve) and define a tabletop exercise.

Tabletop Attendee Roles

- The moderator provides the overall management, control, and direction during the exercise and is the primary authority for decisions related to initiation, suspension, and termination of the tabletop. The moderator will keep the participants focused on the activities at the facility and is responsible for ensuring that the key issues are addressed.
- The facilitators are subject matter experts who are assigned to each breakout group and encourage participants to communicate with others. They keep the discussion on track and within established time limits and contrive to raise awareness around the key issues without dominating the dialog.
- Observers may participate for official or educational purposes. They should not interact with participants, contribute information or opinions, or interfere with the tabletop in any way. If sufficient time is available during the hotwash, they may be asked to briefly share their thoughts on the exercise.
- Participants will be asked to introduce themselves with a brief mention of their occupation.

Agenda

When developing the agenda do not forget to take breaks into consideration and to provide enough time at the end for an adequate hotwash. Also, the participants will need time to complete the participant feedback form. A sample participant evaluation form can be found in HSEEP Volume IV under "Exercise Conduct."

When the participants have left, the moderator will debrief the facilitators (if using breakout groups) and the scribes so that an overview of the proceedings is shared while still fresh in everyone's mind.

TTXs are usually divided into three modules with each module focusing on a different phase of the catastrophe.

Module One: Earthquake and Tsunami

The first module focuses on the earthquake and tsunami and the steps that must be taken to attempt to contain the incident (not possible) and to organize the existing resources in California. It describes the events as laid out above and the ensuing destruction, initial injuries, and deaths.

Module Two: Response and Surge

The second module is designed to simulate the escalation of the event. Players should be instructed to focus on the issues as they are presented and not "play ahead of the scenario." They will need to initiate the requests for support from outside the affected area.

Discussion Periods at the End of Module One and Module Two

Break out into groups or use a single plenary session. It is a good idea to let people take a 5 minute break before the discussion periods. If using the breakout group format:

- Remind groups to assign a recorder and/or reporter. Explain the roles of each.
- A moderator will circulate between the groups and, both facilitators and the moderator can distribute injects as a tool to encourage the group if conversation lags or to provide extra pressure for more sophisticated groups. Give the facilitators a 5 minute warning so they can have the participants wrap up and have information ready to report back.
- Ideally, the discussion session using breakouts will run approximately 20–30 minutes.
- Report back period on key issues or decisions made should not take more than 5 minutes per group.

If using the single group format:

- The moderator will use and select questions directed to the appropriate members of the audience to highlight the key issues for the group discussion.

Module Three: Recovery

The third module focuses on the disruption of services that have occurred during the event and what will need to be done to restore the affected locations to their pre-event status or as close to it as is possible. We know that almost 7 years after Katrina, there are still major issues affecting the City of New Orleans and so total recovery is not always an option or may take a very long time. The key in this module is to look at the "healing" process for infrastructure: the accompanying mental health issues, and the long-term sequelae of the effects of the earthquake and tsunami (e.g., radiation) on the survivors.

Facilitator Questions

These are used by the moderator to drive a discussion during the plenary sessions. They can also be used by facilitators of the breakout groups to ensure maintaining a focus on the issues at hand presented by the scenario and discouraging fixation on a single problem as well as deviation from the mission at hand. The planning team members should design questions focusing on their jurisdiction's preparedness capability. Special sets of questions can also be used for functional breakout groups such as health and medical, emergency management, public safety, and government.

Hot Wash

A hot wash occurs immediately following a tabletop exercise and allows the participants the opportunity to provide immediate feedback. The objective of the hot wash is to review events or key decisions that took place during the exercise and to provide an opportunity for participants to describe any immediate lessons learned and to identify barriers/gaps in mounting an effective response. It enables the moderator to capture thoughts, decisions made, and other events while they remain fresh in the participants' minds and to describe what was learned (Figure 14.8).

Although catastrophes are extremely difficult to simulate in a tabletop exercise, we should strive to approximate the conditions encountered in a catastrophe by simulating some of the accompanying problems discussed earlier—the lights go out, food disappears, nearby toilets are overwhelmed when water pressure disappears. Create as realistic an environment as possible to prepare participants for a catastrophic event.

Consider seeking the assistance of subject matter experts when designing the scenario—for an earthquake consult with seismologists and engineers.

To ensure continuity, create a timeline for additional tabletops with each focusing on a specific set of problems pertinent to the locale.

Finally, remember the circle of life—plan, train on the plan, exercise the plan, evaluate the efficacy of the plan, and then start again. Learn from the mistakes of the previous cycle.

ADDITIONAL COURSE MATERIAL

IS-120.A An Introduction to Exercises

http://training.fema.gov/EMIWeb/IS/IS120A.asp.

Course Overview

IS 120.A introduces the basics of emergency management exercises. It also builds a foundation for subsequent exercise courses, which provide the specifics of the Homeland Security Exercise and Evaluation Program (HSEEP) and the National Standard Exercise Curriculum (NSEC).

This course will introduce the student to the following concepts:

- Managing an exercise program
- Designing and developing an exercise
- Conducting an exercise
- Evaluating an exercise
- Developing and implementing an improvement plan

Figure 14.8 Additional course material.

REFERENCES

1. Gilbraith MW. 2003. *Adult Learning Methods: A Guide for Effective Instruction.* Melbourne: Krieger Publishing Company.
2. Some academics dismiss appeal, value of lectures: February 17, 2012, Washington Post. Available at http://www.sfgate.com/education/article/Some-academics-dismiss-appeal-value-of-lectures-3338136.php.
3. Neil R. Hintze: Thesis for Masters of Homeland Security, Studies at the Naval Post Graduate School, Monterey, CA, March 2008.
4. IML. *The Virtual Terrorism Response Academy,* Interactive Media Lab, Dartmouth College. Available at URL http://iml.dartmouth.edu/education/pcpt/vtra/ops-plus/1.0/ accessed on February 24, 2012.
5. Chrisg.com *Chris Garrett on New Media.* Available at URL http://www.chrisg.com/blog/accessed February 24, 2012.
6. Keyes DC, Burstein JL, Schwartz RB, and Swienton RE. 2005. Exercises and Educational Courses in Terrorism Preparedness. In *Medical Response to Terrorism: Preparedness and Clinical Practice,* Chapter 33, edited by Lippincott Williams & Wilkins, Socher MM and Leap EK. Philadelphia.
7. HSEEP Volume I: *HSEEP Overview and Exercise Program Management.* Available at https://hseep.dhs.gov/support/VolumeI.pdf.
8. HSEEP Volume II: *Exercise Planning and Conduct.* Available at https://hseep.dhs.gov/support/VolumeII.pdf.
9. HSEEP Volume III: *Exercise Evaluation and Improvement Planning.* Available at https://hseep.dhs.gov/support/VolumeIII.pdf.
10. HSEEP Volume IV: *Library—Sample Exercise Materials.* Available at https://hseep.dhs.gov/hseep_vols/default1.aspx?url=home.aspx.
11. HSPD-5 *Homeland Security Presidential Directive-5.* —Subject: Management of Domestic Incidents. Available at http://www.fas.org/irp/offdocs/nspd/hspd-5.html.

CHAPTER 15

Catastrophes in Haiti and Japan

Thomas Kirsch, Nobuaki Kiriu, and Rick Bissell

CONTENTS

The 2010 Haiti Earthquake and Its Complexities 342
Summary Characteristics.. 343
International Disaster and Humanitarian Response Systems 343
The Emergency Response to the Haitian Earthquake 345
    The Haitian Government Response 345
    United Nations Response 346
    The United States Government Response..346
    Department of Defense 348
    NGO/Private Voluntary Organization (PVO) Response............................. 349
    Information and Data Collection/Management 349
Specific Response Functions after the Haitian Earthquake 349
    Search and Rescue Response 349
    Medical Response 350
    Public Health Response 351
    Shelter... 351
    Water and Sanitation 352
    Food... 353
Conclusions and Summary for Haiti... 353
The Great East Japan Earthquake of 11 March 2011 and Its Complexities........... 354
Fukushima Daiichi Nuclear Power Station Failure 356
    Overview 356
Summary Characteristics.. 357
Background: Japan's Emergency Preparedness and Response Systems................ 358
Disaster Healthcare... 359
Overview of the Japanese Response 360
    Search and Rescue 360
    Medical Response 362

Response to the Fukushima Daiichi NPS Failure 366
    March 11 367
    March 12 367
    March 14 368
    March 15 368
    March 16 368
    March 17 368
    March 18 369
    March 19–24 369
    March 25 369
Conclusions 370
References 372

THE 2010 HAITI EARTHQUAKE AND ITS COMPLEXITIES

The Haitian earthquake of January 12, 2010 was a catastrophe for many reasons, but most importantly because it destroyed the capitol city and the government capacities. The management of the response was further challenged because it was far more massive than usual, and the traditional leadership was killed or incapacitated in the event.

The earthquake was not particularly strong, registering as a magnitude 7.1, but it created a "perfect storm" of devastation. It destroyed the capital of the poorest country in the Western hemisphere causing widespread devastation and deaths due to sub-standard construction and lack of urban planning. It incapacitated an already weak government, destroying 28 out of 29 ministry buildings, leaving many civil servants either dead or busy recovering their lives and grieving the loss of family and friends.[1] The United Nations headquarters also collapsed, killing the Special Representative and 102 other senior staff who would generally coordinate international response efforts. An estimated 97,000 dwellings were destroyed and 188,000 buildings were damaged, resulting in 230,000 deaths, 300,000 injured, and over 1 million people displaced.[2] About 2.5% of the country's total population died and another 3% were injured.

Haiti is the poorest country in the Western Hemisphere with more than 75% of the population living on <$2 per day prior to the earthquake.[3] Since 1982, the population of Port-au-Prince has expanded by 42% to an estimated 3.0–3.5 million inhabitants,[4] more than twice the population that the government believes can be reasonably supported. Of these, more than 85% were living in slums.[5] In 2006, 43% of the population lacked access to safe water, 81% did not have access to adequate sanitation[6] and over 2.4 million people were food-insecure.[7] Common public services, such as education, sanitation, and healthcare had been mostly taken over by private sector institutions or non-governmental organizations (NGOs) funded by international donors. As a result, the government is weak, torn by political rivalries, corruption, and severely limited funds. The government had no means to respond effectively on its own; there is no standing army. The police force is small and unprofessional and its small civil protection department was totally destroyed. The government also had practically no financial resources to mobilize private sector responders to assist in the relief efforts.

Because of the fragility of the government, the United Nations established MINUSTAH as a peacekeeping force in Haiti starting in 2004 (after the removal of President Aristide) to strengthen the rule of law and support the government.[8] However, the earthquake destroyed the UN MINUSTAH headquarters killing essentially the entire leadership. The loss of so many senior UN staff crippled the UN's ability to respond in the initial weeks following the earthquake.

Another problem was that the earthquake occurred in America's backyard; only 600 miles south of Florida and 200 miles from Puerto Rico. This proximity to the United States and the unprecedented response of the US press increased national and international focus on the disaster. This led to a massive response by the United States government (USG) (the largest international disaster response ever) and to dozens of non-traditional organizations and thousands of individuals to pour into Haiti further confusing the response.

SUMMARY CHARACTERISTICS

The Japanese have described their catastrophe in terms of four characteristics. In regards to the Haitian earthquake, they are

1. *"Extra large disaster"*: Although the area impacted by the earthquake was relatively small, it occurred in the midst of 1/3 of the total population of the country.
2. *Complex disaster*: Multiple disasters occurred with the loss of the Haitian government, the UN leadership and the destruction of key infrastructure, including the port and airport.
3. *Dispersed disaster*: not Haiti.
4. *The loss of abilities of governing bodies:* The earthquake destroyed the capital city severely damaging the usual response systems and capacities.

INTERNATIONAL DISASTER AND HUMANITARIAN RESPONSE SYSTEMS

When countries call for international assistance with a disaster within their territory, there are specific laws, organizations, and methods used. The primary responsibility for international disaster response rests with the government of the affected country, assisted by the United Nations through the host country Representative and the Office for the Coordination of Humanitarian Assistance (UN) (OCHA). However, most of the actual delivery of services is provided by NGOs, such as Medicien Sans Frontiers (Doctors without Borders), the International Rescue Committee and many Red Cross/Red Crescent societies. Most of these organizations are based in the United States and Europe, but Asian organizations are being created rapidly. These organizations use private donations. However, most of their funds to provide the food, water, shelter, and healthcare needed by the people are contracted by international donors, such as the Office of Foreign Disaster Assistance (OFDA) and World Bank.

The organizational framework employed by the UN OCHA to manage the response is called the "cluster system." The cluster system is a hierarchical and scalable management structure similar to the National Response Framework of the U.S. Government. A "cluster" represents a specific technical area that provides specific services or commodities (see Table 15.1). Each cluster has a lead organization, most headed by UN agencies, which are responsible for coordinating the activities of the NGOs and agencies actually providing services to the people. The cluster system was first introduced in 2005, and it has had limited success, particularly in managing the response to an acute natural disaster. A primary flaw of the cluster system is that the responding NGOs do not work directly for the UN, but contract with other funding organizations and so there is no direct reporting to, or significant consequences that the UN can employ.

Historically, the U.S. Government response to global disasters is coordinated by the OFDA under the United States Agency for International Development (USAID) within the Department of State. OFDA's role is to supplement and support the affected country's government response efforts, while working within the greater United Nation's response system. They also support the US Embassy and coordinate with other donor governments, international organizations, UN agencies, and NGOs. They do not actually provide relief, but assess needs, give grants to NGOs to provide services and assess compliance. The Department of Defense regularly works in concert with USAID/OFDA to respond to international disasters. The Department of Defense (DoD) has unique capabilities in logistics, transportation, assessment, and security that no other agency possesses.

Table 15.1 UN Clusters and Lead Agencies

Cluster Name	Lead Agency
Agriculture	Food and Agricultural Organization (FAO)
Camp Coordination and Camp Management (CCCM)	United Nations High Commissioner for Refugees (UNHCR)/International Organization for Migration (IOM)
Early recovery	United Nations Development Program (UNDP)
Education	United Nations Children's Fund (UNICEF)/Save the children
Emergency shelter	United Nations High Commission for Refugees (UNHCR)/International Federation of the Red Cross (IFRC)
Emergency Telecommunications Cluster (ETC)	OCHA/WFP/UNICEF
Food aid	World Food Programme (of the United Nations) (WFP)
Health	World Health Organization (WHO)
Logistics	World Food Program (WFP)
Nutrition	UNICEF
Protection	United Nations High Commission for Refugees (UNHCR)
Water and Sanitation (WASH)	UNICEF

THE EMERGENCY RESPONSE TO THE HAITIAN EARTHQUAKE

Early on the response was chaotic with the loss of the leadership, the widespread destruction and the severely reduced logistic infrastructure that made moving people and supplies into, and around Port-au-Prince, extremely difficult. Things improved rapidly over the first 2 weeks with the opening of the port and airport and the increasing number of expert personnel, equipment, and supplies. Unlike prior global catastrophes, the military, especially the US military, had the greatest capacities and played a crucial, but sometimes conflicting role in the management of the response.

The Haitian Government Response

The Haitian Government had limited response resources before the earthquake and those that existed were severely impacted. In many countries it is the army that provides the major response capacities, but Haiti has no standing army, and only a small police force, but local police stations collapsed, killing staff and destroying vehicles. The *Système National de Gestion des Risques et des Désastres* (National Disaster Risk Management System) was established in 1999 but is small, sustained heavy losses and the emergency operations center was destroyed. The *Ministère de l'Intérieur et des Collectivités Territoriales* (Ministry for the Interior) has the main responsibility for disaster management and operates through the *Direction de la Protection Civile* (Department of Civil Protection). The *Direction de la Protection Civile* (Department of Civil Protection of Haiti) (DPC) is responsible for operational coordination and is thus similar to the Federal Emergency Management Agency (FEMA) in the United States. However, national coordination is limited by weak capacities and because municipalities are often loyal to mayors, and not the national government. Furthermore, misuse of aid is common with officials using it for their advantage (e.g., in election campaigns) or withholding it from their opponents.

Despite the losses and prior problems, the government attempted to coordinate relief efforts with the assistance of the United Nations and the U.S. Government. A management framework was established in 2 weeks led by the Prime Minister as part of the High Level Coordination Committee. Under this, the Coordination Support Committee and the Presidential Commission on Recovery and Reconstruction (PMCC) were created and included the United Nations, development agencies, international militaries, and bi-lateral donors. However, the government had no capacity to actually directly deliver services to the affected people. The US embassy provided critical logistic and communication support to the Haitian government and collaborated with the World Bank to temporarily fund the government and rebuild the state's capacity to operate. The World Bank took over the payroll functions of the government employees to encourage their return to work.

The government published the "Action Plan for the Reconstruction and the Development of Haiti" with the assistance of the UN, the Inter-American Development Bank, the World Bank and the European Union.[9] The Action Plan estimated that $3.9 billion was needed for the first 18 months and $11.5 billion for long-term reconstruction. On March 31, the plan was presented at an international donors' conference and more than $9 billion was pledged, with $5 billion for 2010–11.

United Nations Response

The UN headquarters collapsed with the earthquake, killing the leadership and destroying offices, records, computers, and essentially everything needed to conduct business. Critical data were lost, and there were no backups available. The focus of the United Nations for the first week was the search and rescue of their colleagues and friends, as well as to personally recover from the damage to their own homes. The next task was to find a new space for work and to set up a complete office. It took 1 week to get UN staff set up near the recovering airport at the Logistics Base (Log Base). This became the emergency operations center (EOC) for the international response, while the Americans still worked out of the heavily fortified embassy. Because of the personal impact to its staff in Haiti, the UN sent in a completely new management team and staff, but with limited Haitian experience.

With the help of quickly-deployed outside personnel, OCHA took charge of the humanitarian response by quickly launching a flash appeal for funding from the international community and starting the "cluster system" to coordinate disaster relief.[10] The two greatest constraints were the disrupted UN leadership and the overwhelming number of inexperienced responding organizations attending the cluster meetings. The UN was also initially thinly staffed to run the cluster system and the cluster leads were often rapidly changed, resulting in the breakdown of continuity and management style. Coordinating the NGOs proved especially difficult due to the sheer number of organizations that arrived. In the health cluster, more than 300 NGOs participated in the meetings, when normally this number would be 15–20. This added significantly to the complexity discussed in other chapters of this book.

Daily meetings were held at the Logistics Base, but initially outdoors due to the lack of facilities. The meetings were held in English and thus the Government of Haiti and local organizations were unable to participate. Because local actors were not included in the response, information on national capacity was absent, resulting in its underestimation and underutilization by humanitarian organizations, just as was described in the Bissell and Wachtendorf chapters describing how catastrophes result in decisions being made by outsiders due to the loss of local capacity. All these early difficulties led to a great deal of duplication in services provided in certain sectors and major gaps and the absence of relief in others. The strong military lead of the relief process was largely due to the inability of the cluster structure to provide a strong decision-making forum with international and national partners.

The United States Government Response

The United States government also faced significant difficulties in its response efforts in Haiti. The overwhelming event, the proximity to the United States and the loss of the United Nations and Haitian government, led the United States government to change the way it traditionally responds to an international disaster. The greatest change was the use of a "Whole of Government" approach that was implemented after the President declared that the entire United States government would do whatever was necessary to help Haiti. This was a significant deviation from all prior foreign responses and there was no experience or management structure existing. Because of this, the management in Washington evolved rapidly over the first 7–10 days as the various agencies tried to work in areas in which they were not traditionally involved. In addition to the routine USAID/OFDA and DoD (all branches response), other responding agencies included the Departments of Homeland Security, State, Transportation, Treasury, and Health and Human Services, US Peace Corps, FEMA, US Army Corps of Engineers, and the United States Geological Survey. These new agencies struggled to incorporate themselves into the international response structure and often were unable to provide significant support. The United States government spent $1.1 billion on the Haiti response in the first 6 months alone, which was 10 times greater than any prior foreign disaster response.

At the time of the earthquake, key leadership positions at USAID and OFDA were either vacant or had just been appointed. The head of USAID had only started work 5 days before the earthquake, and the new USAID Mission Director arrived in Haiti almost exactly 24 hours before the earthquake. There were also many staff and leadership positions still open within the agencies. With the implementation of the whole of government approach, this further blurred the chain of command which led to the appointment of a special ambassador entitled the Office of the Response Coordinator (ORC) intended to coordinate the overall response between the many different departments and agencies. The Ambassador deployed to Haiti on January 16th but the ORC remained critically understaffed and under resourced until February 19th. Unfortunately, this position was completely unrecognized by the traditional responders in USAID and the Embassy and its mission was poorly defined. More importantly the ORC had no independent budget for organizing or implementing plans and projects.

The OFDA sent a Disaster Assessment Response Team into Haiti within 24 hours, starting with 17 members, and eventually expanding to 34. The team is organized along a traditional Incident Command System structure into six major functional areas: Management, Operations, Planning, Logistics, Administration, and Communications. The team included experts in disaster response operations, logistics, communications, information management, safety and security, as well as technical specialists in food and nutrition, shelter and settlements, search and rescue, water and sanitation (WASH), and civil-military liaisons. The core functions of the team are assessment, coordination, and technical support for the response, delivery of relief commodities, grant making, and monitoring and evaluation. The team helped develop and implement a United States government response strategy and coordinated relief efforts with the Haitian government and United Nations, donors such as Department for International Development (UK) (DfID), European Commission–Humanitarian Aid and Civil Protection (ECHO), and the World Bank. By the 6th week of the response, USAID programmed more than $400 million to address immediate food, water, health, and shelter needs for earthquake-affected populations.

Another major deviation from a traditional response was that of senior officials and politicians from the United States government in Washington, DC. Because of the high-profile nature of the event, and the prior criticisms of the United States government response to Hurricane Katrina, many policy makers became enmeshed in the day-to-day running of the disaster response, thus repeating one of the mistakes made in the response to Hurricane Katrina. Moreover, the strategic leadership from Washington was made more difficult by the limited availability of accurate information from Haiti and limited disaster management experience. This has been described by many people in Washington, Haiti, and Miami as the "1,000 mile screwdriver" which made daily operations in the field difficult.

Department of Defense

The US military played a much greater role in the Haitian response than in a prior foreign disaster, spending over $250 million and deploying 22,000 members, with 8,000 on the ground in Haiti. The reasons for this are many including the history of US military involvement in Haiti, the fact that Haiti had essentially no military, the loss of the United Nations and MINUSTAH leadership, and ironically because the deputy-commander of the Southern Command (SOUTHCOM) happened to be in Port-au-Prince during the earthquake. Their major focus was on logistics and security, and included specific activities such as re-opening the airport and port, clearing roads, transporting supplies, and supporting other agencies. The US military, along with militaries from Canada, Argentina, France, and the United Kingdom, provided field hospitals, cutter equipment, hospital ships, and cargo ships and made air deliveries of water, food, medical supplies, and non-food items (see Figure 15.1).

Figure 15.1 US Urban Search and Rescue Team in Port-au-Prince. "Urban Search and Rescue Team surveys the destruction caused by the earthquake in Port-au-Prince before continuing recovery efforts with assistance from US military personnel." (http://www.navy.mil/view_single.asp?id=80521.)

SOUTHCOM is one of 10 unified Combatant Commands in the Department of Defense and is responsible for operations in Central and South America, and the Caribbean. The Haiti response was entitled, "Operation Unified Response" and the US military stood up a Joint Task Force (JTF), which arrived in Haiti 24 hours after the earthquake. Because of their overwhelming presence (8,000 vs. 34 OFDA staff on the ground), the military became deeply involved in all aspects of the response, from leadership, planning, and coordination to the delivery of food to camps.

NGO/Private Voluntary Organization (PVO) Response

For decades, Haiti has depended on NGOs and private enterprises to deliver social services throughout the country. Before the earthquake, it was estimated that up to 3,000 NGOs were working in the country.[11] Traditionally, between 25 and 40 international NGOs respond to a global disaster, but in Haiti more than 400 health-based NGOs alone responded. This further overwhelmed the management infrastructure and bogged the cluster meetings down with the need to repetitively explain just the basics of response to the new NGOs. As numerous NGOs flooded Haiti, there was competition for space and problems of access to coordination and communication structures. Perhaps only 20% of NGOs arriving in Haiti had the necessary experience, skills, and tools to appropriately respond and to work within the UN cluster management system. As a result, a large number of NGOs were delivering aid unsuitable to the situation, or duplicating other's efforts while not addressing pressing needs. Furthermore, in the aftermath of the earthquake, NGOs were neither regulated nor held accountable as they should have been, as evidenced by the problems surrounding the adoption of Haitian children.

Information and Data Collection/Management

The difficulty in collecting data on needs and resources immediately after the earthquake greatly hampered relief efforts, but the lack of compiling data, analysis, and the creation of useful information for planners and responders worsened the problem. The current international system relies heavily on NGOs to collect and report data through the clusters, but NGO staff often have limited assessment skills, the collection methods are not consistent and there are few resources and people identified to analyze and propagate the information. The multiplicity of information sources and reports hindered rather than helped the response.

SPECIFIC RESPONSE FUNCTIONS AFTER THE HAITIAN EARTHQUAKE

Search and Rescue Response

The United States government deployed six urban search and rescue (USAR) teams with 511 members to Haiti. The first arrived on January 13th (24 hours after the event) and the final on the 16th. Four teams were activated by FEMA and had no prior international experience or training. The reported number of lives saved by American USAR teams was 47. International USAR teams were deployed from Iceland, Chile, Spain, France, the Netherlands, Great Britain, and China. Many international teams focused on rescuing non-Haitians at the Hotel Montana and the UN Headquarters. In total, 43 international USAR teams deployed to Haiti and rescued 136 individuals.[12,13] The six teams deployed by the United States alone cost $35 million.

Medical Response

The lessons learned regarding the medical response:

1. Foreign medical teams were critical to providing care because of the widespread destruction of the already very weak healthcare infrastructure.
2. Many international organizations and particularly individuals who responded did not have the proper skill, training or logistical support and potentially added to the difficulties of the response.
3. Medical interventions were routinely done that were far beyond the capacity of the prior Haitian standards and expertise (e.g., complex reconstructive surgery and the widespread use of external fixatures for fracture treatment). This led to great difficulties in providing long-term care as the acute care teams left after a few weeks.

Over 300,000 people were immediately injured by collapsing buildings and needed immediate emergency medical care, often requiring surgical intervention, for severe and critical injuries. However, even before the earthquake, Haiti's governmental healthcare system was barely functioning and healthcare facilities were not equipped to respond to a disaster. Then the healthcare sector was devastated: The Ministère de la Santé Publique et de la Population (MSPP) building collapsed and 60% of hospitals in the capital were severely damaged. The facilities that remained in operation, and later, the clinics and hospitals set up by international teams became quickly overwhelmed.

Local Haitians, NGOs, various militaries, and some foreign government teams provided emergency medical and health-related assistance within 24 hours. Initially, with 300,000 injured and the extremely limited lack of facilities and supplies, care was crude at best. Healthy people also flocked to medical centers that had comfortable provisions (water, electricity, etc.), which further overwhelmed the limited resources. Mobile clinics were eventually used to provide care to people in hard to reach areas. As more and more resources arrived, the care reached a higher level, and then (unfortunately) reached a standard far beyond the capacities of the existing Haitian healthcare system. Since patients still needed care after their operations, post-operative systems became overwhelmed as well. Hospital ships from the United States and other nations arrived, but they too were overwhelmed quickly, mostly because there was almost nowhere to discharge patients to back on land, especially those recovering from complex operations. Many patients were evacuated to the United States for an extremely high level of care under US standards.

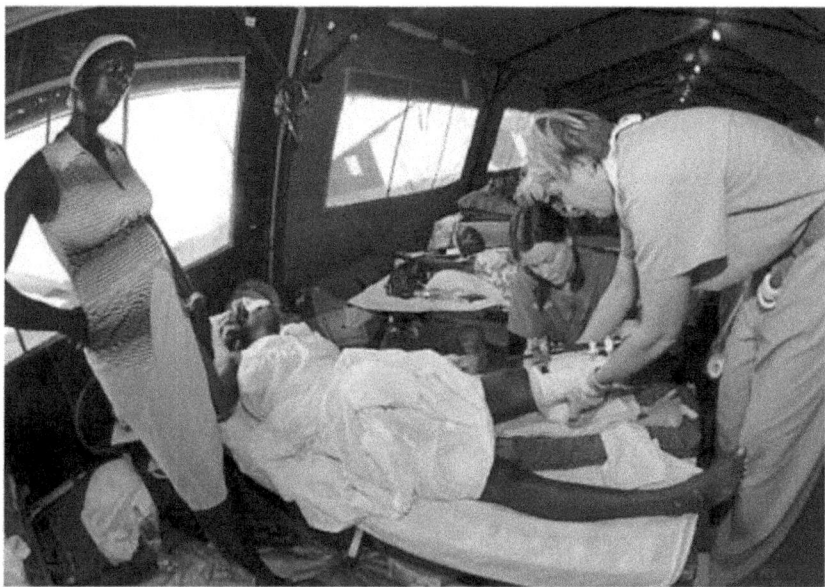

Figure 15.2 Hospital care provided by International Personnel. (Courtesy of: http://www.navy.mil/view_single.asp?id=81958.)

The already extremely weak public healthcare system in Port-au-Prince was destroyed by the earthquake, leaving most of the people without any care as the NGOs left. The need for the long-term and sustainable reconstruction of the healthcare system is a high priority for Haiti (see Figure 15.2).

Public Health Response

In parallel with the initial emergency medical response, efforts were made to meet fundamental public health needs and conduct epidemiologic surveillance. To monitor disease trends and detect outbreaks, Haiti's MSPP, the Pan-American Health Organization (PAHO), the Centers for Disease Control and Prevention (CDC) and other agencies launched an infectious disease surveillance system and started a nation-wide immunization program. Despite this, cholera was imported into Haiti during the response and the resulting epidemic has caused thousands of deaths.[14]

Shelter

Approximately 1.5 million Haitians were displaced by the earthquake, leading to the creation of over 1,000 spontaneous camps in the Port-au-Prince area. Initially many people also left Port-au-Prince to live with family and friends, which put great pressure on rural communities. Emergency shelters such as tents and tarpaulins were rapidly distributed. Transitional shelters made of a concrete

Figure 15.3 Tent City in Haiti. (Courtesy of: http://www.navy.mil/view_single.asp?id=81126.)

foundation and timber or steel frame were built. The Shelter Cluster estimates that on average it reached 100,000 people per week during the first 4 months of the response. The construction of permanent housing has been more controversial because of land rights and politics and because many of the homeless had lived as squatters prior to the earthquake.

The goal after a disaster is to "build back better" and so settlement strategies aim to relieve the overcrowding present in Port-au-Prince before the earthquake and to enforce land use and building safety codes (see Figure 15.3).

Water and Sanitation

Prior to the earthquake, Haitians had limited access to safe drinking water with only half of Port-au-Prince's population receiving tap water through the municipal system.[15] This meant that many people drank from unclear springs, rivers, and wells causing diarrhea, dysentery, and hepatitis. PAHO listed water-borne diseases as one of the leading causes of death in Haiti.[16]

Access to potable water was one of the top priorities of the international community's response. The WASH cluster organized the distribution of water bottles, trucks, and bladders while working to restore the Port-au-Prince water system. Remarkably, in <30 days, Port-au-Prince's municipal water authority was producing 50% more water than before the earthquake due to improved access to fuel.[17] By the end of April, 1.3 million people were receiving treated water.[18]

Figure 15.4 Distribution of Food Aid in Haiti. (Courtesy of: http://www.navy.mil/view_single.asp?id=81124.)

Food

During the emergency phase, the goal was to provide enough food by any means to meet the needs of the people and prevent civil unrest. This meant the delivery of ready-to-eat-meals, food rations, and rice by truck and helicopter. These activities quickly became more organized and used scheduled distribution points and the targeting of vulnerable populations such as women and children. A rapid food security assessment in February showed that half of Haitian households commonly lacked adequate food, and that those in camps had even worse access.[19] By the end of March when the government of Haiti decided to end general food distribution, about 4 million Haitians had received food assistance.[20] An important consideration for providing food aid after a disaster is to ensure that the mass distribution of food stocks does not ruin the local market and negatively impact the rural economy. Food aid distributions have not had a major impact on the price of rice, the most important staple food in Haiti (see Figure 15.4).

CONCLUSIONS AND SUMMARY FOR HAITI

The Haitian earthquake and its response were a true catastrophe with one of the greatest losses of life recorded in modern history and the destruction of the heart of the county's capitol. The earthquake and its vast destruction of critical infrastructure, including much of the standing government, led the country to seek vast quantities of immediate and long-term international assistance. But the response was complicated and disjointed because of its massive scope and the loss of traditional leadership. This event presents one kind of challenge for those who would plan responses to catastrophes ... how to plan a response to an event in which many of the key priority-setting and resource deployment decisions will be made by foreign nationals. In disaster response, most of the world's international assistance organizations expect to be able to work within priority frameworks developed by the host government. In catastrophes, that may well not always be the case. The overarching key lessons include

- Planning for the loss of local, state, and national government and international agency capacities is critical in an era of increasing urban disasters.
- During the acute phase of a disaster response is not the time to completely reorganize the response management system.
- Catastrophic planning needs to include creative ways to improve rarely-needed surge capacity, especially for personnel.
- Because of the need for massive logistical support, the military will always play a key role in catastrophe response. Civilian-military cooperation and coordination mechanisms need to be strengthened.
- The use of untrained and inexperienced organizations and government agencies further complicates the response and may do more harm than good. Nonetheless, response coordination agencies need to re-think how to coordinate and (hopefully productively) utilize such emergent groups.

THE GREAT EAST JAPAN EARTHQUAKE OF 11 MARCH 2011 AND ITS COMPLEXITIES

Japan is one of the most earthquake-prone countries in the world. The island country was formed by the subduction of the Pacific plate under the eastern Asia continental shelf and, as a result, is a land of volcanoes and frequent tremors. On March 11, 2011, at 14:46 (2:46 p.m. local time), an earthquake of magnitude 9.0 occurred offshore of the north-east area of Japan, 130 km east-southeast of the Ojika peninsula (Epicenter: latitude 38.6 north, longitude 142.52 east, 24 km deep, magnitude 9.0 by Richter Scale). Its seismic intensity level by Japan Meteorological Agency Seismic Intensity Scale was measured as seven at its maximum in the Northern area of Miyagi Prefecture. This was the largest earthquake observed in Japan and the seismic ground motion was observed all over Japan, centering in its eastern portion.[21] The source region was approximately 450 km long and 200 km in width. There is a possibility that this source region includes six zones for long-term risk assessment conducted by the Earthquake Research Committee of the Headquarters for Earthquake Research Promotion.[22] One of the zones (Miyagi-oki area) is expected to cause an earthquake about M 7.5 with a probability of 99% within 30 years. It had been expected to be M 8 if it occurs with the next zone. However, an earthquake that interlocks all of those zones simultaneously had not been predicted to occur.[23]

The earthquake generated a massive tsunami. Approximately 30 minutes after the earthquake, the tsunami reached and hit the east coast. The recorded maximum height of the tsunami tide was 9.3 m (30.5 ft) at Soma, Fukushima Prefecture. The traces of higher tides (more than 10 m or 33 ft) have been detected. The run-up height of the tsunami wave was recorded at 40.5 m (132.5 ft), the highest ever observed in Japan.[24]

Taro town in Iwate Prefecture is notorious as a tsunami suffering place having lost many lives over the centuries. So, it built a huge sea wall against tsunamis. After more than 30 years of building, repairs and expansions, it was completed at 10 m (33 ft) of height from the sea level and the total length amounted to 2,433 m (1.52 miles). This wall was called "The Great Wall in Taro." It was able to withstand the tsunami caused by the Great Chilean Earthquake in 1960 and Taro had little damage though other areas had great damage. However, the wall was destroyed by this huge 2011 tsunami, and the number of the victims in Taro amounted to 146 out of 2,466 citizens.[25,26]

Approximately 41 minutes after the earthquake, the first tsunami wave hit the Fukushima Daiichi nuclear power plant complex, located on the coastline in Fukushima prefecture.[27] Of the six reactors in the complex, three were already shut down for previously scheduled maintenance and the other three operating reactors immediately shut down when the earthquake was detected, with power to supply the pumps that circulates the plants' cooling waters being supplied by backup generators.[28] Even though the complex had been designed to be tsunami-proof, the engineering design had not anticipated waves as high as came with this tsunami, and the complex was soon inundated. With the flooding came the destruction of the generators supplying the water pumps, and over the next few days the world watched in horror as the three operating reactors overheated, suffered explosions, and melted down, with the release of significant amounts of both air-borne and water-borne radioactive contamination. After much confusion regarding how to control the plant and protect the public, a 20 km radius mandatory evacuation zone was enforced, affecting approximately 78,000 residents. Another two rings of suggested and optional evacuation covered another 68,000 people.[29]

The death toll of this earthquake and tsunami, as of 14 October, 2011, is 15,824 confirmed dead, with an additional 3,847 people missing and presumed dead, for an estimated death toll of approximately 20,000 people.[30] More than 90% of the deaths were caused by drowning, and approximately 65% of those who perished were age 60 or older.[31] Again, using October 2011 data, 118,640 housing units were completely destroyed, and another 181,836 homes were significantly damaged.[32] The result of the lost or unlivable housing was about 556,000 people homeless and evacuated, reduced 6 months later in October 2011, down to 65,753 homeless.[33,34] The estimated *direct* damage to capital stock (public building and infrastructure, capital, housing, and private corporate facilities) is estimated to be approximately 16–25 trillion yen (around $205–320 billion). This does not include the cost of rehabilitating thousands of square kilometers of cesium-contaminated soils.[35,36]

FUKUSHIMA DAIICHI NUCLEAR POWER STATION FAILURE

Overview

When the Great East Japan Earthquake occurred at 2:46 p.m., three reactors out of six reactors at the Fukushima Daiichi Nuclear Power Station (NPS) complex (reactors 1, 2, and 3) automatically stopped. The other three reactors were already shut down at that time for previously planned maintenance. The external power sources were cut off by the direct impact of the earthquake. However, the emergency generators started to cover them. Forty-one minutes after the earthquake, the first tsunami wave hit the Fukushima Daiichi NPS and more tsunami waves followed one after another. All the facilities, at the complex were inundated, including generators, and it caused the complete loss of electrical power sources. Electricity is needed to power the water pumps that keep the reactor basins cool.

The result was the inability to pump water to the emergency reactor core cooling systems at Reactors 1 and 2 and the loss of the reactor cooling system at Reactor 3. Tokyo Electric Power Company (TEPCO) informed the Nuclear and Industrial Safety Agency (NISA) of these incidents in accordance with the articles of the special law of Emergency Preparedness for Nuclear Disasters. Cooling down of the spent fuel pools of Reactors 1–4 also became difficult.

In spite of all the dramatic, heroic, and ingenious efforts to cool the fuel rods, explosions, thought to be from accumulated hydrogen in the containment vessels, occurred in succession. Reactor 1 exploded on March 12, then Reactor 3 on March 14 and Reactor 4 on March 15. Fire also broke out following the explosion at Reactor 4. Reactor 2 also suffered a huge explosion on March 15. [37,38] As a result of these explosions and fires, radioactive material was released out of the plant. It spread over in the form of airborne plumes and contaminated water. The Japanese government initially assessed the failure as Level 4 on the International Nuclear Event Scale which means an accident with local consequences. As the accident advanced, the level was raised to five by the NISA on March 18 which means an accident with wider consequences, similar to the Three Mile Island accident in 1979. Though other international experts or agencies insisted that the level of this accident should be higher, NISA persisted its assessment. However, the NISA eventually raised the accident level to 7 on April 12 which means Major Accident and is the worst in this scale. This signifies a major release of radioactive material with widespread health and environmental effects requiring implementation of planned and extended countermeasures. This accident was the second Level 7 accident in the history. The first one was the Chernobyl disaster occurred on April 26, 1986.[39,40]

On April 2, a crack was found on a surface of the pit storing electric cables near the intake channel of Reactor 2, and from it contaminated water was flowing out into the sea.[41] In Reactor 4, highly contaminated puddles were found inside the building.[42] While trying to stop this leakage, TEPCO had to discharge the low-level radioactive water accumulated in the Radioactive Waste Treatment Facilities to transfer the highly-concentrated radioactive waste water as an emergency measure.[43] Since that time, soil and structures within at 20–50 km radius of the plant have been found to be contaminated by cesium and other various isotopes. Cold shutdown of all three damaged plants was not achieved until some 6 months later, in the Fall of 2011. Prime Minister Noda declared the completion of cold shutdown of all the reactors on December 16, 2011.[44] The plant failure at Fukushima Daiichi following the tsunamis resulted in tens of thousands of evacuations, many of them permanent, and qualifies as a full-fledged disaster in its own right, even if one were to somehow disregard the effects of the earthquake and tsunami. However, since the nuclear power plant disaster resulted from the tsunami, it is all part of a complex set of interactions resulting from a single event, the earthquake of March 11th, 2011.

SUMMARY CHARACTERISTICS

The Japanese have described this disaster in terms of four characteristics.[45] They are

Unexpected disaster is a term the Japanese are using to describe this earthquake, as in being unexpectedly large (wide area) and powerful. Its primary impact was in the Tohoku region of three prefectures, but in fact its physical effects were felt throughout the entire country, as well as infrastructure, economic, social, and political effects.

Complex disaster: The Great East Japan Earthquake caused the huge tsunami disaster. The nuclear power plant accident followed the tsunami disaster. The nuclear power plant failure caused both physical damage and damage to the reputation of government, due both to rumors and the way that the power plant response was handled. Multiple disasters occurred successively and together they can be described as a hyper-complex disaster.

Dispersed disaster: The damaged areas were dispersed such as local urban areas, rural farming villages, fishing villages, and mountain areas. At the time of the 1995 Great Hanshin-Awaji Earthquake, the damage was concentrated to the urban city area, so the response and recovery operations could be managed intensively in a restricted area. However, it was very difficult to respond to all in the same way in the 2011 earthquake, because of the highly variable needs and circumstances across the broad area affected by this complex event.

The loss of abilities of governing bodies: Some areas were completely swept away by the tsunami. Originally in Tohoku (the North-East area of Japan most directly affected by this event), in particular, in rural areas, there have been chronic issues concerning decreasing population and an aging society. The earthquake and tsunami were the crowning blow. Many public officers including firefighters, emergency medical technicians (EMTs), and medical doctors who worked in public services lost their lives, which resulted not only in the loss of the ability of a local governing body, but also the local government itself. Many local officials, including one mayor, were lost. Recovery and rehabilitation have been deeply insufficient because the adjacent local governing bodies also have suffered from the disaster.

In conclusion, this event has many of the characteristics of a catastrophe, especially if you consider long-term consequences not noted in these four basic characteristics, and the short-term world wide impact the earthquake had on the production of automobiles and some electronic goods, due to the weeks-long or even months-long production halt in certain key components in Japan. This event is also having worldwide effects on the acceptance and utilization of nuclear power.

BACKGROUND: JAPAN'S EMERGENCY PREPAREDNESS AND RESPONSE SYSTEMS[46,47]

As a result of tremendous damage due to the Ise-wan Typhoon in 1959 which claimed more than 5,000 victims, the Japanese national government urged the establishment of a comprehensive and strategic disaster management system and the Disaster Countermeasures Basic Act was enacted in 1961. The disaster management system has been strengthened through the lessons learned from events such as the Great Hanshin-Awaji Earthquake in 1995.

The main contents of the Disaster Countermeasures Basic Act are as follows:

- *Definition of responsibilities for disaster management:* Clear roles and responsibilities of the national and local governments; the relevant stakeholders of the public and private sectors cooperate in implementing various disaster countermeasures.
- *Disaster management organizations and planning systems*
  National level: The Central Disaster Management Council is established in the Prime Minister's Cabinet Office based on the Disaster Countermeasures Basic Act. The council consists of the Prime Minister, who is the chairperson and the Minister of State for Disaster Management, all other ministers, heads of major public institutions, and experts. It promotes comprehensive disaster countermeasures including deliberating important issues on disaster reduction according to requests from the Prime Minister or Minister of State for Disaster Management. One of the most important tasks of the council is to prepare the Basic Disaster Management Plan, which covers comprehensive and long-term disaster reduction issues such as disaster management related systems, disaster reduction projects, early and appropriate disaster recovery and rehabilitation, as well as scientific and technical research. It was entirely revised in 1995 after the Great Hanshin-Awaji Earthquake. The new plan describes tangible countermeasures to take for each stakeholder as the national and local governments, public corporations, and other entities according to the disaster phases. In case of a disaster, the Prime Minister declares the state of emergency and establishes a Headquarters for Major Disaster Management (headed by the Minister of State for Disaster Management) or a Headquarters for Extreme Disaster Management (headed by the Prime Minister) according to the level of damage. Note that the establishment of a headquarters happens only when there is a crisis, and the Prime Minister is the final decision-maker. Also of note is that the Disaster Management Ministry is almost entirely staffed by government workers who rotate through this ministry on a 2-year basis. There is no large professional staff of experienced emergency managers.

Prefectural level: The Prefectural Disaster Management Council is established to formulate and promote implementation of the Local Disaster Management Plan. This plan is made by the council, subject to the local circumstances and based on the Basic Disaster Management Plan. The national Basic Disaster Management Plan provides guidance to the prefectures regarding planning targets and methods.

Municipal level: The Municipal Disaster Management Council is established to formulate and promote implementation of the Local Disaster Management Plan.

Designated government organizations/designated public corporations: Specific NGOs and public corporations are designated as expected to play important roles in the disaster countermeasures. Designated Government Organizations are 24 ministries and agencies. Designated Public Corporations are 56 organizations including independent administrative agencies, Bank of Japan, Japanese Red Cross Society, NHK (Japanese Broadcasting Corporation), electric and gas companies, and Nippon Telegraph and Telephone. Each of them makes a Disaster Management Operations Plan based on the Basic Disaster Management Plan.

- *Promotion of disaster countermeasures*: At the municipal level, the plan is to establish clear roles and authorities of each stakeholder in implementing various disaster countermeasures according to the disaster phases of prevention and preparedness, emergency response, as well as recovery and rehabilitation. In terms of emergency response, municipalities such as cities, towns, and villages have primary responsibility for the disaster countermeasures. The municipal mayors are given authority to order evacuation, set restricted areas and so on. However, in terms of response operations, the prefectural governors are in charge of the rescue activities such as setting shelters or temporary housings, providing water, foods, clothing and bedding, search and rescue, providing medical services, recovering, and management of dead bodies. The municipal mayors support them as per request.[48]
- *Financial measures*: In principle, those who implement the disaster countermeasures bear the responsibility of the relevant costs. However, when a disaster causes extremely severe damage and is designated an "extremely severe disaster," the national government provides special financial support.

DISASTER HEALTHCARE[49,50]

Disaster medicine in Japan has made progress since the Great Hanshin Awaji Earthquake on January 17, 1995 (Kobe). The lack of appropriate medical and management systems caused more than 500 preventable deaths. The lessons learned at that time are as follows:

- There were no medical teams for the super-acute phase, which could offer medical care at the disaster site.
- There were no disaster specialized hospitals, which could manage disaster medicine.
- There were no transport systems for moving severely injured patients from the overwhelmed hospitals inside the disaster-affected area to off-site hospitals.
- There were no efficient communication systems.

Japan has made great efforts to solve all of these problems, with special attention to the first two.

1. The Japanese government decided to establish Disaster Medical Assistance Teams (DMATs), which are mobile, trained medical teams that can rapidly deploy during the acute phase of a sudden-onset disaster (within 48 hours). With the support of the Ministry of Health, Labour and Welfare (MHLW), the DMAT Team Member Training Course was started at the National Hospital Organization Disaster Medical Center in Tokyo in 2005. One DMAT consists of four or five members (usually two medical doctors, two nurses, one logistician), who completed the course. DMATs have four major roles.
   - On-scene life-saving treatment during the super-acute phase
   - Hospital support in the disaster-affected area
   - Transport of the patients inside the disaster-affected area, including transfer to the surgical care unit (SCU)
   - Wide-area medical evacuation.

   In the course of 4 days training, participants not only take part in tabletop exercises, but also in outside training such as the drills for confined space medicine or triage for wide-area medical evacuation. As of June 30, 2011, 5,357 members (medical doctors: 1,802, nurses: 2,128, logisticians: 1,374) are registered who compose 866 teams from 447 facilities. There are 359 members registered as the DMAT supervisors who have specialized knowledge of DMAT operations and are expected to play a guiding role and serve as a person in charge in the on-site operations.

2. The MHLW has tried to support and designate disaster hospitals. The disaster hospital offers higher level and specific treatment for mass casualties including crush syndrome, burn, or trauma. Patients can be taken directly to disaster hospitals or they can be transferred from local hospitals.

OVERVIEW OF THE JAPANESE RESPONSE

Search and Rescue

The size of the task of conducting search and rescue operations in this event is revealed by the massive number of Japanese personnel who were sent to the task by the national government:

National Police Agency: 307,500
Fire and Disaster Management Agency: 27,373 teams with 103,600 firefighters
Japanese Coast Guard: 4,413 rescue boats, 1,564 airplane flights, and 1,510 Special Rescue Team staff
Japan Self-Defense Force (SDF): 107,000*

---

* It is interesting to note that this amounts to almost half of all of the 230,000 total SDF personnel, potentially compromising other security missions.

A JTF was established to coordinate all SDF personnel in air, sea, and ground missions to enhance effectiveness and efficiency of effort. According to data finalized on 30 May, 2011, the total number of people rescued by police, fire departments, Japan Coast Guards, and the SDF amounted to 26,707.[51]

Although the Japanese Government accepted few international rescue teams and expert teams at the time of Hanshin-Awaji Great Earthquake in 1995, for the 2011 Great East Japan Earthquake and Tsunami, it welcomed teams from 28 countries, regions, and organizations including urban search and rescue (US&R) teams from USAID. In particular, US Forces provided Operation Tomodachi (which means friendship in Japanese) that contributed significantly to the response. They were integrated into the JTF and dispatched more than 16,000 corps, approximately 15 ships and approximately 140 airplanes at maximum. In particular, Operation Tomodachi made a strong contribution to reopening the Sendai airport, which became the advance base for shipping emergency supplies to the affected areas. We do not have data stating how may rescues were accomplished by international teams; it may be that these rescues were included in the 26,707 listed above for the Japanese combined search and rescue (SAR) efforts (see Figure 15.5).

As is the case with any massive operation like this, there were numerous difficulties. The almost complete loss of civilian communications modalities meant that it was exceedingly difficult to obtain good information for the construction of a needs assessment. Furthermore, although the national plan calls for SAR activities to be controlled and centered at the municipality and prefecture levels, the losses of key personnel, communications, and emergency response infrastructure

Figure 15.5 Damage in Iwate Prefecture. (Courtesy of Japanese Red Cross Society: http://media.redcross.org/sites/A/Photo+Library/370?encoding=UTF-8.)

meant that the majority of SAR operations needed to be provided by national or international resources. The national emergency countermeasures system depended on Internet-based communications, and this failed completely in most places, as did cell phone services, for at least the first 4 or 5 days. Although the national government's JTF attempted to coordinate the overall deployment of national resources and services, there was much confusion, resulting in some places having an excess of response personnel and others having no external assistance for several days. The rugged terrain of the Tohoku region and the loss of both ports and bridges made it extremely difficult to deploy SAR personnel and equipment, or to transport rescued victims to a place where they could receive adequate support. Although it should probably be expected in a case like this, tsunamis tend to kill people more than injure them, meaning that, in this case, the SAR personnel (including many who had never worked with the deceased) spent much of their time after Day 3 extricating the dead. The mental health sequelae of this situation are yet to be fully seen.

Medical Response[52]

The DMAT main office inside the National Disaster Organization Disaster Medical Center set up the response headquarters at 14:50, 4 minutes after the earthquake. It secured a disaster inspection helicopter at 15:05. It issued the standby request to all the DMATs through the emergency management information system (EMIS) at 15:10. Sendai medical centers in Miyagi and Fukushima Medical University in Fukushima were designated as gathering points and dispatch orders were issued at 16:00. Then Iwate Medical University in Iwate and Tsukuba Medical Center were also designated as gathering points and dispatch orders were issued at 17:15. These disaster hospitals worked as field DMAT headquarters. For the dispatch order, 306 DMATs, about 1,500 members from all the 47 metropolises and prefectures started the operation and arrived at the gathering points by the next noon. Among them, 82 DMATs, 384 members were transported by air. The operation sites were in four prefectures, Iwate, Miyagi, Fukushima, and Ibaraki. The operation period totaled 12 days from March 11 to 22.

Their basic missions were (1) on-scene life-saving treatment in the super-acute phase, (2) hospital support in the disaster-affected area, (3) transport of the patients inside the disaster-affected area, including transfer to the SCU, and (4) wide-area medical evacuation as aforementioned, however, they could not help supporting evacuation activities of admitted patients to other hospitals outside of these basic missions.

The DMAT supervisors entered in each prefectural disaster response headquarters and established the DMAT coordination headquarters. They tried to manage and coordinate the DMAT activities and supported the prefectural medical response. They also supported the headquarters of the disaster hospital designated as a gathering point and the SCU headquarters. The DMAT supervisors also entered into the surrounding prefectural offices to coordinate those facilities, which were not directly damaged by the disaster and received evacuated patients.

The basic missions of DMAT were done as follows:

1. *On-scene life-saving treatment in the super-acute phase*: In this disaster, there were fewer than expected patients who needed life-saving treatment during the super-acute phase. It is one of the critical features of tsunami disasters that victims who were able to run away and survive are often free of wounds. Those who are caught by the waters rarely survive. Sometimes this feature is called "all or nothing." At the great Hanshin-Awaji earthquake, the morbidity/mortality ratio (M/M) was 6.8 (i.e., 6.8 injuries for each fatality) and a deficit in Japanese disaster medicine was pointed out.[53] The M/M in advanced disaster medical systems is expected to be between 10 and 15, or higher. By comparison, in the 1989 Loma Prieta earthquake in California there were 63 injuries per fatality,[54] which shows that the California emergency healthcare system did a better job of keeping the injured from dying. However, in the 2011 earthquake and tsunami in Japan, almost all of the deaths came from the tsunami, which, as noted, leaves little chance for survival. The number of injured who survived was about 5,000 and the estimated death toll is about 20,000 in this disaster and the M/M is about 0.25, or four times as many deaths as injured. This value is extremely low and shows not only the effect of the tsunami portion of this disaster, but also the lower demand for acute injury-focused medical care.
2. *Hospital support in the disaster-affected area*: The communications systems were so devastated in this disaster that the DMAT headquarters had difficulty in gathering accurate information. Under these conditions, the DMATs supported eight hospitals in Iwate, six in Miyagi, three in Fukushima, and three in Ibaraki based on the information from the prefectural disaster response headquarters and the EMIS. Most DMATs entered into their assigned hospital by land routes, but 18 DMATs were transported by helicopters to the three hospitals located along the Iwate coastline. They supported medical treatment and transport of the patients inside the disaster-affected area as well as sending information regarding the conditions around the deployed local area to the prefectural response headquarters and DMAT headquarters. Hospitals were responsible for treating the injured as well as patients with conditions that were not directly related to the disaster.
3. *Transport of the patients inside the disaster-affected area, including transfer to the SCU*: In Japan, some prefectures are introducing the Doctor-Helicopter (called Doctor-heli for short) system as a part of emergency medical services. The Doctor-heli carries emergency room (hospital) (ER) physicians directly to the patient on scene and returns to the ER while performing preliminary care. In this disaster, the DMAT main office asked all of the Doctor-helis for deployment soon after the onset of the earthquake and after all 16 helicopters entered into the disaster-affected area. They were used for transport of more than 140 patients to the hospitals not only inside the disaster-affected area, but also adjacent prefectures. They were also used for transport of DMATs.
4. *Wide-area medical evacuation*: Although the number of surviving severe trauma patients was limited, three SCUs were established in Iwate, Miyagi, and Fukushima prefecture, and two in other prefectures. From March 12 to 15, 136 patients were transferred to an SCU inside the disaster-affected area, and they were triaged there again. Sixteen patients were evacuated outside of the disaster zone. The other 120 patients were re-distributed back to the hospital inside the disaster-affected area. This was seen as a success, given that pre-event plans for the establishment of SCUs in this area had not been completed prior to the earthquake (see Figure 15.6).

Figure 15.6 Japan DMAT providing care in improvised space. (Photo courtesy of Japan DMAT.)

In addition to their four essential roles, the DMATs supported the evacuation and transport of admitted patients out of the isolated hospitals. At Ishinomaki City Hospital, more than 100 patients were transferred on March 14. They were first evacuated to the Ishinomaki sports park and then transported to the Kasuminome air field by helicopter. In the daytime, the Doctor-helis were used for transport and the SDF helicopters took over after sunset. DMATs set up the SCU in the Ishinomaki sports park and mainly supported the transport from the hospital to the park.

In addition to this activity, the DMATs supported the evacuation of admitted patients from the hospitals within 30 km radius from the Fukushima Daiichi NPS. Prior to that, in one hospital inside the evacuation radius, more than 20 patients died during their evacuation due to lack of sufficient care in-transit, for Japan a new kind of preventable death concerning disasters. When the DMATs took over this activity, more than 300 patients were safely transported.

Due to the size and complexity of this event, problems occurred that had not been anticipated in the national disaster health planning process.

1. *Duration of DMAT Activity*: According to the basic plan, the DMATs perform their activities within 48–72 hours in the acute phase and then transfer the continued care tasks to the local healthcare facilities or other medical relief teams. The infrastructure and healthcare facilities were expected to be restored within this time. However, in this disaster, the disaster-affected area was so vast and the damage was so devastating that the transfer could not have been carried out smoothly. Due to the lack of information, there were big gaps between medical demands and supplies. As a matter of fact, there were no medical relief teams to take over after 72 hours. As a result, many DMATs,

whose design, equipment, and staffing were all predicated on a 3-day service period found themselves out of supplies and food well before there was anybody to whom continued patientcare responsibility could be handed over. Adjacent prefectures could not step in hand take up the slack, because they too were dealing with the same issues, in addition to the extremely difficult communications and transportation conditions.

2. *Communications System*: The damage to the communications infrastructure was much more devastating than had been expected. The disruption of communications systems caused much confusion for DMAT and related activities. The lack of accurate information prevented the DMAT system from effective and efficient use of its resources. The DMAT response headquarters had difficulty in deciding where and how many DMATs to dispatch. In some places, there were many DMATs having nothing to do, on the other hand there were no DMATs where medical support was most needed, because they had no way to communicate their needs. The EMIS is the most critical tool for the DMAT, but it did not function well without the Internet. Furthermore, the Miyagi prefecture had not previously introduced the EMIS due to an insufficient budget. There were some cases in which damaged disaster hospitals could not use the EMIS. The DMATs could have supported them earlier if they had been able to send their information by the EMIS.

Japan has a second system for providing emergency care to disaster victims. Approximately 2 years prior to the 2011 earthquake and tsunami in Tohoku, the Japanese Medical Association formed a disaster response program, the Japanese Medical Association Team (JMAT).[55] The concept of the JMAT is that it will help provide care for patients in disaster-affected areas in which DMATs have been operative and are cycling off-duty. The JMAT is a fluid team made up of Medical Association volunteers from the prefectures that have not been affected by the disaster, each of whom agrees to a 3–7 day deployment. The JMAT teams are then placed where they are needed, mostly in hospitals or clinics, each team consisting of one physician, two nurses, and a logistics specialist. In the Tohoku disaster, in the first week after the earthquake, 62 JMAT teams were dispatched to the four affected prefectures, with another 68 standing by for deployment. During the next couple of months, the role of the JMATs morphed at the request of two formed-for-the-occasion central government committees: the Special Headquarters for Measures to Assist the Lives of Disaster Victims (Office of the Prime Minister) formed the Disaster Victim Health Support Council. This helped coordinate the deployment of JMAT resources to meet the short- and medium-term acute and chronic needs of disaster survivors whose normal medical facilities had disappeared, or survivors who had been evacuated to shelters in safer areas. The role of the JMAT in this event was concluded on 15 July, 2011, with the following service statistics: As of 11 July, 2011, 1,377 out of 1,391 registered teams participated, made up of 2,220 physicians, 1,829 nurses, 469 pharmacists, plus 1,626 coordination and general staff members.[56] It is unknown how many patientcare episodes occurred during this time period, but it is clear that this government-coordinated, medical association-sponsored volunteer program provided significant resources and care to a population caught between the support provided during the emergency period and the drawn-out time period of converting to recovery and reconstruction activities (see Figure 15.7).

Figure 15.7 Hospital care in improvised spaces. (Courtesy of: Japanese Red Cross Society: http://media.redcross.org/sites/P/Photo+Library/339?encoding=UTF-8&b=800.)

RESPONSE TO THE FUKUSHIMA DAIICHI NPS FAILURE

Within about 5 hours of the tsunami hitting the Fukushima Daiichi NPS, Prime Minister Kan issued a National Declaration of a Nuclear Emergency Situation.[57] What followed over the next week can be characterized as confusion, missed opportunities, loss of credibility, fear, rumors, heroic but largely ineffective attempts at improvising technical responses, and public evacuations without much planning. Regardless of any previously planned nuclear plant emergency protocols, it was all made much worse by the fact that:

- The tsunami was significantly beyond the presumed severity in the engineering design specifications.
- The communications and transportation infrastructures were severely damaged.
- Information from the TEPCO was scant, and frequently contradictory.[58,59]
- The Prime Minister, perhaps because he had an engineering background, decided to personally intervene.[60]
- The Japanese system of centralizing much of the emergency decision-making into the Prime Minister's cabinet meant that: (1) there was a huge overwhelming drain on a small number of people, because of the triple-disaster character of this event (earthquake/tsunami/nuclear power plants) and (2) at least in the first few days, many important decisions were made without sufficient input from knowledgeable scientists and technical experts.

It is important to note here that catastrophes, like disasters, are a result of the interaction between event dynamics and size, on the one hand, and the capacity to cope with them on the other. One could argue whether the combination of the 2011 earthquake and tsunami in Japan was sufficient for it to qualify as a catastrophe in this capable country, but the addition of the nuclear plant crises clearly pushed Japan's response capacity into overload, with suboptimal outcomes. Could a different kind of command structure have kept this series of events at the sub-catastrophe level? Let us see how the Japanese coped with the power plant failure. Note: We do not have access to internal TEPCO documents.

March 11

14:46 The earthquake occurs, the first tsunami wave hit the Fukushima coastline about 15:35.
19:03: The Prime Minister issued the Declaration of a Nuclear Emergency Situation and established the Nuclear Disaster Management Headquarters and Local Headquarters for Nuclear Emergency Response. He also headed the Nuclear Disaster Management Headquarters.[61]
21:23: The chief Cabinet Secretary announced the evacuation instruction for residents within a 3 km radius from Fukushima Daiichi NPS and shelter-in-place instructions within 3–10 km from the NPS.[62]

Comments: During the 3.5 hours that elapsed between the tsunami hitting the NPS and the Prime Minister issuing the declaration, information was being gathered and assessed. The time from event to the announcement would likely have been shorter if the communications systems had not been damaged. Note that the major decision-making is kept within the cabinet, not Japan's nuclear power authority. Note also that 2.5 hours passed between announcing a nuclear emergency and informing the local population that those within a 3 km radius should evacuate and those within 10 should remain indoors. This delay raised speculation and concern within both local and national populations.

March 12

3:12: The Prime Minister and his Cabinet decided to open the valve of the reactor to release the rising steam pressure inside to protect the reactor vessel and ordered TEPCO to do so.[63]
5:44: The evacuation area was extended to within 10 km from the NPS due to this procedure.[64]
7:11: The Prime Minister arrived at the NPS by helicopter to inspect and directly ordered TEPCO to open the valve.[65,66] Note, this information is contested by some sources.
15:36: An explosion (considered to be caused by hydrogen) occurred at Reactor 1.[67]
18:25: Responding to the explosion, the evacuation area was extended to within 20 km from the NPS.[68]

Comments: It is interesting that the Prime Minister and his cabinet are making technical decisions regarding an NPS in a crisis that clearly has technical, not political remedies. It is also interesting that the first expansion of the evacuation came almost 2.5 hours after the first order to open the pressure release valve, and the second order to further expand the evacuation zone did not come until almost 3 hours after the explosion in Reactor 1. Is this because decision-makers in the Prime Minister's office lacked emergency management experience, they failed to understand the public safety aspects of a radiation release, or simply because they were overwhelmed by the tragic events in the rest of Tohoku?

March 14

    11:01: A hydrogen explosion occurred at Reactor 3.[69]

At night, the president of TEPCO called and asked the Minister of Economy, Trade, and Industry, then, the Chief Cabinet Secretary for the permission to evacuate all the workers inside the NPS for their safety, however, both cabinet ministers refused it.[70]

Comments: We do not have a record of why this decision was made by the ministers.

March 15

    5:25 The Prime Minister announced the establishment of an Integrated Government-TEPCO Headquarters for Measures against the Fukushima NPS Disaster. He set it up inside the main office building of TEPCO.[71]
    About 6:00: A hydrogen explosion occurred at Reactor 4.[72]
    6:14: A huge explosion sound was heard at Reactor 2.[73]
    9:38: A fire occurred at Reactor 4.[74,75]
    11:00: The Prime Minister announced shelter-in-place instructions for all within a 20–30 km radius from the NPS.[76]

Comments: It took 5 days for the Prime Minister to recognize that the management of the response to this event was not something that could be handled without joint decision-making with the NPS's owner-operator TEPCO. Would he have seen the situation more clearly if he and his staff were not simultaneously engaged in decisions about the many response activities for the earthquake and tsunami? (See Figure 15.8.)

March 16

    5:45: A fire occurred again at Reactor 4.[77]
    About 8:30 white smoke due to the boiling of the water of the spent fuel pool started coming up from Reactor 3.[78]

March 17

    9:48: The helicopter of the SDF started spraying sea water over Reactor 3.[79]
    19:35: A fire-engine of the SDF started spraying at Reactor 3.[80]

Figure 15.8 Japanese SDF helping evacuate citizens. (Courtesy of: Japanese Red Cross Society: http://media.redcross.org/sites/A/Photo+Library/334?encoding=UTF-8.)

March 18

A local coordination office was established to strengthen coordination with the SDF and other related organizations.[81]

Comments: It took 8 days for a local coordination office to be established. In the United States and many other countries that have professional emergency management as a core component of response to any large event, including emergencies at nuclear power facilities, it is standing protocol that a local coordination office (various names are used) would be set up within the first few hours of the response. Was this lack of implementation of this kind of protocol due to the lack of a professional emergency management (EM) agency within Japan's national government, or perhaps was it a victim of the huge demands placed on emergency decision-makers by the other concurrent demands in the Tohoku region?

March 19–24

Task forces made up of personnel and equipment from the Tokyo Fire Department and the SDF combined to pour water on the reactor buildings, in an attempt to cool the reactors. More explosions and signs of radiation leakage occurred.[82]

March 25

The Chief Cabinet Secretary announced recommendation for the residents following the shelter-in-place instruction within 20–30 km radius from the NPS to evacuate out of the area voluntarily.[83]

Comments: It took 15 days to *recommend* (not order) evacuation of the population living within a 20–30 km (12.5–18.75 mile) radius. Was it 20 or 30 km? Why the confusing instructions and why so late? Additionally, because this was recommended (instead of ordered), the evacuation was not coordinated by the national government, and had no designated shelter centers outside of the evacuation zone. By this time, public confidence in the pronouncements of both the government and TEPCO was quite low.

Over the weeks of evacuation activities, 113,000 people were moved to myriad other sites.[84] Note that this number is almost equal to the 124,000 people who were evacuated because of the earthquake and tsunami, almost doubling Japan's evacuee population to over 237,000 people.[85] The evacuation, of course, included all hospitalized patients within the zone. From the Futaba Hospital in Okuma Town, 21 patients being evacuated lost their lives during the evacuation process.[86]

It is important to note at this point that the Japanese government concluded on 13 March that it would accept the offers by both the US Nuclear Regulatory Commission and Department of Energy,[87] as well as the International Atomic Energy Agency (IAEA) (14 March)[88] for technical assistance. Technical assistance from all three agencies was immediately dispatched to Japan. However, its value is in doubt, given the reports from both the IAEA and US agencies that they never had adequate access to information while in Japan.

CONCLUSIONS

The March 11, 2011 Tohoku earthquake/tsunami/nuclear power plant event is often referred to in the press as a "triple disaster." It could certainly be seen that way if you look at it as three separate events, each with its own characteristics. However, from the viewpoint of those responsible for directing and coordinating responses to all of the effects of these events at the same time, it was clearly not three separate events. Each event directly affected the ability to respond effectively to the other events, and the combination of them became too much for the national resources to handle effectively in a timely manner. Decision-making became an early victim of this deadly combination of events, leaving responders out in the prefectures struggling to know what to do, and with what resources, in a society that normally has a strong sense of hierarchy in the decision-making process. There was clearly a failure in decision-making on many fronts, primarily, we think, because this tripartite catastrophe was simply too complex for the existing response management structure to manage effectively. The result was mismatched resources, with populations left to evacuate on their own, surviving with whatever shelter and food as they could find for an extended period of time in some cases. When the population near the Fukushima power plants had to evacuate, while doing the best it could, government resources were overwhelmed with sudden responsibility for 237,000 total evacuees. The power plant failure also had other cascading effects:

1. It changed the character of the disaster response, which, in the case of earthquakes and tsunamis, is characterized by the need to cope with damage that has already been done; government was now required to also try to contain an on-going crises that had the potential to be much more deadly.
2. The power plant failure caused sudden power losses that had widespread impact.
3. Losses of electricity led to numerous other emergencies in other prefectures, including collapses of public transport in some areas, and loss of industrial production.
4. Public opinion has turned harshly against furtherance of dependence on nuclear power, causing Japan to have to spend limited resources on the importation of other sources of fuel.
5. The leakage of radioactive materials has contaminated a large area of previously productive agricultural land, and fear of contamination has greatly decreased the world market for Japanese seafood.
6. The costs for decontamination of the affected lands are estimated to be much higher than the total value of TEPCO, meaning that the national government is going to be spending large sums of money that could otherwise have been spent on recovery and rehabilitation of the coastal areas devastated by the tsunamis.

Haiti is one of the world's poorest countries. It did not have earthquake mitigation standards, nor an active and resourced disaster response force. While the earthquake that hit Japan was of much higher magnitude than that in Haiti, and caused a horrendous tsunami, its primary effects were on the relatively lightly populated north-eastern coastline and its communities. The earthquake in Haiti hit right at the governmental and economic heart of the country, its capital Port-au-Prince. As a result, a high percentage of the government's buildings, tools, and human resources were either destroyed or hugely affected. The vacuum that was left was further accentuated by the destruction of such basic infrastructure as existed throughout much of the area, loss of communications, and the losses of more than 200,000 people and more than 300,000 injured. Those statistics would overwhelm any country ... what nation could effectively handle 300,000 suddenly injured people? The overwhelming majority of emergency medical care was provided by people who came in from other countries, often through the limited airport. Communications, resource management, and major tactical decisions were provided by non-Haitians, at least for the first few months. Haiti's catastrophe did not affect the world of economic trade like Japan's catastrophe did in some ways, but the world response to Haiti involved the movement of resources from many countries, a different kind of worldwide impact.

One of the lessons taken from the response to the Haitian earthquake is that the international community of state and non-state responders, which has been working for years to better coordinate multi-actor responses to disaster-affected poorer countries, needs to continue working on strategies and plans for responding to catastrophes in countries that are rendered essentially non-functional, at least in the short term. This kind of preparedness will take very different tracks than preparing for catastrophes within one's own country. The level of complexity is extremely high, due to the multiple responders, multiple languages, non-synching technologies, lack of familiarity with the site and cultural circumstances of the affected country, and the ever-present questions about who has actual authority to make decisions and assure that policies are followed.

Nonetheless, some of the lessons that are being learned from catastrophe planning in the US and Europe could be extrapolated to the international arena, including lessons that are being learned about combining bottom-up and top-down communication and decision-making at the planning and preparedness stages, use of local "experts" to predict the effects of making particular decisions or employing certain techniques or strategies, and being prepared to deal with mass evacuation. Likewise, domestic catastrophe preparedness and response planners would do well to learn from their international response colleagues regarding such tasks as integrating a surge of volunteers, setting up and dividing out response sectors (clusters?), and using simple but effective communication strategies when high-tech ones fail or prove to be insufficient.

Japan is one of the world's most disaster-aware countries, with significant resources and a wealth of mitigation activities aimed at diminishing the damage from its most probable hazards. Even so, it demonstrated that even wealthy, technologically advanced and well-organized societies can be overwhelmed by events we call "catastrophes." Our focus on catastrophes is not, and should not be thought of as kind gestures toward developing countries; rather, our focus on catastrophes is relevant to everyone, regardless of where they live.

REFERENCES

1. Human Rights Watch. Haiti Country Report. 2010. Available from: http://www.hrw.org/sites/default/files/related_material/haiti_1.pdf. Accessed on March 30, 2012.
2. FEMA Haiti Earthquake Response, Quick Look Report. 2010. Available from: http://info.publicintelligence.net/FEMAHaitiQuickLookReport.pdf. Accessed on March 30, 2012.
3. Active Learning Network for Accountability and Performance in Humanitarian Action. 2010. *Haiti Earthquake Response: Context Analysis*. Available from; http://www.alnap.org/pool/files/haiti-context-analysis-final.pdf. Accessed March 30, 2012.
4. Institut Haïtien de Statistique et d'Informatique. 2010. Haiti: Departments, major cities, towns & agglomerations. *City Population Website*. Updated on: 3/15/10. Available from: http://www.citypopulation.de/Haiti.html. Accessed on: March 30, 2012.
5. Active Learning Network for Accountability and Performance in Humanitarian Action. 2010. *Haiti Earthquake Response: Context Analysis*.
6. PAHO. *Haiti: Population Health Assessment prior to the 2010 earthquake*. Available from: http://www.google.com/url?sa=t&rct=j&q=&esrc=s&frm=1&source=web&cd=1&ved=0CCYQFjAA&url=http%3A%2F%2Fnew.paho.org%2Fdisasters%2Findex.php%3Foption%3Dcom_docman%26task%3Ddoc_download%26gid%3D689%26Itemid%3D&ei=4yZzT_GFDIfx0gHBkp3OAQ&usg=AFQjCNG5D7r6OX0CX4aTW7acks1kVPitiw&sig2=fO04CDFm2-yejFdx6L-Maw. Accessed on March 30, 2012.
7. WFP. 2010. Haiti overview. *World Food Programme Website*. Available from: http://www.wfp.org/countries/haiti. Accessed on March 30, 2012.
8. MINUSTAH. Restoring a secure and stable environment. *United Nations Stabilization Mission in Haiti Website*. Available from: http://www.un.org/en/peacekeeping/missions/minustah/. Accessed on March 30, 2012.
9. USAID. Action Plan for Haiti. Available from: http://haiti.usaid.gov/about/action_plan.php. Accessed March 30, 2011.

10. Binder A and Grünewald F. IASC Cluster approach evaluation, 2nd phase, country study, April 2010. Available from: http://www.gppi.net/fileadmin/gppi/GPPi-URD_Cluster_II_Evaluation_HAITI_e.pdf. Accessed March 30, 2012.
11. United States Institute of Peace. Haiti: A Republic of NGOs? Available from: http://www.usip.org/files/resources/PB%2023%20Haiti%20a%20Republic%20of%20NGOs.pdf. Accessed on March 30, 2012.
12. FEMA Haiti Earthquake Response, Quick Look Report. 2010. Available from: http://info.publicintelligence.net/FEMAHaitiQuickLookReport.pdf. Accessed on March 30, 2012.
13. USAID/Haiti. 2010. *Success Story: USAID Supports Urban Search and Rescue Operations in Haiti.* Available from: http://www.usaid.gov/our_work/humanitarian_assistance/disaster_assistance/countries/haiti/template/files/usar_success_story.pdf. Accessed March 30, 2012.
14. Hatian MINISTERE DE LA SANTE PUBLIQUE ET DE LA POPULATION (MSPP). Rapport en Cas du 15 mars, 2012. Available from: http://www.mspp.gouv.ht/site/index.php?option=com_content&view=article&id=120&Itemid=1. Accessed on March 30, 2012.
15. http://www.time.com/time/world/article/0,8599,2003216,00.html.
16. http://www.paho.org/english/dd/ais/cp_332.htm.
17. USAID/DCHA. 2010. *Haiti Earthquake: Fact Sheet # 39.* February 23.
18. USAID. 2010. *Haiti Relief and Recovery: Office of the Response Coordinator Weekly Slide Update.* May 4.
19. CNSA. 2010.
20. WFP. 2010.
21. Japan Meteorological Agency: The 2011 off the Pacific Coast of Tohoku Earthquake and Tsunami-Portal-. Available at http://www.jma.go.jp/jma/en/2011_Earthquake.html. Accessed on September 1, 2011.
22. Cabinet Office: Government of Japan, White Paper on Disaster Management 2011, Executive Summary. Available at http://www.bousai.go.jp/hakusho/WPDM2011_Summary.pdf. Accessed on September 1, 2012.
23. NHK "Science Zero" television crew, Furumura T et al.: Solving the mechanism of the East Japan Great Earthquake, June 25, 2011.
24. Ibid, Cabinet Office, Government of Japan: White Paper on Disaster Management 2011, Executive Summary.
25. Hatamura Y. Unprecedented and Unexpected, lessons learned from the East Japan Great Earthquake, July 20, 2011.
26. Hatamura Y. Expect the 'Unexpected'—Suggestions from failure knowledge, August 25, 2011.
27. Yomiuri Online: Daiichi NPS, 5m flooded by tsunami, 15m max.high. Available from: http://www.yomiuri.co.jp/science/news/20110409-OYT1T00724.htm. Accessed on September 17, 2011.
28. The Nuclear Industry Safety Agency: Earthquake damage information, No. 85, April 10, 2011. Available from: http://www.meti.go.jp/press/2011/04/20110410003/20110410003-1.pdf. Accessed on September 17, 2011.
29. Ibid, Cabinet Office, Government of Japan: White Paper on Disaster Management 2011, Executive Summary.
30. National Police Agency: About the East Japan Great Earthquake. Available from: http://www.npa.go.jp/archive/keibi/biki/index.htm. Accessed on October 14, 2011.
31. Ibid, Cabinet Office, Government of Japan: White Paper on Disaster Management 2011, Executive Summary.

32. Ibid, National Police Agency: About the East Japan Great Earthquake.
33. Ibid, Cabinet Office, Government of Japan: White Paper on Disaster Management 2011, Executive Summary.
34. Fire and Disaster Management Agency: About the East Great Earthquake, No. 140, October 11, 2011. Available from: http://www.rescuenow.net/2011/10/330-2.html. Accessed on October 14, 2011.
35. Ibid, Cabinet Office, Government of Japan: White Paper on Disaster Management 2011, Executive Summary.
36. MSN Sankei News: The total amount of damage 16–25 trillion yen by the Government calculation, not including NPS accident damage, March 23, 2011. Available from: http://sankei.jp.msn.com/economy/news/110323/fnc11032320470016-n1.htm. Accessed on October 15, 2011.
37. The Mainichi Daily News: Sunday Mainichi, an special issue: Meltdown Fukushima daiichi NPS detailed document, June 25, 2011.
38. Nuclear Emergency Response Headquarters, Government of Japan: Report of the Japanese Government to the IAEA Ministerial Conference on Nuclear Safety—The Accident at TEPCO's Fukushima Nuclear Power Stations, June, 2011.
39. Ibid.
40. The Sankei Shimbun: NPS accident raised to "Level 7" equal to Chernobyl, April 12, 2011.
41. Yomiuri Shimbun: Contaminated water flowing out directly into the sea, April 3, 2011.
42. Yomiuri Online: Highly contaminated water inside the Reactor 4 building, influence on the cooling system recovery? April 2, 2011. Available from: http://www.yomiuri.co.jp/national/news/20110402-OYT1T00695.htm. Accessed on October 20, 2011.
43. Yomiuri Shimbun: Low-level radioactive water 11,500 ton discharged into the sea to store the highly contaminated water, April 5, 2011.
44. MSN Sankei News: Prime Minister declared the cold shutdown of Fukushima daiichi NPS, December 16, 2011. Available from: http://sankei.jp.msn.com/politics/news/111216/plc11121616050012-n1.htm. Accessed on February 17, 2012.
45. Michiko Iwabuchi: Doesn't the politics work? The Great East Japan Earthquake 2011.3.11 and the politics, August 25, 2011.
46. Cabinet Office, Government of Japan: Disaster Management of Japan, February, 2011. Available from: http://www.bousai.go.jp/1info/pdf/saigaipanf_e.pdf. Accessed on December 20, 2011.
47. Cabinet Office, Government of Japan: An outline of the Disaster Countermeasures Basic Act, January 23, 2009. Available from: http://www.bousai.go.jp/hou/pdf/090113saitai.pdf. Accessed on December 20, 2011.
48. Houko: Disaster Relief Act. Available from: http://www.houko.com/00/01/S22/118.HTM. Accessed on December 20, 2011.
49. Kondo H et al. Establishing disaster medical assistance teams in Japan. *Prehospital and Disaster Medicine* 2009: 24(6): 556–564.
50. Otomo Y, Koido Y. Disaster medicine in Japan. *Animus* 2011: 68: 3–9.
51. Ibid, Cabinet Office, Government of Japan: White Paper on Disaster Management 2011, Executive Summary.
52. Koido Y et al. The activities and structure of DMAT–Emergency Report: The DMAT activities in the East Japan Great Earthquake, *Monthly Fire Fighting* 2011: 33: 52–55.
53. RA Bissell, L Pinet, M Nelson and M Levy. Evidence of the effectiveness of health sector preparedness in disaster response: The example of four earthquakes. *Family and Community Health (special issue: Disaster Management in Public Health)* 2004: 27(3): 193–203.
54. Ibid.

55. Ishii M. Japan Medical Association Team's (JMAT) first call to action in the great eastern Japan earthquake. *Japan Medical Association Journal* 2011: 54(3): 144–154.
56. Nichii News online: Regular press conference on July 13, 2011 About completion of JMAT operation and future medical support for the affected areas, August 5, 2011. Available from: http://www.med.or.jp/nichinews/n230805d.html. Accessed September 13, 2011.
57. Ibid, Nuclear Emergency Response Headquarters, Government of Japan: Report of the Japanese Government to the IAEA Ministerial Conference on Nuclear Safety—The Accident at TEPCO's Fukushima Nuclear Power Stations.
58. Sassa A. Know-how of 'Crisis management and Press conference'. July 10, 2011.
59. Asahi Shimbun: Crisis management confused. March 13, 2011.
60. Sassa A. They really overthrow Japan, July 25, 2011.
61. Ibid, Cabinet Office, Government of Japan: White Paper on Disaster Management 2011, Executive Summary.
62. Ibid, The Mainichi Daily News: Sunday Mainichi, an special issue: Meltdown Fukushima daiichi NPS detailed document.
63. Prime Minister of Japan and His Cabinet, the press conference of the Chief Cabinet Secretary, March 12, 2011. Available from: http://www.kantei.go.jp/jp/tyoukanpress/201103/12_a2.html. Accessed on September 15, 2011.
64. Yomiuri Shimbun, 3.11 Earthquake document, March 12, 2011.
65. Yomiure Shimbun, Earthquake on March 12, 2011.
66. Ibid, The Mainichi Daily News: Sunday Mainichi, an special issue: Meltdown Fukushima daiichi NPS detailed document.
67. Ibid.
68. Prime Minister of Japan and His Cabinet, Prime Minister's instruction, March 12, 2011. Available from: http://www.kantei.go.jp/saigai/pdf/20110312siji11.pdf. Accessed on September 15, 2011.
69. Ibid, The Mainichi Daily News: Sunday Mainichi, an special issue: Meltdown Fukushima daiichi NPS detailed document.
70. Ibid.
71. Yomiuri Shimbun, Great Earthquake document 3.15, March 15, 2011.
72. Ibid, The Mainichi Daily News: Sunday Mainichi, an special issue: Meltdown Fukushima daiichi NPS detailed document.
73. Ibid.
74. Ibid.
75. Teshima Y and Takahashi K. An analysis of Fukushima Nuclear Accident, June 23, 2011.
76. Ibid, Yomiuri Shimbun, Great Earthquake document 3.15.
77. Ibid, The Mainichi Daily News: Sunday Mainichi, an special issue: Meltdown Fukushima daiichi NPS detailed document.
78. Ibid.
79. Ibid.
80. Ibid.
81. Ibid, Cabinet Office: Government of Japan, White Paper on Disaster Management 2011, Executive Summary.
82. Ibid, The Mainichi Daily News: Sunday Mainichi, an special issue: Meltdown Fukushima daiichi NPS detailed document.
83. Prime Minister of Japan and His Cabinet, the press conference of the Chief Cabinet Secretary, March 25, 2011. Available from: http://www.kantei.go.jp/jp/tyoukanpress/201103/25_a.html. Accessed on September 15, 2011.

84. Shimbun Akahata, Grasp the total number of evacuees by the Nuclear power plant accident accurately, June 17, 2011. Available from: http://www.jcp.or.jp/akahata/aik11/2011-06-17/2011061704_03_1.html. Accessed on October 20, 2011.
85. Mainichi Shimbun: 124,594 the number of evacuees and moved as of June 2, June 15, 2011. Available from: http://mainichi.jp/select/weathernews/20110311/archive/news/2011/06/15/20110616k0000m040039000c.html. Accessed on October 20, 2011.
86. Asahi Shimbun: Patient evacuation without doctors attendance, 21 dead at Futaba hospital, March 18, 2011. Available from: http://www.asahi.com/national/update/0318/TKY201103170566.html. Accessed on October 20, 2011.
87. MSN Sankei News: US nuclear experts visit Japan for maximum support by NRC, March 13, 2011. Available from: http://sankei.jp.msn.com/world/news/110313/amr11031322310005-n1.htm, accessed October 20, 2011.
88. Yomiuri Online: IAEA dispatched Experts team to Fukushima, March 15, 2011. Available from: http://www.yomiuri.co.jp/world/news/20110315-OYT1T00186.htm, accessed October 20, 2011.

CHAPTER 16

Summary and Call to Action

Rick Bissell and Jasmin R. Ruback

CONTENTS

What We Know About Catastrophes 378
Call to Action 380
Some Remaining Questions 383
Conclusions 385

Until recently, we have been relatively naive regarding catastrophes as a continuation of the disasters with which we have frequent contact, rather than seeing catastrophes as a distinct species of mass emergency. As a result, there is precious little of the requisite science, research, and historical record upon which to build solid planning and protocols. Furthermore, we have learned that the emergency management system realigns itself based on events (Pine). Is the current planning for catastrophes going to be enough to keep us from needing to realign again? Lack of familiarity with the dynamics of catastrophes will lead most communities and states/regions, and even most emergency managers to assume that catastrophes can be effectively managed by the use of protocols and techniques designed for disasters, and will be surprised and confused when responses to disaster-designed inputs are ineffective.

Dr. Oliver-Smith warns us that "the potential for mass displacement is real," in fact it is virtually inevitable. As part of a global community, are we ready to have a discussion regarding how society changes after a catastrophe? For example, how might powers and authorities on all levels shift? How could we be impacted by catastrophes occurring on the other side of the world from us? How might the world community respond to a catastrophe in our own lands? The potential for significant increases in catastrophes secondary to the combined effects of various climatic changes, land-use patterns, and human population growth is poorly understood or even discounted by individuals, politicians, planners, and many emergency managers.

Figure 16.1 Satellite image of Hurricane Katrina. (http://www.katrina.noaa.gov/satellite/satellite.html.)

WHAT WE KNOW ABOUT CATASTROPHES

At the international level:

- Countries are willing and able to help respond to a catastrophe but response coordination is extremely complex.
- Catastrophes are hypercomplex and may involve or directly affect many countries at the same time.
- Militaries may play a large role in any catastrophic disaster response.

At the national level:

- The highly complex networks of businesses, governments, individuals, and nongovernmental organizations that contribute to the normal flow of life-sustaining goods and services are too numerous and too decentralized to be brought to bear on the process of delivering emergency supplies and services to all the catastrophe-affected areas under a single coordinating agency or control mechanism. Likewise, the technical and scientific knowledge necessary to make sound decisions for catastrophe response will not all lie in government agencies. This hypercomplexity renders the stove-piped center-of-control plans found in many national government agencies incapable of meeting the needs.
- National governments in large economically advanced countries are not accustomed to requesting immediate aid from other countries. Without pre-designated pathways integrating foreign assistance effectively when it arrives, such aid will be unnecessarily slowed or stopped.

At the state/regional level:

- States/provinces and regions, which carry front-line responsibility for bringing assistance and protection to the citizens of localities that are not capable of providing for their own needs in disasters, in many catastrophes will find themselves unable to perform these functions as per disaster plans, due to their own losses, and the overwhelming quantity of needs provoked by the event.
- The highly complex network of electrical power and fuel supplies, information management, food delivery, medical supply delivery, and finances are much larger than many states and provinces, and are not centrally located in such a manner that states and provinces can exert a strong influence over priorities.
- Even multi-state compacts may be rendered powerless in events in which every member state is affected.
- States and provinces may find themselves in the uncomfortable and virtually uncharted situation of having to make triage decisions about which communities are to receive assistance from the limited resources available, and which populations will be left on their own.
- Tools that states commonly depend on, such as national guard units or disaster medical assistance teams, will be insufficient to meet the needs at hand, and may even be nationalized and moved elsewhere.
- States and localities that have not developed mechanisms for quickly and effectively using spontaneous volunteers will unnecessarily divert human resources when they are most needed.

At the local government level:

- Local government and local services may be so damaged as to lose functionality, or even existence. Community leaders may be lost. This means that local people are essentially "on their own" for an extended period of time. All of the resources and activities that support and protect life will have to be provided by individuals or perhaps neighborhood groups without outside assistance for much longer than the 72 hours benchmark set in nationwide public preparedness training programs.
- For many localities, major resource deployment decisions will be made by outsiders.
- Information is likely to flow from localities to central news or government organizations long before quality information flows back to localities. This is due to many factors, including the loss of most electronic means of communication, and impeded transportation.
- Lack of in-flow from the margins. In disaster studies, we talk about zones of impact, and embrace the concept that beyond the zone of total impact, people who come from zones of marginal impact or the no direct-impact zones just beyond the area of marginal impact will infiltrate into the impact zones with both organized and spontaneous assistance. In catastrophes, the impact zones are so great that no assistance can be expected from the surrounding communities, or even the surrounding states or provinces.
- Massive outward migration. Catastrophes, more than disasters, are likely to result in local conditions being so bad for so long that large numbers of survivors permanently migrate elsewhere as soon as they can. This has significant long-term effects on the processes of reconstruction and recovery.

- Local healthcare may be severely hampered by a combination of damage to facilities, losses of healthcare personnel, and the reality that healthcare supplies will run out quickly and may not be replenished for weeks or even longer. Even in a pandemic catastrophe, in which physical infrastructure is untouched, the lack of adequate supplies and personnel could cripple the local healthcare services at the very moment that demand is the highest.

At the individual level:

- People need to be involved in decision making when determining plans for catastrophes.
- Volunteers need to be included in any planning.
- Consideration of evacuation and relocation will be a large part of any catastrophe.

CALL TO ACTION

It is always easier to conceptualize and prepare well-targeted responses to events if we have enough experience and applied science to be able to predict outcomes of specific planned interventions or programs. Humans have been collecting experience and information on disasters for as long as humans have been around, but the organized compilation of disaster-oriented information did not begin in earnest until the conclusion of World War II. In the ensuing 60+ years, subspecialties in disaster sociology, psychology, hazards geography, disaster medicine, emergency public health, and the emergence of the field of emergency management out of civil defense have all combined to increase our knowledge of how and why things happen in disasters. The extent that we have been able to build a level of confidence in predictions allows us to develop plans and protocols that are generally effective when applied consistently. This is not to say that we can control the turn of events in disasters or always respond effectively, but our abilities to significantly decrease suffering and improve outcomes are increasing. Regarding catastrophes, we are at the point of recognizing and studying the additional challenges they bring, in comparison to disasters, and hence we call on responsible individuals, organizations, and governments to take up the following actions:

Request agencies to be pro-active with funding for catastrophes instead of the reactive post-event:
- Funding for preparedness is often not available unless a specific threat is recognized and the event has occurred. Many threats related to catastrophes are outside of the vision of most of the public and their policy makers. In the United States, the experiences with the 9/11 attacks and Hurricane Katrina have served to motivate recognition that catastrophes are a reality requiring different kinds of responses. It could be argued that the focus on defense-oriented homeland security since 2001 may have diffused the development of a holistic concept of catastrophe, but the visit of Hurricane Katrina 4 years later provided an impetus for a string of funding within FEMA and some states to start planning for catastrophes. The National Science Foundation has not earmarked funding for

catastrophe studies, so researchers struggle to obtain funding for the process of doing the necessary background science. How funding develops or is maintained in the future remains to be seen. It may be helped by the violent climatic changes now being seen in some parts of the world, but many of the warming-related climatic changes are of relatively slow-onset and not the kind of thing that stimulates national politicians to dedicate a long-term string of funding.

Strengthen the ability of our responders to adapt to changing conditions and encourage policy makers to understand that under extreme stress, the concept of control is variable:

- Adequate response to catastrophes will require very high levels of multi-pod understanding and coordination, which does not fit well with many current top-down hierarchical response management modalities. A multi-sector, multi-pod approach is made difficult by the way societal, public safety, economic, and academic functions are divided into hard-walled sectors. As described in the public health and pandemic chapters of this book, in the United States, even public health funding for cross-sectoral disaster planning with emergency management and social services agencies specifies that the funding can only go to the participating health agencies. In most wealthy countries, government is the primary source of system-design and planning work for disasters, and governments have a tendency to see themselves being in control of operations. However, the multi-pod, multi-actor requirements for responding to catastrophes may be best met by having pods for industry (particularly information, power, food, and health related), non-profit public service organizations such as the Red Cross, which can muster and coordinate large numbers of volunteers, and scientific/technology expert groups that can provide science/technology-based advice and problem-solving, using personnel who are already catastrophe-educated. The broad breadth of experience that it took to create the chapters in this book is but an incomplete microcosm of what is needed.

Establish legal frameworks nationally and internationally to protect the welfare and human rights of people affected by catastrophe:

- Many economically advanced countries have an expectation that nearly everybody's needs can be met in disasters, thereby avoiding truly difficult ethical decisions *en mass*. This prepares us poorly for such decision-making in catastrophes in which there will not be adequate resources to meet the needs of large numbers of affected communities and individuals. As discussed in the ethics chapter of this book, catastrophes almost inevitably require gut-wrenching decisions to be made, often with an information base that is both poor in quantity and reliability. Without pre-prepared catastrophe-oriented decision-making protocols that are crafted in quiet times when deliberation can consider the full realm of ethical and moral values, decision makers will themselves become psychological victims of their necessary work, and may be exposed to post-event legal wrangling or vilification. In the United States, some state health departments have taken on the challenge of developing protocols for resource decisions in a pandemic scenario; perhaps some of their work can serve as an example for every other potential body of decision-makers.

Communicate the seriousness of a potential catastrophe and increase resilience by providing pre-event capacity building and on-site training for volunteers:

- Since World War II, we have gathered an increasingly substantial understanding of how individuals and groups respond in disasters, but we are lacking that quantity and quality of literature related to catastrophes. One of the challenges of catastrophe preparedness is that we are largely forced to extrapolate our predictions on human behavior based on the disaster-related literature, without really knowing if disaster findings can predict the behavior of humans in events of such size and quality that it becomes clear that outside help will not arrive any time soon. How long will people selflessly put themselves at risk to help others, before reverting to an ethic of protecting first one's own family or group? How probable is violence when there is both desperation and no local law enforcement? How adequate is the knowledge individuals and communities have regarding how to meet their own basic needs for survival, when electrical power, gasoline deliveries, food and water stocks, and communications are limited or unavailable for some period of time? More research on human behavior and human survival skills is needed related to catastrophe circumstances.

Make mitigation a priority:
- Given the fact that many of the variables that are merging to contribute to increased exposure to catastrophes are relatively slow in their onset (in terms of the typical government 2–4 year planning cycle), it is a serious challenge to stimulate nation-wide and international efforts to mitigate catastrophes. For the same reasons that are well-documented in disaster mitigation, individuals, investors, developers, and governments are often under-motivated to set aside short-term gain for long-term security ... for something that they cannot see happening in their short-term mindset. However, when considering such things as sea level rise, desertification, and aquifer losses, all of which can result in mass suffering and mass migration, it is clear that now is the time to start mitigating these and other hazards. This is a good example of a kind of mitigation that is perhaps not focused on emergency managers' efforts, but rather led by other organizations such as environmental protection groups or agencies. Long-visioned emergency managers can provide significant assistance in this direction using some of our tools such as SLOSH and HAZUS.

Continue to learn from the global community and update plans. Planning never stops, there are always new people to bring to the table and scientific advances to utilize:
- Methods for responding to catastrophes need to be re-thought at an international level. The challenge is that countries tend to work alone. Current work being done in the United States and some European countries may provide early models to explore, as long as information is freely shared. The UN "cluster system" has promise, but it showed considerable weakness in the response to Haiti's earthquake in 2010. Each country will need to address the planning issues within the realities of its own culture, geography, and economy, but collaboration with the surrounding countries may render significant savings in research and development costs, and may allow a much more efficient flow of response resources when catastrophes happen. Wealthy countries may consider the possibility that financially supporting catastrophe preparedness in poorer nations could result in net savings, if the results of the preparedness make the participating low-income countries more capable of managing their own needs in catastrophe, and if such improved response capabilities result in fewer instances of mass migration. All countries, wealthy or not, face the challenge of re-thinking emergency management paradigms, so that they include the specter of catastrophes. Some experience gained in some of the poorer countries that have experienced catastrophes, regarding the coordination of

inflowing response resources, may be profitably shared with wealthier countries that lack such experience.

Include individuals, families, and friends actively in decision making about their future when a catastrophe hits:
- The public needs to be prepared as part of the solution. This call for an improved community and individual resilience is a challenge for countries of all socio-economic development levels. Many people in poorer countries already have skills at surviving harsh conditions, but may lack the wherewithal to survive rapidly changing circumstances. Many people in wealthier countries lack the skills needed to survive a sudden loss of incoming lifeline supplies and services, but could be motivated to learn some of these if they become aware of the potential for personally experiencing catastrophe conditions. Public preparedness programs need to be revised so as to inform participants that, in some events, outside resources will not be available in the previously estimated three days, and that they need to be ready to meet their own needs for a longer period of time. Organized neighborhood disaster committees may be one potential solution. Only when many in a population can meet most of their own needs for an extended period of time, will governments and other relief agencies be able to approximate meeting the needs of those in the most dire conditions.

Improve policies and practices for adaptation, mitigation, and assistance for uprooted people:
- Mass migration will become an increasingly pressing issue; international frameworks are needed now. Regardless of whether the event is slow-onset or rapid, a catastrophe that makes it impossible to continue living in a given place will result in either mass death or mass migration … or both. As addressed in the chapter on mass migration in this book, changing climatic conditions, coupled with continuous population growth and the purposeful targeting of civilians in armed conflicts, guarantee that the globe will experience mass migrations … and human history is replete with examples of these mass movements going badly. Whether the migration is within a country or across national boundaries, governments and international organizations need to be prepared to facilitate resettlement in peaceful and sustainable conditions. Further work is needed in the United Nations now to help such work go more smoothly in the future.

SOME REMAINING QUESTIONS

Beyond the call to action we have just outlined, there are some questions about catastrophe preparedness and response that we recognize as important in guiding new work, but which we have yet to come to grips with, even regarding how to best formulate the questions. That is to say, we have not answered these questions, but they need to be addressed. For the most part, these questions relate to the local level but have distinct higher level implications. They are

- In conducting catastrophe planning, localities must recognize that they could quickly find themselves overwhelmed and totally outside of their own planning parameters and skill levels, and yet facing the reality that any kind of outside help is a long way off. How does one plan to operate outside of the plans?

- How can planners encourage individuals and families to be prepared to be self-sufficient for two weeks or longer for an event that may never happen? What kinds of training are needed? Should stockpiles be in individual homes or neighborhoods? What kinds of leadership or self-governance could be encouraged for such emergencies?
- The reality of catastrophes may be that populations of survivors will need to either survive on their own for an extended period of time or out-migrate. Either option requires substantial planning if it is to be effective ... and both options depend to a certain extent on the skills and behavior of the remaining local population. Good military campaign plans have a section for an organized retreat, if necessary. What is the emergency management equivalent of this kind of planning?
- How do you preplan to evacuate a large population, post-impact, when transportation infrastructure is at a minimum?
- Sometimes it is impossible to remain where people have previously lived and they must permanently relocate. Only through coordinated efforts can a large outmigration work reasonably smoothly, and that requires preplanning. Should this be a part of every jurisdiction's catastrophe preparedness planning requirements?
- If a population relocates, as a unit, it must start the recovery process in a place different from where the population's original response and recovery planning took place. How can populations plan for catastrophe recovery in such a manner that recognizes that they may no longer occupy the same space?
- One of the characteristics of catastrophes that make them hypercomplex is that many of the holders of resources needed for a response are not included in the typical government-led planning efforts. How does one plan in such a way that the owners of resources and technologies are brought into the decision-making processes, both before and during a catastrophe response?

Figure 16.2 Thirteen-story "Paz" apartment tower collapsed in Concepción, Chile in the 2010 earthquake. (Photo courtesy of Rick Bissell.)

CONCLUSIONS

The world is heading into an era in which increasingly grave challenges are likely to threaten large numbers of human beings. Some of the challenges will come on quickly, such as massive storms, earthquakes, and tsunamis, all made the more powerful by virtue of human settlements moving out into ever more vulnerable territory, and, in the case of storms, by increasing atmospheric heat providing the fuel for more frequent and more powerful storms. Some of the challenges will come more slowly, such as sea level rise resulting in losses of large habitable territories and fouling of aquifers. Some other slow-onset catastrophes may come as a result of increased aridity due to higher heat, combined with careless human practices in using both surface water and ground water, resulting in conversion of previously habitable land into deserts or wasteland. These processes are already underway. If one considers, on top of these "natural" causes, the challenges that will hit when petroleum starts disappearing in the next few decades, it is clear that once-rare catastrophes are likely to become more frequent and more damaging.

If it is the desire of humanity to limit suffering and loss wherever and whenever possible, then we need to start now with the many programs and processes that will be needed to mitigate catastrophes where possible, and prepare populations to withstand them where mitigation is insufficient or not possible. It is our contention that a multi-disciplinary and multinational effort is needed, and we hope that this book provides some of the information needed to get started. By bringing together the sciences and disciplines of sociology, psychology, public health, economics, anthropology, ethics, policy studies, and emergency management, the authors of this book hope to contribute to the process of building a literature and knowledge base capable of contributing to the development of a more solid understanding of catastrophes and their potential responses.

Epilogue

During the production phase of this book, Hurricane Sandy hit the Carribean nations of Haiti, Jamaica, Cuba and the Bahamas between October 24th and October 27th, 2012. As the storm moved up along the eastern coast, various modeling trackers projected that the storm would take a disastrous turn inward, somewhere between the Virginia and Connecticut coastlines (Figure E.1).

As it turned out, Superstorm Sandy was a harbinger of things to come to a society ... indeed perhaps a species ... that has been slow to take seriously the signs that we are entering into a new period of history in which, with more frequency than has been the case in the last couple of centuries, natural forces will threaten the well-being and lives of millions of people at a time. The New York/New Jersey area had been warned by scientists and emergency planners for more than two decades that the area was woefully vulnerable to precisely the kind of storm that was now headed that direction, one that brought high winds and a tall surge of water that could inundate the infrastructure that keeps the heavily populated area functioning.

The warning that Superstorm Sandy provided is real. Millions of people from Maryland to Connecticut were without electricity, some for weeks. In the NY/NJ area, the lack of electricity meant the evacuation of hospitals, the loss of elevators for the evacuation of unheated high-rise apartment buildings, the loss of telecommunications with which to request assistance, gas leaks and house fires, the loss of water pressure and of food, in a population that is accustomed to having its substantial needs provided on a daily basis. Few had alternative sources of heat for the winterlike weather that followed Sandy, reserve food to last a week or more, water, or a safe alternative place to go within the tangled transportation infrastructure. Indeed, many were "on their own" without having the wherewithal to meet their basic needs. While consisting of a resilient populous that will rebuild, areas struck were clearly vulnerable to just such a storm.

Superstorm Sandy did not meet the definition of a *catastrophe*, such as the 2010 earthquake in Haiti or the 2011 earthquake/tsunami/nuclear plant meltdown in Japan. However, it does raise many of the questions addressed in this book. What kinds of overwhelming challenges and risks are we likely to be facing in the next few decades of change? What kinds of preparations now can mitigate massive suffering later? What kinds of thinking and strategies are needed to enable societies to respond effectively to meet the needs of those who are affected by megastorms, massive earthquakes, pandemics, food shortages, or even large acts of terrorism, and how would those strategies and methods differ from what is common today? What will be the role of individual citizens in the work of self-protection, and how will governments collaborate with each other to be able to provide the quantity and kinds of assistance that are impossible for a single government ... even the largest governments on earth (see Figure E.2)?

As people dealt with the impact and aftermath of Sandy, the publishers of *Preparedness and Response for Catastrophic Disasters* were working to bring this

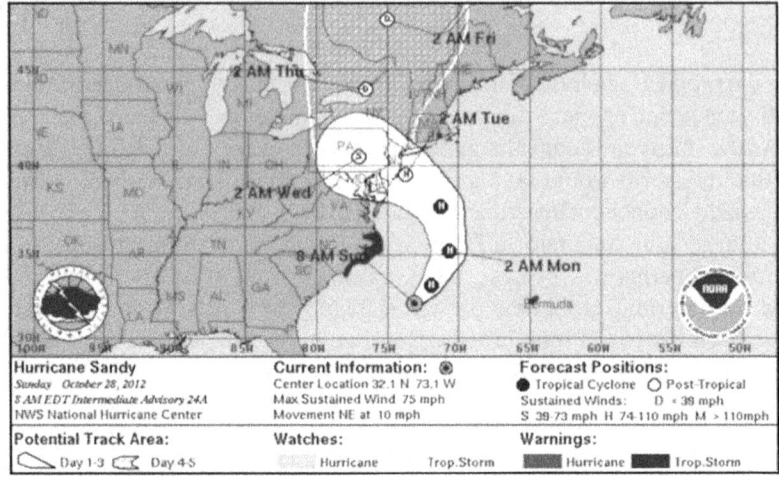

Figure E.1 NOAA projections of Hurricane Sandy's path. Source: NOAA.

Figure E.2 Staten Island, N.Y., Nov. 7, 2012—The TS Kennedy, a maritime academy training ship is moored in New York and serving as a home for 400 DHS volunteers. A provision in the 2006 Post-Katrina Act authorized DHS to create a surge capacity force (SCF) of federal employees to augment a catastrophic disaster response. The force was activated to help with Hurricane Sandy relief efforts. Source: FEMA/Tim Burkitt.

important and insightful volume to press, designed to meet the needs of those who plan on living into the future. This should be primary reading for emergency managers, policy makers, students, and all of us who take seriously the responsibility to look out for both ourselves and others, professionally and personally, regardless of where you are living.

Acronyms and Abbreviations

ACE	Agency Centric Effort
CAN	Collaborative Aid Network
CDC	Centers for Disease Control and Prevention (USA)
CERT	Citizen Emergency Response Team
CPP	Catastrophic Planning Program (a planning methodology devised by FEMA)
DfID	Department for International Development (UK)
DFO	Disaster Field Office
DHHS	Department of Health and Human Services (USA)
DHS	Department of Homeland Security
DOD	Department of Defense (USA)
DPC	*Direction de la Protection Civile* (Department of Civil Protection of Haiti)
ECHO	European Commission–Humanitarian Aid and Civil Protection
ED	Emergency Department (hospital, also called Accident and Emergency in the UK)
EM	Emergency Medicine or Emergency Management, depending on context
EMAC	Emergency Management Assistance Compact
EMIS	Emergency Management Information System
EMON(s)	Emergent Multi-Organizational Network(s)
EMT	Emergency Medical Technician
EMT-P	Emergency Medical Technician-Paramedic
EOC	Emergency Operations Center
ER	Emergency Room (hospital)
FAC	Family Assistance Center
FDIC	Federal Deposit Insurance Corporation (USA)
FEMA	Federal Emergency Management Agency (USA)
GIS	Geographic Information System
HAZUS	A GIS-based software program for estimating and tracking losses and damage in disasters. This is freely distributed by the Federal Emergency Management Agency (FEMA).
HHS	US Department of Health and Human Services. HHS is also abbreviated as DHHS.
HSPD	*Homeland Security Presidential Directive*
ICS	Incident Command System
IMS	Incident Management System
IOM	International Organization for Migration
JTF	Joint Task Force
NHK	Japanese Broadcasting Corporation
NIMS	National Incident Management System (USA)
NMSZ	New Madrid Seismic Zone (a seismic zone in the U.S. Mississippi River basin)

NPS	Nuclear Power Station
NRCC	National Response Coordination Center
NVOAD	National Voluntary Organizations Active in Disasters
NWS	National Weather Service (USA)
OCHA	Office for the Coordination of Humanitarian Assistance (UN)
OEM	Office of Emergency Management
PD-HL	Post-Disaster Humanitarian Logistics
PH	Public Health
PIE	Partially Integrated Effort
PPE	Personal Protective Equipment
PSC	Psycho-socio-cultural
PVO	Private Voluntary Organization
RAP	Resettlement Action Plan
RRCC	Regional Response Coordination Center
RRF	Rapid Reflection Force
SAR	Search and Rescue (also S&R)
SCU	Surgical Care Unit
TCL	Targeted Capabilities List
TEPCO	Tokyo Electric Power Company
UNHCR	United Nations High Commissioner for Refugees
UNICEF	United Nations Children's Fund
USAID	United States Agency for International Development
USAR	Urban Search and Rescue
US&R	Urban Search and Rescue
UTL	Universal Task List
WFP	World Food Programme (of the United Nations)

Index

A

AAR, *see* After Action Report (AAR)
ACE, *see* Agency Centric Effort (ACE)
ADR, *see* Alternative dispute resolution (ADR)
After Action Report (AAR), 331
Agency Centric Effort (ACE), 135
Agent-generated demands, 134
All-hazards planning, 268
Alternative dispute resolution (ADR), 292
Americans with Disabilities Act, 62, 63
Americans with Rehabilitation Act, 62, 63
Anthropogenic hazards, 28
Arenal dam resettlement project, 215–217
ATM systems, 125
Avian influenza, 305

B

Banking systems, 125
Biological moral community dimension, 66
British Petroleum (BP), 199
Building block approach, 327
Bureaucratic model, 40, 41

C

Call to action
    communication, 381–382
    improving policies and practices, 383
    learning from global community and update plans, 382–383
    legal framework establishment, 381
    making mitigation priority, 382
    including people in decision making, 383
    questions, 383–384
    requesting agencies, 380–381
    strengthening responder's ability, 381
Camps, 205
CAN, *see* Collaborative Aid Network (CAN)
Capabilities-based preparedness guidelines approach, 80
Catastrophe impacts on society, 37
    outside involvement, 39
    psychological impact, 38
    sheltering, 38
Catastrophe planning, 257–258
    complexity, 264
    conflicts with, 263–264
    CPP, 271–273
    FEMA, 260
    FEMA organized planning meeting, 263
    IPS, 270–271
    North Atlantic Hypercomplexity approach, 273–277
    planning activities, 262, 263
    practices, 270
Catastrophe readiness and response
    applied ethics, 50–51
    civil rights and anti-discrimination laws, 61–64
    constitutional rights, 58–61
    ethics and law relationship, 58
    ethics typologies, 50
    focusing on vulnerable populations, 71–72
    international law, 64–65
    moral community dimensions, 65–67
    new media and social networking, 56–57
    professional codes of ethics for media, 55–56
    professional duty and self-preservation, 54–55
    professional ethics and codes of conduct, 52–54
    real-time decision making, 51–52
    social inequities, 72–73
    sources of ethical thinking, 48–49
    survival of fittest, 47–48
    U.S. aid to foreign nations, 67–69
    volunteer organizations and private donations, 69–71
Catastrophe response
    citizen involvement initiatives, 262
    critical success factors, 261
    integrating international responders, 262
    strategic thinking, 259–260
    voluntary responders, 260, 262
Catastrophe response planning
    change of focus of planning, 268–269
    innovations, 264
    legislation for, 264–265
    new research, 266–268
    new theory and decision-making tools, 268
    predictive modeling techniques, 269–270
Catastrophe-focused planning models, 276
Catastrophes, 4, 6, 138, 191–193, 225, 282, 284, 336, 377
    advocacy groups, 242
    catastrophic events, 242
    challenges, 242
    characteristics, 138–139
    common factors in, 22–23
    common misconceptions, 226–231

Catastrophes *(Continued)*
    complexity of, 258
    conceptual continuum, 6
    consequences for emergency supply chain, 139–141, 143
    contending with materiel convergence, 146
    critical infrastructure, 152–167
    critical supplies distribution, 144, 145
    dartmouth interactive media laboratory, 322
    demand knowledge, 145–146
    disaster response planning, 144
    disaster *vs.*, 30, 110, 320–321
    drought and desertification, 18–20
    earthquake and tsunami, 336
    emergent groups and networks, 234–239
    existing and emergent responders in, 248–252
    extensive and extended out-migration, 143
    facilitating integration and visibility, 245–247
    FEMA definition, 4
    flattened capital, 139
    global pandemic, 20
    in Haiti, 342–354
    hazards, 27–29, 35–37
    health effects, 177, 178
    help from neighboring cities and counties, 141
    holistic vulnerability, 33–34
    Hurricane Katrina, 13–16, 34
    Hurricane Rita, 13–16
    at individual level, 380
    influenza, 12–13
    at international level, 378
    interruption, 39–40, 141, 142
    Irish potato famine, 10–11
    in Japan, 354–370
    Little Ice Age in Europe, 9–10
    at local government level, 379–380
    local officials, 140
    logistical requirements, 141
    long-term recovery resources, 140
    mass media and political arena, 142
    mass out-migration, 243–244
    middle ages Black Plague, 7–9
    myths and realities, 227
    at national level, 378
    New Madrid Mega-Earthquake, 21–22
    New York, 243
    personal or people convergence, 239
    poverty line in Haiti, 32
    PPD-8, 265–266
    public health, 7
    Quarantelli's criteria, 4
    recommended additional readings, 247
    response and evaluate exercises, 322
    routine professional roles, 140
    Sea Level Rise, 17–18
    social and physical environments, 143
    social vulnerability, 31, 32
    at state/regional level, 379
    suggestions for improvement, 143–144
    supply distribution area, 244
    supporting systems, 146
    surge capacity planning role in, 181–182
    tabletop attendee roles, 336
    terrorism-based, 159
    types, 241
    vulnerability, 31, 35–37
    webinars, 322
    widespread, 132, 139
Catastrophes effects on CI, 162
    earthquakes, 160
    high-mortality pandemic, 161
    infrastructure collapse, 163–164
    mean institutions, 161
    power supplies, 161
    resilience and vulnerability, 161, 162–163
Catastrophic disaster recovery, 294; *see also* Disaster recovery assistance framework
    existing collaborative operation modification, 297
    improving integration of disaster recovery issues, 297–298
    maximizing collective strength, 396–397
    non-traditional stakeholder involvement, 295–296
    shifting resource delivery balance, 294–295
Catastrophic disasters, 131
    aid response effort, 132
    cedar rapids and Iowa, 133
    characteristic of, 282
    events, 132–133
    impacts, 285–286
    logistical operations, 133
    moderate disaster, 132
    physical destruction, 131–132
    preparedness, 158
    widespread catastrophe, 132
Catastrophic Incident Supplement (CIS), 268
Catastrophic Planning Program (CPP), 270, 271, 276; *see also* Integrated Planning System (IPS)
    FEMA regions, 271
    planning approach comparison, 277
    strengths, 272
    weaknesses, 272, 273
CBRNE, *see* Chemical, biological, radiological, nuclear, and explosive (CBRNE)

INDEX

Cernea's model, 209
CERT, *see* Community Emergency Response Teams (CERT)
Chemical, biological, radiological, nuclear, and explosive (CBRNE), 322
CI, *see* Critical infrastructure (CI)
CIS, *see* Catastrophic Incident Supplement (CIS)
Civil hazards, 28
Civil Rights and Anti-Discrimination Laws, 61
    Americans with Disabilities Act, 62, 63
    Americans with Rehabilitation Act, 62, 63
Climate equity, 196
Cluster system, 344
COG, *see* Continuity of government (COG)
Collaborative Aid Network (CAN), 135
Common misconceptions, 226
    in catastrophes, 229–230
    decision-making and response, 230, 231
    disasters, 228, 229
    DRC, 227–228
    high consequent events, 231
    local residents hired by USAID, 230
    pre-tsunami planning, 231
    responses, 226
Community Emergency Response Teams (CERT), 297
Community reconstruction, 206
Community-partnership building, 246
Complex disaster, 343
Consequentialism, *see* Teleological ethics
Constitutional rights, 58
    Eighth Amendment, 60, 61
    First Amendment Rights, 59
    Habeas Corpus, 59
    Right to Due Process, 59
    Right to Equal Protection, 59
Continua of relocation, 201–202
Continuity of government (COG), 155
Continuity of Operations (COOP), 155
Convergence, 137
COOP, *see* Continuity of Operations (COOP)
Coordinating pandemic response, 305
    principles of pandemic response, 305–306
    priority setting, 306–307
Cost-push inflation, 120
CPP, *see* Catastrophic Planning Program (CPP)
CrisisCommons, 57
Critical infrastructure (CI), 152
    catastrophes effects on, 160–161
    education and research, 156
    first echelon, 157–158
    focus on inviting private owners, 166
    food, water, and shelter, 153–154
    fourth echelon, 160
    goods and services, 155–156
    government and finance, 155
    infrastructure collapse, 163–164
    logistics, transportation, and electricity, 154–155
    mitigation, 164–165
    pre-disaster states, 153
    priorities, 157
    public health and healthcare, 156, 157
    recognize hypercomplexity, 165–166
    recognize professional organizations, 167
    recognizing roles of second-echelon CI, 167
    second echelon, 158–159
    socioeconomic and cultural impacts, 161–163
    telecommunications and information technologies, 155
    third echelon, 159–160
    work with non-traditional assets, 167
Critical infrastructure failures in catastrophes, 164
    focus on inviting private owners, 166
    hypercomplexity recognizing, 165–166
    mitigation, 164, 165
    professional organizations recognizing, 167
    second-echelon CI, 167
    work with non-traditional assets, 167
Cry wolf effect, 118

D

Decision-making tools, 268
Demand-pull inflation, 120
Demographic movement, 200, 201
Deontological ethics, 50
Department for International Development (UK) (DfID), 347
Department of Civil Protection of Haiti, *see* *Direction de la Protection Civile* (DPC)
Department of Defense (DOD), 101, 344
Department of Health and Human Services (DHHS), 302
Development-forced displacement and resettlement (DFDR), 189
DFDR, *see* Development-forced displacement and resettlement (DFDR)
DfID, *see* Department for International Development (DfID)
DFO, *see* Disaster field office (DFO)
DHHS, *see* Department of Health and Human Services (DHHS)
DHHS Pandemic Flu Plan, 311
    collaborative PH approach, 314
    components, 312

DHHS Pandemic Flu Plan (*Continued*)
    response portion of, 313
    standardization, 312, 313
DHS, *see* U. S. Department of Homeland Security (DHS)
DHS Pandemic Plan, 314–315
Direction de la Protection Civile (DPC), 345; *see also* Federal Emergency Management Agency (FEMA)
Disaster, 6, 228
    dispersed, 343
    extra large, 343
    management system, 358–359
    natural, 189
    organizations in, 228
    readiness and response organizational framework, 78
    response planning, 144
    victims, 64–65
Disaster agent-generated demands, 145–146
Disaster Countermeasures Basic Act, 358
Disaster fatigue, *see* Donor fatigue
Disaster field office (DFO), 249
Disaster Medical Assistance Team (DMAT), 360
    missions, 363
    problems, 364–365
    roles, 364
    supervisors, 362
Disaster recovery assistance framework
    ADR technique, 292, 293
    comprises, 287
    dimensions, 287
    horizontal and vertical integration, 290–291
    principle challenges, 286
    role of planning in, 292–293, 294
    shortfall in, 284
    Stafford Act, 287
    stakeholder rules, 288
    timing of resource, 288–290, 293–294
    transforming dimensions, 291–292
    understanding of local needs, 288
    weaknesses in, 285
Disaster Recovery Center (DRC), 82
Disaster Research Center, 227
Disease control mechanisms, 175
    animate vectors, 175, 176
    control disease spread, 176–177
    disease spread, 175
    incubation period, 177
    SARS, 176
DMAT, *see* Disaster Medical Assistance Team (DMAT)
DOD, *see* Department of Defense (DOD)
Donor fatigue, 70
Doppler radar, 118
DPC, *see Direction de la Protection Civile* (DPC)
DRC, *see* Disaster Recovery Center (DRC)
Drought and desertification, 18
    in American Southwest, 18
    climate change-generated, 19
    in North American bread basket, 19
    in United States, 19–20

E

Earthquake, 336
    Haiti earthquake, 3
    Japan earthquake, 354
    mega-earthquakes, 199
    New Madrid Mega-Earthquake, 21, 22
ECHO, *see* European Commission–Humanitarian Aid and Civil Protection (ECHO)
EEG, *see* Exercise evaluation guides (EEG)
EM, *see* Emergency management (EM)
EMAC, *see* Emergency Management Assistance Compact (EMAC)
Emergency, 6
Emergency management (EM), 171, 302, 369
Emergency Management Assistance Compact (EMAC), 92
Emergency management information system (EMIS), 362
Emergency management plan (EMP), 332
Emergency operations center (EOC), 249, 331, 346
Emergency operations plan (EOP), 332
Emergency response; *see also* Haitian earthquake
    data collection/management, 349
    DoD, 348, 349
    Haitian Government response, 345–346
    NGO/PVO response, 349
    United Nations response, 346
    US Government response, 346–348
Emergent groups, 234
Emergent multi-organizational network (EMON), 236
    centralized approaches and IMS, 238
    fishing village in Tamil Nadu, 237
    fleeting and volitional member participation, 239
    Town of Kinniya, 237
Emergent organizational networks, 236
Emergent response groups, 235
EMIS, *see* Emergency management information system (EMIS)
EMON, *see* Emergent multi-organizational network (EMON)

EMP, *see* Emergency management plan (EMP)
Environmental
    changes, 195
    disruption, 195
    migrants, 194
EOC, *see* Emergency operations center (EOC)
EOP, *see* Emergency operations plan (EOP)
Epidemiology, 172
Ethics, 49
    applied, 50–51
    in catastrophe readiness and response, 48, 49
    ethics and law relationship, 58
    national security, 73
    population security, 73
    Professional Codes of Ethics, 55
    typologies, 50
Etiology, 7, 172, 173, 174
European Commission–Humanitarian Aid and Civil Protection (ECHO), 347
Evacuation, 88, 89
Exercise cycle, 332
Exercise documentation, 327, 328
Exercise evaluation, 330–331
Exercise evaluation guides (EEG), 331
Exercise planning conferences, 333
Exercise planning team, 324–325
Extinction level event, 6

F

FAC, *see* Family assistance center (FAC)
Facilitation skills, 335
Family assistance center (FAC), 249
FBI, *see* Federal bureau of investigation (FBI)
FDIC, *see* Federal Deposit Insurance Corporation (FDIC)
Federal bureau of investigation (FBI), 322
Federal Deposit Insurance Corporation (FDIC), 125
Federal disaster declaration, 282
Federal Emergency Management Agency (FEMA), 117, 345
    catastrophe planning, 260
    Catastrophic Event Study, 266
    HAZUS logo from, 270
    organized planning meeting, 263
    regions, 271, 331
    roles and responsibilities, 264–265
    whole community, 260, 283
Federal emergency management system, 81
    advantages, 81
    DHS, 82
    Stafford Act, 82
Federalism in preparedness response and recovery, 85

    Barry's analysis, 86–87
    evacuation, 86
    Stafford Act, 86
    State law, 85
    in United States, 85
Federal pandemic plans, 311–312; *see also* Pandemic scenario
    DHHS Pandemic Flu Plan, 312–314
    DHS plan, 314–315
FEMA, *see* Federal Emergency Management Agency (FEMA); US Federal Emergency Management Agency (FEMA)
Financial markets; *see also* Catastrophes
    banking systems, 125–126
    insurance companies, 124–125
    real estate markets, 126–127
First echelon, 157–158
Flood insurance, 124
Forced migration, 187
    and after displacement, 204–205
    mass relocation and legal status, 196–198
Four Stage Framework, 207
Fourth echelon, 160
FSE, *see* Full-scale exercise (FSE)
Fukushima Daiichi NPS, *see* Fukushima Daiichi Nuclear Power Station (Fukushima Daiichi NPS)
Fukushima Daiichi NPS failure, responses to, 366–370
Fukushima Daiichi Nuclear Power Station (Fukushima Daiichi NPS), 356
Full-scale exercise (FSE), 332

G

Gap analysis, 269, 270
GDP, *see* Gross Domestic Product (GDP)
Geographic Information System (GIS), 63, 269
Geographical moral community dimension, 66
Global climate change
    adverse effects of, 199
    mass displacement, 199–200
    mitigation, 200
    vulnerability, 198–199
Global Pandemic, 20–21
Great Wall in Taro, The, 355
Gross Domestic Product (GDP), 121
Ground-based transportation system, 154

H

Haiti earthquake, 3, 70, 342, 353, 354
    catastrophes, 229
    characteristics, 343

Haiti earthquake (*Continued*)
　complexities, 342–343
　consequences on emergency supply chain, 140
　debris removal, 230
　price of cement after, 119
Hazards, 27, 28
　earthquake, 35
　human activities, 37
　nuclear weapon, 35
　physical environment, 36
　vulnerability, 36, 37
HAZUS-MH methodology, 269, 270
Healthcare, 156, 157
Herd immunity, 174
Homeland Security Exercise Evaluation Program (HSEEP), 324
Homeland security exercise evaluation program, 323–324
Homeland Security Presidential Directive-5 (HSPD-5), 324
Homeland Security Presidential Directive-8 (HSPD-8), 324
Horizontal and vertical integration, 290
　to catastrophic disaster recovery, 291
　community types, 290–291
Hot wash, 338
Housing and urban development (HUD), 296
HSEEP, *see* Homeland Security Exercise Evaluation Program (HSEEP)
HSPD-5, *see* Homeland Security Presidential Directive-5 (HSPD-5)
HSPD-8, *see* Homeland Security Presidential Directive-8 (HSPD-8)
HUD, *see* Housing and urban development (HUD)
Hurricane Evacuation (HurrEvac), 270
Hurricane Katrina, 1, 378
　catastrophe-like characteristics, 3
　healthcare issue after, 15
　impacts, 2
　learned lessons, 16
　New Orleans under water, 14
　NIMS approach, 15
　situation, 13
Hurricane Rita, 14, 16
　evacuations, 116
　statewide building code establishment, 98
Hypercomplexity, 165–166

I

IAEA, *see* International Atomic Energy Agency (IAEA)
IAEM, *see* International Association of Emergency Managers (IAEM)
ICE, *see* Instituto Costarricense de Electricidad (ICE)
ICS, *see* Incident Command Structure (ICS)
IDMC, *see* International Displacement Monitoring Center (IDMC)
IDP, *see* Internally displaced person (IDP)
Impoverishment Risks and Reconstruction approach (IRR approach), 209
Improvement plan (IP), 331
IMS, *see* Incident Management System (IMS)
Inadequate inputs approach, 210
Incident Command Structure (ICS), 80, 232–233, 267, 324
Incident Management System (IMS), 232
　challenges, 232
　effectiveness and appropriateness, 232
　ICS, 232–233
Indian Ocean Tsunami, 2–3
Infancy-to-teen concept, 327
Infectious disease vocabulary, 172
　CDC website, 174, 175
　etiology, 172, 173
　malaria vector-borne disease life cycle, 174
　personal protective equipment, 176
　social distancing, quarantine, and isolation, 175
　swamp drainage or insecticides, 173–174
　vector, 173
Inflation, 119, 121
　cost-push inflation, 119, 120
　demand-pull inflation, 119, 120
Influenza, 12, 175, 302
　in Kansas, 12
　pandemic, 12
　situation, 12
　in United States, 13
Information technologies, 155
Infrastructure collapse, 163
　in poor Haiti, 163, 164
　in wealthy Japan, 163, 164
Instituto Costarricense de Electricidad (ICE), 215
Insurance companies, 124
　Alfa Mutual, 124
　flood, 124, 125
　taxpayer, 124
Integrated Planning System (IPS), 270–271; *see also* North Atlantic Hypercomplexity approach
　definite measure of reality, 276
　planning approach comparison, 277
　strengths, 271

INDEX

Inter-organizational partnerships; *see also* Jurisdictional collaborations
  broad-based collaborations, 92
  formal partnerships, 91
  horizontal cooperation, 92
  implementation, 91
  inter-jurisdictional partnerships, 91–92
  mutual aid agreements, 92
  vertical collaborations, 92
Intergovernmental Panel on Climate Change (IPCC), 217
Internally displaced person (IDP), 197
International Association of Emergency Managers (IAEM), 53
International Atomic Energy Agency (IAEA), 370
International Displacement Monitoring Center (IDMC), 196
International human rights law, 64
  disaster victims, 64–65
  non-combatant victims, 65
  policies and standards, 64
IP, *see* Improvement plan (IP)
IPCC, *see* Intergovernmental Panel on Climate Change (IPCC)
IPS, *see* Integrated Planning System (IPS)
Irish Potato Famine
  catastrophes, 11–12
  death toll estimation, 11
  potato blight, 10, 11
  situation, 10
IRR approach, *see* Impoverishment Risks and Reconstruction approach (IRR approach)
Isolation, 175

J

Japan earthquake, 354; *see also* Haiti earthquake
  death toll, 355
  DMAT missions, 363
  Fukushima Daiichi nuclear power plant, 355
  JMAT, 365, 366
  medical response, 362
  search and rescue operations, 360–362
  tsunami, 355
Japanese Medical Association Team (JMAT), 365
JFO, *see* Joint Field Office (JFO)
JMAT, *see* Japanese Medical Association Team (JMAT)
Joint Field Office (JFO), 82
Joint Task Force (JTF), 102, 349, 361

JTF, *see* Joint Task Force (JTF)
Jurisdictional collaborations, 88; *see also* Organizational issues in catastrophic events
  barriers to inter-, 91
  debugging, 91
  decision making, 90
  influencing factors, 90
  inter-organizational conflict, 89
  planning efforts, 88
  private resources use in response, 92–93
  problems and challenges, 88
  public agencies, 89

L

Large non-profit groups, 251
Law enforcement availability, 304–305
Little Ice Age in Europe, 9
  crops failure, 10
  situation, 9
Local governments emergency management system, 84
  Emergency Planning and Community Right, 84
  local planning requirements, 84–85
Logistics, 330
  resources, 154
  systems, 134
Long-haul transportation, 144

M

Managing Medical Surge (MMS), 322
Mass casualty incidents (MCI), 52
Mass displacement, 186, 187
  catastrophes and mass relocations, 191–193
  complexity and causation, 189–191
  DFDR, 188, 189
  disaster-associated mass displacements, 187
  driving forces and policies, 187
  emergency management strategies, 187, 188
  estimation, 195–196
  forced migration and resettlement, 187
  global climate changes and mass relocation, 193–194
  Haitian refugees await relocation, 190
  impoverishment risks and reconstruction model, 208–210
  involuntary migration and recovery, 206–207
  mass relocation, 187
  psychological, social, and cultural impoverishment, 210–211

Mass displacement (*Continued*)
  and resettlement process complexity, 210
  social destruction, 188
  understanding resettlement, 207–208
Mass out-migration, 243–244
Mass relocation, 178, 187
  catastrophes and, 191–193
  consequences of, 202
  cultural identity, 203, 204
  establishing causality in, 190
  global climate changes and, 193–194
Material elements, 203
Material reconstruction, 207
Materiel convergence, 137
  contending with, 146
  lack of standard operating procedure, 138
  massive global response, 137–138
  problem with, 137
MCI, *see* Mass casualty incidents (MCI)
MEA, *see* Millennium Ecosystem Assessment (MEA)
Medical triage, 52
Mega-catastrophe, 91
Mega-earthquakes, 199
Middle ages Black Plague, 7
  in Europe, 8
  improvements, 9
  modern medicine, 9
  situation, 7
Millennium Ecosystem Assessment (MEA), 193
Mitigation, 112
  building codes, 115–116
  land use restrictions, 114–115
  private, 113–114
  public, 114
MMS, *see* Managing Medical Surge (MMS)
Moral community, 65
  biological dimension, 66
  geographical dimension, 66
  increasing factors, 71
  pet rescue, 66, 67
  social vulnerability, 71
  temporal dimension, 66
  in United States, 72
Multi-year planning, 332
Multidimensional stress, 207

N

National Disaster Recovery Framework (NDRF), 283
National Disaster Recovery Framework, 78–79
National exercise program (NEP), 331
National Fire Protection Association (NFPA), 92
National Guard, 83–84
National Incident Management System (NIMS), 15, 80, 314, 324
National Infrastructure Simulation and Analysis Center (NISAC), 270
National level exercise (NLE), 331
National planning, 78
  national disaster recovery framework, 78–79
  National Preparedness Guidelines, 79–80
  NIMS, 80–81
  Scenarios, 329
National recovery policy, 284
  catastrophic disaster impacts, 285–286
  disaster recovery assistance framework, 284
  NDRF, 284–285
National Response Coordination Center (NRCC), 82
National Response Framework (NRF), 284
National Voluntary Organizations Active in Disaster (NVOAD), 69, 297
National Weather Service (NWS), 118
Natural disasters, 189
Natural hazards, 28; *see also* Catastrophes
  direct subsidies, 117–118
  evacuations, 116–117
  GDP, 121–122
  inflation, 119–121
  macroeconomics, 118–119
  mitigation, 112–113, 123–124
  risk, 112
  tax Incentives, 117
  unemployment, 122–123
  warning systems, 118
NDRF, *see* National Disaster Recovery Framework (NDRF)
NEP, *see* National exercise program (NEP)
New Madrid Mega-Earthquake, 21–22
New Madrid Seismic Zone (NMSZ), 171, 271, 274, 331
New Orleans, LA (NOLA), 14
NFPA, *see* National Fire Protection Association (NFPA)
NGO, *see* Non-governmental organization (NGO)
NIMS, *see* National Incident Management System (NIMS)
NISA, *see* Nuclear and Industrial Safety Agency (NISA)
NISAC, *see* National Infrastructure Simulation and Analysis Center (NISAC)
NLE, *see* National level exercise (NLE)
NMSZ, *see* New Madrid Seismic Zone (NMSZ)
NOLA, *see* New Orleans, LA (NOLA)
Non-governmental organization (NGO), 197, 342

INDEX 399

North Atlantic Hypercomplexity approach, 273
   earthquake in NMSZ, 274
   hypercomplexity approach, 274–275
   planning approach comparison, 277
   strengths, 275
   variables differentiate catastrophes, 273–274
   weaknesses, 275
Norwegian Refugee Council (NRC), 196
NRC, *see* Norwegian Refugee Council (NRC)
NRCC, *see* National Response Coordination Center (NRCC)
NRF, *see* National Response Framework (NRF)
Nuclear and Industrial Safety Agency (NISA), 356
   characteristics, 357
   disaster healthcare, 359–360
   disaster management system, 358–359
   failure, 356–357
   failure response, 366
NVOAD, *see* National Voluntary Organizations Active in Disaster (NVOAD)
NWS, *see* National Weather Service (NWS)

O

OCHA, *see* Office for the Coordination of Humanitarian Assistance (OCHA)
OEM, *see* Office of Emergency Management (OEM)
OFDA, *see* Office of U.S. Foreign Disaster Assistance (OFDA)
Office for the Coordination of Humanitarian Assistance (OCHA), 343, 344
Office of Emergency Management (OEM), 250
Office of the Response Coordinator (ORC), 347
Office of U.S. Foreign Disaster Assistance (OFDA), 67
Operational plans (OPLANS), 271
OPLANS, *see* Operational plans (OPLANS)
ORC, *see* Office of the Response Coordinator (ORC)
Organizational issues in catastrophic events, 85
   compelling evacuation, 94
   federal troops deployment, 87
   federalism in preparedness response and recovery, 85–87
   governmental powers, 87–88
   immunity in emergency management, 95
   negligence, 94–95
   officials liability and volunteers, 94
   population return limits to evacuation zones, 93–94
   public officials and volunteers indemnification, 95
   warnings and evacuation communication, 93
Organizational structures, 40; *see also* Catastrophes
   Bureaucratic model, 40
   command and control model, 41
   problem-solving model, 40–41
   unconventional nature, 42

P

Pandemic control
   healthcare needs, 309, 310
   PH and EM personnel collaboration, 309
   societal needs, 310–311
   tasks and tactics, 308
Pandemic flu scenario, 304–305
   containing and controlling, 310
   PPE, 309
Pandemic scenario, 301
   coordinating pandemic response, 305–307
   funding limitations, 315
   importance of care, 301–302
   influenza, 302
   international barriers, 316
   lack of unity between disciplines, 316
   long-range problems, 316–317
   pandemic flu scenario, 304–305
   PPE, 308, 309
   scene safety, 307
   worker protection decisions, 307–308
Partially Integrated Effort (PIE), 135
PD-HL, *see* Post-Disaster Humanitarian Logistics (PD-HL)
People convergence, 239, 242
Personal convergence, 239, 241
Personal protective equipment (PPE), 309
PH, *see* Public health (PH)
PIE, *see* Partially Integrated Effort (PIE)
PKEMRA, *see* Post Katrina Emergency Management Reform Act (PKEMRA)
PMCC, *see* Presidential Commission on Recovery and Reconstruction (PMCC)
Posse Comitatus Act, 87
Post-Disaster Humanitarian Logistics (PD-HL), 133
   agent-and response-generated demands, 134–135
   CANs, 136
   challenge, 134
   characteristics, 136–137
   contingencies, 136
   federal disaster logistics system functions, 134
   flow of supplies, 137
   humanitarian and commercial logistics, 134

Post-Disaster Humanitarian Logistics
    (PD-HL) (*Continued*)
  local distribution, 135
  logistics systems, 134
  PIE, 135–136
  relevant operations, 135
Post-disaster resettlement
  failure factors, 211, 212–213
  success factors, 211, 212
Post Katrina Emergency Management Reform Act (PKEMRA), 284
Post-Katrina Emergency Reform Act, 264–265
PPD-8, *see* Presidential Preparedness Directive-8 (PPD-8)
PPE, *see* Personal protective equipment (PPE)
Predictive modeling techniques, 269–270
Preparedness cycle, 332
Presidential Commission on Recovery and Reconstruction (PMCC), 345
Presidential Preparedness Directive-8 (PPD-8), 265–266
Private Voluntary Organization (PVO), 349
Problem-solving model, 40–41
Professional codes of ethics, 52
  Code of Professional Conduct, 53
  CrisisCommons, 57
  crisis communication, 56
  ethical principles, 55
  media, 56
  mobile applications, 57
  perpetuating disaster myths, 56
  research, 56
  rules, 54
  social networking, 56
  SparkRelief, 57
PSC, *see* Psycho-socio-cultural (PSC)
Psycho-socio-cultural (PSC), 210
Psychological stress, 207
Public health (PH), 171, 172, 302
  basic vocabulary, 172
  catastrophes and, 177–181
  common personal protective equipment, 176
  determinants of health outcome in, 180
  disease control mechanisms, 175–177
  epidemiology, 172
  infectious disease vocabulary, 172–175
  managers, 306, 307
  priorities, 180–181
  role in catastrophes, 171
  secondary health effect causes from, 179
  surge capacity planning role in, 181–182
  surveillance data mapping, 173
  systems, 156, 157
PVO, *see* Private Voluntary Organization (PVO)

Q

Quarantine, 175
Quick Look Report (QLR), 331

R

Radar, 118
RAP, *see* Resettlement action plan (RAP)
Real estate markets, 126–127
Recovery from Catastrophe
  community stakeholders, 97
  Louisiana Recovery Authority, 99
  opportunity for political change, 98, 100
  post-disaster planning, 97
  pre-disaster planning, 96
  rebuilding challenges, 96
  recommendations, 101
  state and local governments funding, 98
  Urban Land Institute's report, 101
Refugee, 197
Regional Response Coordination Center (RRCC), 82
Resettlement, 187, 205
  action plans, 214–215
  arenal dam resettlement project, 215–217
  process complexity, 210
  RAP, 214–215
  reconstruction, and development, 213–214
  sites for, 212
  understanding, 207–208
Resettlement action plan (RAP), 211, 214–215
Response functions; *see also* Haitian earthquake
  food, 353
  medical response, 350–351
  public health response, 351
  search and rescue response, 349–350
  shelter, 351–352
  water and sanitation, 352
Response-generated demands, 145–146
Road Home Program, 99
RRCC, *see* Regional Response Coordination Center (RRCC)
Rwandan refugee camp in east Zaire, 205

S

SAR efforts, *see* Search and rescue efforts (SAR efforts)
SARS, *see* Severe acute respiratory syndrome (SARS)
Scenario-based planning, 269
Scenario-based training, 321–322
Sea, Lake, and Overland Surges from Hurricanes (SLOSH), 270

Sea Level Rise, 17–18
Search and rescue efforts (SAR efforts), 361
Second echelon, 158–159
Severe acute respiratory syndrome (SARS), 176
Simple, measurable, achievable, realistic, and task-oriented (SMART), 333
Simple Triage and Rapid Treatment protocol (START protocol), 52
Single plenary session, 337
Single-agent causality, 189
SITMAN, *see* Situation manual (SITMAN)
Situation manual (SITMAN), 333
SLOSH, *see* Sea, Lake, and Overland Surges from Hurricanes (SLOSH)
Slower onset processes, 195
SMART, *see* Simple, measurable, achievable, realistic, and task-oriented (SMART)
SNS, *see* Strategic national stockpile (SNS)
Social distancing, 175
Social vulnerability; *see also* Catastrophes
    emergency management, 111
    evacuation, 111–112
Sociocultural stress, 207
SOP, *see* Standard operating procedures (SOP)
Southern Command (SOUTHCOM), 348, 349
SparkRelief, 57
Stable electrical power grid, 154
Stafford Act, 87, 265, 287
Standard operating procedures (SOP), 330
START protocol, *see* Simple Triage and Rapid Treatment protocol (START protocol)
State emergency management system, 82
    key function, 82
    state emergency declaration, 83
    state homeland security, 82–83
    State National Guard, 83
State National Guard, 83
Strategic national stockpile (SNS), 310
Surge capacity planning role, 181–182
Surveillance, 172

T

T&EPW, *see* Training and Exercise Plan Workshop (T&EPW)
Tabletop attendee roles, 336
Tabletop exercise (TTX), 332, 333
    structure, 336
    tabletop attendee roles, 336
    tabletop formats and facilitation skills, 335
Targeted Capabilities List (TCL), 80
Task Force for Emergency Readiness Pilot Program (TFER), 298
TCL, *see* Targeted Capabilities List (TCL)
Technological hazards, 28
Telecommunications, 155
Teleological ethics, 50
Temporal moral community dimension, 66
Temporary quarters, 212
TEPCO, *see* Tokyo Electric Power Company (TEPCO)
Terrorism-based catastrophe, 159
TFER, *see* Task Force for Emergency Readiness Pilot Program (TFER)
Third echelon, 159–160
Thirteen-story "Paz" apartment tower collapse, 384
Three Mile Island (TMI), 266
Timing of resource, 288–289, 293–294
    hypothetical, 289
    pre-disaster collaborative relationships, 290
    speed *vs.* deliberation issue, 290
TMI, *see* Three Mile Island (TMI)
TMS theory, 239, 240
Tokyo Electric Power Company (TEPCO), 356
Tornado warning systems, 118
Tort, 94
Tort law, 94
Training and Exercise Plan Workshop (T&EPW), 324
Training and exercises for catastrophes, 321–322, 323
    agenda, 336
    building block approach, 327
    discussion questions, 335
    documentation, 327
    earthquake and tsunami, 336
    exercise evaluation, 330–331
    exercise phases, 332
    exercise planning team, 324–325
    exercise types, 325–326
    facilitator questions, 337
    homeland security exercise evaluation program, 323–324
    hot wash, 338
    logistics, 330
    national level exercise series, 331
    planning timelines, 332
    preparedness cycle, 332
    primer, 327–329
    recovery, 337
    response and surge, 336–337
    role, 323
    scenario, 329–330
    using single plenary session, 337
    situation manual, 333–335
    tabletop attendee roles, 336

Training and exercises for
   catastrophes (Continued)
   tabletop exercise design, 333, 336
   tabletop formats and facilitation skills, 335
   tool for assessing preparedness, 323
Transportation, 154
Transportation resources, 159
Triage, 51–52
Tsunami, 336
   Great Eastern Japan Earthquake and, 23
   Indian Ocean, 2, 70, 138
TTX, see Tabletop exercise (TTX)

U

UNFCCC, see United Nations Framework
   Convention on Climate Change
   (UNFCCC)
United Nations Framework Convention on
   Climate Change (UNFCCC), 199
United States Agency for International
   Development (USAID), 67, 344
United States Office of the Inspector General
   report (USOIG report), 298
United States Public Health Service (USPHS),
   311
Universal Task List (UTL), 80
Urban search and rescue (USAR), 349
Urban search and rescue teams (US&R teams), 361
Urbanization, 205
US&R teams, see Urban search and rescue
   teams (US&R teams)
USAID, see United States Agency for
   International Development (USAID)
USAR, see Urban search and rescue (USAR)
U.S. Aid to Foreign Nations, 67
   OFDA, 67
   Pierre-Louis Prosper, 68, 69
   USAID, 67
U.S. Department of Homeland Security (DHS),
   82, 302
U.S. emergency management system
   federal, 81–82
   government decision makers, 104
   ICS, 103
   intergovernmental relationships, 103
   limitations to DOD response authority,
      102–103
   local governments, 84
   network approach, 105
   policy adoption, 104
   problem recognition, 103
   state, 82–83
   White House report, 101

US Federal Emergency Management Agency
   (FEMA), 2
US government (USG), 343
USG, see US government (USG)
USOIG report, see United States Office of
   the Inspector General report
   (USOIG report)
USPHS, see United States Public Health Service
   (USPHS)
Utilitarian perspective, see Teleological ethics
Utilitarianism, 50
UTL, see Universal Task List (UTL)

V

V-MIMI, see Virtual Medical Incident
   Management Institute (V-MIMI)
Vectors, 175
Very important person (VIP), 330
VIP, see Very important person (VIP)
Virtual Medical Incident Management Institute
   (V-MIMI), 322
Virtual Terrorism Response Academy (VTRA),
   322
Voluntary Organizations Active in Disasters
   (VOAD), 245
Volunteer organizations and private donations, 69
   donor fatigue problem, 70–71
   Haiti earthquake, 70
   relief organizations, 69
VTRA, see Virtual Terrorism Response
   Academy (VTRA)
Vulnerability, 31, 35–37, 191, 192
   environmental issues, 191
   holistic, 33–34
   resilience and, 161, 162–163
   social, 31, 32

W

Wastewater management, 153
Water treatment effectiveness, 180
Webinars, 322
WHO, see World Health Organization (WHO)
Whole community, 260, 283
Whole of Government approach, 347
Widespread catastrophe, 132
World Health Organization (WHO), 304
   pandemic preparedness and response plans, 312
   six-phase alert model, 305–306

Y

Yersinia pestis (*Y. pestis*), 7

Lightning Source UK Ltd.
Milton Keynes UK
UKHW020955141022
410458UK00004B/64